the chinese way in religion

The Religious Life of Man Series
FREDERICK J. STRENG, *SERIES EDITOR*

Texts

Understanding Religious Life, Second Edition
    Frederick J. Streng

The House of Islam, Second Edition
    Kenneth Cragg

Japanese Religion: Unity and Diversity, Third Edition
    H. Byron Earhart

Chinese Religion: An Introduction, Third Edition
    Laurence G. Thompson

The Christian Religious Tradition
    Stephen Reynolds

The Buddhist Religion: A Historical Introduction, Third Edition
    Richard H. Robinson and Willard L. Johnson

The Way of Torah: An Introduction to Judaism, Third Edition
    Jacob Neusner

The Hindu Religious Tradition
    Thomas J. Hopkins

Native American Religions: An Introduction
    Sam D. Gill

Anthologies

The Chinese Way in Religion
    Laurence G. Thompson

Religion in the Japanese Experience: Sources and Interpretations
    H. Byron Earhart

The Buddhist Experience: Sources and Interpretations
    Stephan Beyer

The Life of Torah: Readings in the Jewish Religious Experience
    Jacob Neusner

Islam from Within: Anthology of a Religion
    Kenneth Cragg and R. Marston Speight

Native American Traditions
    Sam D. Gill

the Chinese way in Religion

Laurence G. Thompson

University of Southern California

Wadsworth Publishing Company
Belmont, California
A Division of Wadsworth, Inc.

This book is dedicated to my dear friends
David and Mamie Tai

ISBN 0-8221-0109-2

Library of Congress Catalog Card Number: 72-90753

Printed in the United States of America

Printing (last digit): 9 8 7 6

copyRights and acknowledgments

contents

PART THREE: BUDDHISM

PART FOUR: RELIGION OF THE STATE

PART FIVE: FAMILY RELIGION

PART SIX: POPULAR RELIGION

POSTSCRIPT: RELIGION UNDER COMMUNISM

foreword

The power of religious life is often self-evident to the participant, but very difficult to communicate to the uncommitted observer. Therefore, in an attempt to allow students to understand the thoughts, feelings, and attitudes of participants in the major religious traditions, we present companion volumes of readings in the Religious Life of Man Series.

The aim of this series of readings is to introduce the literature of a tradition, and provide sympathetic interpretations and descriptions of important activities which expose the dynamics and some of the concrete variety in a religious tradition. Every book of readings is selective in the material it includes, and the focus here is on religious life, in the past and present, that defines the religious options available today. The selections seek to reveal the goals, experiences, activities, symbolic imagery, and community life of a religious tradition. Hopefully the reader can thereby imaginatively participate in some of the feelings and experiences which are exposed.

Each of the volumes is edited by a university or college teacher who is also a specialist in the major languages and cultures of a religion. Several volumes have new translations of material made especially for them, and each reading is introduced with a brief comment about its place in the tradition and its general religious significance. Further background is found in the companion textbook in the Religious Life of Man Series; at the same time, these books of readings might well be used in combination with other books and media.

Frederick J. Streng
Series Editor

preface

In this reader, as in our *Chinese Religion: An Introduction*, we have proceeded from the conviction that Chinese religion may most fruitfully be studied as an expression of Chinese culture. We have sought primarily to provide descriptions and analyses that would illustrate this functioning of religion in the culture.

The defect of our approach is some slighting of the textual materials, and this has indeed caused us some uneasiness. So far as the works of the Confucian Canon and the philosophers are concerned, the abundance of available translations may enable the reader to compensate for what is not provided here. The most conspicuous omission in our anthology is that of Buddhist texts. Our problem here was the difficulty of selecting any few pages that would be basic, representative, and intelligible without an inappropriately elaborate apparatus of notes. In the end we settled for more pages of other sorts of materials, and the hope that available studies and translations may supplement.

In any case, the lament of the anthologist (and his critics) must inevitably be that there is so much valuable material left out. He can only hope that he will not be taken to task as well for what he has put in. So far as that is concerned, we have aspired to present a multifaceted image of Chinese religion from earliest antiquity to the present day. Although we have used the same theoretical schema as in our *Introduction*, we have not followed the same order of treatment. We have here proceeded in a roughly historical line, with compromises effected here and there. Thus, for example, the selections from the Confucian *Analects* have been placed under Religion of the State instead of under the Ancient Native Tradition because the prominence of Confucius *in religion* seems most evident in the State cult.

An anthology is by definition the work of many hands, and it is a pleasurable obligation to express our gratitude to the many scholars (and their publishers) who herein illumine our subject. Special appreciation is due the colleagues who read and commented upon the manuscript, Professors Spencer J. Palmer, Brigham Young University; and Willard Johnson, California State University, Long Beach. Professor Frederick J. Streng, editor of the series of which this volume is a part, has again placed us under heavy obligation, with his stimulating suggestions, encouragement, and stubborn refusal to accept anything but the best solution to every problem. Had it been feasible to incorporate every sound idea offered by each of these colleagues, this would indeed have been an ideal book; for the imperfect book that it is in fact, they bear no responsibility.

Laurence G. Thompson
University of Southern California

Table of Chinese Religious History

(*Ruling dynasties*)   (*Major religious events and characteristics*)

I. FORMATION OF NATIVE TRADITION

(*Ruling dynasties*)	(*Major religious events and characteristics*)
Hsia (?–?1751 B.C.) (not yet confirmed by archaeology)	
Shang (?1751–?1111) (last centuries also called Yin)	Oracle bones; ancestor worship already dominant; worship of spirits of natural phenomena
Chou (?1123–221) 722–481, "Spring and Autumn" (period covered by *Ch'un Ch'iu*) 403–221, "Warring States" (feudal system destroyed)	Feudal polity; *Shih Ching, Shu Ching, Yi Ching;* Confucius (551–479); *Ch'un Ch'iu* and commentaries; ?Lao Tzu (*Tao Te Ching*). Formative Age of Philosophy: Mo Tzu (480–390), Meng Tzu (Mencius) (390–305), Chuang Tzu (365–290), Hsün Tzu (340–245), *et al.; Analects, Chung Yung, Ta Hsüeh, Li* texts, *Hsiao Ching*
Ch'in (221–206) (First Emperor unifies China)	First Emperor establishes totalitarian dictatorship, attempts thought control by book burning; rise of "religious Taoism"

II. INTRODUCTION, ASSIMILATION, AND DOMINANCE OF BUDDHISM

(*Ruling dynasties*)	(*Major religious events and characteristics*)
Former Han (206 B.C.–A.D. 9) Later Han (A.D. 23–220)	Imperial polity finally established; first great expansionist empire; Confucianism becomes state orthodoxy; scholars concentrate on texts of Confucian canon; state university founded to teach this canon; great age of credulity and superstition; religious Taoism flourishes; Buddhism enters China and begins missionary work.
Three Kingdoms (220–265) (China partitioned)	Rise of Neo-Taoist philosophy
Tsin (265–420)	Neo-Taoism and Buddhism eclipse Confucianism; Ko Hung (*Pao P'u Tzu*) (253–333?)
China partitioned between Southern (Chinese) and Northern (non-Chinese) Dynasties (420–589)	Buddhism flourishes
Sui (589–618) (China united under Chinese rule)	
T'ang (618–907)	China the world's greatest civilization; Buddhism reaches zenith of its influence, and then its temporal prosperity destroyed by State (845); first stirrings of Confucian renascence

III. RENAISSANCE OF NATIVE TRADITION: DOMINANCE OF NEO-CONFUCIANISM

Five Dynasties (907–960) (brief period of disunion)

(Northern) Sung (960–1127)

Chinese high culture attains its peak; rise of Neo-Confucian philosophy to reassert ancient native tradition against Buddhism

Second partition of China, between Southern Sung (Chinese) and Kin (non-Chinese) (1127–1280)

Continuation of cultural brilliance despite political weakness; Chu Hsi (1130–1200) greatest Neo-Confucian philosopher, whose interpretation of the canon was orthodox until 20th century

Yuan (1280–1368) (all of China under Mongol rule)

Europe gets its first, glamorous impression of Cathay from book of Marco Polo (in China 1275–1292)

Ming (1368–1644) (last Chinese dynasty)

Neo-Confucian orthodoxy dominant; beginning of unbroken contact with Europe: Matteo Ricci, S.J., reaches Peking (1600), followed by hundreds of Catholic missionaries

Ch'ing (1644–1911) (all of China under Manchu rule)

Neo-Confucian orthodoxy strait-jackets Chinese thought; "Rites Controversy"; decline of Catholic missions and proscription of missionary work; Protestant missions begin (1800); China's invasion by Western world (19th and 20th centuries)

IV. DISRUPTION OF TRADITION BY WESTERN IMPACT

Republic of China (confined since 1949 to Taiwan, *i.e.*, Formosa) (1912 to date) People's Republic of China (Communist-controlled mainland) (1949 to date)

Collapse of imperial polity; disruption of tradition

Data on dynasties much simplified. Dates for Hsia and Shang follow Tung, Tso-pin, *Chung-kuo Nien-li Chien-p'u* (Taipei: Yee Wen Publishing Co., 1960); dates of Chou philosophers follow Ch'ien, Mu, *Hsien-Ch'in Chu-tzu Chi-nien* (Hong Kong: University of Hong Kong Press, rev. ed. 1956), Vol. II, final chart.

part one
the ancient native tradition

1.
the archaic religion-1

"Beginnings" are always intriguing, and because the psychology of cultures, like that of individuals, seems inescapably bound up with the molding experiences of infancy and childhood, we must seek the meaning of mature institutions at least partly in those beginnings. This is especially true of the so-called "traditional" civilizations; that is, those of the "premodern" type, which looked backwards rather than to the future for truth and perfection. China, most long-lived of all the traditional civilizations, is the one in which the powerful influences of the beginnings are most obvious. Of course, these beginnings are actually not beginnings at all; if archeology has taken Chinese civilization back to the thirteenth century before the Christian era, it has also revealed preceding layers of prehistoric cultures that may well be termed "Chinese." But our information about these Neolithic (not to speak of the Paleolithic) cultures is very meager. We do know enough to be sure by now that they are the true, indigenous ancestors of the historic Chinese civilization, and that the speculations by Western scholars of earlier generations that archaic Chinese culture was imported from the West are untenable.

Among the many continuities of Neolithic and Bronze Age cultures in North China (listed ·in a recent summary of current knowledge)[1] are elaborate complexes organized apparently more on the basis of lineage-ancestry than on agricultural community needs; scapulimancy; and certain forms of ritual vessels. Some pertinent "discontinuities," or new developments, include chamber burials, human sacrifices, the perfection of bronze metallurgy, and writing.[2]

The following selection is taken from *An Interpretation of the Ancient Chinese Civilization* by Tso-pin Tung (original in English), Taipei, Chinese Association for the United Nations, July 1952; pp. 12-21. It is a summary description of what is known of religion during the earliest historical age (known by writing), that of the last several centuries of the Shang

[1]Kwang-chih Chang, *The Archeology of Ancient China.* Yale Univ., 2nd, rev. ed., 1968, p.236.

[2]Kwang-chih Chang, *loc. cit.*

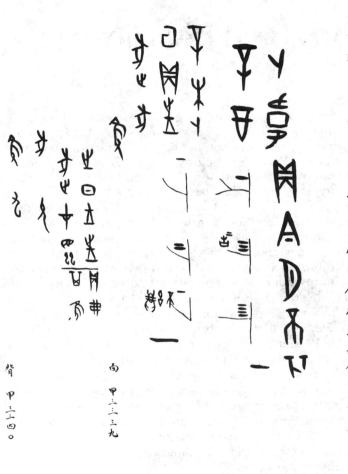

ORACLE BONES

dynasty. Because during this period the capital was located in a place later known as "the waste of Yin," it is often given the designation of Yin. The author of this description, the late professor Tso-pin Tung, was one of the scholars who originally excavated the Yin capital (near the modern town of Anyang, Honan province). He specialized for some thirty years in the decipherment and interpretation of the oracle bones—100,000 pieces of which were found at the site.

As little is known about the family life of the common people, we can only hope that the system of the royal house, of which an outline can be made out of the data furnished by the oracles, could typify the family system prevailing in the Yin dynasty.

What role ancestor worship played in the religious life of that time we shall see later. But ancestor worship was derived from the patrilineal system. The patriarchs that were revered when they were alive became objects of worship when they were dead. Ancestors were of two kinds so far as we can see from the oracles, those of the "lineal" and those of the "collateral." The two kinds of ancestors were worshiped separately. The "lineal" ancestors were called "Ta Tsung"; the collateral ancestors were called "Hsiao Tsung." "Tsung" means "the temple," and "ta" and "hsiao" mean "large" and "small" respectively. The eldest brother that had inherited the throne or had been made the heir apparent normally became "Ta Tsung," but if he had no son, then his brother next in order that had a son would become "Ta Tsung," and he himself would become "Hsiao Tsung." For each generation, only one ancestor was worshiped as "Ta Tsung" together with his spouse. His brother or brothers that had inherited the throne or been made the heir or heirs apparent were worshiped as "Hsiao Tsung," but the wives of "Hsiao Tsung" were not worshiped. . . .

The family system at the time of Yin was patrilineal. Men enjoyed a more privileged position than women. For the oracles about the childbirth of the royal family considered it "propitious" to have a boy and "unpropitious" to have a girl. Clan exogamy was practiced. The king's wives were all called *fu*, women who retained their family names. . . . The one made the legitimate queen and who was the mother of the heir apparent, was to have her own shrine in the family temple after her death, and to be worshiped as one of the ancestors. . . .

We know now that agriculture formed the essential part of the economic life of the Yin people. Cattle were bred mainly for sacrificial purposes . . . Alcoholic drink was made of millet. Whenever there was an offering made to the ancestors, male or female, it must include wine. Not simply wine, but there were also *li*, wine with dregs, and *ch'ang*, scented drink. If the ghosts seemed to appreciate the drink so much, they must have indulged in the habit while living. . . .

[The houses of most of the people consisted of] a sort of pit, about twelve feet deep and twelve feet in diameter, covered at top by the thatched roof. Only the royal family had houses built on the ground. This also applied to the building of ancestral temples. . . .

Ten years of excavation have convinced us of the magnificence of these royal houses. The earth wall and thatch roof are all gone, but the foundation made of earth is in many cases still well kept. The ruins of a terrace made of loess, with several steps of a once long stairway, are still preserved in good condition. In the south are the traces of a gateway, with apparently three entrances facing the terrace. The remarkable fact is that the terrace and the gateway lie exactly on the north-south line of the magnetic meridian[3] . . . The foundation laying of the ancestral temples was a horrible ceremony, for together with the stone plates, were deposited into the earth carriages, horses, living men, etc., as a sort of sacrifice. . . .

The Yin dynasty was a period when ancestor worship was carried to the extreme. But the religion prevalent at that time had a wider scope than mere ancestor worship. Besides the ghosts of ancestors, there seemed to be other supernatural beings that were also worshiped.

First of all, there was the Supreme God, the highest of all deities, that was called *Ti*. The position of *Ti* in heaven was somewhat like that of the king on the earth. *Ti* was also called *Shang Ti*. The omnipotent one dominated over the human lives in at least the following five ways:

a. He sent the rain down to the earth. An agricultural society depends for its food on the timely rain more than anything else. To send down the rain means almost to send down the food. So in the oracles we often find questions about the rain made by the anxious king.

b. He might hold the rain in check and send down famine instead. In the oracles, we find desperate questions and exclamations like these: "Would God send down famine?" "No more rain and God would starve us!"

c. He brought victory to the army. For instance, there was a prayer for victory to *Ti* in an oracle about the king's expeditions against the tribe Kung-fang.

d. He brought fortune to the world.

e. He also brought misfortune to the world.

It was a popular belief that the ancestors of the living men, believed to be in heaven, were in a position to sit near the Supreme One. . . . Since it was up to *Ti* to decide to send down the rain or not, the ancestors might use their influence to prevail upon *Ti* not to send down the rain as a measure of punishment against the sinful sons. . . .

There were also God of Wind, called "*Ti*'s Messenger," and God of Cloud, called "Six Clouds"—meaning the clouds in the East, West, South, North, above the earth and below the earth. The God of Sun was worshiped at sunrise and sunset. There was God of Moon; and the lunar eclipse was considered as a portent of evil. Some of the conspicuous stars and constellations were also worshiped, for instance Adlebaran or Alpha of the Hyades.

In many of the oracles, worship of Yüeh and Ho was mentioned. Though the two characters have been interpreted as names of ancestors, the reading of the contexts convinces us that we should take them at their literal meaning: i.e. Yüeh means the mountain and Ho means the Yellow River. There were gods for the four directions of the compass, as the worship of them is mentioned in the oracles. Gods of different localities and gods of certain big

[3]These building features, with the exception of thatch roofing, have continued to characterize Chinese temple and palace architecture down to modern times. (L.G.T.)

rivers, for instance the Hwan, near the capital were constant objects of worship.

But it was still ancestor worship that held the most important position in the religious life of the Yin people. "To serve the dead as if they were living"—we can say that the piety of the Yin people did reach that degree. The one hundred thousand pieces of oracle bones and shells contain little but the questions the reverential Yin kings put to their ancestors and the answers in the form of cracks which the bones and shells produced when they were scorched. Such questions were asked and such answers received, we can believe, when a solemn ceremony of worship was performed. It was once thought that worship and war were the two most important affairs of the state, and worship of the ancestors was set even above war as a determinant factor of the fate of a nation. Ghosts were diligently worshiped and reverentially feared. Their favor must be won, and their anger propitiated. Ancestor worship is the traditional religion of China that has come down from the Yin dynasty to the present. We should consider this as a special feature of the Chinese civilization.

But the rites of ancestor worship were a very complicated affair. I have studied the subject for over twenty years but there are still many things about it that are beyond my comprehension. . . .

The kings of Yin regarded their ancestors as well as the great ministers in their ancestors' government . . . as still living in the spirit. They retained the same rank and authority, possessed the same emotions, and would enjoy the same good things as they used to enjoy when alive. The only difference seemed to be that the disembodied spirits were endowed with supernatural powers: Their power to grant favours or to inflict punishment was greatly increased after their death. Funeral service was shockingly lavish, for it was thought of as a means to win the favor of the dead. Their tombs were considered to play the same role in their life after death as their palaces, and the temples erected in their honor were meant to be their office buildings where they would hold their court. So in the building of both the tombs and temples, a large number of living persons and horses, carriages and vessels were to be buried in the ground, for it was believed that the dead would need them. Sacrifices were constantly offered to them, and various worship rites were performed from time to time. After the performance of every rite, the question must be put on the oracle bone: "Nothing wrong?" The dutiful son was anxious to know whether he was all right in doing the service, whether anything had been neglected, which might displease his jealous fathers. That question, of course, also implied the prayer that no harm would fall on him and his country because of his possible negligence in serving the dead. Under the reign of Ti-i, at the beginning of each of the five kinds of rites, the prayer must be repeated: "No harms, no misfortunes, no calamities." Indeed, the wish was always being expressed that the sons needed their ancestors' protection.

. . . When [King] Wu-ting was ill, he would think it was his deceased father or grandfather or grandmother who caused his disease. When the crop failed, the question would be put to the oracle: "Is it Kao [i.e. the legendary first ancestor of the Yin kings] who blights our rice?" If such harms could be done by the spirits of the ancestors, they would also enjoy the offerings, listen to the prayers, and send down their blessings. . . . Often the kings would report their disease to the ancestors, with no other purpose, we can believe, than that health might be soon restored to them through the blessing of the supernatural beings. Three of the ancestresses were believed to be tutelary goddesses of childbirth. . . . Prayers were invariably made to them when one of the king's wives was known to be pregnant. It was not so much for the safety of the expectant mother as for the production of a male child that the king prayed. If none of his wives showed any sign of pregnancy, the grandmothers in heaven would also be appealed to. They were indeed the Yin version of the "stork" . . .

It is very curious to note that no records are available about the worship rites of *Ti,* the Supreme God, in the oracles. It seems that the ancestors were expected to intercede for the descendants with the Highest in Heaven. So almost all the elaborate religious rituals of the Yin dynasty were meant for the ancestors. But . . . the temperaments of the kings may differ. While Wu-ting bothered his ancestors with endless questions and prayers, the more rational Tsu-chia paid little heed to the traditional belief and led a more or less enlightened life.

2.
the archaic religion-II

It is now the view of archeologists that there was no sharp break in the cultural development of China when the Shang (or Yin) dynasty was conquered and replaced by the Chou (about 1111 B.C.). We shall use the term "archaic" to characterize the whole long period up to the time of Confucius (roughly 500 B.C.), after whose days we come into what may aptly be called China's Classical Age. The documents we have for the Yin culture consist mostly of bronze vessels, many with short inscriptions, the oracle bones so ably explicated by Tso-pin Tung in our previous selection, and other archeologically excavated artifacts. Archaic China during the later, Chou centuries, is further revealed in a few literary texts, including the *Scriptures of Documents* and *Poetry* (or *Songs*), portions of the *Scripture of Changes*, and the *Spring and Autumn Annals* with its commentaries, especially that called *Tso Chuan*. In all of these works there are numerous passages that give us glimpses of the world view and the religion of the time. It is significant that none of these texts attempts anything like a sustained systematic treatment of such subjects. Speculative philosophy, theology, or creedal formulations have always been foreign to Chinese thought.

In what follows we excerpt a number of passages on several topics from the previously mentioned writings, which have since the early Han dynasty been accorded the status of sacred literature.

1) *Heaven.* "The works of Heaven, it is man who carries them out on its behalf. Heaven arranges the existing rules [of family relations], we carefully regulate our five rules and the five modes of amply practicing them. Heaven regulates the existing rites, we follow our five rites [pertaining to the king, the higher feudatories, the lower feudatories, the ministers and dignitaries, the officers and commoners] and their five constant norms. Together we reverence [them], concordantly we respect them, [then there is] harmony and correctness. Heaven gives charges to those who have virtue, [there are] five [degrees of] garments and their five [classes of] emblems. Heaven punishes those who have guilt, [there are] five punishments and their five applications. In the affairs of government let us be energetic, let us be energetic! Heaven's hearing and seeing work through our people's hearing and seeing, Heaven's discernment and severity work through our people's discernment and severity [against bad rulers]. There is correspondence between the upper and the lower [world]. Be careful, you possessors of the soil (sc. feudal lords)." (Bernhard Karlgren, *The Book of Documents*, p.9; slightly edited)

"When Heaven inspects the people below, it takes as norm their righteousness and sends down life either long or not long. It is not that Heaven prematurely kills the people, the people in the middle cut off their lives. When among the people there are those who do not comply with virtue and do not acknowledge their guilt, Heaven has [always] given its grant of life, determining their virtue. And thus I say: It is as I tell you. Oh, when the kings become successors in taking care of the people, there are none who are not the successors of Heaven; in the standard sacrifices [to the royal spirits], do not perform rites in familiarity." (Ibid., p.26)

There are many references to the Mandate of Heaven in the *Book of Documents*. This concept corresponds in a general way to the Western Divine Right of Kings, but with an all-important difference: The Chinese sovereign held his commission on sufferance; Heaven gave it to reward virtue, and when virtue vanished, Heaven would revoke it and confer it upon a deserving house. Here are a few more statements from this text:

"[The legendary emperor] Yü said: Be quiet in the position which you occupy, if you attend to the smallest beginnings, you will have peace. Your assistants should be virtuous, if you act [through them], there will be a grand response [from the people]. They will wait for your will, and so it will be manifest that you have received your [mandate] from God on High (Shang Ti). Heaven will renew its mandate and apply blessings." (Ibid., p. 11)
    "The lord of Hu violates and despises the five elements, he neglects and discards the three governing forces [of Heaven, Earth and Man]. Heaven therefore cuts off his appointment." (Ibid., p.18)
    "Oh, august Heaven, God on High, has changed his principal son (i.e. chosen the 'Son of Heaven' from another house), and this great state Yin's mandate. Now that the [Chou] king has received the mandate, unbounded is the grace, but also unbounded is the solicitude. Oh, how can he be but careful! Heaven has removed and made an end to the great state Yin's mandate. Now there are many former wise kings of Yin in Heaven. The following kings and following people (i.e. officers) here [still] managed their mandate. [But] in the end (i.e. under the last king) the wise and good men lived in misery. These wise men, wrapping and carrying, leading and supporting the wives and children, and wailing and calling to Heaven, went to where nobody could come out and seize them. Oh, Heaven also had pity on the people of the four quarters, and looking to it with affection and giving its mandate, it employed the zealous ones (that is, the Chou)[1]. (Ibid., p.48f)

2) *Mythology*. Only fragments of what must have been a rich repertory of myths can be found in the remains of the most ancient literature. The most complete story is the origin and history of the Chou, as depicted

---

[1]The foregoing is of course a piece of propaganda by the Chou usurpers to justify having replaced the Yin dynasty. (L.G.T.)

in certain poems of the *Scripture of Poetry* (or *Songs*). Here is one of these, in the translation of James Legge (*The She King*, Bk.II, Ode 1):

> The first birth of [our] people
> Was from Chiang Yüan.
> How did she give birth to [our] people?
> She had presented a pure offering and sacrificed,
> That her childlessness might be taken away.
> She then trod on a toe-print made by God,[2] and was moved,
> In the large place where she rested.
> She became pregnant; she dwelt retired;
> She gave birth to, and nourished [a son],
> who was Hou Chi.
>
> When she had fulfilled her months,
> Her first-born son [came forth] like a lamb.
> There was no bursting, nor rending,
> No injury, no hurt; —
> Showing how wonderful he would be.
> Did not God give her the comfort?
> Had He not accepted her pure offering and sacrifice,
> So that thus easily she brought forth her son?
>
> He was placed in a narrow lane,
> But the sheep and oxen protected him with loving care.
> He was placed in a wide forest,
> Where he was met with by the wood-cutters.
> He was placed on the cold ice,
> And a bird screened and supported him with its wings.
> When the bird went away,
> Hou Chi began to wail.
> His cry was long and loud,
> So that his voice filled the whole way.
>
> When he was able to crawl,
> He looked majestic and intelligent.
> When he was able to feed himself,
> He fell to planting large beans.
>
> The beans grew luxuriantly;
> His rows of paddy shot up beautifully;
> His hemp and wheat grew strong and close;
> His gourds yielded abundantly.
>
> The husbandry of Hou Chi
> Proceeded on the plan of helping [the growth].
> Having cleared away the thick grass,
> He sowed the ground with the yellow cereals.
> He managed the living grain, till it was ready to burst;
> Then he used it as seed, and it sprang up;
> It grew and came into ear;
> It became strong and good;

[2]That is, Ti, or Shang Ti (L.G.T.)

It hung down, every grain complete;—
And thus he was appointed lord of T'ai.

He gave his people the beautiful grains:—
The black millet, and the double-kernelled;
The tall red, and the white.
They planted extensively the black and the double-kernelled,
Which were reaped and stacked on the ground.
They planted extensively the tall red and the white,
Which were carried on their shoulders and backs,
Home for the sacrifices which he founded.

And how as to our sacrifices [to him]?
Some hull [the grain]; some take it from the mortar;
Some sift it; some tread it.
It is rattling in the dishes;
It is distilled, and the steam floats about.
We consult; we observe the rites of purification;
We take southernwood and offer it with the fat;
We sacrifice a ram to the Spirit of the path;
We offer roast flesh and broiled;—
And thus introduce the coming year.

We load the stands with the offerings,
The stands both of wood and of earthenware.
As soon as the fragrance ascends,
God, well pleased, smells the sweet savour.
Fragrant it is, and in its due season!
Hou Chi founded the sacrifice,
And no one, we presume, has given occasion for blame or regret in regard to it,
Down to the present day.

3) *Ancestral sacrifices.* From the studies of the archeologists, we have seen that by Yin times almost all religious rites were already connected with the ancestral cult; in the *Shih Ching (Scripture of Poems or Songs)* we have vivid descriptions of the sacrifices in the ancestral temples of the rulers of the early Chou centuries. We give here the most complete of these descriptions, in the clear and careful translation of James Legge (*Chinese Classics: Vol. IV: The She King,* 2nd edition, London, 1895, pp.368-373 ["Ch'u Tz'u," Mao's No.209]). One notes the mention in this poem of "the representatives of the dead"; these were junior relatives of the deceased—preferably grandsons—who "stood in" for the invisible spirits that were presumed to descend to enjoy the sacrifices; they remained quiet throughout the ceremony, and were treated as the guests of honor. The custom of having such a Personator of the Spirit was not continued after Chou times, but its idea is still present, as may be proved by the practice of the grandson riding home from a funeral, carrying the soul-silk, or the "pre-spirit tablet" of the deceased (see the chapter on Funeral Rites in Taiwan).

Thick grew the tribulus [on the ground],
But they cleared away its thorny bushes.
Why did they this of old?
That we might plant our millet and sacrificial millet;
That our millet might be abundant,
And our sacrificial millet luxuriant.
When our barns are full,
And our stacks can be counted by tens of myriads,
We proceed to make spirits and prepare viands,
For offerings and sacrifice;
We seat the representatives of the dead, and urge them to eat:—
Thus seeking to increase our bright happiness.

With correct and reverent deportment,
The oxen and sheep all pure,
We proceed to the winter and autumnal sacrifices.
Some flay [the victims]; some boil [their flesh];
Some arrange [the meat]; some adjust [the pieces of it].
The priest sacrifices inside the temple gate,
And all the service is complete and brilliant.
Grandly come our progenitors;
Their Spirits happily enjoy the offerings;
Their filial descendant receives blessing:—
They will reward him with great happiness,
With myriads of years, life without end.
They attend to the furnaces[3] with reverence;
They prepare the trays, which are very large;—
Some for the roast meat; some for the broiled.
Wives presiding are still and reverent,
Preparing the numerous [smaller] dishes.
The guests and visitors
Present the cup, and drink all round.
Every form is according to rule;
Every smile and word are as they should be
The Spirits quietly come,
And respond with great blessings:—
Myriads of years as the [fitting] reward.

We are very much exhausted,
And have performed every ceremony without error.
The able priest announces [the will of the Spirits],
And goes to the filial descendant to convey it.
'Fragrant has been your filial sacrifice,
And the Spirits have enjoyed your spirits and viands.
They confer upon you a hundred blessings;
Each as it is desired, each as sure as law.
You have been exact and expeditious;
You have been correct and careful:
They will ever confer on you the choicest favours,
In myriads and tens of myriads.'

[3]For cooking the sacrificial feast. (L.G.T.)

The ceremonies having thus been completed,
And the bells and drums having given their warning,
The filial descendant goes to his place,
And the able priest makes his announcement,
'The Spirits have drunk to the full.'
The great representative of the dead then rises,
And the bells and drums escort his withdrawal,
[On which] the Spirits tranquilly return [to their place].
All the servants, and the presiding wives,
Remove [the trays and dishes] without delay.
The [descendant's] uncles and cousins
All repair to the private feast.

The musicians all go in to perform,
And give their soothing aid at the second blessing.
Your viands are set forth;
There is no dissatisfaction, but all feel happy.
They drink to the full;
Great and small, they bow their heads, [saying],
'The Spirits enjoyed your spirits and viands,
And will cause you to live long.
Your sacrifices, all in their seasons,
Are completely discharged by you.
May your sons and your grandsons
Never fail to perpetuate these services!'

4) *Ceremonialism.* The artifacts of royal tombs give evidences from which the archeologist, with skill and imagination, can reconstruct some of the ceremonial splendor of archaic times. For the early Chou, there are in addition literary passages which give life to these relics. The following is a book from the *Shu Ching* ("Ku Ming," or the Testament, of the Chou king Ch'eng) which we reproduce with a minimum of condensation, in order to leave the reader with a strong impression of the elaborateness and symbolical character of the great religious rites. This is, of course, an enduring feature of Chinese civilization. In the translation to follow, by Bernhard Karlgren (*The Book of Documents*, pp.70-74), we have pictured the burial rites of the third Chou ruler, who died in 1079 B.C. (We have retained all the terminology of the original text, despite its technical character, simply to aid in conveying the overall formality and complexity. Some of the things mentioned are not clearly describable even by specialists.)

The grand guardian gave order to Chung Huan and Nan-kung Mao and made them assist him. The prince of Ts'i, Lü Ki, with two [men with] shield and dagger-axes (i.e. two squires) and tiger braves one hundred men, went to meet the son Chao outside the south gate, and invited him to enter the Bright Room and carefully attend to those who sojourn in the clan temple (i.e. the Spirits). . . . On the 7th day, a kuei-yu (referring to "ten stems and twelve branches" numbering system[4]) day, the leader-premier ordered the officers to make exact the materials [for the burial].

Servants displayed the screen ornamented with axes and the stitched garments (the graveclothes) [of the king]. Between the windows, facing the south, they spread out double bamboo-strip mats with black-and-white silk borders, and the traditional stool with varicolored jades. In the space along the western wall, facing the east, they spread out double smooth [rush] mats with stitched borders, and a traditional stool with striped cowries. In the space along the eastern wall, facing west, they spread out double sumptuous mats with painted borders, and a traditional stool with carved jades. In the western side-room, facing the south, they spread out double young-bamboo mats with dark, ample borders and a traditional stool with lacquer. [There were] quintuple jades and old treasures. The red [sacrificial jade] knife, the large grand [kuei tessera], the great [jade] pi disk, the rounded-top [kuei tessera] and the pointed-top [kuei tessera] were in the space along the western wall, the great jade, the jade of the Yi tribes, the great k'iu-jade and the drawing-tablet of the River were in the space along the east wall, the dancing garments of Yin, the great shell and the big drum were in the western room, the dagger-axe of Tuei, the bow of Ho, the bamboo arrows of Ch'uei were in the eastern room. The grand chariot was in front of the guests' staircase, the adjunct chariot was in front of the eastern staircase, the foremost chariot was before the left gate-room, the next-following chariot was before the right gate-room.

Two men with sparrow-caps holding huei-lances stood inside the Last gate (farthest from the south). Four men with black-mottled caps, holding dagger-axes with the edge upwards, stood on both sides of the staircases and the corners of the [raised] hall-platform. One man, with state cap, holding a liu axe, stood in the eastern part of the [open] hall, one man, with state cap, holding a yüe axe, stood in the western part of the hall, one man, with state cap, holding a k'uei lance, stood at the eastern extreme end of the hall, one man with state cap, holding a k'ü lance, stood at the western extreme end of the hall, one man, with state cap, holding a tuei lance, stood at the side staircase (i.e. north from the hall).

The king had hempen state cap and skirt with black-and-white [axe-shaped] ornaments and ascended by the guests' staircase, the ministers and feudatory rulers had hempen state caps and ant[-coloured] skirts, they entered and went to their positions. The grand guardian, the grand scribe and the grand master of rites all had hempen state caps and red skirts. The grand guardian held the grand kuei-tessera, the high master of rites held a kia-vessel and tsan libation ladle; they ascended by the eastern staircase. The grand scribe held the document (i.e. the late king's testament) and ascended by the guests' staircase. He presented to the king the written down charge. He said: The august sovereign, leaning on the jade stool, brought forward and manifested his last will. He ordered you to follow up the instructions, to look down upon and govern the state of Chou, to follow the great laws, to make the whole world harmonious and concordant, and thus respond to and

---

[4]A system of numbering by two intermeshing sets of symbols, thus: A-1, B-2, C-3, etc. It ran for sixty days (or years) and then repeated itself in an infinite series. (L.G.T.)

extol Wen's and Wu's (i.e. the first two rulers of the dynasty) brilliant instructions. The king bowed down twice, rose and answered saying: Very insignificant am I, the small child, last of our line. How can I govern the [regions of] the four quarters, and thus reverently stand in awe of Heaven's majesty? Then he received the kia-vessel and the libation ladle.

The king thrice strained the wine, thrice sacrificed and thrice he returned to his place. The high master of rites said: It has been enjoyed [by the Spirits]. The grand guardian received the kia-vessel, descended, washed the hands, took another kia-vessel, grasped the libation ladle with chang-tessera handle and with it made the matching libation. He handed the kia-vessel to the assistant master of rites and saluted. The king in response saluted. The grand guardian descended. They removed the utensils. The princes went out through the temple gate and waited. The king came out and was inside the principal gate. The grand guardian led the princes of the western regions to enter [and stand] to the left of the principal gate, the prince of Pi led the princes of the eastern regions to enter [and stand] to the right of the principal gate. They all had black-and-white-figured [robes] and knee-covers which were yellow and red. The guests lifted and presented their kuei-tesserae and at the same time their presents and they said: We, your few servants and guards presume to bring the offerings of our soils. All twice saluted and bowed down the head. The king, as the rightful heir, returned the salute to them one by one. . . . (the feudatory rulers urge the king to retain the Mandate by good rule; and the king charges them to assist him by zealous service) . . . All the princes, having heard the charge, saluted each other and hastily went out. The king took off his cap and assumed again the mourning garments.

The *Tso Chuan* is a long and detailed history of feudal China from 722 to 481 B.C., in particular as that history concerns the State of Lu. One of the most significant things revealed in this work is the surprising lack of "superstitious" elements in the religion of that time. It may be that, because the history deals with affairs of state, and the protagonists are mostly from the aristocratic level of society, the beliefs of the common people are not adequately represented. It may also be that, because the work is supposed to have been written by a disciple of Confucius, the rationalistic and humanistic outlook of the philosopher has colored the presentation. In any case, it is the text we must consider in conjunction with *Shu, Shih,* and *Yi,* as we attempt to find evidences of the archaic beliefs and practices in pre-Confucian China. We shall extract several items on different topics, whose most striking common theme is the assumption that man's actions in nature are religiously important.

5) *Spirits respond to Man's behavior.* In autumn, in the 7th month, there was the descent of a Spirit in the State of Hsin. King Hui asked Ko, the historiographer of the interior, the reason of it, and he replied, "When a

state is about to flourish, intelligent Spirits descend in it, to survey its virtue. When it is going to perish, Spirits also descend in it, to behold its wickedness . . . The king then asked what should be done in the case of this Spirit, and Ko replied, "Present to it its own proper offerings, which are those proper to the day on which it came." . . . The Spirit stayed in Hsin six months, when the duke of Kuo (another feudal state) caused the prayer-master Ying, the superintendent of the ancestral temple Ch'ü, and the historiographer Yin, to sacrifice to it, and the Spirit promised to give him territory. The historiographer Yin said, "Ah! Kuo will perish. I have heard that, when a State is about to flourish, its ruler receives his lessons from the people; and when it is about to perish, he receives his lessons from Spirits. The Spirits are intelligent, correct, and impartial. Their course is regulated by the feelings of men. The slenderness of Kuo's virtue extends to many things; —how can any increase of territory be obtained?" (p. 120, cols. 1 and 2)

6. *Omens and portents*. . . .Two serpents, one inside and one outside, had fought together in the southern gate of the capital, till the inside one was killed. [When] the duke of Lu heard of the circumstances and inquired about [this supernatural event] the answer was, "When men are full of fear, their breath, as it were, blazes up, and brings such things. Monsters and monstrous events take their rise from men. If men afford no cause for them, they do not arise of themselves. When men abandon the constant course of virtue, then monstrosities appear . . ." (p. 92, cols. 1 and 2)

[The portent next referred to is the entry in the *Spring and Autumn Annals*, of which *Tso Chuan* is a commentary, that six fish-hawks flew backwards, past the capital of Sung.] Duke Hsiang asked the historiographer Shu-hsing about this event, saying, "What are they ominous of? What good fortune or bad do they portend?" The historiographer replied, "This year there will be the deaths of many great persons of Lu. Next year Ch'i will be all in disorder. Your lordship will get the presidency of the States, but will not continue to hold it." When he retired, he said to some one, "The king asked me a wrong question. It is not from these developments of the *Yin* and *Yang* that good fortune and evil are produced. They are produced by men themselves. I answered as I did, because I did not venture to go against the duke's idea." (p. 171, col. 1)

[The *Spring and Autumn Annals* for a certain year contains the entry that in the spring there was a great hailstorm.] Chi Wu-tzu asked Shen Feng whether the hail could be stopped, and was answered, "When a sage is in the highest place, there is no hail; or if some should happen to fall, it does not amount to a calamity. Anciently, they stored up the ice, when the sun was in his northern path; and they brought it out when he was in his western . . . At the storing of it, a black bull and black millet were presented to the Ruler of cold; and when it was brought out, a bow of peach wood and arrows of thorn were employed to put away calamitous influences . . . It was deposited with a sacrifice to the [Ruler of] cold; the depositories were opened with the offering of a lamb. . . . Now it is the [cold] wind which makes the ice strong; and it was when the [warm] winds [prevailed] that it was brought forth. The depositories were made close; the use of it was very extensive. In consequence there was not heat out of course in the winter; no lurking cold in the summer; no biting winds in the spring; and no pitiless rains in the autumn. When thunder came, it was not with a shaking crash. There were no calamitous hoarfrosts and hail. Pestilences did not descend [on the land]. The people did not die premature deaths. But now the ice of the streams and pools is what is stored up; [much also] is cast away and not used. The winds go abroad as they ought not to do and carry death with them; so does the thunder come with shaking crash. Who can put a stop to this plague of hail? . . ." (pp. 595, cols. 1 and 2; 596, col. 1)

[The following concerns an eclipse noted in the *Spring and Autumn Annals*, which may be dated to the afternoon of 14 August 524 B.C.] When the eclipse occurred, the priest and the historiographer asked for the offerings of silk which should be employed. Chao Tzu said, "On the occurrence of an eclipse, the Son of Heaven does not have his table fully spread, and causes the drum to be beaten at the altar of the land, while the princes of States present offerings of silk at that altar, and cause the drum to be beaten in their courts. This is the rule." P'ing Tzu opposed it, saying, "Stop; it is only in the first month, before the evil influence has shown itself, that it is the rule, on the occurrence of an eclipse, to beat the drum and present those offerings. On other occasions there is no such rule." The grand historiographer said, "That is just this month. After the sun has passed the equinox and before he has arrived at the solstice, when any calamity happens to the sun, moon, or stars, the various officers put off their elegant robes, the ruler does not have his table fully spread, and withdraws from his principal chamber, till the time [of the eclipse] is past; the musicians beat the drums, the priest presents his offerings, and the historiographer makes an address. . . ." (p. 667, col. 1)

There appeared a comet in Ch'i, and the marquis gave orders for a deprecatory sacrifice.[5] Kan Tzu said to him, "It is of no use; you will only practice a delusion. There is no uncertainty in the ways of Heaven; it does not waver in its purposes:—why should you offer a deprecatory sacrifice? Moreover, there is a broom-star in the sky;—it is for the removal of dirt. If your lordship have nothing about your conduct that can be so described, what have you to deprecate? If you have, what will it be diminished by your deprecation? . . . Let your lordship do nothing contrary to virtue, and from all quarters the States will come to you;—why should you be troubled about a comet? . . . If the conduct be evil and disorderly, the people are sure to fall away, and nothing that priests and historiographers can do will mend the evil." The marquis was pleased, and stopped the sacrfice. (p. 718, cols. 1 and 2)

This year, there had been a cloud, like a multitude of red birds, flying round the sun, which continued for three days. The viscount of Ch'u sent to ask the grand historiographer of Chou about it, who said that it portended evil to the king's person, and that if he offered a deprecatory sacrifice to it, the evil might be removed so as to fall on the chief minister or one of the marshals. The king, however, said, "Of what use would it be to take a disease threatening the heart and lay it upon the limbs. If I had not committed great errors, would Heaven shorten my life? I must receive the penalty of my transgressions; why should I try to move it over to another?" So he did not offer

[5]Sacrifice to appease Heaven by admitting his own faults. (L.G.T.)

the sacrifice. Before this, king Chao had been ill, and an answer was obtained from the tortoise-shell[6] that his illness was occasioned by the [Spirit of the] Ho (i.e. the Yellow River). Notwithstanding, he did not sacrifice to it; and when his great officers begged him to sacrifice to it at the border [altar], he said, "According to the sacrifices commanded by the three dynasties (i.e. Hsia, Shang, and Chou), a State cannot sacrifice to any but the hills and streams within its borders. The [Yangtze] Chiang, the Han, the Chŭ, and the Chang are the rivers to which Ch'u ought to sacrifice. Calamity or prosperity is not to be accounted for by error in this respect. Although I am deficient in virtue, I have not offended against the Ho." Accordingly, he would not sacrifice to it. . . . (p. 810, col. 2) (Confucius commented approvingly on king Chao's attitude.)

7) *Ghosts.* The *locus classicus* for the Chinese notion of the origin of ghosts is a passage of the *Tso Chuan* which we quote here, in abbreviated form:

The people of Cheng frightened one another about Po-yu, saying, "Po-yu is here!" on which they would all run off, not knowing where they were going to. In the second month of the year one man dreamt that Po-yu walked by him in armor and said, On the day *jen-tzu* I will kill Tai, and next year, on *jen-tzu*, I will kill Tuan." When Ssu Tai did die on *jen-tzu*, the terror of the people increased. This year, in the month that the States of Ch'i and Yen made peace, on *jen-yin*, Kung-sun Tuan died, and the people were still more frightened, until prime minister Tzu Ch'an made certain appointments in order to soothe the people, after which their terrors ceased. Someone asked his reason for making these arrangements, and Tzu Ch'an replied, "When a ghost (*kuei*) has a place to go to (*kuei* — a different character), it does not become an evil spirit. I have made such a place for the ghost." . . . When Tzu Ch'an went to the State of Chin, someone asked him whether it was possible for Po-yu to become a ghost. "Yes," replied Tzu Ch'an. "When a man is born, we see in his first movements what is called the animal soul. After this has been produced, it is developed into what is called the spirit. By the use of things the subtle elements are multiplied, and the soul and spirit become strong. They go on in this way, growing in etherealness and brightness, till they become thoroughly spiritual and intelligent. When an ordinary man or woman dies a violent death, the soul and spirit are still able to keep hanging about men in the shape of an evil apparition; how much more might this be expected in the case of Liang Hsiao [another name for Po-yu], a descendant of our former ruler duke Mu, the grandson of Tzu Liang, the son of Tzu Erh, all ministers of our State, engaged in its government for three generations! Although Cheng be not great, and in fact, as the saying is, an insignificant State, yet belonging to a family which had held for three generations the handle of government, his use of things had been extensive, the subtle essences which he had imbibed had been many. His clan also was a great one, and

6See Sec. 8, *Divination.*

his connections were distinguished. Is it not entirely reasonable that, having died a violent death, he should be a ghost?" (p. 618, col. 1)

8) *Divination.* Two divinatory practices were standard at the courts of the feudal states in archaic times. One was by the tortoise shell and the other by the stalks of the milfoil plant. As for the first, we know already of the oracle bones from which scholars like Tso-pin Tung have derived so much information about the late Shang, or Yin period; from the frequent references in *Tso Chuan* we know that this sort of divination continued to be practiced from the Chou dynasty to the time of Confucius. We may quote here from a note by James Legge in his translation of the *Shu Ching* (p. 335, n. 20). He cites a passage by the great Sung philosopher and commentator, Chu Hsi: "The tortoise . . . after great length of years becomes intelligent; and the milfoil plant will yield, when a hundred years old, a hundred stalks from one root, and is also a spiritual and intelligent thing. The two divinations were in reality a questioning of spiritual beings, the plant and the tortoise being employed, because of their mysterious intelligence, to indicate their intimations. The way of divination by the tortoise was by the application of fire to scorch the tortoise-shell till the indications appeared on it; and that by the stalks of the plant was to manipulate in the prescribed ways forty-nine of them, eighteen different times, till the diagrams were formed." (For details on this latter method, see Hellmut Wilhelm, *Change, Eight Lectures on the I Ching*, pp. 98-104.) We give now one of the instances recorded in *Tso Chuan* of divination by the stalks, which clearly shows the oracular use of the *Yi Ching* in Ch'un Ch'iu times:

Duke Li of Ch'en . . . begat Ching-chung, during whose boyhood there came one of the historiographers of Chou to see the marquis of Ch'en, having with him the *Chou Yi*. The marquis made him consult it by the milfoil on the future of the boy when he found the diagram Kuan (☰☷), and then by the change of manipulation, the diagram P'i (☰☷). "Here," he said, "is the deliverance;"—'We behold the light of the State. This is auspicious for one to be the king's guest. (See the *Yi* on the fourth line, counting from the bottom, of the diagram Kuan).' Shall this boy in his generation possess the State of Ch'en? Or if he do not possess this State, does it mean that he shall possess another? Or is the thing foretold not of his own person, but of his descendants? The light is far off, and its brightness appears reflected from something else. K'un (☷) represents the earth; Sun (☴), the top part of the diagram Kuan, wind; Ch'ien (☰), heaven; Sun becoming Ch'ien over earth [as in the diagram P'i], represents mountains. Thus the boy has all the treasures of mountains, and is shone on by the light of heaven:—he will dwell above the earth. Hence it is said, 'We behold the light of the State. This is auspicious for him to be the king's guest.' A king's guest fills the royal courtyard with the display of all the productions of his State, and the offerings of gems and silks,—all excellent things of heaven and earth; hence it is said—'It is auspicious for him to be the king's guest.'

"But there is still that word — 'behold,' and therefore I say the thing perhaps is to be hereafter. And the wind moves and appears upon the earth; — therefore I say it is to be perhaps in another State. If it be in another State, it must be in that of the Chiang; — for the Chiang are the descendants of the Grand-mountain (legendary emperor Yao's chief minister). But the mountains stand up as it were the mates of heaven. There cannot be two things equally great; as Ch'en decays, this boy will flourish." (p. 103, col. 2)

9) *Dream interpretation.* The marquis of Chin saw in a dream a great demon with dishevelled hair reaching to the ground, which beat its breast, and leaped up, saying, "You have slain my descendants unrighteously, and I have presented my request to God in consequence (this would be the Spirit of the founder of the Chao clan)." It then broke the great gate of the palace, advanced to the gate of the State chamber, and entered. The duke was afraid and went into a side-chamber, the door of which it also broke. The duke then awoke, and called for the witch of Sang-t'ien, who told him everything which he had dreamt. "What will be the issue?" asked the duke. "You will not taste the new wheat," she replied. After this the duke became very ill (and a physician was called who told him nothing could be done for his disease). In the sixth month, on the day *ping-wu*, the marquis wished to taste the new wheat, and made the superintendent of his fields present some. While the baker was getting it ready, they called the witch of Sang-t'ien, showed her the wheat, and put her to death. As the marquis was about to taste the wheat, he felt it necessary to go to the privy, into which he fell, and so died. One of the servants that waited on him had dreamt in the morning that he carried the marquis on his back up to heaven. The same at midday carried him on his back out from the privy, and was afterwards buried alive with him!" (p. 374, cols. 1 and 2)

. . . Sheng-pi dreamt that he was crossing the Huan, when some one gave him a gem and a fine pearl, which he ate. He then fell a-crying, and his tears turned to the same gems and fine pearls, till his breast was filled with them. After this he sang:

'Crossing the waters of the Huan,
They gave me a pearl and a gem.
Home let me go! Home let me go!
My breast with pearls and gems is full.'

When he awoke, he was afraid and did not venture to have the dream interpreted. Returning now from Cheng, on the day *jen-shen* he arrived at Li-shen, and had the dream interpreted, saying, "I was afraid it indicated my death, and did not venture to have it interpreted. Now the multitude with me is great, and the dream has followed me three years. It cannot hurt me to tell it." He did so; and in the evening of that day he died. (p. 404, col. 2)

Tzu Ch'an having gone on a complimentary visit to Chin, the marquis was then ill, and Han Hsüan-tzu met the guest, and had a private conversation with him. "Our ruler," he said, "has been ill in bed now, for three months. We have been all running about and sacrificing to all the hills and streams in Chin, but his illness has got worse instead of better. He has now dreamt that a yellow bear entered the door of his chamber;—what evil devil can that be?" "With a prince so intelligent as your ruler," replied Tzu Ch'an, "and with the government in your hands, what evil devil can there be? Anciently, when Yao put K'un to death on mount Yü, his spirit changed into a yellow bear, which entered into the abyss of Yü. He was under the Hsia dynasty the assessor at its sacrifice to Heaven, and in fact the three dynasties all sacrificed to him. Chin, though lord of covenants, has perhaps not yet sacrificed to him." Han Hsüan-tzu on this offered the Hsia sacrifice to Heaven, when the marquis became somewhat better, and gave to Tzu Ch'an the two square tripods of Lü (as gifts). (p. 617, col. 2)

10) Superstition vs rationalism. The duke wished, in consequence of the drought, to burn a witch and a person much emaciated. Tsang Wenchung said to him, "That is not the proper preparation in a time of drought. Put in good repair your walls, the inner and outer; lessen your food; be sparing in all your expenditure. Be in earnest to be economical, and encourage people to help one another;—this is the most important preparation. What have the witch and the emaciated person to do with the matter? If Heaven wish to put them to death, it had better not have given them life. If they can really produce drought, to burn them will increase the calamity." The duke followed his advice; and that year, the scarcity was not very great. (Legge has here a note, pointing out that "in the *Li Chi,* II, Pt. II.iii.29, there is an account of exposing in the sun, in a time of drought, a person in a state of emaciation, with the hope that Heaven would have pity on him, and send down rain.") (p. 180, cols. 1 and 2)

11) Magic. The people of Ch'u required the duke [of Lu] to bring graveclothes with his own hand [for their deceased king]. He was troubled about it, but Mu Shu said to him, "Have all about the coffin sprinkled, and then take the grave-clothes there. They will be but so much cloth or silk set forth at court." Accordingly a sorcerer was employed, who first executed the sprinkling with a branch of a peach tree and some reeds. . . . (p. 547, col. 2)

Tzu Ch'an of Cheng, in consequence of the fire, celebrated a great sacrifice at the altar of the land, and ordered exorcisms and deprecatory sacrifices throughout the State, in order to remove entirely the plague of the fire . . . (p. 671, col. 2)

12) Man's Heaven-endowed nature. The viscount of Lü said, "I have heard that men receive at birth the exact and correct principles of Heaven and Earth, and these are what is called their appointed nature. Men of ability nourish those rules so as to secure blessing, while those devoid of ability violate them so as to bring on themselves calamity. Therefore superior men diligently attend to the rules of propriety, and men of an inferior position do their best. In regard to the rules of propriety, there is nothing like using the greatest respectfulness. In doing one's best, there is nothing like being earnestly sincere. That respectfulness consists in nourishing one's spirit; that earnestness, in keeping one's duties in life. The great affairs of a State are sacrifice and war. At sacrifices in the ancestral temple, the officers receive the roasted flesh; in war they receive that offered at the altar of the land:— these are the great ceremonies in worshipping the Spirits. . . . (pp. 381f.)

13) Vast significance of the li, being based upon cosmic order. (Li is here rendered by Legge as "ceremonies" to bring out the religious character of the word, as against the more limited "rules of propriety" by which he translates it very often.)

    Tzu T'ai-shu had an interview with Chao Chien-tzu, and was asked by him about the ceremonies of bowing, yielding precedence, and moving from one position to another. "These," said Tzu T'ai-shu, "are matters of deportment (*yi*) and not of ceremony (*li*)." "Allow me to ask," said Chien-tzu, "what are we to understand by ceremonies." The reply was, "I have heard our great officer Tzu Ch'an say, 'Ceremonies are founded in the regular procedure of Heaven, the right phenomena of earth, and the actions of men.' Heaven and earth have their regular ways, and men take these for their pattern, imitating the brilliant bodies of Heaven, and according with the natural diversities of the Earth. Heaven and Earth produce the six atmospheric conditions, and make use of the five material elements. Those conditions and elements become the five tastes, are manifested in the five colors, and displayed in the five notes. When these are in excess, there ensue obscurity and confusion, and the people lose their proper nature. The rules of ceremony were therefore framed to support that nature. There were the six domestic animals, the five beasts of the chase, and the three classes of victims, to maintain the tastes. There were the nine emblematic ornaments of robes, with their six colors and five methods of display, to maintain the five colors. There were the nine songs, the eight winds, the seven sounds, and the six pitch-pipes, to maintain the five notes. There were ruler and minister, high and low, in imitation of the distinctive characteristics of the earth. There were husband and wife, with the home and the world abroad, the spheres of their respective duties. There were father and son, elder and younger brother, aunt and sister, maternal uncles and aunts, father-in-law and connections of one's children with other members of their mother's family, and brothers-in-law,— to resemble the bright luminaries of heaven. There were duties of government and administration, services specially for the people, legislative vigour, the force of conduct, and attention to what was required by the times,— in accordance with the phaenomena of the four seasons. There were punishments and penalties, and the terrors of legal proceedings, making the people stand in awe, resembling the destructive forces of thunder and lightning. There were mildness and gentleness, kindness and harmony, in imitation of the producing and nourishing action of Heaven. There were love and hatred, pleasure and anger, grief and joy, produced by the six atmospheric conditions. Therefore the sage kings carefully imitated these relations and analogies in forming ceremonies, to regulate those six impulses. To grief there belong crying and tears; to joy, song and dancing; to pleasure, beneficence; to anger, fighting and struggling. Pleasure is born of love, and anger of hatred. Therefore the sage kings were careful judges of their conduct, and sincere in their orders, appointing misery and happiness, rewards and punishments, to regulate the death and life of the people. Life is a good thing; death is an evil thing. The good thing brings joy; the evil thing gives grief. When there is no failure in the joy and grief, we have a state in harmony with the nature of Heaven and Earth, which consequently can endure long."

Chien Tzu said, "Extreme is the greatness of ceremonies!" "Ceremonies," replied Tzu T'ai-shu, "determine the relations of high and low; they are the warp and woof of Heaven and Earth; they are the life of the people. Hence it was that the ancient kings valued them, and hence it is that the man who can now bend, now straighten, himself so as to accord with ceremonies is called a complete man. Right is it that ceremonies should be called great!" (pp. 708f)

A classical statement of the social relationships is included in this second passage on the importance of *li* (this time rendered as "rules of propriety"):

[Yen Tzu said:] "Their rise (the *li*) was contemporaneous with that of Heaven and Earth. That the ruler order and the subject obey, the father be kind and the son dutiful, the elder brother loving and the younger respectful, the husband be harmonious and the wife gentle, the mother-in-law be kind and the daughter-in-law obedient;— these are things in propriety. That the ruler in ordering order nothing against the right, and the subject obey without any duplicity; that the father be kind and at the same time reverent, and the son be dutiful and at the same time able to remonstrate; that the elder brother, while loving, be friendly, and the younger docile, while respectful; that the husband be righteous, while harmonious, and the wife correct, while gentle; that the mother-in-law be condescending, while kind, and the daughter-in-law be winning, while obedient;— these are excellent things in propriety." "Good!" said the duke; "henceforth I have heard the highest style of propriety." Yen Tzu replied, "It was what the ancient kings received from Heaven and Earth for the government of their people, and therefore they ranked it in the highest place." (pp. 718f)

14) *Dragons.* The dragon has been such a prominent symbol in Chinese culture from the ancient bronze vessels to contemporary decorative motifs, that we include in these excerpts from *Tso Chuan* two interesting passages on the subject. That the dragon symbolizes water, that he is beneficent as well as terrible, and that he is one of the most important symbols of the Imperial rule, is of course well known; the true origin of the symbol in China is still a subject for conjecture.

There were great floods in Cheng; and some dragons fought in the pool of Wei, outside the Shih gate. The people asked leave to sacrifice to them; but Tzu Ch'an refused it, saying, "If we are fighting, the dragons do not look at us; when dragons are fighting, why should we look at them? We may offer a deprecatory sacrifice, but that is their abode.[7] If we do not seek anything of the dragons, they will not seek anything from us." (p. 675, col. 2)

In autumn, a dragon appeared in the suburbs of Chiang, on which Wei Hsien-tzu asked Ts'ai Mo, the grand historiographer, saying, "I have heard that of all the scaly tribes the dragon is the most knowing, because it cannot be got alive. Is it true to say that it is thus knowing?" Mo replied, "This is only men's want of knowledge; it is not that the dragon is really knowing. Anciently they kept dragons, and hence there were in the kingdom the families of Ch'üan-lung (Dragon-rearer) and Yü-lung (Dragon-ruler)." Hsien-tzu said, "I have heard myself of those two families, but do not know their history; —what is the meaning of their names?" The historiographer replied, "Formerly, there was Shu-an of Liu, who had a distant descendant called Tung-fu, very fond of dragons, and able to find out their tastes and likings, so as to supply them with meat and drink. Many dragons came to him, and he, according to their nature, reared them in the service of the [legendary] emperor Shun, who gave him the surname of Tung, and the clan-name of Ch'üan-lung. He was also invested with the principality of Tsung-ch'uan, and the family of Tsung Yi is of his posterity. Thus in the time of the emperor Shun, and for generations after, dragons were reared.

"We come then to K'ung-chia of the Hsia dynasty who was so obedient and acceptable to God (*Ti*), that God gave him teams of dragons; two from the Ho (Yellow River) and two from the Han,— in pairs, male and female. K'ung-chia could not feed them, and no members of the Ch'üan-lung family were to be found. But amid the remains of the family of T'ao-t'ang (Yao) was a descendant called Liu Lei, who had learned the art of rearing dragons from the family of Ch'üan-lung. With this he undertook to serve K'ung-chia, and was able to feed the dragons. The sovereign esteemed his service, gave him the clan-name of Yü-lung, and appointed him to the place of the descendants of Chu-wei. One of the female dragons died, and he secretly preserved it as minced meat in brine, supplying with it the table of the sovereign of Hsia, who enjoyed it, and required him to find others for the same use. On this Liu Lei was afraid, and removed to Lu Hsien. The family of Fan is descended from him."

Hsien Tzu said, "What is the reason that there are none now?" Mo replied, "Every kind of creatures must have its own officers, who carefully attend to the laws of its nature, morning and evening thinking of them, and who, if for a single day they fail in their duties, should be liable to death, lose their offices, and have no support. When the officers rest in the performance of their appointed duties, the creatures come to them abundantly. If they neglect and abandon those duties, the creatures cease to appear, and lie concealed — their production is restrained and stopped. In this way there were the officers of the five elementary principles (i.e. the *wu hsing*) who were called the five officers, received their several clan-names and surnames, and were appointed dukes of the highest rank. They were sacrificed to, after death, as Spirits, and received honour and offerings, at the altars of the land and grain, and at the five regular sacrifices. The chief officer of wood

---

[7]A deprecatory sacrifice is irrelevant: the dragons are simply acting like dragons in the sky where they live, and their actions are not caused by man's faults. (L.G.T.)

was called Pao-mang; of fire, Chu-jung; of metal, Ju-shou; of water, Hsüan-ming; of earth, Hou-t'u. The dragon is a creature of the water; there is no longer an officer of the water; and therefore it is not got alive. . . . (Here the speaker goes for support to the *Yi Ching*, where the dragon is mentioned several times in elucidating the diagrams, and concludes): If the dragon had not constantly—morning and evening—appeared, who could have thus described it?" (p. 731, cols. 1 and 2)[8]

[8]The foregoing excerpts from *Tso Chuan* are from the translation of James Legge, *The Ch'un Ts'ew with the Tso Chuen* (The Chinese Classics, Vol. V, Oxford 1872.)

3.
ancient festivals and holy places

From the numerous passages in the early literature that mention matters connected with religion, modern scholars have attempted reconstructions of the religious system of Chou times. Unfortunately it is difficult to understand the texts that survive from the most ancient times. In 213 B.C. the First Emperor of the Ch'in dynasty had burned all copies of all the historical records of the feudal states which Ch'in had vanquished, along with the *Shih*, the *Shu*, and the works of the philosophers of the late Chou period. This destruction seems to have been fairly thorough, due to the rarity of copies in times when there was of course no printing, and a "book" consisted of many ruler-shaped slips of bamboo, each bearing a single line of characters, and all strung together with thongs. When the scholars of Han times attempted to reconstruct the texts that had been in existence only a generation or so before, they faced serious problems. In fact, those problems have remained to vex scholars down through the ages.

One result of this situation is that in many cases we see Chou China through the eyes of the Han scholars. Such texts as the *Li* Scriptures, for example, which are so important for the student of the Chou religion, have to be considered as systematizing reconstructions by the Han scholars, who in many cases were giving their own best guesses rather than quoting from original sources. The break between Chou China and Han China was decisive: It is the beliefs and practices of the latter—including the soon to be powerful influence of the newly-arrived Buddhism—that molded Chinese civilization up to our times.

Among those who have tried to give a more or less extended and systematic interpretation of Chou religion, despite the problem of sources, Marcel Granet is one of the most famous. He attempted to apply the methodologies of historical sociology, anthropology, and comparative religion to ancient China, a sort of daring that few Sinologists have exhibited. He has been admired for this bold and imaginative approach; he has also been reproved for a lack of critical care in the use of his sources, particularly in failing to distinguish between the actual Chou texts and the "best guesses" of Han (and even later) scholars. We include the following material from Granet's influential book, *Festivals and Songs of Ancient China*, (E.P. Dutton & Co., Inc. N.Y. 1932) pp. 166-190, because it seems to us a reasonable, if imaginative, interpretation of certain religious problems, and a case where textual criticisms are of minimal concern.

THE SEASONAL RHYTHM

The old Chinese festivals are seasonal and rural. Apparently those which took place in spring were the most important, but they were also held in autumn. Have they any connection with the course of the sun? The answer is in the negative: They are not connected with any solar terms. . . . Are they connected with the cycle of vegetation? If they are, it seems difficult to understand why their content differs so little whether they belong to spring or autumn . . . Are they connected with the cycle of agriculture? Judging by their uniformity, it would hardly seem that some are festivals connected with sowing, for example, and others with harvesting, or with tillage, or with weaving. The theory that they are dependent upon the rhythm of peasant life is more plausible.

Actually, it is certain that there is a link between these festivals and the ritual of marriage. Now, it appears from the disputes of scholars that, in the opinion of the Chinese, spring and autumn were regarded as the favourable periods for the celebration of marriages—or rather those times during the spring and autumn when the peasants changed from one manner of life to another quite different. A tradition is set forth thus: "When the white frost falls, women's work is finished; then marriages may be made. When the ice melts, the work of the field begins and the gathering of mulberry leaves: at this time marriage rites approach their end." The women's work to which reference is made is that connected with the production of silk, which comes to an end at the same time as the work in the fields. "When the white frost begins to fall all work stops." The men no longer remain scattered through the fields, but—after a great celebration—"all return to their homes." During the dead season they spend their time in indoor occupations such as twisting rope while the women work at weaving hemp: When the cloth is woven and ready for sale, when the spring clothes are finished and ready to be worn at the spring rites—then is the time that girls, ceasing to spin, follow the youths of the neighborhood to the festivals, the time when the ice melts—and the peasants begin to give up living in their villages.

The times when individuals changed their occupations and their dwelling, and formed themselves into new groups were doubtless pathetic times, and social activities must then have taken on a new solemnity. The festivals which correspond to these momentous periods may, perhaps, mark the time of the rhythm of the life of the peasants. How far this theory is able to take us we are able to judge from a fortunate example.

The termination of work in the fields and the return to the village were the occasion of festivities with which we are acquainted in their official form, the festival of the *Pa Cha.* . . . At first the festival marked the close of the actual year, the end of the cycle of production, [i.e. the tenth month] and, later, that of the civil year, the arbitrary conclusion of the astronomic cycle [i.e. the twelfth month].

The celebration had all the characteristics of an orgy. Those who took part in it ate and drank to repletion. In olden times sexual rites were a feature. . . . During the festivities "the people of the whole country were as if mad." There were dances and music; the weapon dance and the banner dance were accompanied by the clay drum. There were even kinds of ceremonial masquerades in which people represented, for example, cats and leopards. There was a shooting match in which the targets were painted figures of animals, and success therein paved the way to feudal honours. This complex, lively, dramatic festival, which seems at first to be connected with the harvest and the chase, has two main features upon which I propose to lay stress. This is a concluding festival, it is a festival of thanksgiving.

In it a general thanksgiving was made. The ceremonies described by the *Yüeh ling* [a section of *Li Chi*] include prayers for the year (harvest) to come, offered to the celestial Tsung; the offering of many victims in sacrifice to the god of the public fields, as well as the *La* sacrifice (offering of venison) made at the gates of the villages and towns to the Ancestors and to the five spirits of the house. The catalogue of the *Chiao t'ê chêng* [in *Li Chi*]—none too lucid as regards detail—mentions first eight (*pa*) varieties of sacrifices (*cha*) offered mainly to the first husbandman (men?) (Shên Nung?); then to the minister (s?) of agriculture (Hou Chi?), to the hundred seeds, to the workers in the fields, to the bounds (or the guard-huts built on the edges of the fields), to all the animals (birds and beasts). The list is completed by comment inserted in the text: "They presented themselves (for the purpose of sacrificing to them) before (persons representing) cats and leopards" because the former eat field-mice and the latter boars. From the invocation used it is evident that the ceremony also had reference to the earth, water, insects, plants and trees. According to the *Chou li*, the music which was played was meant for feathered creatures and the spirits of rivers and lakes; hairless creatures and the spirits of mountains and forests (or of mountain forests); scaly creatures and the spirits of mounds and hills (or of cliffs and shores); to hairy creatures and the spirits of plains and uplands; horned creatures and the spirits of the earth; to stellar beings and heavenly gods (*shên*). Thus thanksgiving was made to all classes of beings, animate and inanimate, imaginary and real, in groups and separated. Also, to *Cha*, the etymology of which was obscure, was given the meaning of "to seek." "Throughout the whole country search was made for the *Kuei* and the *Shên* and sacrifices and offerings were made to them." It is also said that sacrifices were offered to the hundred things, that is to say, to all things. . . .

In the same way, everyone contributed to the sacrifices and everyone took part in them. The people of the whole state gave in proportion to the yield of the harvest; the vassals sent their gifts to the emperor by envoys. The envoys took part in the ceremonies; the sovereign prepared a grand drinking bout for his adherents, the flesh of the sacrificial victims being set out on tables. "The field-workers were rewarded (for their toil) in such a way as to give them rest." The heads of districts collected all the people in the arena. All the basic rules of the social order were displayed during the ceremony: filial piety, respect for elders, respect for rank, a spirit of deference, a desire for purity, feelings of reverence. Those present were divided into two groups, one group taking the side of the Master of the Ceremony, the other that of the guests. The position of the guests was fixed by an orientation whose influence, it was believed, connected each group with the opposing forces of the universe—heaven and earth, sun and moon, *yang* and *yin*—which decide the rotation and the opposition of the seasons. The leaders of the two groups and their assistants offered goblets to one another in turn. Two companies of musicians played one after the other and then together. The effect of this festival was general harmony; it was said to mark the highest point of Benevolence (*jên*, the virtue of man in his social state), the perfection of justice (*i*, the law of human relationships).

From all that is known of this thanksgiving festival it is evident that it made obvious the unity of the All, the world of matter and the world of men, and that the consciousness of this unity was the result of setting over against each other things arranged according to opposites. Sacrifice was offered to everything, and everything was used in the sacrifice; all were bound to serve as offerings and all shared in the offerings. While they took part in the offerings, the members of the human group were divided into two groups, just as the things in nature were divided into two categories.

From another point of view, the *Pa Cha* are a concluding festival. This brings the agricultural year to an end. Mourning is worn for it, and this is the reason why white clothes are donned with a girdle of hemp and a staff of hazelwood. It is thus that the aging year is conducted to its end. . . . As the purpose of the festival is to give back vigour to things that have grown old, weary with producing, so to men, as the reward of their toil, is given rest. One invocation ran: "May the Earth return to its place! May the Waters withdraw into their channels! May summer Insects not bestir themselves! May Trees and Plants return into the lakes!"—mysterious phrases, of which a perfectly intelligible explanation may be found elsewhere. . . .

When men take their rest they give rest also to things, and they conceive this rest of nature in the likeness of their own. Because they live during the winter snug in their homes, shut up in their clan village, they look upon the dead season as a period of universal confinement, during which all things return to their original dwellings, live there shut up with their own kind, and have no further dealings one with the other. Each species, now shut in, is beyond the reach of any other, remote from all outside contact, placed under an interdict: The earth, dedicated, no longer yields to human toil; exclusive rights of ownership no longer hold good at a distance; there are no longer any ties save between beings in close proximity and of the same nature. While men are reviving their powers in the intimacy of their family circle, and, in contact with their own people, are restoring in themselves the genius of their race, they believe that in the same way the various classes of beings, also dwelling among their intimates, regain their particular attributes, and that their revived nature is being prepared for the spring. Thus the formula of the *Pa Cha* which effected universal separation, effected also universal revival.

. . . The natural laws conceived by the Chinese upon the model of the rules governing their own life, appeared to them to be constant when they themselves remained subject to the laws appropriate to men. The rhythm of their life decided the alternation of the seasons; their festival of rest gave nature authority to rest; their winter seclusion assured the independence of species for the season; irregularity in their customs would have thrown the universe into disorder. . . . Chinese peasants did not shut themselves up in the winter with any magical purpose in view or anticipate that the effect of their action would be to shut up unseasonable rain and prevent it from falling, but, being accustomed to remain in seclusion in their homes during this season, when it never rained, they therefore assumed that the practices of nature were identical with those of men. From this standpoint their various customs were so many rules of practice whose influence extended to the material world. The regular rhythm of their life was, as a matter of fact, an exact copy of the regular progress of things; but this regularity in nature was made intelligible to them by the uniform course of their own lives, and because of that same course they judged regularity to be incumbent upon the whole universe. In the same way, their faith in the efficacy of their observances was due to the confidence and the respect inspired in them by their customs. It is therefore not surprising that the seasonal festivals, which mark first of all the emotional moments in the life of the community, should also have had an effect upon Nature, nor that the means by which this effect is brought about, far from having been devised and adapted for such a purpose, merely arise from customs instituted for the purpose of providing for human needs.

THE HOLY PLACES

It has long been known that Mountains and Rivers played an important part in the official religion and in the popular beliefs of the Chinese. From the most remote antiquity, we are told, Mountains and Rivers have been objects of worship in China. This statement is liable to be misinterpreted: There is a danger that it may be understood to mean that special worship was offered to them and that individual cults sprang up in connection with this sacred mountain or that sacred river. . . . Let us see what the texts say:

"Mountains, forests, rivers, valleys, heights, hills, have the power to produce clouds, to make rain and wind, and to cause portents to appear: of all these things it is said that they are *Shên*, sacred powers." "It is the sacred powers of mountains and rivers who are entreated by means of sacrifices when floods, droughts, or epidemics befall." . . .

It is true that the mountain-tops are wrapped in cloud, and that mists are given to hanging over forests and valleys; is it by observation that the source of rain has been discovered to lie in the places where clouds appear to form? But is not the power to avert pestilence also attributed to mountains and rivers? It may be affirmed that this power is dependent upon the others. The spread of infection is due to too much or too little moisture. In fact, the power of mountains and rivers is not as specialized as it would be if it were based upon observation of the facts of nature. They are not merely storehouses of rain, they are rather controllers of the regularity of the seasons. In the natural order they occupy a position analogous to that of the ruler in human society. . . .

The fact of the matter is that their power is only another aspect of the power of the prince. When the prince lacks virtue there is no order among men; when the mountain lacks power, rain does not fall in its appointed time. But if any should propose to punish the mountain for failing in its duty, he would be holding the wrong person responsible. Disorder in nature is only the result of disorder in society; it is the prince who should hold himself to blame both when rain fails and when it rains too much. . . . The virtue of mountains and rivers is thus entirely dependent upon the virtue of the prince. If they guarantee to the people life and health it is through no innate qualities of their own, for no such qualities are inherent in the essence of their being. In everything they are dependent upon human government; they are worth what it is worth; they last as long as it lasts. . . .

Such were the beliefs connected with the princely worship of mountains and rivers. Their relation with the beliefs connected with seasonal festivals is easily understood. While the princes, on whom rested the double responsibility of maintaining good order in society and in the universe, thought to make use of the potency of mountains and rivers to uphold their rule, the seasonal festivals, which brought together, close to the mountains and rivers, the members of a local community, while they served in the first place to display the ordered course of the life of the community, further assured the orderly functioning of nature. . . . Since sacred mountains and rivers never possessed any power other than that delegated to them by the ruling authority, must it not also be true that the holy places had no virtue of their own. Their sanctity was entirely due to the fact that the local communities which gathered there rendered effective in these places, which had witnessed their reunions from generation to generation, the principle of the sacred forces set in motion by the seasonal festivals.

Thanks to these festivals they hoped to avoid plagues, ensure rain in due season, and to be granted children. Believing their livelihood, both present and future, to be guaranteed by the favour of the hallowed place of their assemblies, the members of the local community felt themselves bound to it by a relationship teeming with benefits, which caused them to adhere to it as faithful vassals to a powerful lord. When they were gathered together to keep these festivals from which so much good resulted, each one, hoping for all these benefits, ascribed a variety of virtues to mountains, rivers, and woods, with which he was familiar and which seemed to him worthy of reverence. He endeavored to assimilate and to woo the protecting power which, it seemed to him, invested the spot where at all times his people had attained their loftiest desires. . . .

. . . Certain princely families bore the name of a holy place from whose influence had been derived the special virtue of their traditional ancestor. . . . Thus it sometimes happens that the name, indicating the genius of the race, springs directly from the holy place, while at others it is supplied by the miscellaneous things connected with the festivals held there. Is there any very real difference between the two cases? Should not the holy places be regarded as *ancestral centers* where the genius of the family was felt to be, and whence those belonging to that race thought to obtain, on the occasion of the festival, that which would ensure the fecundity of their women? . . .

As the feudal princes looked upon their mountains and rivers as the principle of their authority made manifest, so the local communities realized in their holy places the genius of their race. By reason of the age of the ties which bound them to these places dedicated to their solemn assemblies they had come to regard them as ancestral centres, while the regularity of the festivals held there gave them the impression that here dwelt the powers in control of nature. Distributors of souls, controllers of the seasons, it was from them that the indigenous groups drew alike their existence and their continuance.

These holy places were revered not for their rivers, their mountains, and their woods; they maintained their venerable character through having been the traditional link of the seasonal festivals. They appeared as the witnesses and the protectors of the social covenant renewed at regular intervals by these assemblies. Hence their majesty. Hence also it happened that when princely rule was set up, and to the prince, surety for the unity of the people, was ascribed a like majesty, they supposed a sort of partnership between the holy places and the prince.

4.
the moral law and the moral life

Elsewhere in this reader we have furnished some selections which illustrate the particularly Taoist usage of the important term Tao (see chapter 7: The Taoist Sages); here we give a few passages showing the most important implications of that term in the vocabulary of the Confucian School—which means, for the past 2,000 years, of the educated class as a whole. The work from which we quote is one of the Four Books, and of all the Confucian Scriptures, it contains the most eloquent statement of the moral position of man in a moral universe. The book is called *Chung Yung*, a title usually translated as The Doctrine of the Mean; Hung-ming Ku, the translator we cite, prefers to call it *The Conduct of Life*:

Confucius remarked: "The life of the moral man *(chün-tzu)* is an exemplification of the universal moral order *(chung yung)*. The life of the vulgar person, on the other hand, is a contradiction of the universal moral order. The moral man's life is an exemplification of the universal order, because he is a moral person who unceasingly cultivates his true self or moral being. The vulgar person's life is a contradiction of the universal order, because he is a vulgar person who in his heart has no regard for, or fear of, the moral law."

Confucius remarked: "To find the central clue to our moral being which unites us to the universal order, that indeed is the highest human achievement. People are seldom capable of it for long."

[Confucius remarked:] "The man with the true force of moral character *(chün-tzu)* is one who is easy and accomodating and yet without weakness or indiscrimination. How unflinchingly firm he is in his strength! He is independent without any bias. How unflinchingly firm he is in his strength! When there is moral social order *(tao)* in the country, if he enters public life he does not change from what he was when in retirement. When there is no moral social order in the country he holds on his way without changing even unto death. How unflinchingly firm he is in his strength!"

Confucius remarked: "There are men who seek for some abstruse meaning in religion and philosophy and live a life singular in order that they may leave a name to posterity. This is what I never would do. There are again good men who try to live in conformity with the moral law, but who, when they have gone half way, throw it up. I never could give it up. Lastly, there are truly moral men who unconsciously live a life in entire harmony with the universal moral order and who live unknown to the world and unnoticed of men without any concern. It is only men of holy, divine natures who are capable of this."

The moral law is to be found everywhere, and yet it is a secret. The simple intelligence of ordinary men and women of the people may understand something of the moral law; but in its utmost reaches there is something which even the wisest and holiest of men cannot understand. The ignoble natures of ordinary men and women of the people may be able to carry out the moral law; but in its utmost reaches even the wisest and holiest of men cannot live up to it.

Great as the Universe is, man, with the infinite moral nature in him, is never satisfied. For there is nothing so great but the mind of the moral man can conceive of something still greater which nothing in the world can hold. There is nothing so small but the mind of moral man can conceive of something still smaller which nothing in the world can split. The Book of Songs says:

"The hawk soars to the heavens above and fishes dive to the depths below."

That is to say, there is no place in the highest heavens above nor in the deepest waters below where the moral law does not reign. The moral law takes its rise in the relation between man and woman; but in its utmost reaches it reigns supreme over heaven and earth.

Confucius remarked: "The moral law *(tao)* is not something away from the actuality of human life. When men take up something away from the actuality of human life as the moral law, that is not the moral law. . . . Wherefore the moral man in dealing with men appeals to the common human nature and changes the manner of their lives and nothing more.

"When a man carries out the principles of conscientiousness *(chung)* and reciprocity *(shu)* he is not far from the moral law. What you do not wish others should do unto you, do not do unto them.

"There are four things in the moral life of a man, not one of which I have been able to carry out in my life. To serve my father as I would expect my son to serve me: that I have not been able to do. To serve my sovereign as I would expect a minister under me to serve me: that I have not been able to do. To act towards my elder brother as I would expect my younger brother to act towards me: that I have not been able to do. To be the first to behave towards friends as I would expect them to behave towards me: that I have not been able to do.

"In the discharge of the ordinary duties of life and in the exercise of care in ordinary conversation, whenever there is shortcoming, never fail to strive for improvement, and when there is much to be said, always say less than what is superfluous; words having respect to actions and actions having respect to words. Is it not just this thorough genuineness and absence of pretence which characterizes the moral man?"

The moral man conforms himself to his life circumstances; he does not desire anything outside of his position. . . . He puts in order his own personal conduct and seeks nothing from others; hence he has no complaint to make. He complains not against Heaven nor rails against men. Thus it is that the moral man lives out the even tenor of his life, calmly waiting for the appointment of Heaven *(ming)*, whereas the vulgar person takes to dangerous courses, expecting the uncertain chances of luck.

Confucius remarked: "In the practice of archery we have something resembling the principle in a moral man's life. When the archer misses the center of the target he turns round and seeks for the cause of his failure within himself."

[Confucius remarked:] "There is only one way for a man to be true to himself. If he does not know what is good, a man cannot be true to himself. Truth is the Law of Heaven (t'ien chih tao). Acquired truth is the law of man (jen chih tao). He who intuitively apprehends truth is one who, without effort, hits what is right, and without thinking understands what he wants to know; whose life is easily and naturally in harmony with the moral law. Such a one is what we call a saint or a man of divine nature. He who acquires truth is one who finds out what is good and holds fast to it."

[Confucius remarked:] "Thus it is that he who possesses great moral qualities will certainly attain to corresponding high position; to corresponding great prosperity; to corresponding great name; to corresponding great age. For Heaven in giving life to all created things is surely bountiful to them according to their qualities. Hence the tree that is full of life It fosters and sustains, while that which is ready to fall It cuts off and destroys.

Confucius remarked: "The power of spiritual forces in the Universe— how active it is everywhere! Invisible to the eyes, and impalpable to the senses, it is inherent in all things, and nothing can escape its operation." It is the fact that there are these forces which makes men in all countries fast and purify themselves, and with solemnity of dress institute services of sacrifice and religious worship. Like the rush of mighty waters, the presence of unseen Powers is felt: sometimes above us, sometimes around us. In the Book of Songs it is said:

"The presence of the Spirit:
It cannot be surmised,
Inspiring fear and awe."

Such is the evidence of things invisible that it is impossible to doubt the spiritual nature of man.

It is only he, in the world, who possesses absolute truth (chih ch'êng) who can get to the bottom of the law of his being (hsing). He who is able to get to the bottom of the law of his being will be able to get to the bottom of the law of being of other men. He who is able to get to the bottom of the law of being of men will be able to get to the bottom of the laws of physical nature. He who is able to get to the bottom of the laws of physical nature will be able to influence the forces of creation of the Universe. He who can influence the forces of creation of the Universe is one with the Powers of the Universe.

Truth (ch'êng) means the realisation of our being; and moral law means the law of our being. Truth is the beginning and end (the substance) of existence. Without truth there is no existence. It is for this reason that the moral man values truth. Truth is not only the realisation of our own being; it is that by which things outside of us have an existence. The realization of our being is moral sense. The realization of things outside of us is intellect. These, moral sense and intellect, are the powers or faculties of our being. They combine the inner or subjective and outer or objective use of the power of the mind. Therefore with truth everything done is right.

Thus absolute truth is indestructible. Being indestructible, it is eternal. Being eternal, it is self-existent. Being self-existent, it is infinite. Being infinite, it is vast and deep. Being vast and deep, it is transcendental and intelligent. It is because it is vast and deep that it contains all existence. . . . Such being the nature of absolute truth, it manifests itself without being evident; it produces effects without action; it accomplishes its ends without being conscious.

The principle in the course and operation of nature *(t'ien ti chih tao)* may be summed up in one word: It exists for its own sake without any double or ulterior motive.

Oh, how great is the divine moral law in man! Vast and illimitable, it gives birth and life to all created things . . . All the institutions of human society and civilization—laws, customs, and usages—have their origin there. All these institutions wait for the man before they can be put into practice. Hence it is said: Unless there be highest moral power, the highest moral law cannot be realized.

Every system of moral laws must be based upon the man's own consciousness. It must be verified by the common experience of men. Examined into by comparing it with the teachings of acknowledged great and wise men of the past, there must be no divergence. Applying it to the operations and processes of nature in the physical universe, there must be no contradiction. Confronted with the spiritual powers of the universe, a man must be able to maintain it without any doubt. . . . Wherefore it is that it is true of the really great moral man, that every act of his life becomes an example for generations; everything he does becomes a statute for generations, and every word he utters becomes a law for generations.

[The] moral laws form one system with the laws by which Heaven and Earth support and contain, overshadow and canopy all things; with the laws by which the seasons succeed each other and the sun and moon appear with the alternations of day and night; with the laws by which all created things are produced and develop themselves each in its order and system without injuring one another; that the operations of Nature *(tao)* take their course without conflict or confusion; the lesser forces flowing everywhere like river currents, while the great forces of Creation go silently and steadily on. It is this—one system running through all—that makes the Universe so impressively great.

5.
shamanism in ancient china

The terms shaman and shamanism have been widely used in writings about religion, but without any complete agreement as to their meanings.[1] Some characteristics of the shaman often described are possession by a spirit, speaking in a voice and tongue of that spirit, dancing—often to the beat of a drum, visiting the spirit world in search of a soul and bringing back the message of that soul. The shaman is set apart from normal men by his peculiar susceptibility to possession by a spirit or spirits. Often this characteristic has been enough to cause a writer to label "mediums" of any kind shamans.

Mediumship has been at least as common in China as in the West. Whether shamanism, more carefully defined, is really common in Chinese religion is another question. In the following selection, we have some interesting comments on this problem, as it can be studied in the ancient literature. It is taken from Arthur Waley's *The Nine Songs, A Study of Shamanism in Ancient China*, George Allen & Unwin Ltd. (London 1955) introduction, pp. 9-16, condensed.

In ancient China, intermediaries used in the cult of Spirits were called *wu*. They figure in old texts as experts in exorcism, prophecy, fortune-telling, rain-making and interpretation of dreams. Some *wu* danced, and they are sometimes defined as people who danced in order to bring down Spirits. But it is clear that dancing was not invariably a part of their technique . . . They were also magic healers and in later times at any rate one of their methods of doctoring was to go, as Siberian shamans do, to the underworld and find out how the Powers of Death could be propitiated. Indeed the functions of Chinese *wu* were so like those of Siberian and Tunguz shamans that it is convenient . . . to use shaman as a translation of *wu*.

Early references to shamans, though fairly frequent, unfortunately tell us little or nothing about how they set to work. The Spirit talks to or through the shaman; but whether the shaman receives these divine communications when in a state of trance or whether some incorporeal part of him climbs to Heaven and there converses with the deity is not made clear. Nor are we told how one becomes a shaman. There is a second century B.C. story of a woman upon whom a Spirit first descended when she was ill, and it appears that afterwards it was only during spells of illness that she shamanized. The *maladie initiatique* is of course a common stage in the career of shamans,

[1]See discussions in Mircea Eliade, *Shamanism: Archaic Techniques of Ecstasy.* Translation of *Le Chamanisme et les Techniques Archaïques de l'Extase* by Willard R. Trask (New York & London, 1964); and J.H. Kamstra, *Encounter or Syncretism: the Initial Growth of Japanese Buddhism* (Leiden, 1967), pp. 9-15.

magicians and saints in many parts of the world, and shamans used often to be described as neurotics by European writers. With this view of them it is interesting to contrast the following passage from a discourse on the relations between men and Spirits supposed to have been delivered about 500 B.C. The shaman, according to this text,[2] is a person upon whom a Bright Spirit has descended, attracted to him because he is 'particularly vigorous and lively, staunch in adherence to principle, reverent and just; so wise that in all matters high and low he always takes the right side, so saintly *(shêng)* that he spreads around him a radiance that reaches far and wide . . .' This is of course an idealized picture, perhaps intended to apply only to shamans of a Golden Age in the past . . .

But to return to the question of how one becomes a shaman. The frequent expression 'shaman family' seems to suggest that the profession was often hereditary. But in Ch'i (northern Shantung) such an expression would have had no meaning, for there every family was a shaman family: 'among the common people the eldest daughter is not allowed to marry. She is called the "shaman-child" *(wu-êrh)* and is in charge of the family's religious rites. This custom still (i.e. *c.*A.D.80) prevails.'[3]

Spirits constantly appear to men in dreams or simply as daylight apparitions and communicate freely, without the aid of a shaman; and the conditions under which they required a shaman as a necessary intermediary are not at all clear . . .

For even the most meager description of a shamanistic séance we have to wait till the fourth century A.D. In the biography[4] of a certain Hsia T'ung there is an account of two shaman girls who practiced in what is now Chehkiang, south of the Yangtze delta. 'They were of remarkable beauty, wore magnificent costumes and sang and danced well. They also had the power to become invisible. At nightfall, to the accompaniment of bells and drums, strings and flutes, they would slit their tongues with a knife, "swallow knives, spit fire from their mouths, fill the whole place with clouds till there was complete darkness," or produce flashes of dazzling light.' Hsia T'ung, who disapproved of shamans, having been tricked by his relatives into coming to a performance which a cousin was giving to propitiate the soul of one of his ancestors, found the two girls 'already leaping and whirling in the courtyard. There were spirit conversations, ghostly laughter . . . exchange of wine-pledges turn and turn about.' . . . This account is probably not accurate in its details, for . . . there is, I think, no evidence that such feats [as tongue-slitting and belly-ripping] formed part of the traditional shaman-technique in China.

The prejudice against shamanism which is displayed in this story went hand in hand with the rise and spread of Confucianism. It was founded, I think, on the saying attributed more than one place to Confucius that one should 'revere Spirits, but keep them at a distance.' When in 32-31 B.C. shamanistic performances at the Chinese Court were abolished, this saying was quoted by the minister who sponsored the reform. Opponents of shamanism

---

[2]*Küo Yü,* Ch'u Yu, Part II (Waley's note).

[3]*Han Shu,* 28B.30b (Waley's note).

[4]*Chin Shu,* 94.3 (Waley's note).

also had a theory that 'when a ruler is addicted to the use of shamans, cases of baleful haunting become more frequent.'[5]

After the establishment of Confucianism as a State religion in the first century B.C. the governing classes tended more and more to look down upon shamans, regarding them at the best as socially inferior—putting them on the same low level as professional entertainers, musicians, craftsmen and other specialized technicians, who were not regarded as gentlemen *(chün-tzu)*, or at the worst were looked upon as impostors who traded on the credulity of the masses. . . .

[In the Nine Songs, a section of the poetic anthology called *Ch'u Tz'u*, or Songs of the South, dating from third or fourth century B.C.,] shamanism assumes a particular form not known, I think, in the classic chamanistic areas—Siberia, Manchuria, Central Asia. The shaman's relation with the Spirit is represented as a kind of love-affair. . . .

It is clear at any rate that the relation between the shaman and the deity is a fleeting one . . . The typical form is this: First the shaman (a man if the deity is female, a girl if the deity is male) sees the Spirit descending and goes out to meet it, riding an equipage sometimes drawn by strange or mythical creatures. In the next part of the song the shaman's meeting with the Spirit (a sort of mantic honeymoon) is over. The Spirit has proved fickle and the shaman wanders about love-lorn, waiting in vain for the lover's return. Between these two parts may have come the shaman's main ecstatic dance.

The songs contain a number of meaningless cries or exclamations, and at the cesura of each line is the exclamation *hsi* which may . . . represent the panting of the shaman in trance, a sound very familiar to anyone who has attended mediumistic seances in Europe. Almost always it appears to be the shaman who is speaking in the songs. It may not always be he who does the actual singing; singers *(ch'ang)* are mentioned several times, and may sometimes have sung his (or her) words . . . One might expect the Spirit to speak through the shaman's mouth. The shaman, says a writer of the first century A.D., 'strikes the Dark Strings (probably a shaman name for some kind of zithern) and brings down the dead, who speak through his mouth.'[6] And there are numerous stories of divinities and dead men speaking through shamans. . . .

The Nine Songs owe their preservation to the fact that like other early Chinese songs they were interpreted allegorically. The shaman becomes a virtuous minister who after having for a time enjoyed the favour of his prince is discarded by him. The best-known similar case outside China is of course the Song of Songs, which would never have found its way into both the Jewish and the Christian Bibles if it had not been allegorized to meet the needs of later times. It was in this allegorical sense that the Nine Songs were understood till well into the twentieth century, although it was recognized from the second century A.D. onwards that the moral interpretation was only a sort of ultimate meaning, and that taken in their literal sense they were *wu* (shaman) songs. . . .

[5]*Kuan Tzu*, 3 (Waley's note).
[6]*Lun Hêng*, 20 (Waley's note).

6.
ancient cosmology and religion according to han scholars

We have already alluded to the great difficulty of arriving at a satisfactory picture of Chou religion from the evidence of the contemporary texts. We have mentioned that we are compelled to view the picture in large part through the eyes of the Han scholars; they themselves were attempting to reconstruct the beliefs and practices of a past from which they were separated by a gulf whose bridge had been burned by the First Emperor of Ch'in.

We wish now to give some idea of this sort of reconstruction, which will not only reveal what the Han scholars conceived ancient civilization to have been like, but equally important, the sort of thinking that was characteristic of the new age of Han itself. Or at least this sort of thinking was characteristic of the intellectual level of Han society. It may serve as representative of the religious outlook of the literati just before the Native Tradition was engaged by the very different thought of Buddhism.

The material to follow is from a book called *Po Hu T'ung: The Comprehensive Discussions in the White Tiger Hall*, E. J. Brill, (Leiden, 2 vols., 1949 & 1952), by Tjan Tjoe Som [Tseng Chu-sen]. The "comprehensive discussions" of the title refer to a council of scholars on the Classics called by the Later Han Emperor Hsiao-chang in A.D. 79 to consider and render authoritative exegeses of various uncertain points in the Scriptures. We give first a few words of explanation by the author, and then some selections from his translations of various parts of the *Po Hu T'ung* text itself. We have condensed and edited.

[The *Po Hu T'ung*] gives us an idea of the way in which the Classics were interpreted in the Han period. We have often heard of the combination of Classical *(ching)* and Apocryphal *(wei)* Books, of the *ching* being the warp and the *wei* being the woof, the former constituting the outer, the latter the inner study; nowhere else can we find such a clear and comprehensive illustration of this curious method of interpretation as in the *Po hu t'ung*.

It gives us an idea of the cosmology of the Han, that curious blending of naturalism and ethics, in which such great emphasis was laid on correct ritual behavior, and in which the King figured as the living link and mediator between the world in Heaven and everything under Heaven. Even if the *Po hu t'ung* is unsatisfactory in its descriptions of details, probably no other text presents so complete a picture of this cosmology as a system. . . . (pp.175f)

(Concerning the Apocryphal Books *(wei)* mentioned above): It would . . . not be too far wrong to assume that the contents of the *wei* on the whole were already current during the second century B.C., but that they did not take the shape of the written documents with their bizarre titles until later, while at the same time new elements, especially historical allusions, were introduced.[1]

In the process of amalgamation of the diverse beliefs into one universal system during the Former Han, the *wei* with their cosmological speculations and their classifications provided the background against which the scholars tried to understand and explain the Classics. On the whole the Classics did not provide a systematic and organic world-conception. . . . All the same we must assume that in general the Schools, including the Confucians, were arguing and disputing with each other against the background of the same world-conception, though we do not exactly know what it was. When in the Han Confucianism was made the official creed the situation changed. Political unity having been established, a new world-conception had to be found, corresponding with that unity, and not or not sufficiently furnished by the Classics. The *wei* united the beliefs current in the Han, many elements of which had been handed down from non-Confucian Schools of pre-Han times. They became complements to the Classics indeed, and not only interpretations of the Classical texts, which, somehow, despite their ambiguous wording, did not bear stretching beyond a certain degree of elasticity. Thus on the one hand the *wei* 'popularized' the Classics by proving that they did not conflict with the prevailing beliefs, on the other hand these beliefs were 'authorized' by enlisting the support of the Classics. . . . (p.118)

The Five Deities

What is meant by the Five Deities *(wu-ssu)?* They are the outer door, the inner door, the well, the hearth, and the impluvium.[2] Why are they worshipped? Because they are the places where men dwell, by which they go in and out, and where they drink and eat. Therefore they are worshipped as spirits. How do we know that the Five Deities are called outer door, inner door, well, hearth, and impluvium? The "Yüeh ling" *(a chapter of Li Chi)* says: "[In spring] they sacrifice to the inner door, [in summer] to the hearth, [in the middle of the year] to the impluvium, [in autumn] to the outer door, and [in winter] to the well."

Why is it that only [those with the rank of] great officer and higher have the right to sacrifice [to the Five Deities]? A common officer has a lowly position and a meagre remuneration, [so] he only sacrifices to his ancestors. The *Li* says: "The Son of Heaven sacrifices to Heaven and Earth, the Feudal Lords sacrifice to the mountains and rivers, the Ministers and great officers to the Five Deities, the common officers sacrifice to their ancestors." (Another text says:) . . . "There should be no presuming to resume any sacrifice which has been abolished [by proper authority], nor to abolish any which

[1]Readers desiring a thorough treatment of this subject should see Fung Yu-lan, translated from Chinese by Derk Bodde, *A History of Chinese Philosophy* (Princeton Univ., vol. II, 1953), chap.III. (L.G.T.)

[2]So rendered by our translator. The term literally means "the central place where the rainwater drops down from the roof." However, it is usually understood as indicating the middle of the room or hall. (L.G.T.)

has been so established. A sacrifice which it is not proper to offer, and which yet is offered, is called a licentious sacrifice. A licentious sacrifice brings no blessing."

Why are the Five Deities successively sacrificed to in the course of the year? They follow [the succession of] the Five Elements. . . . (pp.376f)

The Gods of the Earth and of the Millet (she chi)

Why is it that the King has a God of the Earth and of the Millet? [They are the gods whom he can ask] for prosperity for the benefit of all under Heaven, and whom he can thank for their works. Without land man would not [be able to] eat. Land [,however,] is wide and extensive, and cannot be worshipped everywhere. The species of grain are too numerous, and cannot be sacrificed to one by one. Therefore a tumulus of earth is erected for an altar of the God of the Earth in order to make manifest the holder of the earth. Millet is the most important of the species of grain. Therefore an altar of the God of Millet is erected, to which sacrifices are made. The use of millet is most general because it has absorbed the equi-balanced and harmonious influences of the yin and the yang. Therefore it is considered the principal [of the species of grain].[3]

Why are there two sacrifices [to the Gods of the Earth and of the Millet] in a year? In spring [the sacrifice] means a request [for prosperity], in autumn it means a thanksgiving [for the received boon]. . . .

Why is it that the King and the Feudal Lords each have two altars of the God of the Earth? Both are Lords holding land. Therefore a text says: "The King has two altars of the God of the Earth; he erects one altar for all under Heaven, called the 'Great Altar of the God of the Earth' *t'ai-shê*, and another for himself, called the 'King's Altar of the God of the Earth' *wang-shê*. (Similarly the Feudal Lords.) To the Great Altar thanks are offered for its works on behalf of all under Heaven. To the King's Altar thanks are offered for its works on behalf of the capital. The Great Altar is more honourable than the King's Altar. . . .

Why must the King and the Feudal Lords have a Warning God of the Earth? (*chieh-shê*, the God of Earth of a vanquished State) To remind that there is preservation and loss, and to indicate that those who do well will succeed and those who do evil will fail. Therefore a text says: "Of the God of the Earth of a vanquished state the upper part is covered, and round the lower part a palisade is built." Another text says: "The God of the Earth of a vanquished state is roofed in." It indicates that it is separated from [the influences of] Heaven and Earth. . . . The *Li* says: "The Gods of the Earth and of the Millet of a vanquished state must be used as a screen for the ancestral temple." It means that they are treated contemptuously.

Why is the altar of the Gods of the Earth and of the Millet outside the middle and inside the outer gate [of the palace]? To honour [the gods] and

[3]For the archaic myth in which "Prince Millet" is portrayed as the ancestor of the Chou, see the *Shih Ching* poem we have included in the Archaic Religion II chapter, as translated by James Legge (L.G.T.)

yet to be near to them. They are [treated in] the same [way] as the ancestors. . . . A text says: "To the right there is the altar of the Gods of the Earth and of the Millet, to the left there is the ancestral temple."

Why is it that the altar of the God of the Earth has no roof? To keep it in contact with the fluids of Heaven and Earth. Therefore a text says: "The Great Altar of the Son of Heaven must [be open to] receive the hoarfrost, the dew, the wind, and the rain, so that it can be in contact with the fluids of Heaven and Earth." Why is there a tree on the altar of the Gods of the Earth and of the Millet? That it may [thereby] be honoured and recognized. [Thus] the people may see it from afar and worship it. [The tree is] also the expression of [the god's beneficent] capacities. . . .

Why does the King sacrifice in person to the Gods of the Earth and of the Millet? The God of the Earth is the spirit of the earth. The earth produces the ten thousand things, and is the host of all under Heaven. Out of reverence for it [the King] therefore sacrifices in person.

What is the size of the altar? A text says: "The altar of the Gods of the Earth and of the Millet of the Son of Heaven is fifty feet wide [on each side], that of the Feudal Lords is one half thereof." What is its colour? A text says: "The Son of Heaven has a Great Altar; it is green on the east, red on the south, white on the west, black on the north. The top is covered with yellow earth. Thus, when [the Son of Heaven] is going to enfeoff a Feudal Lord [with a territory] in the east, he takes [a clod of] green earth [from his altar], wraps it in a white *mao* [leaf, and gives it to him]. For each [Feudal Lord receiving a fief the Son of Heaven] takes [earth] from the [corresponding] side [of his altar], with which [the Feudal Lord constructs the mound for his [own altar of the] God of the Earth. . . .

Is music used at the sacrifice to the Gods of the Earth and of the Millet? The text says: "Music [the instruments of which are] executed in metal and stone, finding its expression in tunes and notes, and used in the ancestral temple and at the altar of the Gods of the Earth and of the Millet." (pp.379-386)

The Five Elements

What is meant by the 'Five Elements' *wu-hsing?* Metal, wood, water, fire, and earth. The word *hsing* (which is a verb) is used to bring out the meaning that [in accordance] with Heaven the fluids have been 'put into motion' *hsing*. Earth aids Heaven as the wife serves her husband, and the Minister serves his Lord. . . .

Water has its position in the northern quarter. The north is [the place] where the yin-fluid lies beneath the Yellow Sources, having as its task the nourishment of the ten thousand things. 'Water' *shui* means *chun* 'level.' It nourishes the things equally, possessing the propensity of always being level.

Wood [has its position] in the eastern quarter. The east is [the place] where the yang-fluid begins to move, and the ten thousand things begin their life. 'Wood' *mu* means *cho* 'to knock'; the yang-fluid moves and jumps, knocking against the earth to break out.

Fire [has its position] in the southern quarter. The south is [the place] where the yang is superior, and the ten thousand things hang down their [luxuriant] branches. 'Fire' *huo* means *wei-sui* 'to follow as a result'; it means that the ten thousand things have fully unfurled themselves. *Huo* also means *hua* 'to change'; the yang-fluid holding sway, the ten thousand things transform themselves and change.

Metal [has its position] in the western quarter. The west is [the place] where the yin begins to rise, and [the development of] the ten thousand things is called to a stop. 'Metal' *chin* means *chin* 'to stop.'

Earth [has its position] in the center. The center is [occupied by] the earth. The earth has as its task to bring forth the ten thousand things. 'Earth' *t'u* means *t'u* 'to bring forth.' . . . (pp.429f)

Why is it that the Five Elements alternate their 'kingship'? Because they engender each other in succession, so that [each of them has] an end and a beginning. Wood engenders fire, fire engenders earth, earth engenders metal, metal engenders water, water engenders wood. . . . It is said that each of the Five Elements by its nature is either the yin or the yang. Since wood engenders fire, why is it that [fire] repays it by consuming its mother? The reply is: Metal conquers wood, and fire on behalf of wood wishes to destroy metal; [but] metal is hard and strong difficult to smelt, therefore [wood,] the mother, sacrificing its own body, comes to the aid of fire to burn metal. . . .

Why is it that wood is 'king' for seventy-two days? Earth is 'king' during the four last months of the seasons, each time for eighteen days; together [with each of the other four elements it governs] for ninety days, which makes one season. [Each of the four elements together with earth is] 'king' for ninety days. . . . (pp.437-439)

The Five Elements having a constant existence, why does fire suddenly disappear? Water is the elder yin; [it represents] punishment, therefore it is constantly existent. Metal is the younger yin, wood the younger yang; their fluids are weak and admit of no change; therefore they are also constantly existent. Fire is the elder yang, infinitesimal and fine, a representation of the Lord of men, representing him as honoured and constantly hidden, as the Son of Heaven abides in the confines of the nine double [walls], guarded by his subjects. [As fire is] concealed in wood, [so the Lord of men] reposes in consideration for others. Wood grows of its own nature, metal requires [the force of] man to be taken out and shaped because the yin, being lowly, cannot of itself take shape. . . .

Why is it that Heaven is light within and dark without, whereas man is light without and dark within? It means that Heaven and man exercise their influence by their desire to supplement each other. . . . (pp.440f)

[Here follows an interesting series explaining the way nature gives the pattern for human social behavior; we give only a few examples]:

According to what pattern does the son succeed after the death of his father? He patterns himself after wood, which, terminating [its rule, is succeeded by] fire [taking up] 'kingship.'

According to what pattern does the son obey his father, the Minister obey his Lord, and the wife obey her husband? They pattern themselves after Earth, which obeys Heaven.

According to what pattern does the King bestow his favours first on his relatives and close associates, and afterwards on the distant? He patterns himself on the rain from Heaven, from which the highest [parts of the earth] first receive [the benefit].

According to what pattern does the son wear mourning for his parents? He patterns himself on wood, which withers in the absence of water.

According to what pattern does the mourning last three years? It patterns itself after [the fact that there is] one intercalary month in three years, by which the Way of Heaven is terminated. (pp.442-445)

District Archery Contests

Why does the Son of Heaven in person practice archery? To aid the yang-fluid in stimulating the ten thousand things. In spring the yang-fluid is small and weak, and it is to be feared that the [ten thousand] things, meeting obstructions, will not be able to come out by their own strength. Now in archery [the arrow proceeds] from the inside to the outside, it pierces and enters the solid and hard [target, thus] resembling the bringing forth of [nascent] things. Therefore by means of archery they are stimulated [to come out]. (p.474)

Calamities and Extraordinary Events

Why does Heaven [send down] calamities and [cause] extraordinary events? It is to warn the Lord of men and make him conscious of his deeds, so that he may wish to repent his faults, attend to his spiritual power, and exercise deeper solicitude. A text says: "When the conduct [of the Son of Heaven] shows shortcomings, and his passion goes against Heaven, it will provoke calamities to come down as a warning to men." (p.489)

When the sun is eclipsed, why must it be rescued? Because the yin is encroaching upon the yang. A drum is beaten and a victim is sacrificed to the God of the Earth. This god is the personification of the assembled yin [-forces]. It is tied with a red cord, and a drum is beaten to attack it; [thus] with [the help of] the yang the yin is reproved. Therefore the *Ch'un Ch'iu* says: "[In the sixth month, the first day of the moon] the sun was eclipsed. Drums were beaten and victims offered to the God of the Earth." (The translator notes that while one commentator suggests that "the god is first reproved by the beating of the drum, and afterwards treated with ceremony by the offering of victims," two of the classical commentaries—which themselves attained scriptural status—hold that "the use of victims is against the rites.") (p.491)

Divination with the Milfoil and the Tortoise-shell

From the Son of Heaven down to the common officer every one has to practise divination with the milfoil [stalks] and the tortoise-shell because in important matters where decisions have to be taken on dubious points one must show that one is not going to act of one's own accord. The *Shang shu*

(Shu Ching) says: "If thou hast doubts about any great matter consult with thy Minister, consult with the common people, consult the tortoise-shell and the milfoil." (Another text says:) "To determine [the issues for] good or evil [of all events] in all under Heaven, to make all under Heaven full of strenuous endeavors, there are no [agencies] better than divination with the milfoil or the tortoise-shell." . . .

Why is it that from among the number of dry plants and hard bony material only the milfoil and the tortoise-shell are used [for divination]? They are the longest-living things between Heaven and Earth, therefore they are consulted. . . .

Why is it that at the divination with the milfoil the drawing of the figures must take place in the ancestral temple? Because, observing the rules attached to one's status, one applies for wisdom to the most exalted. Therefore [the stalks are] consulted through the medium of the ancestors.

What is the place [taken by the divinator] to divine an [auspicious] time? [The divinator] takes his place in the west, and faces east; this is his position at the divination with the milfoil. During the divination he turns to the west, after it he turns back, and faces east. His standing in the east and his facing the west when he is consulting the stalks [as, when he is consulting the tortoise-shell,] means that the younger [east] consults the elder [west].

With a cap of white deer-skin and white silk nether-garments gathered at the waist, [thus the divinator] applies [for advice] to the plain material [constituted by the milfoil and the tortoise-shell]. . . .

Why are the tortoise-shell and the stalks buried after they have been used up? Out of reverence, to avoid that the things which have been honoured should be polluted by men. (pp.522-526)

Heaven and Earth

What does *t'ien* 'Heaven' mean? *T'ien* means *chên* 'to govern.' Resting on high, [Heaven] regulates [all that is] below it, governing on behalf of man. Earth is created out of the primeval fluid, and is the ancestor of the ten thousand things. *Ti* 'Earth' means *shih* 'to spend,' *ti* 'to examine.' Responding [to Heaven] it spends [its nourishing powers] and brings about transformations; it investigates and examines unerringly; reverencing the beginning it honors the end; therefore it is called *ti*.

The ten thousand things contain the capacity of mutation and change. In the very beginning there was first the Great Origin *(t'ai-ch'u)*, then came the Great Beginning *(t'ai-shih)*; when the assuming of form was completed it was called the Great Simplicity *(t'ai-su)*. It was [still] chaotic, undivided, invisible, inaudible. Then it divided, and after the clear and the muddy were separated the infinitesimal and sparkling [elements] emerged and dispersed, and the multitudes of things were endowed with life.

The infinitesimal [elements] became the Three Luminary Bodies and the Five Elements. The Five Elements produced the emotions and instincts; the emotions and instincts produced harmony and equilibrium; harmony and equilibrium produced intelligence and understanding; intelligence and understanding produced the spiritual power [proceeding from the possession] of the Way; this again produced cultural refinement. . . . (pp.591f)

7.
the taoist sages

No term in Chinese studies has been so ambiguously used as Taoism. For the most part, it has been applied without distinction both to the ancient philosophical maxims of the *Tao Tê Ching* (by "Lao Tzu") and the poetical imagery of *Chuang Tzu,* and to the heterogeneous beliefs and practices of modern folk religion. It is especially the blanket use of the term Taoism that has confused the real character of this folk religion. In addition one needs to differentiate the institutionalized Taoist "Church," a historically continuous body of professional religious, with its many similarities to the Buddhist sangha and monachism. Taoism may be used to refer to the vast corpus of writings developed through the centuries, which contains a variety of texts concerned with inner and outer alchemy and other subjects centering upon the quest for immortality. And finally, Taoism may represent an entire Great Tradition of fundamental importance in Chinese high culture, standing in relief against the Confucian tradition.

We shall present here only a few words from the seminal classics of Lao Tzu and Chuang Tzu, to illustrate the world view that was to inspire Taoist religious developments. It may be worth noting that there is no solid historical information about either of these two Sages and that their words were collected in books that appeared toward the end of the Chou dynasty (several centuries B.C.). The relationship of the two is so enigmatic that it is hard to decide whether Chuang Tzu is in effect writing an exegesis upon texts of Lao Tzu, or Lao Tzu is a reduction to provocative aphorisms of Chuang Tzu—or whether, upon close examination, they represent two basically different outlooks.

LAO TZU[1]

Tao

There was Something that brought order out of Chaos before Heaven and Earth were born. Silent! Void! Sufficient unto Itself and changeless, yet

[1]In this chapter, all translations are mine except where indicated otherwise. (L.G.T.)

inexhaustively pervasive. It can be called the Mother of the world. Not knowing its name, I just call it Tao. One must needs call it The Great. . . . Man takes his way from Earth, Earth takes its way from Heaven, Heaven takes its way from Tao. Tao is what It is. (chap. 25)

    Tao produced one, one produced a second, the second produced a third, and from these came all things. All things are composed of yin and yang and derive their being from the harmonizing of these Ethers. (chap. 42)

> The grandest forms of active force
> From Tao come, their only source.
> Who can of Tao the nature tell?
> Our sight it flies, our touch as well.
> Eluding sight, eluding touch,
> The forms of things all in it crouch;
> Eluding touch, eluding sight,
> There are their semblances, all right.
> Profound it is, dark and obscure;
> Things' essences all there endure.
> Those essences the truth enfold
> Of what, when seen, shall then be told.
> Now it is so; 'twas so of old.
> Its name—what passes not away;
> So, in their beautiful array,
> Things form and never know decay.
> How know I that it is so with all the beauties of existing things? By this nature of the Tao. (chap. 21, J. Legge's transl.)

Like waters in flood the Great Tao is everywhere. How can it be limited to "left" or "right"? The ten thousand beings depend on It for their existence and It never fails them. (chap. 34)

    Tao is forever passive, yet in the natural order nothing is lacking. (chap. 37)

    To respond is the way to act in accordance with Tao. To be meek is the way to function in accordance with Tao. Everything in the world comes from something that exists—but existing things come from non-existence. (chap. 40)

Paradoxes of Appearance and Reality

> The old poem has it:
> The Tao, when brightest seen, seems light to lack;
> Who progress in it makes, seems drawing back;
> Its even way is like a rugged track.
> Its highest virtue from the vale doth rise;
> Its greatest beauty seems to offend the eyes;
> And he has most whose lot the least supplies.
> Its firmest virtue seems but poor and low;
> Its solid truth seems change to undergo;
> Its largest square doth yet no corner show;
> A vessel great, it is the slowest made;
> Loud is its sound, but never word it said;
> A semblance great, the shadow of a shade.
> Hidden is the Tao, and nameless, but it is only Tao that skillfully imparts and completes the nature of all things. (chap. 41, J. Legge's poem)

Whatever is perfect may seem imperfect — but its functioning is unimpaired. Whatever is completely filled may seem empty — but when you use it it is inexhaustible. Something that is perfectly straight seems bent; the greatest skill seems simple; the most moving eloquence is seemingly unpolished. (chap. 45)

Indifference of Nature

Nature is amoral: It treats all things indifferently.[2]
The Sage is amoral: He treats all people indifferently. (chap. 5)

Noninterference With the Natural Order

Don't be always "doing something" — then everything will be in order. (chap. 3)
The softest things in the world overcome the hardest. Only nonbeing can enter nonspace. From this I know the advantage of noninterference with the natural order. Few in the world reach the stage of being able to teach without words and to benefit the world by noninterference with the natural order. (chap. 43)

How to Succeed Without Really Trying

Heaven and Earth have existed for a long time. The reason they have been able to exist for so long is that they do not live for Self; therefore they can live for a long time. In the same way the Sage puts himself last — but finds himself first; leaves himself out — but finds himself still remaining. Is it not because he is selfless that his self is fulfilled? (chap. 7)
Therefore the Sage, holding to one thing—humility—is the model for the world. He doesn't show off, and therefore he is famous. He doesn't assert that he is right, and therefore his authority is displayed. He doesn't boast, and therefore he gets the credit. He doesn't sympathize[3] with others, and therefore he lives long. Because he is not competitive there is none in the world that can compete with him. The old saying, "If you are pliant you will succeed," is not idle talk! True success resides in this. (chap. 22)

The Progress of Morality Is Really Regress

Losing wholeness and naturalness (*Tao*) man comes to particularize his view (*tê*). Losing the particular applications of virtue he comes to a theoretical concept of Goodness (*jen*). Losing the ideal of Goodness man's highest value becomes Righteousness (*yi*). When he loses even that he sinks to the level of Ceremony (*li*). Now ceremony is evidence that Conscientiousness (*chung*) and Sincerity (*hsin*) have worn thin, and that moral breakdown is imminent. (chap. 38)[4]

---

[2]Literally, like straw dogs — items used in sacrifices and then thrown away. (L.G.T.)
[3]Cp. above, Indifference of Nature.
[4]These terms, capitalized in translation and their romanized forms given, figure as most important in the Confucian Way of Life. (L.G.T.)

The Way of Salvation

Devoting oneself to study, one accumulates knowledge day by day; but devoting oneself to Tao one diminishes his knowledge day by day. When one diminishes and diminishes one's knowledge, one finally reaches the level of noninterference with the natural order. When one does not interfere, everything is naturally in order. (chap. 48)

Seeing what is the simple truth, embrace this uncarved block. Diminishing Self, have few desires. (chap. 19)

Empty yourself of all passions and maintain your inner stillness. We see that all creatures, after completing their life's activities, return to their origin. All plants, after completing their blooming, return to their roots. This returning to the root is called stillness. It is what is meant by fulfilling destiny. To fulfill one's destiny is called the invariable law. To know this invariable law is to be enlightened, while not to know the invariable law is recklessly to court disaster. To know the invariable law is to be tolerant, to be tolerant is to be equable. The equable one is the ruler, and to be the ruler is to be over all, like Heaven. Heaven follows Tao, and Tao endures forever. One like this will not perish though his body dies. (chap. 16)

One who knows Tao does not talk about it; one who talks about it is one who knows it not. Block the road, shut your gate, subdue your ardor, do away with your inner divisions, dim your light, and become one with the dusty world.[5] This is called realizing the original identity of all things. Because it cannot be monopolized, it cannot be abandoned; it cannot be used for profit, it cannot bring harm; it can neither exalt nor degrade one — therefore it is the noblest thing in the world. (chap. 56)

The Sage

The Sage desires to be desireless, and does not esteem hard-to-get things. He studies to be unlearned. He returns to that which the mass of men have passed by. He assists all creatures in their natural ways, but dares not interfere with the natural order. (chap. 64)

To know that one does not really know is to be superior. Not to know that one's knowledge is deficient is to be sick. Only if we recognize this sickness as sickness can we become free of sickness. The Sage is not sick: Recognizing sickness as sickness, he is free of sickness. (chap. 71)

He who has in himself abundantly the attributes of the Tao is like an infant. Poisonous insects will not sting him; fierce beasts will not seize him; birds of prey will not strike him. The infant's bones are weak and yet its grasp is firm. It knows not the union of male and female, and yet its virile member may be excited; showing the perfection of its physical essence. All day long it will cry without its throat becoming hoarse — showing the harmony of its constitution.

> To him by whom this harmony is known,
> The secret of the unchanging Tao is shown,
> And in the knowledge wisdom finds its throne.

[5]Usually taken metaphorically as a description of meditational practices. (L.G.T.)

All life-increasing arts to evil turn;
Where the mind makes the vital breath to burn,
False is the strength, and o'er it we should mourn.
When things have become strong, they then become old, which may be said to be contrary to the Tao. Whatever is contrary to the Tao soon ends. (chap. 55, J. Legge's transl.)

Words to the Wise

At birth man is soft and supple; when he dies he becomes hard and rigid. So it is with all living things. The plants when they sprout are soft and tender, but after they die are withered and dry. Therefore hardness and rigidity are the characteristics of death, while softness and suppleness are the characteristics of life. So it is that when a soldier fights too hard he will not win, and a tree that resists the wind without bending will break. The mighty shall be laid low and the meek exalted. (chap. 76)

CHUANG TZU

Tao

Tao cannot be existence, for existence cannot be nonexistence, [which is the necessary cause for existence]. Tao is merely a metaphor used for convenience, while causation and nonaction pertain only to things which have existence. How can these be characteristics of Tao itself? If words could suffice, then we could exhaust the subject of Tao with a day's discussion. But words not sufficing, our day's discussion will only exhaust the subject of existing things. Tao is beyond all existing things, and neither words nor silence can convey its nature. Neither by words nor by silence shall you know it — discussion has its limitations. (chap. 25)

Existence and Nonexistence

Starlight asked Nonentity, saying, Master, do you exist? or do you not exist? He got no answer to this question, however, and looked steadfastly to the appearance of the other, which was that of a deep void. All day long he looked to it, but could see nothing; he listened for it, but could hear nothing; he clutched at it, but got hold of nothing. Starlight then said, Perfect! Who can attain to this? I can conceive the ideas of existence and nonexistence, but I cannot conceive the idea of nonexisting nonexistence. Yet he has achieved this state—how is this possible? (chap. 22, J. Legge's transl., modified)

Cosmology and Salvation

In the Beginning even nonexistence did not exist. Then came the Nameless (i.e. Tao) from which one thing was produced. But this one thing was without form. Now that by virtue of which beings are produced is called their particular character (*tê*). This formless thing dividing up continuously is what is called the conferring of life. By the alternate resting and movement (of yin and yang?) beings were produced. The principle of production according to which beings are completed is called form. The bodily forms had within them spirits or souls (*shên*), each specifically differentiated, which are called the individual natures. When our individual nature is perfected it reverts to its original character (*tê*), and to regain that original character is to return to the beginning of things. This is to be void of differentiations, which is to be great.[6] (chap. 12)

Change Is the Essence of Things

The Tao has no beginning or end, but beings are produced and die, without reaching perfection. They change from being nothing to being what they are, without any permanent form. The years cannot be recalled, time cannot be halted. Things contract and expand, fill and empty, and the process, when it has come to an end, begins anew. That which we call righteousness among men refers to this principle of all life. The life of creatures speeds by like a galloping horse. Not a movement but brings change, not a moment but brings alteration. What should one do or not do? Assuredly one should accept this process of natural change. (chap. 10)

Noninterference With the Natural Order

The Emperor of the Southern Sea was named Shu ("having Form"). The Emperor of the Northern Sea was named Hu ("having no Form"). The Emperor of the intermediary region was named Hun-t'un (meaning a chaos, neither quite formed nor yet completely unformed). Shu and Hu at times met together on the territory of Hun-t'un, who entertained them very well. Shu and Hu planned to repay the kindness of Hun-t'un. They said, Men all have seven orifices, for seeing, hearing, eating, and breathing. He is the only one who doesn't have them. Let's try and bore them for him. So each day they bored a hole — but on the seventh day Hun-t'un died. (chap. 7)

Seeking Tao

Kuang Ch'eng Tzu ("broadly-complete Master") said . . . Come and I will tell you the perfect Tao. Its essence is surrounded with the deepest obscurity; its highest reach is in darkness and silence. There is nothing to be seen; nothing to be heard. When it holds the spirit in its arms in stillness, then the bodily form of itself will become correct. You must be still; you must be pure; not subjecting your body to toil, not agitating your vital force — then you may live for long. When your eyes see nothing, your ears hear nothing, and your mind knows nothing, your spirit will keep your body, and the body will live long. Watch over what is within you, shut up the avenues that connect you with what is external[7] — much knowledge is pernicious. . . . Watch

[6]See above, Lao Tzu's characterization of Tao as The Great.
[7]Cp. Lao Tzu, above, chap. 56.

over and keep your body, and all things will of themselves give it vigour. I maintain the original unity of these elements, and dwell in the harmony of them. In this way I have cultivated myself for one thousand and two hundred years, and my bodily form has undergone no decay. (chap. 11, J. Legge's transl.)

[The mythical Emperor] Huang Ti, enjoying himself to the north of the Red River, climbed to the heights of the K'un-lun Mountains,[8] and gazed towards the south. When he was returning home he lost his Dark, Mysterious Pearl (i.e. Tao). He had Intellect search for it, but it could not be found. He had the fabulously keen-eyed Li Chu search for it, but it could not be found. He had the great debater Chieh Kou search for it, but it could not be found. Then he had Amorphous search for it — and Amorphous found it. Huang Ti said, How strange, that it was Amorphous who was finally able to find it! (chap. 12)

The Taoist Saint

We must have pure men (*chen-jen*), and only then can we have pure knowledge. But what is a pure man? The pure men of old acted without calculation, not seeking to secure results. They laid no plans. Therefore, failing, they had no cause for regret; succeeding, no cause for congratulation. And thus they could scale heights without fear; enter water without becoming wet; fire, without feeling hot. So far had their wisdom advanced towards Tao. The pure men of old slept without dreams, and waked without anxiety. They ate without discrimination, breathing deep breaths. For pure men draw breaths from their uttermost depths; the vulgar only from their throats. Out of the crooked, words are retched up like vomit. If men's passions are deep, their divinity is shallow. The pure men of old did not know what it was to love life or hate death. They did not rejoice in birth, nor strive to put off dissolution. Quickly come, and quickly go—no more. They did not forget whence it was they had sprung, neither did they seek to hasten their return thither. Cheerfully they played their allotted parts, waiting patiently for the end. This is what is called not to lead the heart astray from Tao, nor to let the human seek to supplement the divine. And this is what is meant by a pure man. (chap. 6, H. A. Giles's transl.)

Not seeking fame, not scheming, not holding office, not aspiring after knowledge: He is completely unrestricted, yet his movements leave no trace; he realizes his potential to the full, but unselfconsciously. He is simply passive (literally, empty). The Perfected Man (*chih-jen*) uses his mind as a mirror—not grasping, not welcoming, just reflecting without retaining. Therefore he is able to surpass all other beings without coming to harm. (chap. 7)

Wang Ni said, the Perfected Man is a god (*shen*). Though it were so hot that even the lakes should be on fire, he would not feel hot. Though it were so cold that the great rivers Ho and Han should be frozen solid, he would not feel the cold. Though thunderbolts should split the mountains and typhoons

---

[8]Real mountains in the far west of China; but in Taoism the home of the Immortals and other supernatural beings. (L.G.T.)

roil the seas, he would not be perturbed. Being like this, he mounts the clouds, rides the sun and moon, and journeys beyond the four seas. Neither death nor life move him. (chap. 2)

Taoist Yogic Concentration

Yen Hui (the favorite disciple of Confucius) said, 'I am making progress.' Confucius replied, 'What do you mean?' 'I have ceased to think of benevolence (*jen*) and righteousness,' was the reply. 'Very well; but that is not enough.' Another day, Hui again saw Confucius, and said, 'I am making progress.' 'What do you mean?' 'I have lost all thought of ceremonies and music.' 'Very well, but that is not enough.' A third day, Hui again saw the Master, and said, 'I am making progress.' 'What do you mean? 'I sit and forget everything.'

Confucius changed countenance, and said, 'What do you mean by saying that you sit and forget everything?' Yen Hui replied, 'My connection with the body and its parts is dissolved; my perceptive organs are discarded. Thus leaving my material form, and bidding farewell to my knowledge, I am become one with the Great Pervader (i.e. Tao). This I call sitting and forgetting all things.' Confucius said, 'One with that Pervader, you are free from all likings; so transformed, you are become impermanent. You have, indeed, become superior to me! I must ask leave to follow in your steps.'[9] (chap. 6, J. Legge's transl.)

Nieh Ch'ueh asked P'i Yi about Tao. P'i Yi replied, Assume the correct posture and make your mind one-pointed, and then you will feel a natural inner peace. Concentrate your mind and regulate your body, and spirits will come to dwell in you, the attributes of Tao will be perfected in you, and Tao itself will live in you. You will have the vacant look of a newborn calf, nor will you seek to know the whys of things. He had not yet finished speaking when Nieh Ch'ueh already dozed off. P'i Yi, greatly pleased, left him and went on his way singing this song:

> Like stump of rotten tree his frame,
> Like lime when slaked his mind became.
> Real his wisdom, solid, true,
> Nor cares what's hidden to pursue.
> O dim and dark his aimless mind!
> No one from him can counsel find.
> What sort of man is he? (chap. 22, J. Legge's poem)

Progress of Civilization Is Really Regress

Horses, living in the open country, eat grass and drink water. When they are happy they intertwine their necks and caress one another. When they are angry they turn their backs and kick each other. This is all that horses naturally know to do. But now, if we put them in crossbars and yokes, and place the armored band about their foreheads, then they know to try to break the

[9]It is perhaps needless to point out that Chuang Tzu's stories of Confucius are both apocryphal and tongue in cheek. (L.G.T.)

crossbars, snap the yoke, tear the carriage-top, spit out the bit, and steal the reins. Therefore it is the crime of Po Lo (a famous horse trainer) that horses have learned to become criminals.

Again, in the time of [the mythical Emperor] Ho Hsü people simply rested without thinking what they were doing, and went nowhere in particular when they walked. They were happy when they had had enough to eat, and amused themselves by drumming on their bellies. This was all that people naturally knew to do. But then Sages appeared, teaching the yielding and bowing of the rites and music to rectify conditions in the world. They dangled moral perfection and righteousness before them to console the hearts of the world. It was then that people first began to dance about on tiptoe with eagerness for knowledge, and to struggle with each other for profits, so that there was no stopping them. This is all the fault of the Sages. (chap. 9)

Taoist Criticism of the Confucian Way

Confucius went to see Lao Tzu and talked about moral perfection and righteousness. Lao Tzu replied, When one winnows chaff and the dust gets in his eyes, then one can't distinguish the sky from the earth or one direction from another. When mosquitoes and gadflies bite one's skin, then one can't sleep the whole night long. Now your "moral perfection" and "righteousness" are aggravating—they exasperate me more than anything in the world. If you, Sir, would only bring about that all men would not lose their original innocent nature! If you Sir, would only relax and let yourself be blown about as the wind blows! Then the natural attributes of all men would establish themselves. Why do you play the hero, going about as though carrying a great drum on your back and trying to save the lost children? The snow goose does not bathe every day in order to stay white, nor does the crow blacken himself every day in order to stay black. The original untouched black and white are unquestionably just what they are. To care about one's reputation cannot be considered an adequate Way of life. When a spring runs dry and the fish are stranded together on dry land, they may try to keep each other moist by their gasping breaths and wet each other with the drops of foam. But it would be much better if they could simply forget each other in the rivers and lakes. (chap. 14)

Chuang Tzu on His Deathbed

When Chuang Tzu was about to die, his disciples expressed a wish to give him a splendid funeral. But Chuang Tzu said, With Heaven and Earth for my coffin and shell; with the sun, moon, and stars as my regalia; and with all creation to escort me to the grave—are not my funeral paraphernalia ready to hand?

We fear, argued the disciples, lest the carrion kite should eat the body of our Master; to which Chuang Tzu replied, Above ground I shall be food for kites; below I shall be food for mole-crickets and ants. Why rob one to feed the other? (chap. 32, H. A. Giles's transl.)

8.
eaRLy ReLiGious taoism

Whatever the implications one may find in the frequently enigmatic and ambiguous texts of *Lao Tzu* and *Chuang Tzu*, the development of Taoism as a religious movement involved other factors than the teachings of the Sages. The great goal of religious Taoism was immortality, or at least increased longevity.

The serious study of religious Taoism is a relatively new pursuit for both Western and Chinese scholars. The pioneer in this field was the distinguished French sinologue, Henri Maspero, whose tragic death in Buchenwald during World War II cut short a promising series of publications that were beginning to give us our first real understanding. Fortunately, an equally eminent savant, Paul Demiéville, undertook the laborious task of collating many of the vast number of scattered notes and papers left by Maspero, and saw three volumes of posthumous articles through the press. We give here a translation of one of these articles, which was in its original form intended as part of a series of lectures on the historical development of Chinese religion. It is a lucid summary of the origins of early religious Taoism and its salient characteristics through its most flourishing period, the Six Dynasties, or the third through sixth centuries of the Christian era. (Chapter entitled "Le taoïsme," in the volume called *Les religions chinoises*, Paris, 1950, pp. 49-63, is condensed and edited.)

The profound disorders of Chinese society which marked the last centuries of the Chou dynasty had provoked a religious crisis between the fifth and third centuries B.C., particularly among the literati class. Many of them, dissatisfied with the official religion, and its crude concept of the connections between man and the gods, sought to escape the painful impression of bargaining that the current ideas of sacrifice gave them, and denying any personality or consciousness to the gods, substituted for them unconscious magico-religious forces; but, in their desire to explain the world rationally and scientifically, they often ended by losing sight of religious facts themselves, so that their ideas were far from acceptable to everyone.

Completely opposite were all those who, more inclined to personal religion, were less interested in the problems of man in society and the universe than in those of individual conscience, of the inner life, of personal ethics, refusing to admit that all that was higher than man was impersonal and unconscious. They found, besides, in the experiences of sorcerers and sorceresses, experts in serving as mediums between gods and men, an empirical proof of the existence of personal and conscious divinities, since by the techniques of possession one could enter into direct and personal relations with

such divinities. Religion for them was no longer a matter of some lords officiating in the name of their subjects, to obtain a certain material happiness
for the whole of society. They came to think of it as the business of everyone:
Each should try to get from the gods, by a personal contact, efficacious help
in assuring a certain individual spiritual happiness, in this life at first, and
then in the life to come. For the problem of the destiny of man after death,
with which the official religion did not concern itself very much, had assumed
a capital importance in their eyes.

It was known that man had numerous souls which separated at death;
but what became of each of them was not very well known. Several beliefs
existed concurrently: life in the tomb; subterranean life in the Yellow
Springs, in the dark prisons of the Earl Earth; a happy life in Heaven near the
Lord on High. It seems that these diverse destinies were ranked in some way
according to mortal rank: The common people went to the Yellow Springs
in the Nine Darknesses; kings and princes, thanks to special ceremonies,
rose up near the Lord on High; the great lords who were not entitled to these
rites, but who wished to avoid the destiny of the commoners, would have an
existence in their funerary temple, near the tomb. But this ranking was itself
only one belief among others . . .

Thus, in this life, no personal intercourse with the gods, and after death
a sort of Sheol where all, good and bad, huddled together in darkness, being
guarded jealously by the god of the Soil who ended by devouring them: That
was all that the official religion offered to souls tormented by a need for personal religion and by anxiety about their fate beyond the grave. Now this
was especially crucial: Even if souls escaped from the perils which menaced
them, the personality after death could not subsist, since the various souls
were separated. In the desire to survive whole and not in dispersed fragments,
and in the impossibility of surmounting the difficulty presented by the multi-
plicity of souls, they turned to the aspiration to conserve all the spirits who
inhabited man, in the interior of the body that was to be transformed, by an
appropriate technique, into an immortal body. Thus the religious effort
clashed in the beginning with the necessity to have recourse to techniques
which were often complicated; the importance of techniques never ceased
to be believed in, and, in Taoism, the technical quest sometimes nearly
smothered the religious quest. What the Taoists sought to obtain is the
immortality of the physical body, the abode of the souls and spirits: It contained material which it seemed to them necessary to retain.

Since antiquity, sorcerers had communicated with the gods by sending
their souls to their vicinity. Clothed in the costume of the divinity who was
to possess them, they entered into trance by various means, of which the
best known is a dance that grew faster and faster, to the sound of drum and
flutes, described in a collection of ancient poetry, the *Nine Songs*. They
mimed the journey thus, and when they fell, exhausted and unconscious, it
was because the god whom they had gone to seek in his dwelling place, and
with whom their connections seemed to be complicated by a love affair,
had taken possession of them; and whatever they did and said was then
supposed to be the acts and words of the god himself. . . .

It is from this school that the Taoists, who could witness such practices
every day, learned to send the souls from their bodies in order to scour the

world in search of the gods as far as the skies; but this was not without profoundly transforming the procedures and the aims of sorcery. It is probable that their ecstatic techniques, as well as their dietetic regimens, had something to do with those of the sorcerers and sorceresses. One proof is one of the terms by which the Taoists called ecstacy: the "entry of a spirit" (*kuei-ju*); this term is only explicable if the Taoist ecstacy is descended from the possession of the sorcerers, for such an expression fits Taoist ecstacy very poorly. Possession is well conceived as "the entry of a spirit" among sorcerers; it is accompanied, it seems, by the idea of sexual union. . . . The spirit enters into the body of the sorceress, speaks through her mouth, moves her limbs. There is nothing of all that in Taoist ecstacy: the mystical union with the impersonal Tao would necessarily exclude all trace of eroticism, and even the idea of the entry of a spirit is inadequate: The Tao has nothing "to enter," it is already in us as in all things. Another expression designating Taoist ecstacy, "forgetfulness" (*wang*), is likewise borrowed from the sorcerers: It is found in one of the *Nine Songs*. This is almost all we know of the connections between sorcery and the origins of [religious] Taoism.

What characterizes the Taoists is that they soon sought to go beyond extravagant rites to obtain mystical trances. Some, like Hsi K'ang and his friends in the third century [A.D.], the Seven Sages of the Bamboo Grove, tried to get out of themselves by means of wine. Others claimed to get to this stage by individual meditation, as in the school of Chuang Tzu and Lieh Tzu, the great masters of mystical Taoism of the fourth and third centuries B.C. This school attributed to an ancient master whose name was unknown — Lao Tzu — the invention of their mystical technique, which consisted, as it seems to me, of entering into trance and obtaining ecstacy without any exterior stimulation. But a long preparation was necessary for that, analogous to the *via purgativa* of the Christian mystics . . . The soul must be liberated from all exterior influence by the fasting of the heart . . . Indeed, to the heart (which is for the Chinese the organ of intelligence, of the spirit) when it has been emptied of all that comes from the exterior, one gives nothing more to absorb, nothing about which to think. . . . The "fasting of the heart" is opposed, in Chuang Tzu, to the "fasting of sacrifices," the ritual abstinence which preceded the sacrifices, as among the Moslem mystics purification of the soul is opposed to ritual purification.

In these ecstacies and in mystical union, the Taoist masters of the school of Lao Tzu had surpassed the simple relations with the gods that one went to visit in their home. They entered into contact, beyond the gods, with the first principle of all things, the *Tao*. This principle, under the influence of the doctrines of the literati . . . they conceived as an impersonal and unconscious one, at the same time transcendent and immanent. They thus arrived at immortality by a sort of shortcut, for, united with the eternal *Tao*, they participated in its eternity.

The mass of the Taoists did not follow them to such heights. This mystical and philosophical Taoism could only attract a few very great spirits. One among the disciples of Chuang Tzu, the best philosopher of the school, asked of him "the process of preserving life and nothing else." It was to this indeed that most of the Taoist believers clung: To avoid death and to make the body last forever. Such was the goal of almost all those who "studied the Tao." For Chuang Tzu, these were only "worldly people": "I pity," said he, "the worldly people who think that the processes of Nourishing the Body suffice to secure eternal life. In truth, Nourishing the Body does not so suffice." (Chap. 19)

But the generality of the Taoists did not look at it so closely, and the recipes for immortality multiplied. They were of all sorts: dietetic recipes, alchemical recipes, respiratory recipes, magical formulas, cults of all kinds: they tried everything. And as they did not ask for a spectacular immortality such as that of some great saints who had been able to "mount to heaven in plain day," these procedures seemed to be quite sufficient, and had their adepts. It was admitted, in fact, that in order not to disturb social life, where death is a normal event, he who had obtained immortality ought not to make a parade of that immortality. He should, on the contrary, make a semblance of having died; in reality, he substituted a sword or a cane which took on the aspect of his body and which was buried in its place, while the body, become immortal, would go to the paradise of the Immortals.

But even this immortality acquired by an apparent death (this was called the Deliverance of the Corpse) was not given to all the faithful. Not only did it require laborious efforts to attain, but also drugs which were expensive. The Taoist life, filled with detailed practices, was incompatible with the worldly life. Now Taoism quickly became a universal religion conducive to the salvation equally of all believers, rich or poor, religious or worldly, so that there were two degrees in the religious life. Some were content to take part in the collective ceremonies by which their sins were washed away and a happy life in the other world was prepared: These were the Taoist People (*tao-min*); others, adding to this participation the meticulous practices of personal religion, and the combinations of physiological techniques, sought a high rank in the hierarchy of the immortals: These were the Taoist Adepts (*tao-shih*).

The religious ceremonies of ancient Taoism, prior to the Christian era, are not well known to us. Towards the middle of the second century of the Christian era, a master (*tao-shih*) named Chang Chüeh, had a revelation that the advent of the Great Peace (*t'ai-p'ing*), which should be the commencement of the earthly paradise, would come with the day that the Yellow Heaven replaced the Blue Heaven in the government, and that this replacement would be produced upon the next renewal of the sexagenary cycle (the Chinese do not count by centuries, but by cycles of sixty years), the year A.D. 184; he began to preach repentance of sins and instituted public ceremonies of penitence. The missionaries that he sent throughout the empire recruited for him adherents by the hundreds of thousands; they were made to wear a turban of yellow cloth, in order that the Yellow Heaven could recognize them as his own (whence the sobriquet given to them, the Yellow Turbans), and he exacted from them a fine of five bushels of rice per year, in order to atone for their past faults (whence the name, "Doctrine of the five bushels of rice" which remained connected to his sect). In twenty years, all of eastern China was converted, that is to say, probably the various existing Taoist communities all rallied to those of Chang Chüeh; but Chang Chüeh did not profit from his success; an excellent religious leader, he had no ability as a military leader. He seems besides to have believed that the Great Peace would be established spontaneously and without struggle, for it does not seem that the Yellow Turbans were in the least prepared to revolt. In 183, the Han Court, worried by his progress, attacked him; the imperial generals besieged him in the town where he resided; he was killed there at the end of several months, and the revolt, deprived of its leader, was drowned in blood. Some islands remained, one in the north under the command of a certain Chang Yen, which, after a score of years, ended by submitting to the Wei [dynasty] at the beginning of the third century, another in the west, directed by a personage named Chang Lu, which lasted a little longer and which was also subdued by the future founder of the Wei dynasty in A.D. 214. The organization of Chang Lu was, under a different name, completely the same as that of Chang Chüeh: This identity leads us to believe that both had simply adapted to their own purposes the organization of all the Taoist sects that had preceded them, an organization which survived their attempt at unification.

The outlines of the Taoist church in the time of the Six Dynasties and under the T'ang still had many of the features of those of the Yellow Turban sect during the Later Han. Around the sixth century A.D. the faithful were grouped by cult communities into a sort of parishes. The leader of each community was the Master or Instructor (*shih*). The officials (*chu kuan*) formed a hierarchy in three degrees, for the rich and very pious faithful, for the moderately well-off faithful, for the pious but poor faithful: the male and female Capped (*nan kuan* and *nü kuan*), the Patrons (*chu chê*) and the Teachers of the Talismans (*lu shêng*); the first and third grades required a sort of initiation at the age of eighteen years. The officials of the first and second grades were charged with giving financial assistance to the faithful in need, particularly in case of sickness; they also had to bear the expense of the banquet at the beginning of the year. The mass of the faithful formed the Taoist People (*tao-min*). The officials were subordinate to the Instructor; they marked this by going to pay him homage each year on a set day, under pain of demotion in the hierarchy.

The role of the Instructors was somewhat like that of our parish priests. The office was hereditary from father to son, or, in the lack of a son, from eldest to younger brother, excluding the children of wives of the second rank [i.e. concubines]. They were the solid supports of the whole organization; and they are the direct ancestors of the Instructors of today, such as exist still in certain provinces, and whom, for example, De Groot found in Amoy always under the same name (*shih-kung*, pronounced locally *sai-kung*, "Sir Instructor") and always filling the same role. It is possible that, in that time as today, the father began the education of his son, and then sent him to a well known master for the finishing touches, and from whom at the age of eighteen years he received the initiation which gave him the right to perform his functions.

The religious life of the community was very full. There were first of all the yearly Three Assemblies (*san-hui*), the seventh day of the first and of the seventh month, and the fifteenth day of the tenth month, for each of the Three Agents (*san kuan*), Heaven, Earth, and Water, who examined the merits and demerits of men and fixed their good or bad fortune; then the five days of the dead, when ceremonies were performed for the salvation of the ancestors (first day of the first month, fifth day of the fifth month, seventh day of the seventh month, first day of the tenth month, and a day during the twelfth month); on New Year's Day there was a great ceremonial banquet for the prosperity of the community during the year which had just begun. To these nine festivals which were celebrated regularly on fixed dates there were added others at variable dates. Those called "Kitchens" (ch'u) were religious feasts offered by the families to the Instructor and a group of the faithful, on the occasion of births or deaths. The Services (chiao) were offerings of cakes and pieces of cloth to obtain special favors: asking for children, for the healing of sicknesses, or asking for rain in times of drought, thanksgiving for favors rendered, etc. . . .; an altar was prepared in the open air, and the Instructor recited prayers.

The most important festivals were the Fasts (chai), for the purpose of delivering the living faithful from their sins, or delivering the souls of the dead and securing their salvation. As early as Han times, the Yellow Turbans had purification ceremonies in which the Master, holding in his hand a bamboo wand of nine joints (the number of Heaven), performed incantations on water which he gave the sick person to drink, [these] prostrating themselves with their heads to the ground to reflect on their sins; this was in order to cure them, for the sickness was a chastisement for unexpiated sins. Among the Yellow Turbans of the West, the hierarch communicated the names of the sick to the Three Agents (Heaven, Earth, Water) by three "letters to the Three Agents," one of which was carried to the top of a mountain, another buried, and the third immersed [in water], the first rudimentary schema of the great festival of the Fast of the Three Originals (san-yuan chai) of the following centuries.

Under the Six Dynasties, the origin of all the collective festivals was attributed en bloc to the "Three Chang," that is to say the leaders of the Yellow Turbans of the second century; [but] the rituals are certainly more recent. Some of the Fasts were obligatory, such as the Fast of the Gold Talisman celebrated each year on behalf of the sovereign to ward off disasters, eclipses, floods, famine, and to contribute to the establishment of the Great Peace (t'ai-p'ing), and the Fast of the Jade Talisman which had for its object the salvation of all men, believers or infidels; others were celebrated upon request of the faithful, such as the Fast of Mud and Charcoal, intended to heal the sicknesses which were the consequence of sin, or the Fast of the Yellow Talisman by which the souls of the ancestors to the seventh generation were delivered from hell.

The Fast of the Yellow Talisman was a long and costly ceremony; others were less expensive, being paid for by the poor believers. However it is not necessary to believe that the great ceremonies were reserved for rich families: The Taoist communities were, it seems, quite united, and it was a pious work for the rich to assist the poor in their sicknesses and miseries, and to help them act for their salvation and for that of their ancestors. And the fact that it required at least eight persons to celebrate the Fasts often obliged them to complete the number by first offering places to their parents, and then to people of other families.

Those who led a pure life, free from sins, those who repented sincerely of their sins, and who attended zealously to services of penitence, would be saved: After their death, they would escape the Dark Prisons; they would descend to the Agent Earth, but would carry out there the duties of officers and employees, above the crowd of unbelievers who putrefied in the gloom. They could not get out until they had been redeemed by their descendants; they then rose to Heaven where they occupied inferior posts in the celestial hierarchy. This is because all, even the Taoist faithful, are mortal and one can only enter directly into paradise if one knows how to escape mortality. That is what the Taoist Adepts (*tao-shih*) strove to attain by a series of exercises and practices designed to "nourish the Vital Principle" and to render the body immortal.

I cannot describe here all these innumerable practices. The principle was replacement of the elements of the body, gross and consequently mortal, by the subtle and immortal elements. All things are composed of breaths. The Nine Breaths in the beginning were mingled in Chaos. When the world was constituted, the breaths separated, the purer rising and forming the sky, the grosser descending and forming the earth. The body of man is composed of gross breaths; but that which gives him life, which animates him, is the Original Breath, the pure breath which penetrates into him with the first respiration. Upon entering the body, it mingles with the Essence that each one distills in some way in himself, and this union forms the Spirit, the principal director of existence which lasts throughout life and dissolves at death when the breath and the Essence separate. This body is like the Universe, it is made exactly like it, and like it, it is filled with divinities who are the same as those of the Universe. In order to live forever, it is necessary to prolong [the life of] the body, to prevent the spirit from being annihilated by separation of the Breath and the Essence, and to preserve all the gods in one's own interior in order to maintain the unity of one's personality which their dispersion would destroy. From this come three series of practices: "Nourishing the Vital Principle" (*yang-hsing*), "nourishing the Spirit" (*yang-shen*), and "Concentrating on the One" (*shou-yi*).

In order to "nourish the Vital Principle," it is necessary to prevent the causes of death: The major one of these is cereals, for the breath of cereals causes malevolent demons to be born inside of us, the Three Worms or the Three Cadavers, which gnaw on us, the first on the brain, the second on the heart, and the third on the abdomen, thus causing our death. "Discontinue cereals" is the essential dietetic regimen, accompanied by drugs and respiratory exercises whose aim is to succeed in "Nourishing the Breath." Little by little, one replaces the gross breaths of the body with the pure Original Breath: The body becomes light and, when the replacement is complete, one becomes immortal. Alchemy also helps: When one absorbs perfectly pure cinnabar, the bones turn to gold and the flesh to jade, and the body is incorruptible.

Moreover, in nourishing the breaths, one strengthens the breath in oneself; in conducting the breath, inhaled through the nose through the body to the abdomen where it mingles with the Essence, and in causing it to rise up again through the spinal marrow to the brain, one strengthens the union of the Breath and the Essence and one "Nourishes the Spirit," preventing its dissolution.

Finally, by concentration, meditation and ecstacy, one enters into relations with the gods inside oneself. One sees first the petty gods of no importance; in the measure that one progresses, one sees more important gods; when one sees the great Triad of gods who reside in the middle of the brain, immortality is assured. Some want still more: After having practiced meditation which will lead to entering into relations with the gods, they go further, and in their meditation, abandon spirit to itself after having eliminated all influence of the exterior world. These, rejoining the great masters of the school of Lao Tzu, arrive at a mystical union with the Tao. Indissolubly united with the Tao, they have no need of a body to be immortals. They participate in the omnipotence of the Tao, they are masters of life and death, of transforming themselves at their pleasure and of transforming the world; but, like the Tao, they have no self-will and practice Non-Action; they let the world follow its "way," its Tao, which is the best possible when nothing interferes. They renounce all personal immortality and are absorbed into the Tao. These are the great saints of Taoism.

9.
an introduction to taoist yoga

The primary goal of "religious Taoism" was the prolongation of life, or even immortality. To accomplish this, the Taoist Adepts used various techniques: most importantly, respiratory, sexual, dietary, and alchemical. The latter was closely similar to, and very likely the ultimate source of, the alchemy of the European middle ages; but its interest was in production of an elixir of immortality rather than in the riches to be won by transmuting base metal into gold. No doubt in China, as in the West, the experiments of the alchemists were directly responsible for many discoveries in prescientific chemistry and pharmacology. The dietary regimen is discussed briefly in the selection by Maspero (see p. 61). The sexual and respiratory techniques have continued to the present time to be central practices of serious seekers of long life or immortality. As for the sexual techniques, the reader may consult the translation of a modern text, the *Hsing Ming Fa Chüeh Ming Chih*, or *Secrets of Cultivating Essential Nature and Eternal Life*, given by Lu, K'uan-yü (Charles Luk), in his *Taoist Yoga: Alchemy and Immortality* (London, 1970). There is more than a possibility that the Tantric practices of attaining salvation through sexual congress, as found in both Hinduism and Indian Buddhism, may derive from the ancient Taoist disciplines of China.[1]

Here we give a comprehensive account of the most basic of the Taoist techniques, yogic breathing. The author of this article, Chung-yuan Chang, is a leading authority on the subjects of Taoism and Ch'an (Zen), and the relationships between the two. "An Introduction to Taoist Yoga" was published in the *Review of Religion*, Vol. XX (1956), pp. 131-148.[2]

I. It is a general impression that Yoga as practiced in China is of Indian origin and was brought in with Buddhism, but when we examine the works of Lao Tzu and Chuang Tzu, we find they contain both the basic philosophy of Yoga and adumbrations of its techniques. Yoga, as the Indian philosophers interpreted it, was a Way of abstract meditation and transcendental wisdom, "these two means being just like two bullocks tied to the yoke of a cart and leading to a destination."[3] Of course this partnership was a commonplace in Taoist thinking many centuries before the introduction of Buddhism from

[1]For discussion of this matter, see R. H. van Gulik, *Sexual Life in Ancient China* (Leiden, 1961), Appendix I, "Indian and Chinese Sexual Mysticism."
[2]A considerably modified version of this material was later published by the author in his book, *Creativity and Taoism* (New York, The Julian Press, 1963, chapter 4).
[3]S. Radhakrishnan, ed., *History of Philosophy Eastern and Western* (London, 1952), p. 180.

India. Particularly do we find the Yoga emphasis on breathing exercises well suggested in the writings of Taoist founders. An examination of the writings of Lao Tzu and Chuang Tzu in any detail gives ample credence to this contention. References to the three basic elements of Indian Yoga — abstract meditation, transcendental wisdom, and breathing techniques — are clearly and unmistakably set forth.

If we look, for example, at the thought in Chapter XVI of the *Tao Te Ching*[4] we can see how the theory of Yoga was well developed in China by the time of Lao Tzu.

> Devote yourself to the utmost Void;
> Contemplate earnestly in Quietness.
> All things are together in action,
> But I look into their nonaction.
> For things are continuously moving, restless,
> Yet each is proceeding back to its origin.
> Proceeding back to the origin means quietness.
> To be in quietness is to see "Being-for-itself."
> "Being-for-itself" is the all-changing-changeless.
> To understand the all-changing-changeless is to be enlightened.
> Failure to understand leads to absurdity and disaster.
> The all-changing-changeless is all-embracing.
> To embrace all is to be selfless.
> To be selfless is to be all-pervading.
> To be all-pervading is to be transcendent.
> To be transcendent is to attain *Tao*.
> To have attained *Tao* is to be long-lasting.
> When he loses himself among all these the Man of *Tao* does not cease to exist.

In this chapter Lao Tzu looks into the two aspects of things — subjectively into his own Self and objectively into all other things — and he awakens into a new consciousness. One's mind is always in action, but Lao Tzu keeps his mind in the extreme quietude of nonaction. In nonaction his mind sees its own nature and becomes being for itself. This being for itself, or Self Nature, is part of the universe. It interfuses with other things, with the nature of the "ten thousand things." Because this interfusion is all-pervading and all-embracing, the subject is included in the object and the object in the subject. Therefore Lao Tzu speaks of the selfless. When one is selfless, in the Taoist sense, he is in the realm of Non-Being or Void.

On the other hand, all objects, all things, are seen first as objects in action, growing and flourishing. But when one looks into their origins, their roots, one sees their non-action. The flow is from movement to quietude. Objects themselves fade into the Non-Being or Void. When subject and object have both entered the realm of Non-Being we have abstract meditation — one of the basic requisites of Yoga. When the individual achieves this point in the practice of Yoga and is conscious of the realm of Non-Being, he has entered the region of transcendental wisdom. "To be transcendent is to attain *Tao*."

[4]The *Tao Te Ching* is most difficult to translate, and, to do it complete justice, the translator should have experienced spiritually the concepts of the author, as well as understanding them intellectually. The writer of this paper, in the preparation of this translation, has tried to convey the meaning through his own experience.

We also find references to meditative breathing in the *Tao Te Ching*. In Chapter X we read:

> Can you concentrate on your breathing to reach harmony
>   And become as an innocent babe?
> Can you clean the Dark Mirror within yourself
>   And make it of perfect purity? . . .
> Can you enter and leave the realm of Non-Being
>   And leave nothing to be retained there?

To achieve the Void, Lao Tzu himself recommends breathing exercises. To be sure, none of the details of such exercises are set forth, but that such techniques existed and were familiar to Lao Tzu we can hardly doubt. In the works of Chuang Tzu these ideas are developed in greater detail. Chuang Tzu, for example, describes the "fasting mind" in his Chapter IV. Here also he speaks of concentration, breathing, and the concept of enlightenment in some detail:

> Concentrate on your meditation. Do not listen with your ear but listen with your mind — not with your mind, but with your breath. Let hearing stop with the ear, the mind stop with its pictures. To concentrate on breathing is to prepare the emptiness for receiving things — the *Tao*. It is because *Tao* abides only in emptiness. This emptiness is the fasting mind. . . .
> Look at emptiness! In the chamber of emptiness there is produced light. The feeling of gaiety lives in repose. It not only permeates this repose but extends outward even while one is sitting still. Let the eye and the ear turn their communication within but eliminate all consciousness from without. The spirits and gods will dwell in this emptiness, as will the inner man (the Real Self). This is the way of transforming all things. . . .[5]

These notions of concentration and light are further explained in Chapter XXIII: "When one has reached extreme repose one gives forth a heavenly light. One who has developed this heavenly light sees his inner man (Real Self). Only through such cultivation can man reach eternity."

In these two quotations we can make out clearly the three important points of Yoga, i.e., breathing to enforce the process of abstract meditation toward the attainment of "extreme repose," or emptiness; from emptiness, or repose, one comes to enlightenment, sees the Real Self, and is associated and interfused with the universal forces of the gods and the spirits. This is the process of self-transformation leading to a highly integrated personality.

Although Chuang Tzu emphasized the method of breathing (the perfect man breathes "from the heels"), he was opposed to those who used breathing techniques to achieve longevity, without any understanding of the philosophy underlying the techniques. In an interesting passage he criticizes these men:

> Men who blow and breathe noisily, and inhale and exhale silently, in order to release the old air and obtain new air, who hibernate like bears and stretch their necks like birds — these men are simply striving for longevity. Such scholars indulge in breathing exercises in order to develop their physiques, wishing to live as long as Peng Tzu. They are given over to such practices (Chapter XV).

[5]This and subsequent translations from Chuang Tzu are by the author of this paper.

But breathing exercises were more than this, more than mere hygienic aids. Ideally, they were an aid to attaining spiritual self-recognition, to becoming one with the universe and its natural forces. It was essential to understand the philosophy behind the technique. In the Confucian canon, too, as, for example, in the works of Hsun Tzu (*ca.* 198 — *ca.* 238 B.C.), we frequently find a critical attitude toward those scholars who practice breathing exercises merely as an aid to longevity or physical well-being. Mencius (371?-289? B.C.) recognized a relationship between breathing and the personality, although he does not go into any detail, preferring to keep his discourse on a purely philosophical level.

We can look outside purely philosophical and speculative writing for confirmation of the early existence of some concepts of meditative breathing in China. We find, for example, a famous poem by Ch'ü Yüan (d. *ca.* 288 B.C.), entitled "Wandering in the Distance," which suggests a close connection between the concept of *Tao* and breathing exercises as an aid to its attainment. The poem, freely translated, reads:

> Eat six kinds of air and drink pure dew in order to preserve the purity of the soul. Breathe in the essence of the air and breathe the foul air out. The *Tao* can be received but it cannot be taught. The *Tao* is small and without content, and yet it is large without limit. Do not confuse your soul—it will be spontaneous. Concentrate on the breath and *Tao* will remain with you in the middle of the night.[6]

Moreover, when Buddhism was introduced into China, during the third and fourth centuries A.D., most Buddhist philosophers used Chuang Tzu to interpret Buddhism. We have, for example, the Buddhist monk Hui-yüan (334-416). When he attempted to explain the Buddhist theory of reality, he was obliged to resort to the teachings of Chuang Tzu to make his teachings intelligible. The practice of turning to Lao Tzu or Chuang Tzu to interpret Buddha became so widespread that the term *ko yi*, or "method of analogy," became the accepted description of this species of inter-religious influence.

Tao-an (312-385), in his introduction to the *Sutra on Breathing,* used typical "method of analogy" techniques in explaining Indian meditative breathing to the Chinese. Note the great use of Taoist terminology in the following passage:

> The breathing technique known as Anāpāna refers to the inhaling and exhaling the breath. *Tao* and *Tê* rest in all places, there is no place that they are not to be found. Anāpāna is the use of breathing to achieve inward integration. There are four meditation techniques which make use of the functions of the body. Through breathing exercises we pass through the six stages toward integration. Bodily exercises lead through four stages toward concentration. These steps consist of taking away and taking away until we have reached the point of complete non-activity. The stages consist of forgetting and forgetting until we

---

[6]From the *Ch'u Tz'u* ("Collection of the Poetry of Ch'ü yuan, Sung Yu, and Others"), Author's translation.

have done away with all desire. By non-activity we come into accord with things. By non-desire comes harmony in our affairs. By being in accord with things we can see into their nature. Through harmony in our affairs we can accomplish our missions. Accomplishing our mission, we make all *that is* consider itself as the *other.* Seeing into the nature of things, we cause the whole world to forget the self. Thus we eliminate the other and we eliminate the self. This is to achieve integration into the One.[7]

This quotation of Tao-an ostensibly describes Buddhist Yoga, but it describes very closely the Taoist concept of the achievement of non-being. It is not merely a matter of borrowed terminology. The goal of Oneness is a mutual goal of the Buddhist yogi and the Taoist meditative breathing practitioner. Methods of achieving the goal, as the Buddhist put it, by "taking away and taking away" and by "forgetting and forgetting" are the classic Taoist roads toward Enlightenment. They are the well-known methods of *wu wei* (non-activity) and *wu yü* (non-desire). It is not merely a coincidence or a matter of convenience that the Buddhists turned to the Taoist classics when they sought to interpret their teachings to the Chinese. These teachings, in no greatly different form, were already familiar to the Taoist.

II. From what we have said above it would seem that Buddhist Yoga and Taoist Yoga were very similar. Indeed, this is true, in the sense that the goals of both are one and the same. But the similarity does not go all the way. The systems of the two Yogas are quite different in many respects. The Taoist system of meditative breathing was a product of its native ground. We have not merely the works of Lao Tzu and Chuang Tzu, but many other roots. There is, for example, the well known *I Ching* ("Book of Changes") and the widely prevalent theories of the Five Elements and the Yin-Yang Schools, as well as the works of the Chinese alchemists, numerologists, and diviners. Above all, there were the Chinese cosmological theories and the macrocosmic-microcosmic view of man as the universe contained in the individual.

The fundamental, or in any event the earliest, text of the Taoist Yoga, or meditative breathing school, is the third century *Chou Yi T'san-t'ung-ch'i* ("Synthesis and Agreement with the Chou Changes"), the work of Wei Pe-yang. It is a difficult and complicated work, dealing in the arcane and the alchemical, but it is worthy of study for those who wish to understand the foundations of Chinese Yoga. It deals with all of the theories mentioned above as contributing to the meditative breathing school — from abstruse cosmological speculation to alchemical practices and number and word magic.

First, let us look at the macrocosmic-microcosmic theory which serves as the basis of Chinese Yoga. The classic work on this subject is known as the *Huai-nan-tzu,*[8] dating from the second century B.C. This work discusses the position of man in the universe. We read:

What is spiritual is received from the Heaven while the body and its material form are derived from the earth. We say: "From the One came the Two. The Two evolved into the Three and the Three into all things. All things hold up *yin* and

[7]*Tripitaka,* Lv, 43. Author's translation.
[8]Ch. VII. Author's translation.

clasp *yang*." It is the harmony of the spirits of *yin* and *yang* on which all harmony depends. It is said, "At one month the embryo is formed; at two months it has skin; in the third and fourth month tissue and shape evolve; in the fifth muscle: in the sixth bone; in the seventh physical completion; in the eighth movement; in the ninth activity; and in the tenth birth." The body being completed, the internal organs have their form. . . . The senses are the outward, and the internal organs the inward regulators . . . each has its fixed rules. The roundness of the head is like the Heavens; the firmness of the foot is like the earth. . . .

Heaven has four seasons, five elements, nine divisions, three hundred and sixty days. Similarly, man has four limbs, five internal organs, nine orifices, and three hundred and sixty joints. Heaven has wind, rain, cold, heat; man, similarly, has joy, anger, taking, giving. . . . Man forms a trinity with Heaven and Earth, and his mind is the master. . . . In the sun there is a bird standing on three legs, and in the moon a toad with three legs. . . .

Thus, man is a microcosmic universe. This idea occurs frequently, indeed constantly, in Taoism, and the meditative breathing school proved no exception in using this concept for its own purposes. Through meditative breathing, man achieved the natural integration with the universe that was destined for him and foreshadowed in so many ways, according to early Taoist theory.

In early Chou times a system of eight trigrams (solid and broken lines) and sixty-four hexagrams, supposedly simulating the cracks in tortoise shell, were developed for use in prophetic rituals. Gradually these trigrams and hexagrams took on complicated symbolic meanings. The nature of these meanings is propounded in the famous *I Ching*. Arbitrary numerical categories were established and assigned fixed symbols. These symbols were picked up and used by the founders of Chinese Yoga. Let us look at a few examples of this categorizing impulse as it is displayed in the *I Ching* and note the parallels in typical Yoga theory.

The four primary trigrams, as set forth in the *I Ching*, are *chen, li, tui,* and *k'an*. These are correlated with the four seasons and the four directions, as well as with arbitrarily derived numbers. The yogi took these categories, for example, and assigned them to the internal organs, such as heart, kidney, liver, and lung. Thereon was built an elaborate relationship with the *I Ching* categories of south, north, east, and west, the four seasons, and other corresponding categories.

FOUR BASIC TRIGRAMS AND THEIR MEANING IN I-CHING.

Trigram	Direction	Season	Number
chen	east	spring	8
li	south	summer	7
tui	west	autumn	9
k'an	north	winter	6

APPLICATION TO THE SYSTEM OF YOGA

Five Elements	Inner Organs	Animal	Five Greatnesses	Constant Virtue
wood	liver	blue dragon	great beginning	love
fire	heart (mercury)	red bird	great change	propriety
metal	lung	white tiger	great simplicity	righteousness
water	kidney (lead)	black turtle	great origin	wisdom
earth	spleen		great ultimate	faith

In *Synthesis and Agreement* the four directions also are used to denote four of the elements and four appropriate animals. East is associated with wood; west with metal, north with water, and south with fire. East is the blue dragon or the liver, west, the white tiger or the lung; south, the red bird or the heart; and north is the black turtle or the kidney. From the *I Ching* we learn that the *chen* trigram suggests the idea of movement. From *chen* the circulation through other trigrams, *li, tui,* and *k'an* sets forth. Thus, in its Appendix V, we read:

> All things issue forth in *chen,* which is East. . . . *Li* suggests the brightness where all things come to see each other. This trigram represents the South. . . . *Tui* is the West and Autumn, the season in which all things are moving by their joy. We say, "*Tui* refers to the spirit of joy." . . . *K'an* refers to water. It is the trigram of the north, where all things return to rest and comfort. We say, "Rest and comfort indicate *K'an*".[9]

Man's breath, according to the Taoist yogi, circulates among the inner organs, even as movement and quietude complete its circulation among the four trigrams, and as the ether of the world circulates among the four seasons and the four directions. The breath is the unifying principle which makes a Oneness of the microcosm of the body. Generally, however, the yogi prefers the category five to that of four. The fifth category represents a unifying principle in the center of the other four. The Taoists correlate the fifth category with the spleen, or earth. This is the storage place of all the energies and source of supply of vital force to all the other organs.

In an apocryphal addition to the *I Ching* known as the *Yi-wei Ch'ien-tso-tu* ("Apocryphal Treatise on the 'Change'") commented on by Cheng Hsüan as early as the second century, we find a metaphysical category of four which was later picked up by the Taoist yogi. The relevant passage in the *Yi-wei Ch'ien-tso-tu*[10] reads as follows:

> In olden times the Sages worked upon the principles of *yin* and *yang* to determine the principles of growth and decline and began *ch'ien* and *k'un* to

---

[9]Author's translation.
[10]I, 7-9. Author's translation.

encompass the fundamentals of Heaven and Earth. But that which has form is produced of the formless. Whence came *ch'ien* and *k'un*? In answer we may say that first there was the Great Principle of Change, then the Great Beginning, then the Great Origin, and then the Great Simplicity.

The yogi has, typically, added a fifth (spleen-earth) category. This is the Great Ultimate, the unifying whole.

The Confucian element in Chinese Yoga appears in the adoption of the five constant virtues of love, righteousness, propriety, wisdom, and good faith. East is love, west is righteousness, south is propriety, north is wisdom, and the central category is good faith.

The various threads of earlier Chinese theory (the Yin-Yang School, conventional Taoism, the Five Elements School, the *I Ching*, numerological theories, etc.) were first brought together as components of the new Chinese school of meditative breathing in the *Synthesis and Agreement*, the work which we have mentioned above as the basic classic of the school. As to the value of the word-magic involved, we will not attempt to make any comment here, but limit ourselves to descriptive commentary rather than symbolic interpretation. That the symbolism is a rich and complex one, will be obvious, I believe, even from the very simple suggestion of some of its aspects which I have outlined here.

Why, then, since we have spent some time indicating the four (or five) elements which go into the Taoist-Yogi concept of the microcosm of the inner man or Real Self — why, the initiate to Chinese Yoga may ask, do we commonly find merely two internal elements suggested as polar aspects of the internal unity? Symbolic word-play of this sort is, of course, subject to endless variation. This instance is a relatively logical one. The five internal elements combine, by the force of the central, unifying principal, into one. The four outer elements form two pairs which become the polar focuses. East and south combine, and west and north combine. The dragon, that is, goes toward the fire, and the tiger goes to the water. Here we have the two centers: fire, represented by the Trigram *li*, and water, represented by Trigram *k'an*. The former is the symbol of the heart, the latter of the kidney. According to the Taoist Yogi, the unification of *li* and *k'an* or the heart and the kidney is called the "small circulation" of breathing technique. Centered here is one of the important functions of Taoist Yoga. The theory of the "small circulation" breathing, arbitrarily correlated with the various categories of season, element, direction, ethical principles, animals, with their appropriate trigrams, patently displays the influences we have named above of indigenous Chinese speculation — Confucian ethics, Taoist cosmological views, and the lesser magical theories of the alchemical and divinatory practitioners.

For the Taoist yogi, in addition to the "small circulation," there is the idea of the "grand circulation." This grand circulation commences at the tip of the spine and moves upward along the spine to the head, forward and downward through the face and ventral surface back to the tip of the spine. One portion of this movement is, of course, rising, the other falling. The rising movement is known as the *yang* movement, the falling movement is known as the *yin* movement. *Yin* and *yang*, of course, are the basic polar dichotomies of Chinese thinking, representing the pairing of positive and negative, masculine and feminine, ascending and descending, etc. This rising and falling movement is symbolically paralleled with the waxing and waning of the seasons of the year. The influential Yin and Yang School of Chinese thinking and the *I Ching* combine to bring a characteristic contribution to *Taoist Yoga.*

In the *I Ching* we find an arrangement of twelve hexagrams to represent the circular movement of *yin* and *yang* and, at the same time, to indicate the movement of the seasons. *Yin* is represented in the diagram below by a broken line (— —) and *yang* (——) by a solid line.

Hexagram						
Name	fu	lin	t'ai	ta-chuang	kuai	ch'ien
Month	11th	12th	1st	2nd	3rd	4th

Hexagram						
Name	kou	tun	fou	kuan	po	k'un
Month	5th	6th	7th	8th	9th	10th

In the upper row we see that the influence of *yang*, the unbroken line at the bottom of each hexagram, beginning at *fu*, steadily increases in succeeding symbols until, in the last hexagram (*ch'ien*), it is complete and all the lines are *yang*. At the same time there is a decrease in the influence of *yin*, represented by the broken line.

The second row illustrates exactly the reverse situation. Here we have a decreasing *yang* and an increasing *yin*, until, in the last hexagram, there is only *yin*, represented by the broken line. Scholars of the Yin-Yang School identified the twelve hexagrams with the twelve months of the year, beginning, as shown in the diagram, with *fu* as the eleventh month, when *yang* begins its influence, and ending with *k'un*, the tenth month, when *yin* reaches its point of complete dominance. Here we have a graphic representative of the fluctuating influence of *yin* and *yang* during the course of a year.

This whole symbolic *Gestalt* was taken over by the Taoist yogi, who adapted the increasing and decreasing influence of *yin* and *yang* to their concept of the circulation of the breath around the body. Since *yang* symbolizes a rising movement, the yogi takes the hexagram *fu* as the starting point of the grand circulation at the tip of the spine. The following hexagrams are assigned positions along the spine upward through the various stages to *ch'ien* at the top of the head. Thus does the *yang* influence rise to its peak at the apex of the grand circulation. When the breath descends through the face, chest, and ventral surface back to the tip of the spine the influence of *yin* waxes. Corresponding hexagrams are placed along the downward course, indicating that the *yin* element is increasing. At the last stage, *k'un*, the *yin* element reaches its utmost influence and the circulation returns to its starting point.

For the Chinese yogi this circulation of the "breath" throughout the body is divided into two "courses." The rising circulation, from the tip of the spine to the top of the head (or, more precisely, to the upper lip) is known as the *To Mu*, or Controlled Course. The descending circulation, from the head (from the lower lip) to the tip of the spine, is known as the *Jen Mu*, or Involuntary Course. These concepts are purely imaginative, of course, but the yogi visualizes it as the supposed path of the circulation of breath. This circulation of the "breath" may be better described as a circulation of a heat current, which is felt by the practitioner. The upward movement is also known as the movement of *yang* and the downward movement as the movement of *yin*. When the practitioner is able to complete this circulation, it means that a complete cycle of *yin* and *yang* has been achieved. This completed cycle is considered the attainment of *Tao*.

We can see from this brief description of the "grand circulation" breathing exercises that they were deeply influenced by the Yin-Yang School and by the ideas in the *I Ching*. In short, we see that the theory of the small circulation and the grand circulation breathing (the basis of Taoist Yoga) can, in large measure, be traced back to the influence of the Taoist and Confucian classics and other native Chinese sources — the work of the numerologists, alchemists, and others.

III. The objective that the Yogi holds before himself in his exercises is the complete elimination of thought. Rather, he tries to "get behind" his thoughts, i.e., transcend himself by looking into the storage house of the unconscious, where he sees his Real Self. If one understands the philosophy of Taoism and is "enlightened" to the Real Self there is no need of the system of Yoga. But most people cannot attain enlightenment through sudden revelation, and they need a technique to help them eliminate the floating thoughts which obscure their true vision. The one important technique is that of concentration. According to Taoist Yoga one picks a spot, such as the *Ming Tang*, or the Hall of Light, the spot between the eyes, and bends his concentration upon it to attain the vision of the heavenly light. Concentration upon a particular spot rules out other thoughts, and the mind is opened and the light shines within. However, the concentration-spot need not be the *Ming-Tang*. It may be various other parts of the body (the tip of the nose, the navel, the tip of the spine) or other outside objects. Usually the spot is that between the eyes, or, more commonly, just below the navel. The spot below the navel is known as the *Ch'i Hai*, or Sea of Breath. *Ch'i Hai* is the most important center and is known as the Regular Red Field. It is the lowest of the three Red Fields supposed to lie within the body. The other two, the Middle Red Field and the Higher Red Field, are in the region of the heart and the center of the brain. The Higher Red Field is located in the middle of the nine sections, or "courts" of the brain, and is known as the Mud Pill Court. Between the Middle Red Field and the Lower Red Field is the *Huang Ting*, or Yellow Court, in the region of the navel. This is the source of life (the umbilicus). "Mercury" from the heart above and "lead" from the *Ch'i Hai* below combine here to create the elixir of life. *Huang Ting* is the storage house of this elixir.

There are numerous dorsal centers in addition to the internal centers mentioned above. Three are the most important. They are *Wei-lu*, the tip

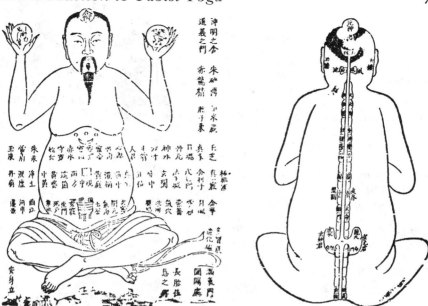

DIAGRAM I (Left): FRONT VIEW. The practitioner of Yoga sitting in a characteristic position. On the abdomen are indicated the positions of the Middle Red Field (new moon and three stars), the Yellow Court (square), and the Lower Red Field (cauldron). The Upper Red Field is located in the head. In the right hand is a Moon, symbolized, as is common in Chinese mythology, by a rabbit. In the left hand is the Sun, symbolized by the three-legged bird mentioned in the *Huai-nan-tzu*. The sun and moon are brought symbolically into a unity within the Yogin. The three rows of Chinese characters beneath the Middle Red Field, the Yellow Court, and the Lower Red Field are a variety of synonomous names for these centers. The Middle Red Field, for example, is also known as Spiritual Gate, Sea of Nature, Stream of the Heart, Heavenly Prince, Jade Mushroom, Red Mercury, etc., some twenty-four synonyms in all for the Middle Red Field alone. The Yellow Court is also known as the Old Grandmother, the Mysterious Gate, the Empty Middle, etc. The Lower Red Field, symbolized by a crucible, or cauldron, for melting and transmuting lead, is also known as the Sea of Breath, Earth Cauldron, Gate of Life, Flower Pool, Genuine Lead, etc. Around the figure are quotations from Taoist texts, recondite and mystical in character. Typically they read: "The House of the Spirit is the Door of Righteousness."

DIAGRAM II (Right): REAR VIEW. This diagram illustrates the important "centers" of the ascending, or Controlled Course, of the grand circulation. These centers are located along the spine. The lowest, at the tip of the spine is *Wei Lu*, the "Gate of the Tail." Another important center, located half-way up the spine and in the region of the kidneys, is *Chia Chi* ("beside the spine"). It is the center for transmitting the upward and downward breath currents. A third center is located in the head, and is known as *Yuan Shen* ("Primordial Spirit"). It is the seat of Nirvana (the Upper Red Field in the front view). Alternative names are: Heavenly Valley, The Jade Mountain, and many others. Also indicated on the diagram are the subsidiary centers in the genital region (between *Wei Lu* and *Chia Chi*, and known variously as The Dark First Prince, the Mysterious Prince, etc.) and in the neck (The Jade Pillow Gate, Heavenly Pillar, etc.). Details of these centers and their significance vary from authority to authority.

of the spine, the beginning of the Controlled Course which sends the heat current upward and the end of the Involuntary Course by which the heat current descends to its beginning. The point behind the kidney on either side of the spine are the centers called the *Chia Chi* ("beside the spine"). In the neck is a third center known as the House of Wind (*Feng fu*). This is the last gate through which the upward heat current passes moving to the Higher Red Field. The accompanying diagrams[11] indicate the centers, seen from the front and the back.

A brief comparison of Taoist Yoga "centers" with those characteristically used in Tantric Yoga may be of interest to those more familiar with the Indian system. Edward Conze[12] points out that there are four main internal centers in Indian Tantric Yoga practice: in the region of the navel, in the heart, in the neck, and in the head. The corresponding centers in Chinese Yoga are easily discernible in the accompanying diagrams. Sir John Woodroffe, in his *The Serpent Power*,[13] identifies six centers: "Inside the Meru, or spinal column, are the six main centres of Tattvik operations . . . Muladhara, Svadhishthana, Manipura, Anahata, Vishuddha, and Ajna." The first is the tip of the spine, the second is the genital region, the third the navel, the fourth the heart, the fifth in the throat, and the sixth between the eyes. All, indeed, have obvious Taoist Yoga counterparts easily definable in the accompanying diagrams. The question arises which influenced which? Conze points out that Tantric Yoga was not organized until the fifth or sixth century.[14] It is most interesting that the *Synthesis and Agreement*, published in the third century and the basis of Chinese Yoga, nowhere mentions Indian practices. Even the *Wu Chen P'ien* ("Enlightenment of Truth"), published about 1095, has references to what we know as Indian Yoga, but only in the slightest and most allusive fashion. Later works indicate a familiarity on the part of the authors with Indian practices. The excellent but little known *Hsing Ming Ch'ih Kuei* ("Meaning of Nature and Destiny"), by an unknown author.[15] published in the sixteenth century, shows a complete knowledge of Indian Yoga and has a picture of Lao Tzu, Confucius, and Buddha sitting together in meditation — with Buddha in the central position. Much evidence suggests that Chinese Yoga developed along a highly independent course in the early centuries of its existence, as well as having independent roots in Chinese culture. Possibly Tibetan texts unavailable to the author or further light from Indian sources can better clarify this point.

[11]The two pictorial diagrams reproduced here are from the *Hsing Ming Ch'ih Kuei* ("meaning of Nature and Destiny") mentioned later in the text. These pictures from the original work were published in a later edition (1669), in the Princeton University Library.

[12]*Buddhism: Its Essence and Development* (New York, 1951), p. 198.

[13]Published under the pseudonym Arthur Avalon (London, 1919).

[14]Conze, *op. cit.*, p. 176.

[15]The pictures reproduced by Richard Wilhelm, in *The Secret of the Golden Flower* (London, 1947), pp. 29, 41, 51, 63, were taken from this work. The "Inner Process" chart, published by Erwin Rousselle, "Seelische Fuhrung im Lebenden Taoism," *Eranos Jahrbuch 1933* (Zürich, 1934), Tafel 1, p. 150, is taken from a Taoist temple picture, and deviates in a number of important points from the classical texts.

A rather more detailed word on breathing techniques is probably necessary for a rounded understanding of Chinese Yoga. Taoist meditative theory emphasizes light, rhythmic breathing — so light that "a feather will not stir before the breath." This is known as *t'ai hsi* breathing, or "breathing of the embryo." When one inhales, the air is sent to the bottom of the lungs, even lower, as if to breathe with the abdomen. The Lower Red Field beneath the navel, the "Sea of Breath," is supplied with this air. When one exhales, the diaphragm rises and the abdomen pulls in. This is the contrary of ordinary "chest" breathing. In practice, breaths are counted for training purposes, but as the technique is perfected this is dropped. One feels that one is not breathing at all.

By this concept breath can circulate anywhere throughout the body — typically in the great circulation through the spine to the top of the head and down the front. Actually air, of course, cannot go through bone and flesh. It is, rather, a heat current, moving upward and downward. Even the idea of the "heat current" is not a very convincing one to the Western reader, but the writer was told on good scientific authority that concentration upon the blood vessels can make a measurable difference in the temperature of the spot. The Chinese yogin can send a heat current in a circular pattern around the navel which stimulates the practitioner in a short period into a trancelike state.

The writer has tried to present information on the Taoist system of Yoga. It is to be hoped that the phenomenon will be scientifically investigated some day on a truly objective basis which will enable the indifferent or the unsympathetic to form unbiased judgments of the theory and its practice.

IV. A concrete example of the practice of Chinese Yoga may serve as a fitting conclusion.

There is an interesting and authentic story[16] of a student who actually achieved Enlightenment through an interesting discipline under his master. In the Ming Dynasty (about the sixteenth century) there was a student who sought Enlightenment. One day he passed by a cave on a mountain top and saw a Taoist Master practicing meditation. He went up to him and made a bow, but the Master ignored his politeness. The student realized immediately that the Master must have achieved the highest stage. Immediately he sat down opposite him and practiced meditation. After a time the Master got up to make some tea. When the tea was ready the Master took a cup for himself and then put the cup back and resumed his meditation. The visitor came up, took a cup of tea and returned the cup the same as the Master had. Neither of them uttered a single word. In the evening the Master got up and prepared his dinner. When it was ready he took a bowl and ate. The visitor came forward and took a bowl and ate with him. After dinner they both sat back again. In the middle of the night the Master got up and took a stroll around the mountain pass. His guest did the same thing, both of them returning to their original places. The next day was very much the same. They meditated together, shared their simple meals in silence. After seven days the Master spoke, saying: "Sir, where do you come from?" The man replied, "The South." The next question was, "What makes you come here?" The man

[16]Quoted from *Cheng Chung-yin* in his "Random Notes" section of the periodical, *Chia Hsün* ("Message of Enlightenment"), Shanghai, VIII (August, 1954), 10.

said, "To see you." "My face is just like this," the Master said. "There is nothing particular there." "I have already recognized that well," the man replied. The Master explained that during his stay of thirty years in his cave he had never met such a congenial companion. The man stayed with him and learned from him. One night as the disciple walked along the mountain path he felt a sudden lightning circulating within him. There was a roar of thunder in the top of his head. The mountain, the mountain stream, the world, and his very self all vanished. This experience lasted "for about the time it would take for five inches of incense to burn." After that he felt that he was an entirely different man and that he was purified by his own light. The student was told that even this light must be put aside. His Master, indeed, had experienced it frequently over the course of thirty years and had learned to pay no attention to it.

This story exemplifies the path through meditative breathing toward the final achievement, the Enlightenment. The quiescence of the student and the master symbolizes the need for meditation and clearing the mind of all thought. Those who look inward may suddenly even forget that they are looking. This is when the body and the heart are completely freed and all entanglements disappear. Greetings from guests are ignored, distinctions of name disappear, the face of the master disappears, even the purpose of meditation itself is forgotten. When one has advanced this far one's heart is empty, the essence of one's nature is manifest, and the light of consciousness transforms itself into the light of essence.

Taoist Yoga[17] is a product of Chinese culture. If we wish to evaluate it in a socio-cultural context we must know something of its origins. Philosophically we must look back to Lao Tzu and Chuang Tzu. But Lao Tzu and Chuang Tzu were philosophers in a true sense and not magic theorists. They suggested the possibility of Yoga-like practices as an aid to attaining spiritual enlightenment, but they did not attempt to elaborate techniques or build up fanciful symbolisms. This work was chiefly the product of far lesser minds, who gave themselves over unthinkingly to the pursuit of vain and non-spiritual ends. That they accomplished something in the field of spiritual experience seems undeniable to the author, but it must be admitted that much of their work was the mere product of "medieval" alchemical hopes. It was an attempt at "scientific" explanation of phenomena without adequate scientific basis for judging, and it inevitably flew off into the excesses that are apt to be the chief pitfall of abstract speculation.

As to the value of Yoga practices, the author is personally convinced, not, however, in any proselytizing sense. The point of Yoga is the attainment of *Tao*. The value of Yoga is entirely as a means to an end; if *Tao* can be attained by other means, all well and good. Yoga can be put aside as an unnecessary aid. If it helps the individual in his effort to understand himself and see somewhat more clearly his relationship to the universe around him, then it serves the end of any spiritual exercise — self-realization.

[17]The word Yoga is not generally used by the modern Chinese, who refer, rather, to "quiet sitting" or meditative breathing. The term, however, was early introduced into Chinese, through Buddhist texts, such as Yogācāryabhūmi-śāstra, the work of Asaṅga (fourth century A.D.) in India and translated by Hsüan-tsang (596-664), in the transliterated form as *yü chia*. This expression is not now in wide use. In this paper the author has used the word Yoga as being most generally familiar to Western readers.

10.
Buddhism Becomes
chinese

As the only foreign religion that ever—at least until the twentieth century—became truly assimilated into the Chinese civilization, Buddhism has a special interest. In order for assimilation to take place, Buddhism had to undergo a process of Sinicization which resulted in a religion that was quite different from the Indian original. At the same time, it not only yielded to certain Chinese cultural imperatives, but it spread into that Chinese culture and colored it. We see the two processes at work most clearly in the early centuries, between Han and T'ang (roughly A.D. 250 to A.D. 600), a period when China was divided between numerous ephemeral states, "barbarian" (i.e. non-Chinese) in the north, and Chinese in the south; when the sway of Confucian orthodoxy was tenuous at best, because the Confucian State had disintegrated; when conditions encouraged escapism of all sorts in thought and behavior; when both "philosophical" and "religious" Taoism were popular. The selection that follows brings out the most salient features of this crucial period of Buddhism's penetration into Chinese culture.

The Conflict of Buddhism with Native Chinese Ideologies by Richard Mather first appeared in the *Review of Religion, XX* (1955-56), pp. 25-37.

INTRODUCTION

In the West the notion of conflict is well defined and can be documented from both our political and religious history. The notion can be traced in part, I believe, to a generally assumed world view inherited from the Hebrew-Christian tradition, which, stated in its barest terms, sees the created world set over against a transcendent Creator, and man, who was made in the Creator's image, set in a triple relation of confrontation: (1) to God, in which his reaction is, more often than not, one of anxious rebellion, (2) to nature, against which he is pitted in a life-and-death struggle for mastery, and (3) to other men, among whom his relation is often that of a competitor.

In China conflict is certainly not unknown, but it is less well defined, and, in using the term to describe Buddhism's relation to native ideologies, we should be warned at the start that it is not quite comparable with the conflict, let us say, between the early Christian community and the Roman emperors, in which context the slogan was born that "the blood of the martyrs is the seed of the Church." None of the Chinese religions has, to my knowledge, produced any extensive martyrology, and this illuminates in a striking way their different notion of conflict. If, as their world view describes it, Ultimate Reality is completely contained within the framework of the self-created, self-sustaining natural-social order, with its immanent principle of operation, the Tao, then all conflicts appearing on the periphery, since they cannot originate outside the order of Reality, will, if followed back to the Source or Center, be found to be in harmony.

Most Chinese Buddhists, therefore, clung to the traditional harmonious world view. They saw no real conflict of the new religion with China's best traditions. On the contrary, it represented for them a needed complement, offering a penetrating and consoling analysis of neglected problems like suffering and death, and affording a metaphysical basis for morality without altering accepted standards. A vast number of non-Buddhists as well were willing to accept the new religion as a colorful variation on a familiar theme— the cultivation of goodness.

A few discerning critics, however, saw in the Indian doctrine of Nirvāna a complete negation of the Chinese world view itself, for which no harmonious integration within the system was possible. Nirvāna, the sole Buddhist Reality, lay outside the Chinese order of reality altogether. The empirical world and its inner principle, which the Chinese assumed to be all of Reality, was, according to Indian Buddhism, sheer illusion. Reactions of the critics, therefore, were mostly of two sorts: (1) during the first three or four centuries of our era, while the Buddhist community was predominantly foreign, they ignored it as a mere barbarism which would eventually yield to the civilizing influence of Chinese culture: (2) especially after about A.D. 400, when Chinese Buddhists were a conspicuous segment of the population and even gentry families and members of the imperial household were being attracted to its support, they attempted belatedly to suppress it root and branch. This may seem odd in a system built on harmonious compromise, until we realize that it was precisely because the critics saw this delicately balanced system, which for hem was the system of the universe itself, being turned upside down, the catastrophic omens of which were everywhere apparent, that they reacted in alarm.

Though particular criticisms arose over many separate issues, the underlying complaint was invariably the same: the adherence of Buddhist monks and nuns to an other-worldly ideal, which caused them to repudiate the actual world with its obligations and to practice principles contrary to nature, was a dangerous threat not only to society and the state, but to the harmony of the universe as well. For every issue raised, however, the Buddhist had a ready answer: Truth is one, but the traditional Chinese view of it is too circumscribed. In the words of the popular *Vimalakīrtī Sūtra*, "The Buddha preaches with one voice, but all beings understand according to their several capacities."[1] Confucius, according to one apologist, accommodated his teaching to a crassly materialistic society and hence addressed himself only to "salvaging abuses in their final stages," while the Buddha "illumined their root causes."[2] Lao-tzu, wrote another, confined his teaching to the "fulfilment of life," while the Buddha "illumined the ideal" beyond the relativities of life.[3] Thus they felt Buddhism did not contradict any of China's sages. It merely went deeper than they dared to go.

Beginning with the basic conflict in world view, I shall briefly trace the controversy as it centered about particular issues.

METAPHYSICAL ISSUES

Interestingly enough, the earlier critics of Buddhism, while recognizing in concrete situations conflicts with their own ideology, rarely discussed the underlying metaphysical conflict. The first clear expression of it which I have discovered is by the Neo-Confucianist, Chang Tsai (1020-1077), in his "Western Inscription." "As for those who speak about Nirvāna," he wrote, "they mean by this a *departure* (from the universe) which leads to no return," while the Confucian sage is "one who completely understands the course that lies *within* (the cosmic cycle), who embodies it in himself . . . and who to the highest degree preserves its spirituality."[4] Though Chang Tsai would have quickly rejected the thought, his view of the sage "embodying" the Tao and "preserving its spirituality" was very close to the concept of the monk's relation to Nirvāna held by Chinese Buddhists themselves, and may have owed something to it. Hui-yüan (334-416), the founder of the Pure Land Sect, expressed this relation as the "embodiment of the Ultimate" (*t'ĭ chi*). The Ultimate, or Nirvāna, however world-denying or transcendent it may have been to Indian Buddhists, is clearly identified in Hui-yüan's mind with the immanent principle of the universe, the Tao.[5] Embodying the Ultimate in the world of relativity, the monk is able to transcend mortality and shower benefits on the world. What could be more sagelike than this?

Discussions of the immanence or transcendence of Nirvāna probably made scant impression on the average unlettered Chinese who embraced Buddhism in the early days, but one thing appealed to him mightily, namely, life after death—rebirth in the jeweled splendors of the Western Paradise of the faithful, and amid the unintermittent tortures of Avīcī Hell for the violent and oppressive. All schools of Indian Buddhism denied the survival of a personal entity or "soul" from one incarnation to the next. Only one component of the pseudo-personality survived, namely consciousness, *vijñāna* (Chinese

[1] *Taishō* 475 (vol. 14) 538a: quoted by Tao-an (*Kuang hung ming chi* 8.25b) and others.
[2] Sun Ch'o, in *Hung ming chi* (hereafter abbreviated *HMC*) 3.17b.
[3] Ming Seng-shao, *HMC* 6.14a.
[4] Fung Yu-lan, *History of Chinese Philosophy* (Princeton, 1953), II.497 (italics mine.)
[5] *HMC* 5.12b-15b; cf. Liebenthal, "Shih Hui-yüan's Buddhism as set forth in his Writings," *JAOS* 70 (1950), 247, 258.

shìh). Chinese Buddhists, on the other hand, linked this surviving consciousness to the native concept of the departed spirit, or *shèn*, calling it the "conscious spirit" (*shìh-shèn*), or "spirit-consciousness" (*shèn-shìh*), and from it developed a purely indigenous doctrine of immortality.[6] It was not surprising, however, that Confucian and Taoist intellectuals should view this new departure with disfavor, since the calm acceptance of one's fated span was a measure of one's adjustment to the cosmic cycle. Even Taoist efforts at prolonging the span consisted primarily of a more thorough adjustment to the cycle. Personal survival after death would upset the balance of the universe quite as much as the survival of summer weather into winter.

The controversy, already alive in the second century,[7] reached its most articulate stage over the publication in the southern capital of Fan Chen's essay on "The Destruction of the Soul (at Death)," *Shèn mièh lùn,* toward the close of the fifth century, to which literally scores of rebuttals were composed, one by the Emperor Liang Wu-ti himself.[8] Recognizing this doctrine as Buddhism's most powerful appeal in China, Fan Chen concentrated his attack on it, marshalling simple logic and homely analogy to demonstrate that the soul is an inseparable function of the body, and that both belong to the natural cycle. "When we come," he wrote, "it is not because we cause it to come, and when we go it is not because we drive it away. We but ride on the principle of Heaven."[9]

Buddhist apologists for the doctrine insisted on the separate and eternal existence of the soul. They discovered dim intimations of immortality in China's own custom of recalling the departed spirit,[10] and in the writings of Lao-tzŭ and Chuang-tzŭ.[11] Far from accepting the charge that they were upsetting the traditionally calm acquiescence to fate, they claimed their approach to the Great Change was even less perturbed than the traditional one. The anonymous author of the "Rectification of False Charges," *Chèng wū lùn,* describes the Buddhist attitude as one of fearless repose in the midst of calamity. Quoting the *Book of Changes* he wrote, "'Rejoicing in heaven (the Buddhist) knows his fate,' content with the times he dwells in resignation, and that is all." But the others, on the contrary, mourn death and dread its finality, thereby merely aggravating their perturbation over it.[12]

SOCIAL ISSUES

Almost from the beginnings of Chinese monasticism objections were leveled against its obvious upsetting of the family system. Mou-tzŭ's

[6]See Bodde, "The Chinese View of Immortality," *Review of Religion* 6 (1942), 371 ff.: also Liebenthal, *op. cit.,* p. 252.

[7]See Mou-tzu (*HMC* 1.8b-9a): Pelliot, "Meou-tseu ou les doutes levés," *TP* 19 (1920), 301 f.

[8]Fan Chen's treatise is found in *Nan shih* 57.20ab, and *Liang shu* 48.5b-10a; most of the rebuttals are in *HMC* 9 and 10. It has been translated by Balasz in *Sinica* 7 (1932), 220-34, and in part by Ch'en in *HJAS* 15 (1952). See note 11 below.

[9]Fung, *op. cit.,* II.291 f.

[10]Mou-tzu, *HMC* 1.8b; Pelliot, *op. cit.,* pp. 301 f.

[11]See Ch'en, "Anti-Buddhist Propaganda during the Nan-ch'ao," *HJAS* 15 (1952), 174, and Liebenthal, *op. cit.,* pp. 251 f.

[12]*HMC* 1.29b; *Chou I* 7-3a (Legge, *SBE* 16.354).

questioner in the late second century raised the issues of abandoning the care
of parents and family, disfiguring (by shaving and burning) the body be-
queathed whole by one's parents, cutting off the family line, and giving away
the family partrimony. Mou-tzŭ's reply was that "if there is a great good (to
be gained), one does not hesitate at small (obstacles)." This was for him
merely an application of the Confucian principle of "doing what is appropriate to the moment" (*shih i*).[13]

Later apologists quoted the *Classic of Filial Piety* itself to the effect
that the highest form of filial devotion was to achieve the happiness of one's
parents and to bring glory to the family name by establishing oneself.[14] Only
a slight extension of meaning was required to interpret this as acquiring religious merit for oneself and one's family. One writer affirmed, moreover,
that of the twelve divisions of the Buddhist canon, the fourth is concerned
solely with encouraging filial piety. "Its solicitude may be said to be unsur-
passed," he wrote, "yet the irreligious, without having investigated the
sources or having had any experience (of what they are talking about), proceed with blind assertions and false statements to make attacks and raise
objections."[15]

While we may regard this as a somewhat sanguine view of the filial
solicitude of the Buddhist scriptures, it is true that both Indian and Chinese
texts on monastic discipline mention a requirement of parental consent
before young men or women may be ordained.[16] Legislation in the Toba
domain even provided for monks and nuns to observe mourning rites for
their parents.[17] Devout families, of course, were not averse to offering their
sons and daughters to the Church, and in times of distress, as at the close of
the first quarter of the sixth century in the north, many did so to ease the strain
at home and to evade forced labor and the draft.[18]

ECONOMIC ISSUES

The sight of large numbers of able-bodied men and women flocking from
their farms and mulberry groves to the monasteries and convents, the deed-
ing of large tracts of arable land to tax-free temples, and the investment of
huge sums in bronze images and pagodas could hardly be expected to arouse
the enthusiasm of officials charged with tax-collection and recruitment. Before the fifth century, when the monastic establishments were comparatively
modest, not many overt attacks were made. But by 405, when Kumārajīva
became State Preceptor in the later Ch'in state, it was estimated by one writer
that in the heavily non-Chinese northwest nine-tenths of the population were

[13]*HMC* 1.7a. The reference seems to be to the *Doctrine of the Mean* 25 (Legge 1.419).
See Pelliot, *op. cit.,* p. 298.

[14]*Hsiao ching* 1 (Legge, *SBE* 3.466). The passage was quoted by An-ling-shou to her
father (Wright, *HJAS* 15.195) and by Sun Ch'o (*HMC* 3.18a), both of the fourth
century.

[15]*HMC* 3.18a.

[16]*Mahāvagga* 1.55 (Oldenberg, *Vinaya Texts, SBE* 1.210); *Szu fen lü tsang* 34
(*Taishō* 22.810a, cited in Wright, *ibid.*).

[17]Ware, "Wei Shou on Buddhism," *TP* 33 (1930), 158.

[18]*Ibid.* 178 f.

Buddhist.[19] And after the early Toba rulers adopted the foreign religion as a sort of state cult, appointing a Chief Monk and constructing an official temple at the capital in 398,[20] the rapid expansion of the Church in the north threatened to get out of hand. Urged on by the Taoist minister, Ts'ui Hao (d. 450), the Toba Emperor, T'ai-wu-ti, published his repressive edicts of 444 and 446, which were directed not only against the clergy but against their lay supporters as well. The immediate occasion for the first edict was the discovery of arms and supplies in a certain monastery near Ch'ang-an, in the territory of a local chieftain then in revolt against Toba rule,[21] and the issue of the economic and political role of monasteries was dramatically raised. Though the edict of 446 called for the virtual annihilation of Buddhist property and personnel, the intervention of a sympathetic prince, and the willingness of local officials, many of whom doubtless had investments in monastery property, to turn their backs, enabled most of the monks to return safely to lay life, while some, like T'an Yao, continued to practice their religion in secret.[22] The proscription was short-lived and was followed by further official patronage.

But the economic loss involved in the dislocation of the normal division of labor, with its primary stress on agriculture, continued, at least until the ninth century, to be a conspicuous source of irritation. Fu I (555-639), in his memorial to T'ang Kao-tsu in 624, recommended that the estimated 100,000 monks and nuns of his day be made to marry and produce sons for the army and silk and food for the empire.[23] When we read that in the devastating proscription under T'ang Wu-tsung in 845, in which 4600 larger and 40,000 smaller monasteries were ordered demolished, 260,500 monks and nuns secularized, 150,000 temple slaves and thousands of acres of temple land redistributed among tax-paying families, tens of thousands of catties in bronze images and bells melted down for coinage, iron images recast into agricultural implements, and gold and silver ornaments returned to the state coffers, we can gain some impression of the sheer material wealth tied up in the Church at that time.[24] After 845 reprisals against the Church were mostly in the form of quota limitation rather than attempted extirpation.[25] The temporal power of the Church had been permanently broken.

I have mentioned the implications of the discovery by the Toba Emperor, T'ai-wu-ti, of a stockpile of bows and arrows and other goods in a Ch'ang-an monastery. While the smaller Buddhist sects shared with their Taoist counterparts a history of guilt by association with rebellion,[26] there was a deeper

[19]*Chin shu* 117, 10 b; *Tzu-chih t'ung chien* 114, 1 b.

[20]Eberhard, *Das Toba-reich Nordchinas* (Leiden, 1949) p. 229.

[21]Ware, *op. cit.*, p. 139.

[22]*Ibid.*, p. 143.

[23]A. F. Wright, "Fu I and the Rejection of Buddhism," *Jour. of the Hist. of Ideas* 12 (1951), 41.

[24]J. J. M. de Groot, *Sectarianism and Religious Persecution in China* (Amsterdam, 1903), pp. 36-40.

[25]E. g., the measures of the first Ming Emperor, *ibid.*, 81 f.

[26]E. g., the popular messianic Maitreya Cult in the north during the fifth and sixth centuries, see Eberhard, *History of China* (Berkeley, 1950), p. 156.

underlying mistrust of the principle of monasticism itself, with its extraterritorial immunity from Chinese law.[27] The origin of this immunity was undoubtedly the predominantly foreign constituency of the earlier religious communities, but as more and more Chinese joined the Order the problem became more acute.

Controversy began in the south during the reigns of the Eastern Chin Emperors, Ch'eng-ti and K'ang-ti (326-345), when Yü Ping (d. 344) raised the question of *lèse-majesté* over the failure of Buddhist monks to kowtow in the presence of the Emperor. At that time the pro-Buddhist minister, Ho Ch'ung (d. 346), defended the monks on the ground that they should not be forced for the sake of outward ceremonial to compromise their method of cultivating inward goodness, a method which involved severing all worldly ties.[28] Later, in the year 402, the usurper, Huan Hsüan, anxious to buttress his authority, took up the argument with the significant observation that honors paid to the emblems of royalty were by no means an empty gesture, since the ability to "comprehend life and regulate objects" resides in the ruler, and in the role of life-giver he is the embodiment of Heaven and Earth. How could the monks accept his life-giving favors and neglect the honor due to him?[29] Huan Hsüan observed further that in the old days the first foreign devotees of Buddhism were permitted to observe their barbaric customs unmolested, but, now that Chinese emperors themselves were believers, they should make Chinese custom standard for all.[30]

It was primarily in answer to Huan Hsüan that Hüi-yuan wrote his treatise, "Why a Śramana does not do Obeisance to Kings," *Shā-mén pú chìng wáng che lùn*.[31] In it he marks a dualism between the Taoist principle of "conforming to transformations (both of nature and of the sovereign)," *shùn-huà*, and the Buddhist principle of "seeking the Ideal (beyond all transformation)," *ch'iù-tsūng*. The Buddhist layman takes the first course,[32] the monk the latter.[33] But in doing so his nonconformity is not disloyalty; he merely transcends the dualism. For the Ideal he seeks is Ultimate Reality itself (Nirvāna or Tao). During his quest he deviates from accepted patterns which involve him with other beings in endless rebirth and suffering. At the end of his quest he "embodies the Ultimate" (*tī-chī*), and is in a better position than kings to bestow favors on other beings. Heaven and Earth can give life, and kings can preserve it, but neither of these can grant immortality or freedom from suffering. The śramana, however, can do both. Therefore he treats kings and commoners with equal compassion and equal ceremony.[34]

Needless to say, this type of argument was lost on many hearers who saw in it a confirmation of their worst suspicions, namely that the monks were a group of "super-emperors" offering the inducements of heaven and the

[27]Ware, *op. cit.*, p. 158.
[28]*HMC* 12.112-142.
[29]*Ibid.*, 14b-15a.
[30]*Ibid.*, 17b-18a.
[31]*HMC* 5-9b-19a.
[32]*Ibid.*, 10b-11b.
[33]*Ibid.*, 11b-12b.
[34]*Ibid.*, 12b-15b.

restraints of hell in full usurpation of the emperor's prerogatives as sole
rewarder and punisher. Fu I, in the memorial to T'ang Kao-tsu referred to
above, reminded his emperor of a passage in the *Book of Documents* that
states. "The sovereign alone creates blessings and intimidations . . . and
if his subjects (do the same) . . . they damage his house and bring misfortune
on his kingdom."[35] He even hinted darkly that through their connections at
court the clergy threatened to seize political control from the gentry.[36] In
actuality, however, the struggle seems not to have been altogether one of
gentry versus clergy, or Chinese versus foreigners, but the lines were drawn
between factions among the gentry themselves, some of whom favored, and
some of whom feared the Church.[37]

In the Toba state the monks got neatly around the loyalty issue by
declaring the emperor to be an incarnation of Maitreya and publicly venerat-
ing him as such.[38]

CULTURAL AND MORAL ISSUES

After the proscription of 845, the sphere in which Buddhist influence was
principally felt was in the culture and mores of ordinary people, among
whom it had by now become permanently acclimated, with its impressive
artistic monuments, its colorful temple ceremonies and festivals, its masses
for the dead, and its contributions to folklore and mythology.

From the very beginning the process of acculturation was upsetting to
China's intellectuals. Since, until very recent times, China has never exhibited
the kind of xenophobia with which we are familiar in the West, the almost
chauvinistic contempt for "barbarian" culture characterizing nearly all
critiques of Buddhism in China seems paradoxical enough. But it was precisely because the Chinese intellectuals did not champion a nationalistic
culture, but insisted instead on maintaining a *universal* one, that divergent
practices were rejected, not so much on the grounds that they were Indian or
Parthian or Kuchean, as that they represented *no* culture. If the foreign missionaries had accepted this universal culture and lived by its principles, no
objections would have been raised. The cultured man (and he is inseparable
from the moral man) is one who accepts the pattern of the universe, as it has
been perceived and transmitted by sage kings and emperors, and cultivates
it within himself. Among other things, this involves developing a proper
balance between the physical, mental, and emotional forces of human nature.

---

[35]*Shang-shu* 7.4b (Legge, *SBE* 3.144); de Groot, *op. cit.,* 38; Wright, "Fu I," p. 41.
Fu I's argument had been anticipated a century earlier by Hsün Chi, of the Liang
Dynasty, who had written "the most powerful and scathing attack leveled against
Buddhism up to this time" (Ch'en, *op. cit.,* p. 191).

[36]See Wright, *op. cit.,* p. 42, and de Groot, *op. cit.,* pp. 40 f..

[37]Eberhard, *Toba-reich,* p. 239.

[38]Ware, *op. cit.,* p. 129; Eberhard, *op. cit.,* p. 229.

Now the Buddhists were making men and women act contrary to their nature by living as celibates, and by mutilation and even self-immolation.[39] and were thereby upsetting the universal pattern. It was not simply a matter of cultural inferiority, but of cultural nihilism. The argument had appeared already in Mou-tzu, where it was countered by the extraordinary observation that even one of China's own commentators had acknowledged that the pole star is in the middle of the heavens but to the *north* of China, which proves that China is not in the middle of the world. Those, therefore, who honor Buddha are not necessarily moving off center, nor is the gold of India necessarily incompatible with the jade of China.[40]

China's cultural Great Wall, erected over centuries of relative isolation from other major cultures, was not, however, to be breached in a day. During the fourth century, and intermittently on down to the thirteenth, controversy raged between Taoists and Buddhists over the tract, "The Conversion of the Barbarians," *Huà-hù-ching*, which had claimed that Lao-tzu, in his mission to the king of Kashmir, adapted his teaching to people completely lacking in the amenities of life, and hence the doctrine which he developed there (later known as Buddhism) was totally negative. It could not in any sense apply to those who had benefited from the influences of culture. In 467 another Taoist, Ku Huan (390-ca. 483), added fuel to the fire with his "Treatise on Barbarians and Chinese," *I-hsià-lùn*,[41] in which he stated: "Buddhism and Taoism may be equal in aiming at conversion, but there is a difference between the methods of barbarians and Chinese . . . Buddhism is a means of destroying evil; Taoism is a device to develop goodness. . . ."[42] The implication is unmistakable that one religion is suitable for boors and the other for the cultured.

It is to the credit of the apologists for Buddhism that they were able to extricate themselves from the cultural isolation in which their opponents stood all unaware. In doing so they represented one of the most salutary contributions Buddhism ever made to Chinese culture.

> To Ku Huan's charge, Chu Chao replied: "I beg to inquire, the cruelty of branding (criminals)—is this a Sogdian or Indian form of punishment? The pain of shedding blood—was it not begotten in the (Chinese states of) Ch'i and Chin? The atrocity of ripping up (pregnant women)—did this idea originate with those who button the lapel on the left? . . . If we probe their nature and sentiments, Chinese and barbarians are one and the same. I resent the false assumption that the one is civilized and the other boorish."[43]

[39]Cf. the case of the monk Hui-i, who drenched himself with oil and burned to death in a public square in Nanking in 463 reciting the story of Bhaiṣajya-rāja from the *Lotus Sūtra* (Goodrich, *A Short History of the Chinese People* (New York, 1951) p. 106; Hu Shih, "Buddhistic Influence on Chinese Religious Life," *Chin. Soc. and Pol. Sci. Rev.* 9, 1925, 148 f. It was this aspect of Buddhism which provoked the sharpest attack from Han Yü in his famous memorial to T'ang Hsien-ti in 819 (translated in Giles, *Gems of Chinese Literature: Prose*, London, 1926, 127).

[40]*HMC* 1.10ab; Pelliot, *op. cit.*, pp. 303 f.

[41]Largely preserved in rebuttals (see *HMC* 6 and 7).

[42]Ch'en, *op. cit.*, pp. 170 f.

[43]*HMC* 7-5a.

On the positive side, many of the Buddhist clergy, especially in the south during the period of division (317-589), came from the educated classes and were prominent figures among the intellectual élite at the capital and at K'uai-chi in modern Chekiang.[44] The Buddhist historians Seng-yu (d. 518) and Hui-chiao (d. 554) were at great pains to demonstrate the intellectual respectability of the Buddhist religion and its adaptability to the Chinese scene.[45]

CONCLUSION

In describing here the *conflict* which Buddhism encountered with China's native ideologies I hope not in any sense to have distorted the normal view of the essential unity of the "Three Religions" held nearly universally in all periods by the educated and illiterate alike in China. While certain vocal critics deplored what they considered the wholesale abandonment of the traditional view of a real, self-contained, and basically good universe, with social, economic, and political responsibilities built into the nature of things, they remained a minority, and their counsels were only sporadically, though sometimes devastatingly, applied against the foreign cult.

What was probably a majority view among non-Buddhist intellectuals was expressed by Liu Tsung-yüan (773-819), who, though a close friend of the implacable foe of Buddhism, Han Yü, did not share the latter's views on the subject. He wrote:

> There is much in Buddhism which could not well be denounced; namely, all those tenets which are based on principles common to our own sacred books. It is precisely to these essentials, at once in perfect harmony with human nature and the teachings of Confucius, that I give my adhesion. . . . Now Han Yü objects to the commandments. He objects to the bald pates of the priests, their dark robes, their renunciation of domestic ties, their idleness, and life generally at the expense of others. So do I. But Han Yü misses the kernel while railing at the husk. He sees the lode but not the ore. I see both; hence my partiality for the faith.
>
> Again, intercourse with men of this religion does not necessarily imply conversion. Even if it did, Buddhism admits no rivalry for place or power. The majority of its adherents love only to lead a simple life of contemplation amid the charms of hill and stream. And when I turn my gaze towards the hurry-scurry of the age, in its daily race for the seals and tassels of office, I ask myself if I am to reject those in order to take my place among the ranks of these. . . .[46]

For Liu Tsung-yüan and scores of other officials similarly caught in the net of political intrigue,[47] this sentiment was expressed out of a burning personal conviction hardly to be matched by any conventional allegiance to Confucian orthodoxy.

[44]See Wright, "Biography and Hagiography, Hui-chiao's Lives of Eminent Monks," *Silver Jubilee Volume, Zinbun-kagaku-kenkyūsyo*, Kyōto University, 1954, p. 397.

[45]*Ibid.*, p. 392.

[46]Giles, *op. cit.*, pp. 140 f.

[47]On the verge of high political power, Liu Tsung-yüan became involved in an aborted coup d'état and was banished to a distant post at the age of thirty-three, dying fourteen years later in obscurity. Against this background his interest in Buddhism becomes most meaningful. (See Crump, "Lyou Dzūng-ywán," *JAOS* 67 (1947) 166-171.

(Bibliographic note: Chinese references are cited from the Commercial Press *Szu pu ts'ung k'an* edition, unless otherwise indicated.)

11.

Buddhism in T'ang China

The fortunes of Buddhism are generally conceded to have reached their limits in the China of the T'ang dynasty (618-907). At the same time, in accordance with the ancient Chinese insight that the very height of *yang's* expansion means the beginning of its displacement by *yin*, it was during the mid-ninth century that the great suppression of Buddhism occurred which was to mean the end of its spiritual and temporal predominance. A glimpse of Buddhism in the midninth century will therefore give us some conception both of the glory of the institution and the tragedy of its fall. We are extremely fortunate that such a glimpse has been preserved for us in the diary of a Japanese monk, sent by the Court to study and obtain sacred literature, who traveled in China between 838 and 847. This diary is the source of the notes below. The translation is by Edwin O. Reischauer (*Ennin's Diary. The Record of a Pilgrimage to China in Search of the Law,* Ronald Press, New York, 1955); we condense and slightly edit the text.

The Lantern Festival (First Moon, Fifteenth Day)[1]

At night they burned lamps in the private homes along the streets[2] to the east and west. It was not unlike New Year's Eve in Japan. In the monastery they burned lamps and offered them to the Buddha. They also paid reverence to the pictures of their teachers. Laymen did likewise.

In this monastery they erected a lamp tower in front of the Buddha Hall. Below the steps, in the courtyard, and along the sides of the galleries they burned oil. The lamp cups were quite beyond count. In the streets men and women did not fear the late hour, but entered the monastery and looked around, and in accordance with their lot cast coppers before the lamps which had been offered. After looking around they went on to other monasteries and looked around and worshiped and cast their coppers.

The halls of the various monasteries and the various cloisters all vie with one another in the burning of lamps. Those who come always give coppers before departing. The Wu-liang-i-ssu (temple name) sets up a "spoon-and-bamboo lamp."[3] I estimated that it has a thousand lamps. The

[1]This festival marks the end of the many rituals connected with the New Year season. (L.G.T.)

[2]Ennin is in the great city of Yang-chou, on the lower Yangtze River. (L.G.T.)

[3]Translator's note says: Apparently this was a tree-like tower constructed of bamboo, with metal or pottery spoons for burning oil tied to the ends of the bamboo branches.

spoon-and-bamboo lamp is constructed like a tree and looks like a pagoda. The way in which it is bound together is most ingenious. It is about seven or eight feet in height. [This festival] lasts for a period of three nights from this night to the night of the seventeenth. (p. 71)

. . . 17th Day . . . After the forenoon meal they spread out in front of the halls of the monastery the treasures [of the establishment], laying out forty-two portraits of sages and saints and all sorts of rare colored silks beyond count. As for the countenances of the sages and saints, some were concentrating with closed eyes, others with faces uplifted were gazing into the distance, others looking to the side seemed to be speaking, and others with lowered visages regarded the ground. The forty-two pictures had forty-two different types of countenances. As for the differences in their sitting postures, some sat in the full cross-legged position and others in the half cross-legged position. Their postures thus differed. Besides the forty-two sages and saints, there were pictures of Fugen and Monju (i.e., the celestial Bodhisattvas Samantabhadra and Mañjusri) and of *Gumyō-chō* and *Karyō-binga-chō* (mythical Indian birds).

At sunset they lit lamps and offered them to the pictures of the saints. At night they chanted praises and worshipped Buddha and recited Sanskrit hymns of praise. The monks reciting Sanskrit came in together, some of them holding golden lotuses and jeweled banners, and sat in a row in front of [the pictures of] the saints and intoned together Sanskrit hymns of praise. They went through the night without resting, lighting a cup lamp in front of each saint. (pp. 71-73)

Visit to Wu-t'ai Shan

Mt. Wu-t'ai is in the far northern province of Shansi, close to Mongolia. It has for centuries been a center for pilgrimage by both Chinese and Mongol Buddhists. It is the heart of the cult of the Bodhisattva Manjusri—Wen-shu in its Chinese pronunciation, or Monju in the Japanese version of Ennin. For a detailed account of a pilgrimage to Wu-t'ai Shan by a twentieth century Western Buddhist, see John Blofeld, *The Wheel of Life*, chapter 6.

(A.D. 840, Fourth Moon) 28th Day. We entered an open valley and went west for thirty *li* (Chinese miles), arriving at the T'ing-tien Common Cloister[4] at 10 A.M. Before entering the cloister we saw toward the northwest the central terrace,[5] and bowing to the ground, we worshiped it. This then is the region of Monjushiri. There are no trees to be seen on the rounded heights of the five summits, and they look like overturned bronze bowls. On looking at them from afar, our tears flowed involuntarily. The trees and strange flowers are unlike those anywhere else, and it is a most unusual

[4]Translator's note says: [Common cloisters] appear to have been a type of Buddhist inn erected on the approaches to Mt. Wu-t'ai for the convenience of clerical and lay pilgrims.

[5]Wu-t'ai literally means Five Terraces; this then refers to the central terrace or peak of the group. (L.G.T.)

region. This then is the gold-colored world of Mt. Ch'ing-liang,[6] where Monjushiri manifested himself for our benefit . . .

Since we entered the mountains at 4 P.M. on the twenty-third day up until today we have been going along mountain valleys for a total of six days and, without getting through the mountains, have reached Wu-t'ai. (pp. 214f)

Fifth Moon: 2nd Day. We went to the Commandments Cloister (referring to Vinaya) [of the Chu-lin-ssu — a temple, still standing, according to the translator, about seven kilometers south of the western terrace] and, ascending to the balcony, worshiped the mandara[7] of seventy-two sages, saints, and deities [made] for the benefit of the nation. The coloring is exquisite. Next they opened up the Wan-sheng ("Myriad Saints") Ordination Platform. It is made of jade and is three feet high and octagonal. . . . The beams, rafters, and pillars are painted exquisitely. We called on the venerable monk in charge of the platform. His Buddhist name is Ling-chüeh, and he is one hundred years old, having been a monk for seventy-two years. His visage is unusual, and he is indeed a Consecrated Reverence. When he saw his guests, he was courteous. I am told that during the sixth moon last year three monks of the Nalanda Monastery in India came to Wu-t'ai and saw a nimbus in the form of a five-colored cloud shining about his person . . . (pp. 217f)

16th Day. Early in the morning we left the Chu-lin-ssu and, following a valley, went ten *li* east and ten *li* toward the northeast to the Ta-hua-yen-ssu and entered the K'u-yüan ("Living Quarters Cloister") and lodged there. After the forenoon meal we went to the Nieh-p'an-yüan ("Nirvana Cloister") and saw abbot Fa-chien lecturing on the *Mo-ho-chih-kuan* in a fairly high [two]-storied hall. More than forty monks seated in rows were listening to him lecture. . . . It was impressive and beautiful in the hall beyond description. . . .

[Abbot] Chih-yüan Ho-shang of his own accord said, "The Learned Doctor Saichō of Japan went to T'ien-t'ai in the twentieth year of Chen-yüan (804) in search of the Law. Lord Lu, the Prefect of T'ai-chou, himself provided him with paper and scribes, and they copied several hundred scrolls which he gave to the Learned Doctor [Sai]chō. The Learned Doctor, on obtaining the commentaries, returned to his native land." Then he asked about the prosperity of the Tendai [Sect] in Japan, and I related in brief how Nan-yo Ta-shih (considered to be the second patriarch of T'ien-t'ai sect) was [re]born in Japan. The congregation rejoiced greatly, and the Abbot [Chih]-yüan, on hearing me tell of the [re]birth of Nan-yo Ta-shih in Japan and the spread of Buddhism there, was extremely happy. . . .

After drinking tea we went to the Nieh-p'an ("Nirvana") Place of Ritual and worshiped the representation of [the Buddha attaining] Nirvana. The sixteen-foot figure [of the Buddha] lying on his right side beneath a pair of trees in the grove, the figure of Maya swooning to the ground in anguish, the Four [Heavenly] Kings and the eight classes of demigods, and a crowd of saints, some holding up their hands and weeping bitterly, some

[6]Translator's note: Another name for Mt. Wu-t'ai. "Gold-colored world" is a term for the paradise of Monju.

[7]Or *mandala,* a sacred cosmological diagram. (L.G.T.)

with their eyes closed in an attitude of contemplation, everything that was described in the scriptures, was completely portrayed in these figures.

We also saw a picture of Ta-hsieh Ho-shang, who formerly performed Buddhist practices on this mountain. He made fifty pilgrimages around the five terraces and lived on the summit of the central terrace for three years, both winter and summer, without descending. Finally, with the aid of His Holiness [Monju], he was able to put on some large shoes. They were a foot high and a foot and a half long, and the larger pair was twenty-five pounds and the smaller ten pounds. At present they are placed in front of the picture. The Priest formerly made 15,000 robes and gave them to 15,000 monks, and he arranged 75,000 offerings [of food for monks]. Now they have made his picture and put it in a high balcony and make offerings to it.

. . . When one enters this region of His Holiness [Monju], if one sees a very lowly man, one does not dare to feel contemptuous, and if one meets a donkey, one wonders if it might be a manifestation of Monju. Everything before one's eyes raises thoughts of the manifestations of Monju. The holy land makes one have a spontaneous feeling of respect for the region. (pp. 222-225)

17th Day. . . . In the evening I went with several other monks up to the P'u-sa-t'ang-yüan ("Cloister of the Bodhisattva Hall") and saw the Devotions Priest. He is seventy years old, but at first glance could be around forty. They say that his being ripe of age but hale and hearty is because he has the power of "devotion." We opened the hall and worshiped an image of His Holiness the Bodhisattva Monju. Its appearance is solemn and majestic beyond compare. The figure riding on a lion fills the five-bay hall (that is, a building with a length of five bays between six main columns). The lion is supernatural. Its body is majestic, and it seems to be walking, and vapors come from its mouth. We looked at it for quite a while, and it looked just as if it were moving.

The venerable monk told us that, when they first made the Bodhisattva, they would make it and it would crack. Six times they cast it, and six times it cracked to pieces. The master was disappointed and said, "Being of the highest skill, I am known throughout the empire, and all admit my unique ability. My whole life I have cast Buddhist images, and never before have I had them crack. When making the image this time, I observed religious abstinence with my whole heart and used all the finesse of my craft . . . but now I have made it six times and six times it has completely cracked. Clearly it does not meet the desire of His Holiness [Monju]. If this be correct, I humbly pray that His Holiness the Bodhisattva Monju show his true appearance to me in person. If I gaze directly on his golden countenance, then I shall copy it to make [the image]. When he had finished making this prayer, he opened his eyes and saw the Bodhisattva Monju riding on a gold-colored lion right before him. After a little while [Monju] mounted on a cloud of five colors and flew away up into space . . . After [the master] had made this image, he placed it in the hall, and with tears welling up in his dewy eyes, he said, "Marvelous! What has never been seen before, I have now been able to see. I pray always to be the disciple of Monjushiri, generation after generation and rebirth after rebirth." And so saying, he died.

Later this image emitted light from time to time and continually manifested auspicious signs. Each time there was a sign it was recorded in detail and reported to the throne, and on Imperial command Buddhist scarves were bestowed. . . . Because of this, each year an Imperial Commissioner sends one hundred Buddhist scarves, which are bestowed on the monks of the monastery, and each year the Imperial Commissioner on separate Imperial command sends incense, flowers, precious baldachins, pearl [decorated] banners and baldachins, jades, jewels, precious crowns of the "seven treasures," engraved golden incense burners, large and small mirrors, flowered carpets, white cotton cloth, marvelous imitation flowers and fruits, and the like. . . . The things sent yearly by various other official or private patrons from the provinces, prefectures, or regional commanderies are quite beyond count. . . . (pp. 231-234)

Miracle of Buddhist Relics

At the entrance to the mountain was a small monastery called the Shih-men-ssu . . . in which there was a monk who for many years had been reciting the *Lotus Sutra*. Recently some Buddhist relics were revealed to him, and everybody in the whole city came to make offerings. The monastery was overflowing with monks and laymen . . .

The origin of the discovery of the relics [was as follows]: The scripture-reciting monk was sitting in his room at night, reciting the scriptures, when three beams of light shone in and illumined the whole room and lighted up the whole monastery. Seeking the source of the light, [he discovered that] it came from the foot of the . . . cliff west of the monastery. After several days the monk followed the light to the cliff and dug down into the ground for over ten feet and came upon three jars of relics of the Buddha. . . . He brought them back and placed them in the Buddha Hall and made offerings to them. The noble and lowly, and the men and women of T'ai-yüan city and the various villages, and the officials, both high and low, all came and paid reverence and made offerings. Everyone said, "This has been revealed because of the wondrous strength of the Priest in his devotion to the *Lotus Sutra*." . . . (pp. 271f)

Reverencing Relics, Buddha's Teeth

The Ta-chuang-yen-ssu ([a monastery] in the southwestern corner of the capital, Ch'ang-an) held an offering to the tooth of the Buddha Shakamuni from the eighth day of the third moon until the fifteenth day. The Chien-fu-ssu[8] held an offering to the tooth of Buddha. From the eighth day to the fifteenth day Lan-t'ien-hsien (a county seat to the southeast of Ch'ang-an) had tea and food without restrictions, and monks and laymen came from every direction to eat. T'i-hsü Fa-shih, the Archbishop of the Streets of the Left (a governmental title) served as the head of the festival. The Various monasteries took part, each arranging fine offerings. All sorts of medicines and foods, rare fruits and flowers, and many kinds of incense were carefully prepared and offered to the Buddha's tooth. They were

[8]*ssu* means Buddhist monastery. (L.G.T.)

spread out beyond count in the gallery around the storied offering hall. The Buddha's tooth was in the . . . storied hall. All the Reverences of the city were in the storied hall adoring it and making praises. The whole city came to worship and make offerings. . . .

We monks in search of the Law went on the tenth day and performed adoration. We went up into the storied hall of the Buddha's tooth and saw the Buddha's tooth ourselves and reverently held it and worshiped it. . . .

The Hsing-fu-ssu west of the Sung-shu-chieh ("Pine Tree Street") also holds an offering to the Buddha's tooth from the eighth day to the fifteenth day of the second moon, and the Ch'ung-sheng-ssu hold another offering to the Buddha's tooth. In all there are four teeth of the Buddha in the city. The Buddha's tooth at the Ch'ung-sheng-ssu was brought from heaven by Prince Nata and given to the Preceptor [Tao]-hsüan of the Chung-nan Mountains. The Buddha's tooth at the Chuang-yen-ssu was brought from India in the flesh of a [person's] thigh. The Protector of the Law, the deity Kabira, was able to bring it. Another was brought by Fa-chieh Ho-shang from the land of Khotan, and another was brought from Tibet. . . . (pp. 300-302)

Church and State in Harmony: A Maigre Feast

A.D. 838, Twelfth Moon, 8th Day. Today was a national anniversary day, and accordingly fifty strings of cash were given to the K'ai-yüan-ssu (in Yang-chou) to arrange a maigre feast for five hundred monks. Early in the morning the monastic congregations gathered in this monastery and seated themselves in rows in the flanking buildings on the east, north, and west. At 8 A.M. the Minister of State and the General entered the monastery by the great gate. The Minister of State and the General walked in slowly side by side. Soldiers in ranks guarded them on all sides, and all the officials of the prefecture and of the regional commandery followed behind. They came as far as the foot of the steps in front of the lecture hall, and then the Minister of State and the General parted, the Minister of State going to the east and entering behind a curtain on the east side [of the courtyard], and the General going to the west and entering behind a curtain on the west side. They quickly changed their slippers, washed their hands, and came out again. In front of the hall were two bridges. The Minister of State mounted the eastern bridge and the General the western bridge, and thus the two of them circled around from the east and west and met at the center door of the hall. They took their seats and worshiped the Buddha.

After that, several tens of monks lined up in rows at both the east and west doors of the hall. Each one held artificial lotus flowers and green banners. A monk struck a stone triangle and chanted, "All be worshipful and reverence the three eternal treasures."[9] After that the Minister of State and the General arose and took censers, and the prefectural officials all followed after them, taking incense cups. They divided, going to the east and west, with the Minister of State going towards the east. The monks who

[9]Buddha, Dharma, Buddhist community. (L.G.T.)

were carrying flowered banners preceded him, chanting in unison a two-line hymn in Sanskrit, "The wonderful body of the *Nyorai* (i.e. Tathagata—an appellation of the Buddha)," etc. A venerable monk followed first [behind the Minister of State] and then the soldiers guarding him. They went along the gallery under the eaves. After all the monks had burned incense, they returned toward the hall by this route, chanting Sanskrit hymns without cease. . . .

During this time, there was beautiful responsive chanting of Sanskrit hymns by [the groups of monks] on the east and west. The leader of the chants, standing alone and motionless, struck a stone triangle, and the Sanskrit [chanting] stopped. Then they again recited, "Honor the three eternal treasures." The Minister of State and the General sat down together in their original seats. When they burned incense, the incense burners in which their incense was placed stood side by side. A venerable monk, Yüan-Ch'eng Ho-shang, read a prayer, after which the leader of the chants intoned hymns in behalf of the eight classes of demi-gods. The purport of the wording was to glorify the spirit of the [late] Emperor (on whose behalf the national holiday was declared). At the end of each verse he recited, "Honor the three eternal treasures." The Minister of State and the officials rose to their feet together and did reverence to the Buddha, chanting three or four times. Then all [were free] to do as they wished.

The Minister of State and the others, taking the soldiers [with them], went into the great hall behind the [lecture] hall and dined. The congregation of five hundred monks dined in the galleries. The numbers of monks invited varied in accordance with the size of the monastery. The large monasteries had thirty, the middle-sized monasteries twenty-five, and the small monasteries twenty. All were seated together as groups in long rows, and managers were dispatched from each monastery to attend to the serving of their respective groups. . . . The maigre feast was not served in a single place, but was served and eaten at the same time [in all places], and then [the monks] arose and dispersed, each one going to his own monastery. (pp. 61-63)

Portents of the Persecution to Come

In 841 a new emperor, known in history as Wu-tsung, ascended the throne. Ennin's diary for 842 contains the following ominous entry:

On the 9th day of the Tenth moon an Imperial edict was issued [to the effect that] all the monks and nuns of the empire who understand alchemy, the art of incantations, and the black arts, who have fled from the army, who have on their bodies the scars of flagellations and tattoo marks [for former offenses], [who have been condemned to] various forms of labor, who have formerly committed sexual offenses or maintain wives, or who do not observe the Buddhist rules, should all be forced to return to lay life. If monks and nuns have money, grains, fields, or estates, these should be surrendered to the government. If they regret [the loss of] their wealth and wish to return to lay life [in order to retain it], in accordance with their wishes, they are to be forced to return to lay life and are to pay the "double tax" and perform the corvee. . . . (pp. 321f)

The manifestations of Imperial displeasure with the Buddhist establishment grew increasingly serious. The edict quoted in the following incident is illustrative of arguments used by anti-Buddhist literati through the ages:

843, Sixth Moon, 11th Day. It was the present Emperor's birthday, and a maigre feast was held in the Palace. Reverences and Taoist priests from the two halves of the capital debated in the Imperial presence. . . . Two Taoist priests were granted purple robes on Imperial decree, but none of the Reverences was allowed to wear the purple.

. . . The General Manager of the Crown Prince's Household, Wei Tsung-ch'ing, compiled a commentary on the *Nirvana Sutra* in twenty scrolls and presented it to the throne. When the Emperor saw the commentary, he burned it and issued a decree, ordering the Imperial Secretariat and Imperial Chancellery to go to [Wei's] house and find the original draft and burn it. The text of this edict is as follows:

'An Imperial Edict.

Wei Tsung-ch'ing . . . stands among those of honorable degree and should conform to the Confucian way of life, but he is drowned in evil doctrines, which stir up depraved customs. He has opened the door to delusions and has gone completely against the doctrines of the sages. How deep is the depravity among those of high office! So much the more should We proscribe that which is not the words of the sages. Why should foreign religions be propagated? . . .

The Buddha was a western barbarian in origin, and his teachings spread the doctrine of "nonbirth." Confucius, however, was a Chinese sage, and the Classics provide words of profit. Wei Tsung-ch'ing, while being an ordinary Confucianist, a scholar, an official, and [a man of] distinguished family, has not been able to spread [the teachings of] Confucius and Mo-tzu, but, on the contrary, believes blindly in Buddhism and has foolishly made compilations from barbarian writings and has rashly presented them. How much more have the common people of China been steeped for long in these ways! In truth, their delusions should all be stopped, and they should be made to return to their pristine simplicity. . . .' (pp. 330-332)

In the tightening of the measures against Buddhism, Taoist rivals played a conspicuous part:

844, Third Moon. In order to destroy Lu-fu (a place in northern China which was in revolt) the Emperor summoned eighty-one Taoist priests [to perform sacrifices]. He also had a "ritual place of the nine heavens" constructed in the open on the Palace grounds. Eighty benches were piled up high and covered with elegantly colored [drapes], and at the twelve hours [of the day] ceremonies were held and sacrifices made to the heavenly deities (of Taoism). Dried meats, wine, and meat were used in the sacrifices to the Huo-lo Heaven. [The ceremony] started on the first Day of the fourth Moon and lasted until the fifteenth day of the seventh moon. . . .

The present Emperor is a biased believer in Taoism and hates Buddhism. He does not like to see monks and does not wish to hear about the "three treasures." Buddhist images and scriptures have been placed since early times in the place of ritual inside the Ch'ang-sheng Hall, and three sets of seven monks who are versed in devotions have been drawn from the monasteries of the two halves of the city and assigned in rotation to perform devotions there each day without cease, both day and night. However, the present Emperor has had the scriptures burned and the Buddhist images smashed. He has routed out the monks and sent them back to their respective monasteries and in the place of ritual has put images of the heavenly deities (Taoist) and of Lao-tzu and has had Taoist monks read Taoist scriptures and practice Taoist arts. . . . (pp. 341f)

844, Seventh Moon. Another Imperial edict was issued ordering that throughout the land the mountain monasteries, the common Buddha halls, and the fasting halls at the public wells and in the villages which were less than two hundred *ken* [in size] and not officially registered, were to be destroyed and their monks and nuns all forced to return to lay life and to perform the local corvee. . . . In the wards within the city of Ch'ang-an there are more than three hundred Buddha halls . . . But in accordance with the edict they are being destroyed. . . . There [also] was an Imperial edict ordering the destruction of all the revered stone pillars and the grave monuments of monks. [Another] Imperial edict called upon the University for Sons of the State (*Kuo-tzu-chien*), the Scholars (of the National Academy), those who had achieved the status of Accomplished Literati (i.e. received the "doctorate," *chin-shih*) of the land, and those of learning, to take up Taoism, but so far not a single person has done so. (pp. 347f)

The details of the mounting persecution related by Ennin are fascinating and important, but we can only reproduce a few more passages here:

845, Third Moon, entry of Third Day: Several days later an Imperial edict was issued to the effect that monks and nuns of the land under fifty were all to be forced to return to lay life and to be sent back to their places of origin. . . . (p. 357) Fourth Moon: Because it was being carried out on Imperial order, beginning on the first day of the fourth moon the monks and nuns under forty returned to lay life and were sent back to their places of origin. Each day three hundred monks returned to lay life, and on the fifteenth day the monks and nuns under forty had all disappeared. Beginning on the sixteenth day the monks and nuns under fifty returned to lay life, and by the tenth day of the Fifth Moon they had all disappeared. Beginning on the eleventh day those over fifty who lacked documents from the the Bureau of Sacrifices returned to lay life. . . . (pp. 361f)

Sixth Moon, 28th Day. We reached Yang-chou and saw the monks and nuns of the city being sent back to their places of origin with their heads wrapped up. The monasteries are to be destroyed, and their money, estates, and bells are being confiscated by the government. Recently a document came on Imperial command saying that the bronze and iron Buddhas of the land were all to be smashed and weighed and handed over to the Salt and Iron Bureau and a record of this made and reported to the throne. (p. 373)

Eighth Moon, 16th Day. We went north for 1,300 *li* at one stretch, going all the way through mountains and waste lands. . . . Teng-chou is the northeastern extremity of China. . . . Although it is a remote place, it has been no different from the capital in the regulation of monks and nuns, the destruction of the monasteries, the banning of the scriptures, the breaking of the images, and the confiscation of the property of the monasteries. Moreover they have peeled off the gold from the Buddhas and smashed the bronze and iron Buddhas and measured their weight. What a pity! What limit was there to the bronze, iron, and gold Buddhas of the land? And yet, in accordance with the Imperial edict, all have been destroyed and have been turned into trash. (p.382)

Epilogue: The Persecution Terminated

Ennin remained in China long enough to see normalcy return. The emperor Wu-tsung died and was succeeded by Hsüan-tsung in 847. But, although the *Diary* thus ends on a happier note, irreparable damage had been done, damage from which Buddhism as an institution never completely recovered.

846, Fifth Moon, first Day. The new Emperor, whose surname is Li, had a great amnesty in the fifth moon. There also was an Imperial edict that each prefecture of the land was to build two monasteries and that the regional commanderies were permitted to build three, and each monastery was to have fifty monks. The monks over fifty years of age who had been returned to lay life last year were allowed to take Buddhist orders as of old, and on those who had reached eighty years were bestowed five strings of cash by the state. . . . (pp. 391f)

12.
some symbols in Buddhist icons

Paintings and statues of Buddhist figures are, it is apparent, complex symbols of the Buddhist religion. Buddhism, like most of the major religions, has made extensive use of the visual symbol to convey its message, and there is indeed a rich repertory of gestures and attributes, colors and designs, noticed by everyone who looks at Buddhist icons in temples or in the illustrations of books. In the following notes we have drawn attention to only a few of the most important and most frequently encountered of these, specifically those gestures (called *mudrā*) and attributes most usually characterizing the Buddhas and the bodhisattvas which are the principal icons of temple halls and devotional pictures in Chinese Buddhism. These may serve to aid the student in identifying the figures, and in emphasizing to him that further study is needed if he is to gain a real understanding of Buddhist art.

We have taken these notes from the book entitled *Mudrā: A Study of Symbolic Gestures in Japanese Buddhist Sculpture* (New York, Bollingen Foundation, 1960), by E. Dale Saunders. We have extracted from this study certain points specifically relevant to our particular interest, editing for this purpose (terms given are always the Chinese ones, for example).

. . . The mudrā of the first Buddhist statues in India had no precise iconographic meaning. Moreover, the number of symbolic gestures used during the early times of Gandhāra, at Amarāvatī, and at Mathurā appears to have been very small. But little by little the mudrā multiplied, and a specific nomenclature as well as a more exact iconographic signification was attributed to them. This organization had taken place in large part by the seventh century A.D. Before Esotericism, around the beginning of the Christian era, the symbols used in the aniconic representations of the Buddha, such as the wheel, the lotus, etc., were replaced by the figuration of the historical Buddha in human form. Mudrā were used especially to clarify the symbolic sense of the statue. On the gestures then devolved, to a certain extent, the former identifying role of the symbols employed in aniconic representations. Despite their small number, these first mudrā were to furnish the principal symbolic gestures that spread beyond the Indian frontiers. . . .

Besides their role as metaphysical symbols, the mudrā may, in certain cases, permit the identification of specific Buddhas . . . mudrā and attributes, although not absolute evidence of identity, help to individualize the various Buddhas by completing with other iconographic details the symbolic framework of statues. The possibility of identifying by means of gestures and attributes is more and more manifest as Buddhist iconography evolves: Certain attributes and certain mudrā are associated, if not infallibly, at least frequently enough to draw certain generalities of identification. . . .

The spread of Buddhism throughout Asia imposed on the mudrā considerable modifications of form and meaning. . . . [these] modifications . . . may be explained in several ways. It is possible that in China the artists who continued the Indian tradition had only superficial notions of Indian iconography; they were doubtless even less aware of the texts which underlay the elaboration of these statues. Working from simple instructions, they were probably but little preoccupied with precision in things artistic. . . . By the seventh century, accurate drawings of Indian Buddhist statues were brought back to China by returning pilgrims. Despite this fact, in non-Indian Asia 'the iconographic tradition became obliterated . . . little by little there were created works so far from the traditional pose and so devoid of significant attributes that they escaped any attempt at a very precise definition.'[1] . . . The freedom of interpretation which characterizes Chinese and Japanese works as contrasted with Indian works sometimes resulted in considerable iconographic modification. . . . The meaning of a specific mudrā during a geographical evolution may be clarified, to a certain point, by examining statues and images. But the meaning of the mudrā during its evolution in time — a problem of no less importance — is more difficult to fathom, for the sacred texts and the ritual commentaries do not permit the student to follow the development of the mudrā in an uninterrupted line. . . . The meaning, especially ritual, of the mudrā differs according to the sect which employs it. The same is true for the meaning of the iconographic gesture. It will be necessary, then, in attributing any symbolism to a mudrā, to take into consideration the close relationship between the rites and iconography, the latter being largely the representation in art of the former. Given a variety of meanings of the same ritual gesture, care must be taken not to attach, a priori, a definitive meaning to the iconographic mudrā, but maximum attention must be given to the sect of which the statue is an icon and the period in which the statue was created. . . .

'. . . Only the gesture and the attitude make the personage intelligible to us as a symbol of a religious or metaphysical idea. That is why it is indispensable to know the attitudes and the gestures that are most often met with in Buddhist imagery in order to understand the meaning of the statues.'[2] (pp. 43-48)

THE PRINCIPAL SYMBOLIC GESTURES

1 — Mudrā of the fulfilling of the vow (Sanskrit: *Varamudrā, varadamudrā;* Chinese: *Shih-yüan-yin*)

---

[1]Quoted from O. Sirén, *La Sculpture chinoise du Ve au XIVe siècle* (Paris & Brussels, 1925), p. 132.
[2]*Ibid.,* p. 133.

In this mudrā the hand is lowered, the palm turned outward in a gesture of offering. . . . The palm should be completely exposed to the spectator, open and empty; the fingers may be bent as if to support a round object. When the personage who makes this gesture is standing, he holds his arm slightly extended to the front. In seated statues, the hand remains at about breast level, a little to the side, the palm up; very often the other hand holds a corner of the *kesa* (monk's stole). . . .

The *shih-yüan-yin* indicates the charity of the Buddha, for it is the gesture of dispensing favors. . . . Beginning with the idea of the charity accorded by the Buddha, this mudrā grants all desires and becomes, by extension, the symbol of the 'Gift of Truth' made by the Buddha, Truth of the Doctrine, Truth of the means to salvation. . . . the emphasis is put on the fulfillment of the Vow, i.e., the original Vow of the historical Buddha to strive for the salvation of all Sentient Beings. . . .

This gesture is characteristic of several divinities, the most important being Kuan-yin (Avalokiteśvara). . . . In paintings, Kuan-yin is sometimes depicted letting drop from the ends of the fingers of her right hand the nectar of life which the divinity diffuses around her for the Beings who worship her: This is the expression of the Compassion of Kuan-yin. Early, in India, this miracle was cited 'for the great relief of the hosts in the world of the dead.' According to the *Kāraṇḍa-vyūha:* 'Then Avalokiteśvara approaches the City (of the Dead), it freezes up; the guardian is kind; Avalokiteśvara the Compassionate causes to flow from her fingers ten *vaitaraṇi*, the water of the eight elements, a true water of life, which will permit the dead to reconstitute themselves. When they partake of this water, they are re-embodied. When Avalokiteśvara has saved them, they are transported into the Sukhāvatī Heaven, where the Bodhisattva finds them.'[3] (pp. 51-54)

2 — Mudrā which grants the absence of fear (Sanskrit: *Abhayamudrā, abhayaṃdadamudrā;* Chinese: *Shih-wu-wei-yin*)

[3]Quoted from Marie-Thérèse de Mallman, *Introduction à l'étude d'Avalokiteśvara* Paris, 1948), p. 263. (The nectar of life is more often contained in a vase which she holds—see Attributes: Vase. L.G.T.)

[This mudrā] would seem to sustain the theory that symbolic gestures originally sprang from natural movements. Certainly the outstretched hand is an almost universal iconographic symbol. In the Mediterranean world, for example, the outstretched right hand of the king has magical power; there must be a close connection with the power of salvation in the right hand of the Roman emperors. . . . God, as savior, makes the same gesture. . . . In Semitic religious ritual . . . this gesture was used as a magic blessing having apotropaic powers. . . . In Persia, the cosmocrator Ahura Mazda in the world ring stretches out his right hand in a similar gesture of power. . . . By this sign Christ is designated as the all-powerful monarch, cosmocrator and pantocrator . . . And, like Christ the lawgiver and pantocrator, the Buddha assumes the double role of lawgiver and protector. . . .

[The mudrā] is formed . . . in the following way: 'The right hand exposes the palm; the five fingers, stretched vertically at the level of the shoulder, face toward the outside. . . . This mudrā has the power of giving tranquillity and absence of fear to all Beings.' . . . This position of the hands, perhaps the most frequent of all the mudrā, is characteristic of standing statues, in which it is often associated with the [preceding] *shih-yüan-yin*. The reason that these two mudrā are used together . . . is probably due to the community of symbolic meaning as much as to the suitability of a double gesture to the artistic equilibrium of the statue.

Traditionally, the position of the hand in the *shih-wu-wei-yin* derives from the legend of the malevolent Devadatta, who, wishing to hurt the Buddha, caused an elephant to become drunk. As the elephant was about to trample him, Śākyamuni raised his right hand, with the fingers close together. This gesture not only stopped the elephant in his tracks, but completely subdued him. . . . With the notion of fearlessness as a point of departure, the symbolism of this gesture becomes by extension that of intrepidity . . . It is the gift of living without fear given by the Buddha to Sentient Beings. . . . On a positive plane, this is intrepidity, courage, and audacity. This mudrā, which was able to protect the Buddha against the elephant, will protect the believer against the assaults of evil.

. . . There is no doubt but what this mudrā, in view of its preponderance in almost all of Asia, appropriated to itself a symbolism other than that of fearlessness alone. For example, it is manifest from the earlier Chinese Buddhist bronzes that in point of fact the *shih-wu-wei-yin* was used . . . to symbolize the preaching of the Law. . . .

This mudrā occurs on statues of many divinities. It is the particular position of the *Dīpaṃkara* Buddha, the twenty-fourth predecessor of the historical Buddha, who, holding his garment at the shoulder or at the hip with the left hand, makes the *shih-wu-wei-yin* with his right hand. It is supposed that he appears whenever any subsequent Buddha preaches the *Lotus Sutra*. . . . Already, in India, Avalokiteśvara (Kuan-yin) raises his right hand to reassure; his left hand is held at breast level. The *shih-wu- wei-yin* serves at times to hold the rosary, or the lotus, two common attributes of this divinity. . . . It is also a mudrā characteristic of Baishajyaguru (Yao-shih Fo, Buddha of Healing) . . . It is one of the most frequent gestures on statues of Amitābha (A-mi-t'o Fo); but oftentimes, in statues of this divinity too, one notes the compound gesture [of *shih-yüan-yin* and *shih-wu-wei-yin*], respectively in the left and the right hands. . . . The compound gesture is found on statues of Shakyamuni, of Lochana (Lu-shê-na) Buddha, of Maitreya (Mi-lo Fo) (rarely); of Mañjuśrī (Wen Shu P'u-sa) [Bodhisattva]; and of Kṣitigarbha (Ti-tsang Wang). . . . In China, numerous Wei [dynasty] Buddhas, the identification of which remains sometimes uncertain, exhibit this hand gesture, which, under the Wei and Sui, was by far the most common mudrā. (pp. 55-65)

3—Mudrā of appeasement (Sanskrit: *vitarkamudrā, vyākhyānamudrā;* Chinese: *an-wei-yin*)

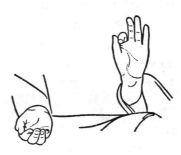

The *an-wei-yin* is formed in the following manner: The hand (right, generally) is raised, the palm outward, the fingers straight, with the exception of the thumb, which touches the end either of the inflected index or of the middle finger, sometimes even of the ring. . . . The *an-wei-yin* is also called the *shuo-fa-yin*, the mudrā of the exposition of the Law. The *shuo-fa-yin* corresponds exactly to the Sanskrit designation of vitarka . . . the mudrā of argumentation. . . . the *vitarkamudrā* is consequently the gesture which indicates the exposition of the Law, the deliberation on the Doctrine. It is the mudrā of the Buddha who explains the Law to the faithful. It is very natural, then, to pass from the idea of instruction to that of teaching. . . .

The *shuo-fa-yin* of the 'Esoteric Amitābha' . . . may be noted to be actually a form of meditation mudrā . . . in which the two hands are joined in the lap, the thumbs touching the index, middle, or ring fingers, thereby forming a circle. Either by separating the hands and raising them both in front of the breast, or by raising one and lowering the other in front of the body, this meditation mudrā turns into two *shuo-fa-yin*. One may see in this relationship of forms a similar concatenation of symbolism, for after the Enlightenment, during which the Buddha sat in the meditation pose, he began to preach, breaking from meditation into predication: In a like manner the meditation mudrā breaks into the *shuo-fa-yin*. . . .

Like the [preceding] *shih-wu-wei-in*, the *an-wei-yin* would seem to support the theory that ritual, symbolic gestures originate in natural gestures. There are numerous examples of the presence of the *an-wei-yin* type in the Mediterranean world from ancient times until the present . . . In the Christian tradition, the sign of the cross, the so-called *benedictio latina*, is a reflection of this earlier gesture in Christian iconography, although it should be noted that this same sign occurs in profane circles as well. . . . The universal connection of this gesture with speech must modify both Christian and Buddhist thinking about it, for the Christ, who, like the Buddha, makes this gesture, should be considered not so much a benedictory or blessing figure as a speaking and teaching one . . .

The circle formed by the thumb and the index, a complete form, having neither beginning nor end, is that of perfection; it resembles the Law of the Buddha, which is perfect and eternal. It is very certainly here a question of a mudrā form which recalls the Wheel, one of the attributes which symbolize traditionally the predication of the Law or the teaching of the Doctrine. . . . In Esotericism . . . the gesture is liable to an extended interpretation: The circle of perfection represents the exercise of the perfect wisdom of the Buddha, and the accomplishment of his vows. The gesture also expresses his great compassion. The left hand represents concentration; the thumb, which corresponds to vacuity and symbolizes superior intelligence, unites with the middle finger, which corresponds to fire and symbolizes the vows of the Buddha. The right hand represents wisdom; the thumb, which corresponds to meditation, unites with the index, which corresponds to air and symbolizes the efforts of the Buddha. The act of joining the thumb and the index is symbolical of the diligence and the reflection which the Buddha brings to his function (of Enlightened One).

. . . By this mudrā, . . . Amitābha welcomes souls into paradise: this is the hand which gives and which welcomes. . . . [It is] characteristic of several secondary divinities: Kuan-yin, Maitreya and Brahmā as a Buddhist divinity. Yao-shih Fo sometimes makes the gesture of the *an-wei-yin* by joining the thumb and the index or sometimes the ring finger. . . . Wen Shu P'u-sa also makes this gesture with his left hand, by joining the middle finger and the thumb. . . . (pp. 66-75)

4—The diamond handclasp (Sanskrit: *vajra-añjalikarmamudrā, añjali-mudrā;* Chinese: *chin-kang ho-chang*)

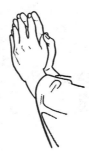

This mudrā is formed by joining the hands, which are held vertically at the level of the breast, palm against palm, fingers against fingers, interlocked at the tips, the right thumb covering the left. (In one form the hands are simply joined.) The arms may be somewhat advanced. . . .

These gestures . . . are mudrā of adoration. . . . [They] may derive from Hindu etiquette, in which it is a gesture of offering, or adoration, and of salutation. . . . In Buddhism this gesture serves to give homage to divinities accompanying offerings or prayers . . . it is universally prevalent in countries of Buddhist obedience. [In Esoteric Buddhism] the designation *chin-kang ho-chang*, as a gesture formed by the union of the two hands, recalls the coexistence of the two inseparable worlds, which are really one: the Diamond World and the Matrix World . . . On the other hand, the *chin-kang ho-chang* as a simple gesture symbolizes the world of ideas, which, like the diamond, is indestructible, eternal, static. . . .

In these gestures of adoration, the union of the right hand (world of the Buddha) with the left hand (world of Beings) represents the fundamental unity which exists between the Diamond World and the Matrix World. This unity is a representation of the Esoteric principle of duality-nonduality. The hands are in fact two; but they are joined to form only one unit, a unity, moreover, parallel to that which exists between the Buddha and Beings. This notion is reflected in the . . . gesture utilized by the Zen sect: Just as the two palms are held firmly closed against each other, in the same manner the Zen adept focuses himself in interior contemplation. . . .

The *chin-kang ho-chang* is a gesture of adoration, a gesture which gives honor to a superior state. Consequently it is never represented on a statue of the Buddha. It is a gesture which belongs rather to Bodhisattvas and to lesser personages (Guardian Kings, holy men, etc.) who give homage either to the Buddha or to the Doctrine. . . . (pp. 76-79)

5 — Mudrā of touching the ground (Sanskrit: *bhūmisparśamudrā;* Chinese: *Ch'u-ti-yin*)

The *ch'u-ti-yin*, a gesture of the right hand, is peculiar to seated statues. It is formed by presenting the hand pendent in front of the right knee with the palm turned inward, the fingers extended downward touching or 'designating' the ground. Sometimes the lowered hand rests on the right knee. Sometimes it remains a little away from the knee, while the left hand holds

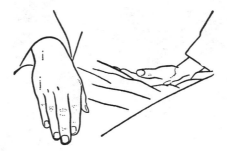

a section of the stole at the level of the breast or lies in the lap, where it may form the so-called Diamond Fist. The left hand may also lie on the left knee or at the level of the navel. . . .

The *ch'u-ti-yin* is characteristic of seated statues, but there is another gesture which iconographically and symbolically is akin to it; this is the *an-shan-yin,* 'the gesture which "represses" the mountain,' a mudrā often found in standing statues. The gesture is regularly formed by the left hand, but sometimes it is made by the right as well. The arm is lowered in the fashion of the *ch'u-ti-yin,* the wrist is flexed in such a way as to present the palm of the hand more or less parallel to the ground—not unlike a natural gesture of suppressing. It is, in fact, the mudrā which signifies the 'subjugation of the mountain' (the earth). To the extent that this mudrā symbolizes the victory over demons, it has the same meaning as the *ch'u-ti-yin.* . . .

. . . This symbolism doubtlessly finds its origin in the following legend: At the moment when the historical Buddha was on the point of proving his Buddha perfection, the gods of the earth warned him that he would be attacked by demons. But the Buddha calmed them, saying that he would suppress these evil-doing gods by his power alone; that is, by his *bodhi* knowledge. At this point the demon king appeared and challenged him to put his words into action. The Buddha, pointing to the ground with his finger, called upon the gods of the earth, who rose up and killed the demons. Other versions describe the Buddha seated in *padmāsana* under the *bodhi* tree and touching the earth . . . Śākyamuni remains unshakable by virtue of his former merits and his boundless kindness. Māra . . . following the defeat of his demon army, nevertheless presses his claim for the *bodhi* throne. He calls upon his troops as witnesses. The Buddha, without supporters, takes Earth as his witness by touching the ground. Whereupon, personified, Earth, trembling in six ways, proclaims the Buddha the rightful occupant of the *bodhi* throne. . . .

The principal divinities which employ the *ch'u-ti-yin* are Śākyamuni and the Esoteric Akṣobhya. . . . (pp. 80-83)

6 — Mudrā of concentration (Sanskrit: *dhyānamudrā;* Chinese: *ting-yin*)

(Author notes there are various forms of this mudrā—which is found only in connection with seated figures; he calls these types A, B, and C:) Type A: The hands lie in the lap, one on top of the other, the palms up. Type B: The hands lie in the lap, one on the other, the palms up; the thumbs, extending

toward each other, sometimes touch, or are raised to form a triangle with the palms of the hands. Type C: The hands lie in the lap, one on the other, palms up. The last two phalanges of the indexes are in a vertical position and touch back to back. The thumbs join at the end of the indexes forming thus two circles. This last is found in the Esoteric images. . . .

The position of the hands in the mudrā of concentration derives, in accordance with the tradition, from the attitude which the historical Buddha assumed when he devoted himself to final meditation under the *bodhi* tree. . . . (We omit enumeration of many details of the symbolism when used in the Esoteric School.)

Amitābha is perhaps the most important of all the divinities that display the *ting-yin*. . . . Numerous Buddhas, and Bodhisattvas, holy men, and sages form the *ting-yin* at times to recall the legend of the historical Buddha, at other times to invoke the Esoteric power of the gesture. The mudra also symbolizes Zen meditation . . . the *ting-yin*, of ecclesiastic and secular use, is rarely sufficient to identify the personage who makes it. (pp. 85-93)

7—Mudra of turning the wheel of the Law (Sanskrit: *Dharmacakra-mudrā;* Chinese: *chuan-fa-lun-yin*)

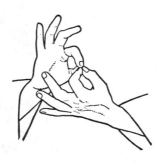

The *chuan-fa-lun-yin* is characterized by a diversity of forms during the course of its development across Asia. . . . in general, the right hand is held at the level of the breast, palm facing outward, while the index and the thumb, joined at the tips to form the mystic circle, touch one of the fingers of the left hand, whose palm is turned inward. . . .

By virtue not only of its designation ('turning the wheel of the Law') but also of its form (the two circles recalling the aspect of the wheel), the Esoteric significance of this mudrā is based on the symbolism of the wheel. This attribute, which may be appropriately classified under the heading of the gesture to which it is so closely associated, is charged with meaning since the earliest antiquity. Before Buddhism, the wheel had doubtless already taken on with the Indo-Europeans a role emblematic of the sun and of fire. And so it is that in Buddhism Vairocana (Lu-shê-na Fo), who carries this attribute, marks his clearly solar nature; he dissipates lies and error, just as the sun dissipates morning clouds. . . .

Even in the pre-Buddhist period, the *cakravartin* . . . the king who causes the wheel to turn, uses the wheel as a symbol or distinctive arm. Legend has it that at his investiture a golden wheel fell from the sky. The *cakravartin* is nevertheless inferior to the Buddha, who as *dharmacakravartin*, the one who causes the wheel of the Law to turn, conquers the world for Buddhism by universalizing the Doctrine. . . . Only he who sets the wheel in motion, who performs the creative act, may be a monarch reigning over the whole world. So the indestructible Wheel of the Cosmos illustrates the action of the Buddhist Doctrine, which crushes all illusion and all superstition, as the wheel crushes all it passes over. . . .(We omit much more of interest here on the symbolism of the wheel in Buddhism.)

Buddhist art utilizes first the symbol of the wheel and then the *chuan-fa-lun-yin* in order to recall the precise moment of the Buddhist legend at which the Buddha, having triumphed over the attacks of the evil demon, Mara, attains *bodhi*, and gives his first sermon in the Deer Park at Benares. This is the moment in which the Buddha puts into motion the wheel of the Law. . . . The *chuan-fa-lun-yin* mudrā appropriates for itself the symbolism of the wheel and acknowledges the omnipotence and the sovereignty of the Buddha by affirming his identification with a universal monarch. [In Esoteric Buddhism] it recalls the 'principal' unity of the Matrix World and the Diamond World. . . . This gesture is also called the *shuo-fa-yin*, mudrā of the exposition of the Law. . . .

The *chuan-fa-lun-yin* . . . is with one exception reserved to the exclusive use of the Buddhas; that exception is the Bodhisattva Mi-lo (Maitreya). Mi-lo as the future Buddha makes the *chuan-fa-lun-yin*, for it is he who in time to come will turn the wheel of the Law. . . . (pp. 94-100)

8—Mudrā of the knowledge fist (Sanskrit: *vajramudrā*[?], *jñāna-mudrā*[?] *bodhaśrīmudrā*[?]; Chinese: *chih-ch'üan-yin*)

The statue of Vairocana (Lu-she-na Fo) on which the *chih-ch'üan-yin* figures is in a seated position, the soles of the feet facing upward; this is the posture of interior concentration (*padmāsana*). To make this gesture, the right thumb is inflected onto the right palm, where it is enfolded and grasped by the other fingers so as to form a solid fist the center of which is the thumb. This is called the 'adamantine, diamond fist'. The left hand is held at the level of the navel, the palm turned toward the right, the raised index (i.e. the 'Diamond Finger') is inserted as far as the first joint into the fist formed by the right hand, which is now superposed over the left. The left index is held by the right little finger. The right index is grasped at the first joint by the right thumb in such a way as to bend the index. This mudrā is called . . . 'first

Knowledge mudrā which conducts souls to enlightenment'; or the . . . 'mudrā which is capable of suppressing darkness and spiritual shadows'; or the . . . 'mudrā of the great and marvelous Knowledge of Vairocana.'

(It is a mudrā of the Esoteric School, and) closely associated with Vairocana. . . . According to the Esoteric symbolism of this gesture, the left index (World of Beings) is surrounded and protected by the fingers of the right hand (World of the Buddha[s]). The five fingers of the right hand represent the Five Elements . . . [and] the five organs of the senses. . . . (There is much more to this symbolism, for which we have not the space.) (pp. 102-104)

THE ATTRIBUTES

We list here the attributes discussed by the author, with a word or two in each case to indicate the general nature of their significance:

Alms bowl—"the principal attribute" of Shakyamuni and Amitābha.

Ax—weapon to protect Law from evil; "carried by secondary divinities."

Bell—stands for impermanence (its sound is perishable); attribute of Guardian Kings and multi-armed Kuan-yin.

Arrow—weapon against evil.

Conch shell—a trumpet; "symbolizes not only the act of diffusing the Law but also its universality and its strength."

Fly whisk—"symbolizes obedience to the Law, particularly the observance of 'not-hurting' . . . for the historical Buddha, the fly whisk, like the parasol, is a symbol of his royalty"; "it is often carried by ecclesiastical dignitaries. It symbolizes the spiritual direction which the master exercises over his subordinates in order to lead them toward enlightenment."

Jewel—grants all wishes; especially characteristic of Kuan-yin.

Lance and trident—arms against evil.

Lotus—"The lotus grows in mud, yet rises immaculate to the surface of the water to bloom: thus it symbolizes purity and perfection." (There is much more to this symbolism; the lotus is also found invariably as the throne of Buddhist divinities)

Mirror—"the image of void."

Reliquary—the stupa in form of a pagoda; identifiable with the Buddha himself. A rich symbolism; as an attribute, mostly associated with the Guardian Kings.

Rope—the lasso to catch and lead sentient beings to salvation.

Rosary—eighteen beads symbolizes the Eighteen Arhats; most common is 108 beads, symbolizing the 108 passions (and other ideas); "But more probably 108 is chosen because it is traditionally an ideal number, a multiple of nine, which iteself bears the greatest potential of variation."

Scroll and Brush—Buddhist sutras.

Sistrum—to warn away creatures that might otherwise be stepped on; "in China, [it] is used in the ceremony for the salvation of ancestors. It is carried by a monk who represents Ti-tsang going through the Hells, forcing the demons to open the doors of cells where the damned are caught." Attribute of Ti-tsang, Wen Shu, multi-armed Kuan-yin, Yao-shih Fo.

Sword—weapon against evil, and symbol of victory of Buddhist Wisdom.

Vajra—principally found in Esoteric Buddhism, where it has diversified meanings; in general it stands for the imperishability of the diamond, which is the Truth of Buddhism. It occurs in many different forms, with a varied symbolism.

Vase—symbol of the illusory self, empty and receptive to the Faith; on another view, it contains the nectar of life, being a characteristic attribute of Kuan-yin; there are other meanings too. (pp. 143-195)

13.
the Laughing Buddha

The figure of "the laughing Buddha" is perhaps the most widely known icon, at least among foreigners, of Chinese religion. Even those who have not the slightest notion about Buddhism or Chinese religion are familiar with the fat, grinning monk, who may be found as a "curio," a paperweight or ashtray decoration, or even as an element in an advertisement or trademark. Visitors to Buddhist temples always find this figure facing them in the entrance hall, an incongruous intrusion, it would seem, into the lofty symbols of the religion. But whether debased to the most vulgar artistic and commercial level, or enthroned in a monastery, the laughing Buddha is a figure that arouses our curiosity.

Investigation of the laughing Buddha reveals many significant aspects of the Sinification of Buddhism, and of that most Chinese of Buddhist developments, Ch'an (or Zen, in Japanese pronunciation). The following essay is taken from Ferdinand D. Lessing, *Yung-Ho-Kung. An Iconography of the Lamaist Cathedral in Peking;* the Sino-Swedish Expedition Publications (Stockholm, 1942), Vol. 1, pp.15-35; we have condensed and edited the text.

When entering [the first Hall] we naturally look first towards the center of the Hall where we hope to encounter some exalted deity of noble bearing whose very appearance would prepare us for greater revelations to come. Instead of this we discover an almost dwarfish image of disproportionate growth, a caricature of a monk, as we should infer from his bald pate, or perhaps a mere court jester to the gods, judging by the broad smile shining over his somewhat coarse features. . . . [This is] a genuine Chinese, man and god in person, the fulfillment of the hopes of the pious Buddhist, Lord Maitreya, the Saviour-Buddha, manifested in the flesh of a humble monk. His most familiar names are: the Pot-bellied Buddha Maitreya, Ta-tu-tzu Mi-lo-fo, and Pu-tai Ho-shang, the "Hemp-bag bonze." His legend abounds in genuine Ch'an features, proving that it was the Ch'an monks who substituted his distinctly Chinese personality for their colourless, outlandish Ch'ieh-lan (the original protective deity derived from Indian Buddhist mythology).

Artistic considerations no longer played a part in these changes. . . So another step towards the Sinification of Buddhism had been taken: The first god to greet the Chinese worshipper was bone of his bones, and flesh of his flesh, and it was on him that the hope of Buddhism rested. . . .

To understand fully the apocryphal newcomer in the Chinese pantheon occupying this throne and his curious career, we must delve into the interesting legend of the person represented. . . . All the "biographies" agree that Pu-tai was a native of Ssu-ming in the Prefecture of Fêng-hua of the Province of Chêkiang and that he lived in the first half of the tenth century. He had no permanent residence except for a sojourn of three years in the Yüeh-lin-ssu in the Prefecture of Fêng-hua.

His real name was unknown, as were those of so many wandering monks of that time. One source says that he used to call himself Ch'i-tz'u, a truly Ch'an (Zen) name, which might mean: "Congruent with This," "This" meaning either his own person or the inexpressible something, the Buddha within us, the Godhead, the Absolute.

It seems that his occasional predictions contributed to his popularity. He gave them by word of mouth or indicated them by his behaviour. They were considered infallible.

We are told that when rain was expected the monk wore wet sandals and hastened on as if seeking shelter. When he was seen wearing wooden sandals with nails under the soles, or sleeping on the market-bridge in a squatting posture with his head resting on his knees (as he is sometimes depicted), the approach of warm weather was indicated. His supposed ability to predict the weather even in this indirect manner probably gained him favour with the farmer.

Almost all sources describe him as obese, with wrinkled forehead, and a white protruding belly which he left uncovered.

There was one feature in his bodily appearance which more than others attracted general attention, although he was not the only person distinguished by it. Wherever he went, he wore a *pu-tai*. This word means literally a hemp (cloth) bag, but at that time it also meant a glutton, just as today we have the *chiu-nang fan-tai* "wine-bag and rice-sack," as an epithet for a person who is immoderate in eating and drinking. The liking of the Chinese for facetious puns and their propensity for nicknames gave our monk the sobriquet Pu-tai Ho-shang, "Hemp-bag Bonze." It is under this name that he has won his country-wide popularity. . . .

Two sources state that he carried his hemp bag on a stick over his shoulder and wandered through the hamlets and markets begging for everything he saw. Whatever he received, pickles, fish and meat, he would promptly taste, putting the remainder in his bag. This bag also served as a container for rubbish, even stones and bricks. At times he even seems to have indulged in barter or trade.

This bag was naturally an object of curiosity with old and young, and particularly with the country urchins who tried to snatch it from him. One source relates that once a crowd of sixteen boys shouted at him . . . chased him, and vied with each other in seizing his bag. Another source speaking of eighteen children adds, mysteriously, that it was not known whence they came.

At times Pu-tai would open the bag, displaying its heterogeneous contents to people, strewing alms, alms-bowl, clogs, bricks, stones—everything on the ground, saying, "Look here, look here." Then he would pick up each article one after the other and ask, "What is this? What is this?"

This scene with the children survives both in art and pantomime. The number sixteen is significant. It corresponds with one of the various groups of the Arhats (Chinese, Lohan), to which Pu-tai and Dharmatāla were added later. . . . Statues representing the reclining Pu-tai surrounded by children show either six or as many as eighteen. In the first case they are explained as the six receptive faculties *(indriya)*, in the second as the eighteen *dhātus:* six receptive faculties *(indriya)*, six sense-objects *(vishaya)*, six resulting "bases" *(dhātus)*. . . .

One expects his utterances to shed more light on his character, particularly those connected with events related in the legends about him. They are, however, very brief and for the most part of that enigmatical type characteristic of the masters of Ch'an in which the corresponding sources abound . . . So we find that the ever-recurrent question: "What was the idea of the Patriarch's (i.e. Bodhidharma's) coming from the West?" was also put to Ch'i-tz'u. Instead of answering it directly he put down his bag and stood there, crossing his hands in front of his breast. "Is there nothing else to it?" the interlocutor asked him. Thereupon the master took up his bag "with his fingers," shouldered it and left. He probably intended to indicate that Bodhidharma's aim in coming to China could be stated in definite terms as little as that of Ch'an Buddhism in general.

This method of answering a question by "the great silence," so familiar to the student of Ch'an Buddhism . . . is found in another episode from his life. The bonze Pai-lu, "White Deer," asked him the simple question, "What is it about your bag?" The master placed the bag on the ground. "What do you mean by putting down your bag?" the other asked. Thereupon Pu-tai shouldered it again and went away. The same happened to the bonze Pao-fu who asked him about the gist of Buddhism. Pu-tai sometimes followed this habit of responding to a question by not giving any direct answer, but by breaking off the conversation altogether even when he himself had begun it.

Once he overtook a monk wandering along the road. Tapping him on the back, he begged him, "Give me a cash."[1] These words are . . . a Zenist *kung-an* (Japanese, *kōan*), subject for meditation. The source continues: The bonze, turning his back, said, "If the truth *(or path, tao)* is found, I will give you a cash." The master put down his bag and stood there with crossed hands.

His taciturn mood alternated, however, as the sources assure us, with moments when he was more communicative, though he always remained laconic.

Once, when he was wandering in Min (Fukien), a layman of the name of Ch'en, a great worshipper of his, elicited from him the following information: "How old are you?" The master replied: "My bag here is as old as space." When asked for further details, he answered: "My surname is Li (the name legend ascribes to the reputed author of the *Tao-tê-ching*, Lao Tzu). I was born on the eighth day of the second moon." The comparison of space with a bag or more precisely with bellows is found in a frequently quoted passage of the *Tao-te-ching*, Ch.5: "Heaven and Earth and all that lies between is like a bellows in that it is empty, but gives a supply that never fails." The word in question means a sack which is open at both ends. It may also mean a bellows. . . .

There is another incident related in Pu-tai's legend which has some analogy to a story told about Diogenes. Once he stood on a road . . . When he was asked by a monk, "What are you doing here?" he replied, "I am waiting for a man." The bonze said, "Here he is." The master took an orange from

[1]The smallest coin. (L.G.T.)

his robe and offered it to him. As soon as the other reached for it Pu-tai withdrew his hand and said: "You are not that man." But when the monk asked, "What kind of man is it (for whom you are waiting)?" he received the surprising reply, "Give me a cash." . . .

But there are other episodes which give us a different picture of his attitude towards current beliefs, and they refer, characteristically enough, to the Messianic hope of the Buddhists, which is focused around Maitreya [Mi-lo-fo], the Coming Buddha.

The scene with the urchins examining the contents of his bag . . . concludes: "Thereupon he wrapped up some excrements with the words: "This is the ground of the inner court of Maitreya." The inner court is a part of Maitreya's palace that plays some rôle in the eschatological ideas of the Buddhists. This palace in which the Bodhisattva is believed to reside is made of gold . . . Similar crude comparisons are also found in other writers. We mention e.g. Chuang Tzu's characteristic statement about ubiquitous Tao. Still, we are at a loss how to explain this saying of the monk in this connection. Was it really purported to be iconoclastic, like the sayings and doings of so many of his fellow-monks since the advent of Bodhidharma almost 500 years before? Viewed in the light of another episode . . . we feel inclined to think so. Once, it is said, he pointed to a privy, saying: "Conversion (or: begging alms) does not amount to as much as these excretions." . . .

But how did it happen that a man of this mentality became a god, even Maitreya himself? That he did not escape the fate of other religious characters, more eminent than he . . . of being made into something which he either did not believe to exist at all or considered to be irrelevant to religious thinking. The answer is that he, too, fell a victim to idealization through religious fiction. . . .

One source states: The magistrate Wang Jen of P'u-t'ien saw him . . . The monk gave him a religious poem *(chieh=gatha)* which reads:

> Mi-lo (i.e. Maitreya), true Mi-lo,
> Reborn innumerable times,
> From time to time manifested to men,
> The men of the age do not recognize you.

Insignificant as such words may seem to the average unbelieving person, they assume magic suggestiveness when raised above the level of every day affairs and connected with such a momentous event as death. Taken as a swan-song, they are capable of surrounding their author with a glamour of mysticism and winning him a nimbus of immortality. . . .

According to one source Pu-tai entered Nirvana sitting on a rock in the Eastern vestibule of the temple Yüeh-lin-ssu in the second year of Chên-ming of the Later Liang Dynasty (AD.916). . . . [In the same source we find] miraculous features accompanying his funeral rites. A beadle of that district who formerly had taken offense at the conduct of the idle mendicant, had upon three occasions given him a scolding and deprived him of his bag, which he burned, but, to his surprise, Pu-tai had reappeared each time with that same old bag. After the saint's death, the beadle, repenting of his harshness, bought a coffin for his funeral. But the whole crowd present was unable to move the coffin. Thereupon they substituted a man by the name of T'ung (which means "boy") who had always shown respect to the Master. It appeared that for him the coffin was as light as a feather. . . . Are we justified to . . . assume that "a (virgin) boy" or "(virgin) boys" were the only ones able to carry the coffin of him who is stated in the text to have remained virgin all his life? The "universal" character of this legend is well enough known to be discussed here. The reader may be reminded of the coffin of the Buddha, Shākyamuni , about which a similar legend is on record.

Because of his popularity, the credulous crowd was only too willing to believe the rumours denying his death. The fact that these regions in those times were rich in religious characters of a similar type with whom Pu-tai may have been confounded seems to offer a sufficient explanation for the origin of such stories. So he is reported to have been seen by people in other districts. To one of them he said, "By mistake, I have taken this sandal with me. Take it back with you." When the man returned, he learned that the master had already died. The people inspected his tomb at Feng-shan, and lo! they found only one sandal in it. . . . The circumstance of the single sandal found in the tomb is frequent in Chinese resurrection stories and has its well-known analogies elsewhere.

It is, therefore, apparent that this and similar stories have been borrowed from older legends in order to strengthen the belief aroused by his famous poem that he was a "preincarnation," so to speak, of Maitreya.

One source speaks of the cult of his relics: "And so they took a flask of celadon[2] used for consecrated water and his mendicant's rattlestaff with six rings, which they found near the pagoda marking his tomb, and preserved them as sacred relics in the temple where he had breathed his last." This is evidently the beginning of his deification. . . .

More miracle stories were rife and enhanced his fame. Already looked upon with amazement, because, when lying on the snow (apparently to sleep), his body remained unaffected by it, this amazement grew into real awe when it became known that a man named Chiang Mo-ho, when bathing with him in a brook, had discovered an eye on his back, which could but be the eye of "transcendent wisdom" *(prajñā-cakshus)*. Utterly surprised, the layman exclaimed, "You are a Buddha!" The Master hushed him: "Don't tell anyone." . . . Another source tells the same story with this variant: Chiang, rubbing (Pu-tai's) back (with a towel) suddenly discovered four eyes shining brightly. Startled he did obeisance to him and exclaimed: "Reverend Sir, you are a Buddha." The Master said, "Don't tell people. That I have been with you for three, four years, that may be called a great 'grace.' I must leave you. Don't be sad." The number four is probably introduced here with the intention to outdo the older version. Four eyes in addition to Pu-tai's natural eyes would symbolize the fivefold eye *(pañ-cacakshus)* of a Buddha.

But two other factors cooperated in raising him above the level of his contemporaries, and even higher than the most illustrious of his predecessors: the poems composed by, or ascribed to him, and the drawings made of him. . . . All [the poems] express that spirit of Ch'an . . .

[2]A green porcelain ware. (L.G.T.)

[A poem in one source] is one of a whole series of parting stanzas with which Pu-tai answers questions of his hospitable friend Ch'en. Here it answers the question about the Buddha-nature.

The first stanza describes the universality of the mind, a favourite subject with the Ch'an mystic; the second develops the state of mind of the wandering monk; the third asserts the futility of cherished scholastic distinctions. The fourth stanza carrying the ideas set forth in the third, describes the state of the "saint" who is fundamentally not different from the profane man, living in the same world with him. The fifth stanza is an exhortation to strive "after that one great aim."

1. This mind, mind, mind is the Buddha,
   The transcendental something in the worlds of the ten quarters.
   In all directions it operates miraculously in the pitiful sentient beings,
   And all the *dharmas* are not real, as the mind is.

2. Ascending, transcending, free and independent, bound for no destination,
   With all-embracing wisdom he moves, the man who left his family.
   If he beholds before his eyes the Real Great Way,
   He does not even regard the tiny (tip of a) hair as real: a miracle indeed.

3. The ten thousand *dharmas,* how are they different, and the mind, how is it
   distinguishable?
   What is the use of searching the meaning of the *sutras?*
   The mind-king in its original state severs the manifold knowledge.
   Only he is wise who understands (or: by whom is illustrated?) the state of
   Nonlearning.

4. Since there is neither profane nor saint, what should one do?
   Abstain from differentiation, and there is the state of the saint, which is
   solitude.
   That priceless pearl of the mind in its original state is round and pure.
   All differences caused by qualities are futile names.

5. It is MAN who makes TAO (the "truth," "way") great, and TAO stands out
   in clarity.
   Numberless pure and noble (men) praise TAO.
   Dragging (your) pilgrim's staff (feel) like ascending the path leading home.
   Do not worry that nowhere (you) hear a sound.

The same sources give us another poem:

One alms-bowl contains the rice of a thousand families;
A lonely body wanders ten thousand *li.*
(Only) a few people cast friendly looks upon me
For the road I ask the white clouds.

. . . But these poems, even in combination with the legends relating prophecies and miracles, would hardly have been sufficient to secure him a permanent place in tradition and a comparatively high rank in the pantheon, if pictorial art had not come to their aid.

"Thereupon" [says the source] (continuing the story about his reappearance after his burial), "priests and laymen vied with each other in drawing his portrait. Even now in the eastern side hall of the Great Hall of the Yüeh-lin-ssu (where he died) a full portrait of him has been preserved." Another source states expressly that the portraits drawn by the people were wor-shipped, and our oldest source declares that his poem about Maitreya led to the belief that he had pointed towards himself as the actual Maitreya.

The *Kao-seng-chuan (Lives of Eminent Monks)* says that his portrait was frequently painted by people "in the region of the Yang-tzu and the Che-chiang rivers" (modern Che-kiang), the cradle of so many religious innova-tions. The cult of the Arhats, among whom Pu-tai is a belated guest, spread from there over China. . . .

We omit several extracts from the author's sources, which give a cir-cumstantial and obviously fictional account of the portrait and other matters further illustrating the deification of the monk Pu-tai.

This is apparently all the information we have about the inception of his iconographic portrait. What it resembled we can only vaguely imagine from his literary picture, as nothing genuine seems to have survived of those pre-sumably crude wall-paintings which were originally mere "sgraffiti" or scrib-blings of a more or less perishable nature made by novices or visitors. But perhaps it is quite safe to assume that they inspired, indirectly, the oldest real paintings which have come down to us. Such a type, with his grotesque features and his ragged, dirty garb, appealed to the Chinese genius with its leaning for the bizarre, which often enough, for instance in the traditional Arhat type, gives us the erroneous impression of intentional caricature. Inten-tional caricaturing is doubtless to be found in many more recent reproduc-tions, as the type underwent certain remarkable changes in the course of time.

For the earliest drawings or paintings just mentioned no outside influ-ences need be assumed. It seems, however, quite possible, or even probable, that the statuary was inspired by some squatty *Yaksha* type, as Lucian Scher-man was the first to surmise.[3] Certain statues of the sitting Pu-tai show essential similarities to that of the Yaksha Jambhala, and it may be that later images of the monk represent a crossing between the Chinese paintings and some Yaksha. The peach seen in the hand of Pu-tai has very probably been substituted by the Chinese for the lemon held by Jambhala which had less meaning for them. One of the oldest Chinese stone figures in existence, dat-ing from the Sung Dynasty, is found at Yen-hsia-tung in the province of Che-kiang. It shows the type familiar to us.

This short-limbed *(kharva)* Yaksha-type goes back, as Scherman sur-mises for good reasons, to a popular type of Silenos, the friend of children, who has survived in Buddhist iconography since the age of Gandharan art, though we are not yet able to give an uninterrupted history of his evolution. It may be observed, however, that the broad grin Pu-tai displays in the more

[3]"Die Dickbauchtypen," in *Jahrbuch der asiatischen Kunst*, Vol.I, pp.120-136.

recent images is contradictory both to the description of the legend and to the traditional type of Jambhala (who, particularly as *Ucchushma*, is expressly described as frowning, *kṛta-bhṛkuṭin*); whereas it would fit the popular conception of a Silenos. The "winebag" characteristic of Silenos, was often misunderstood and converted into a fold or corner of his garb. That would explain the feature noticeable in images of Pu-tai showing him without his chief attribute, the bag, instead of which he clutches a corner of his "monastic robe" with his left hand.

Statues of him have usually neither nimbus nor aureola, nor the ornaments of Maitreya either. There are, however, statues where the solemn combines with the grotesque: the fat, half-nude monk wears a crown, much in the same way as the "real" Maitreya as "crownprince" (*yuva-rāja*, i.e. as designated successor of Gautama or Shākyamuni).

. . . Summing up, it seems that Pu-tai Ho-shang was a figurehead representing a whole category of similar characters of the Ch'an school, posing as religious eccentrics, commanding a deep respect with the populace willing to worship them and to credit them with superhuman qualities. As a matter of fact one Chinese text enumerates four Pu-tais:

1. Ch'i-tz'u, in the T'ang dynasty.
2. Liao-ming, a fat monk, Sung dynasty.
3. Pu-tai, Yüan dynasty (considered to be a reincarnation of Nos. 1 and 2).
4. Chang's son of Tsao-yang, said to resemble a painted Pu-tai.

This statement, if correct . . . would be another proof of the undoubtable fact that the popularity of the fat monk grew rapidly. He eclipsed the entire crowd of older, nobler, and more famous colleagues, among whom were quite a few very popular figures, for he was Maitreya, the Buddha-to-Come, who, temporarily in a humble guise and in an unpretentious manner, preached the message of Ch'an Buddhism in the language of the people. Ch'an, as Dr. Hu Shih has justly pointed out, is the Chinese version of the Buddhist gospel, and Pu-tai, or the Pu-tais, were the last of its apostles, the Messiahs of the Latter Days. Systematic mythology required a definite place and rank for this preincarnation in the pantheon, and so he became not only one of the last Arhats, but also the first saint to greet the worshipper visiting the temple.

This then is Pu-tai Ho-shang, the Hemp-bag Monk, alias the Pot-bellied Maitreya, mendicant, friar, philosopher, poet, hero of legends, guardian of the temple, saint and saviour in disguise, one of those Eulenspiegels in which Chinese folklore is so rich and who lived up to Lao-Tzu's saying: "The highest wisdom is like foolishness, the greatest eloquence like stuttering."

In China he is still one of the most favourite figures of popular religion, known everywhere and to everyone. A thousand years have not dimmed his popularity, on the contrary, they have increased it. This appears even in commonplace sayings of everyday life. If a mother proudly refers to her fat baby as a *Tz'u-wa-wa*, "a porcelain doll," she has in mind the numerous ugly porcelain figures of the monk.

14.
Zen and Amidism in Chinese Buddhism

The syncretistic character of Chinese Buddism is something that has been noted by many writers. In recent centuries the dominant forms have been the pietistic Pure Land (*ching-t'u*), or what is often called Amidism because recitation of the name of Amitabha Buddha is the heart of this form, and Ch'an, which we shall call by the better-known Japanese pronunciation Zen. To the Westerner, with his experience of dogmatic sectarianism, nothing would seem more unlikely than the easy ecumenical relationship of these utterly different practices. Even in Japan, where both Amidism and Zen flourish—as well as various other sects—there is a clearcut separation between the different sects. So we may consider that the Chinese way is indeed uniquely Chinese.

The following material is extracted from an autobiography by the English Buddhist, John Blofeld, entitled *The Wheel of Life*, Rider and Co., (London, 1959), pp. 87-90. His conversation with the Venerable Hsü Yün, no doubt the most eminent Buddhist monk of this century, will illustrate the Chinese attitude better than any abstract discussion.

The present Abbott [of the Nan Hua Monastery in North Kwangtung province] was no other than the Venerable Hsü Yün, who was believed to be well over a hundred years old, though still able to walk as much as thirty miles a day. He was renowned all over China as the greatest living Master of Zen; so I was delighted to hear the unexpected news that he had just returned after an absence of several months spent in a distant province. Not long after my arrival, I excitedly followed the Reverend Receiver of Guests to pay my respects to this almost mythical personage. I beheld a middle-sized man with a short, wispy beard and remarkably penetrating eyes. He was not precisely youthful-looking as I had been led to expect, but had one of those ageless faces not uncommon in China. Nobody could have guessed that he was already a centenarian. Finding myself in his presence, I became virtually tongue-tied and had to rack my brains for something to say, although there was so much that I could profitably have asked him. At last, I managed to ask:

'Is this famous monastery *purely* Zen, Your Reverence?'

'Oh yes,' he answered in a surprisingly vigorous voice. 'It is a great center of Zen.'

'So you do not worship Amida Buddha or keep his statue here?'

The question seemed to puzzle him, for he took some time to reply.

'But certainly we keep his statue here. Every morning and evening we perform rites before it and repeat the sacred name while circumambulating the altar.'

'Then the monastery is not *purely* Zen,' I persisted, puzzled in my turn.
'Why not? It is like every other Zen monastery in China. Why should it be different? Hundreds of years ago there were many sects, but the teachings have long been synthesized — which is as it should be. If by Zen you mean the practice of Zen meditation, why, that is the very essence of Buddhism. It leads to a direct perception of Reality in *this* life, enabling us to transcend duality and go straight to the One Mind. This One Mind, otherwise known as our Original Nature, belongs to everybody and everything. But the method is very hard — hard even for those who practice it night and day for years on end. How many people are prepared or even able to do that? The monastery also has to serve the needs of simple people, illiterate people. How many of them would understand if we taught only the highest method? I speak of the farmers on our own land here and of the simple pilgrims who come for the great annual festivals. To them we offer that other way—repetition of the sacred name—which is yet the same way adapted for simple minds. They believe that by such repetition they will gain the Western Paradise and there receive divine teaching from Amida Buddha himself — teaching which will lead them directly to *Nirvana*.'

At once reluctantly and somewhat daringly I answered: 'I see. But isn't that a kind of — well, a sort of — of — er — deception? Good, no doubt, but —'

I broke off, not so much in confusion as because the Venerable Hsü Yün was roaring with laughter.

'Deception? Deception? Ha, ha, ha, ha-ha! Not at all. Not a bit. No, of course not.'

'Then, Your Reverence, if you too believe in the Western Heaven and so on, why do you' trouble to teach the much harder road to Zen?'

'I do not understand the distinction you are making. They are identical.'

'But —,'

'Listen, Mr. P'u, Zen manifests self-strength; Amidism manifests other-strength. You rely on your own efforts, or you rely on the saving power of Amida. Is that right?'

'Yes. But they are — I mean, they seem — entirely different from each other.'

I became aware that some of the other monks were beginning to look at me coldly, as though I were showing unpardonable rudeness in pertinaciously arguing with this renowned scholar and saint; but the Master, who was quite unperturbed, seemed to be enjoying himself.

'Why insist so much on this difference?' he asked. 'You know that in reality there is nought but the One Mind. You may choose to regard it as *in* you or *out* of you, but "in" and "out" have no ultimate significance whatever — just as you, Mr. P'u, and I and Amida Buddha have no *real* separateness. In ordinary life, self is self and other is other; in reality they are the same. Take Bodhidharma who sat for nine years in front of a blank wall. What did he contemplate? What did he see? Nothing but his Original Self, the true Self beyond duality. Thus he saw Reality face to face. He was thereby freed from the Wheel and entered *Nirvana*, never to be reborn — unless voluntarily as a Bodhisattva.'

'Yet, Reverence, I do not think that Bodhidharma spoke of Amida. Or am I wrong?'

'True, true. He did not. But when Farmer Wang comes to me for teaching, am I to speak to him of his Original Self or of Reality and so on? What do such terms mean to him? Morning and evening, he repeats the sacred name, concentrating on it until he grows oblivious of all else. Even in the fields, as he stoops to tend the rice, he repeats the name. In time, after a month, a year, a decade, a lifetime or several lifetimes, he achieves such a state of perfect concentration that duality is transcended and he, too, comes face to face with Reality. He calls the power by which he hopes to achieve this Amida; you call it Zen; I may call it Original Mind. What is the difference? The power he thought was outside himself was inside all the time.'

Deeply struck by this argument and anxious, perhaps, to display my acquaintance with the Zen way of putting things, I exclaimed:

'I see, I see. Bodhidharma entered the shrine-room from the sitting-room. Farmer Wang entered it through the kitchen, but they both arrived at the same place. I see.'

'No,' answered the Zen Master, 'you do not see. They didn't arrive at any place. They just discovered that there is no place for them to reach.'

This reply made me feel proud of myself. It seemed I *had* grasped the point correctly, for the Master had condescended to answer with one of those Zen paradoxes which force the hearer into even deeper understanding. His broad smile was enough to show that he was really satisfied with my reply.

'After all,' I added complacently, 'it's all a matter of *words*.'

Instead of nodding approvingly, the Venerable Hsü Yün turned away from me suddenly and began speaking on quite a different subject to one of his disciples. His withdrawal was so pointed that, for a moment, I felt hurt as by a harsh snub. Then I saw the point and almost laughed aloud. 'Of course that's it,' I said to myself. 'The significance of that turning away is as clear as clear can be. It means, "On the contrary, it is all a matter of no words—*silence*." Of course that was it.' I prostrated my self and walked out to find the room allotted to me for the night.

15.
the religious vocation

Many observers have expressed their opinions about the caliber of the Buddhist Sangha in China in modern times, and many reasons have been advanced why its members choose this career. There is no need to doubt that in such a large and ancient institution there will be found persons of all sorts, and that their reasons for having joined the Order will be varied.

What we mean to emphasize, by including the following selection here, is that one should not underestimate the importance of a true vocation for some among the Sangha. If we accept the universality, the humanness of religious needs, the fact that man is by nature *homo religiosus,* then we will not be surprised to find those in every culture who turn to the religious life simply because that part of their nature is dominant.

This brief testament, *Diary of a Chinese Buddhist Nun: T'ze Kuang,* appeared originally in Chinese in the prominent Buddhist periodical *Hai Ch'ao Yin* (Sound of the Tide), Vol. II, Nos. 11-12 (February 1923). The translation by Y. Y. Tsu was published in *The Journal of Religion,* VII, 5-6 (October 1927), pp. 612-618.

[1]*26th Day of 10th Moon.* — Today is the one hundredth day after brother Wen's death; we held a memorial service for him in the "Paradise Nunnery." Just three years ago this day, brother started on his honeymoon trip with his bride . . . . alas, what a dream life is! This morning I accompanied sister-in-law to the nunnery, we lunched with the nuns, sharing their meager meal (because we asked them not to prepare specially for us), and afterward joined them in their devotional service amid the music of the bells and the fragrance

---

[1]TRANSLATOR'S NOTE.—The diary covers seventeen days within three months in the life of a young woman that led to her "taking the veil" of a nun. The Chinese equivalent for taking the veil is "shaving the head," or "discarding the hair," the hair being looked upon as symbol of worldly vanity. There is no reason to doubt that the document is genuine. The Chinese terms for family relations, such as Wen Ku for elder brother Wen, and Wen Sao for sister-in-law or wife of elder brother Wen, have a charm untranslatable in English. The term for addressing a Buddhist monk or nun is Fa Shih, which means "teacher of law," so "Chin Kuang Fa Shih" will be Teacher of Law Chin Kuang; for brevity it is usually shortened into "Chin Shih," Teacher Chin. In the translation, Fa Shih, for a nun, is given as "Sister" for convenience. Excepting for one small portion omitted in the entry for 29th of 11th Moon, the Chinese text has been faithfully followed in the translation. The *Hai Ch'ao Yin* is the official organ of the modern Buddhist movement in China, and under the powerful editorship of Tai Hsu, the St. Paul of Chinese Buddhism, it has a high standing in Buddhist and literary circles. It contains valuable material for a student of comparative religion and psychology of religion.

of the burning incense. On our way home my heart felt the longing for the quiet and serene life of the nunnery, and wondered whether it could be mine also. . . . .

4th Day of 11th Moon. — Morning: read prayers with mother and sister-in-law for two hours. Since brother's death sister-in-law has been fasting, reading prayers, and constantly talking with me about the Buddhist life. When the great sorrow came to her, she almost wanted to give up living; now she seems determined to follow Buddha's way. Afternoon: Sister Chin Kuang called, and we urged her to spend the night with us. Sister Chin Kuang has a beautiful personality, sympathetic and serene, is of the same age with sister-in-law, and literary. We find much in common and are good friends. Often we would ask her about her past, but she kept it to herself. This evening she told us that she was the daughter of Li family, a high official in the Manchu Dynasty, married at seventeen to Mr. Shen, but finding no happiness in her husband's house, she secured the consent of her family and entered the nunnery on the first day of the tenth moon in the fourth year of the Republic [1915], five months after her wedding! We talked together until midnight.

7th Day of 11th Moon. — Sister-in-law and I got mother's consent to invite Sister Chin Kuang to our house to teach us the sutras, and so in the afternoon we went to the nunnery and explained our errand to her. She spoke to the Abbess, who gladly agreed. It began to rain, and so we were asked to pass the night there. In the evening Sister Chin Kuang showed us two photographs. One was of herself before she shaved off her hair — such refined presence and elegant bearing — and on the margin was written, "Taken three days before initiation. From now on, my worldly self remains in the picture only." The second photograph shows her with the shaven head and dress of a nun, and on the margin was written: "Taken two days after initiation; almost a different person from the one in the other picture." I shared a room with another nun, Hui Kuang. She is fifteen only, bright and pretty, early lost her mother, was ill-treated by her stepmother, and now finds her happiness in a nun's life.

8th Day of 11th Moon. — Rose at 4 A.M. Watched the nuns at their early matins. After breakfast, sat in meditation before Buddha with the others until 10 A.M. At that time a Mrs. Wang called, and seeing sister-in-law and myself, inquired whether we were there preparing for initiation. I replied, "I hope that such may be my good fortune some day." Sister-in-law was delighted to know that I had the same desire as she. Sister Chin Kuang had her head shaved preparatory to coming to our house, and as we watched the procedure, she showed us a box in which her beautiful original hair was kept, which she said would be burnt with her body after death. We came home and arranged an altar for Buddha.

12th Day of 11th Moon. — Rose at 4:30 A.M. Sister-in-law has already formed the practice of spending an early morning hour in silent meditation and prayer. At six, breakfast. Afterward had our morning service with Sister Chin Kuang. I can repeat a number of sutras, only the rhythm is not so smooth. Afternoon, Mr. Chen came to say that brother Wen's grave was prepared and that the burial would take place on the twenty-fifth, etc. It was a hard day for sister-in-law, but she felt much comforted by our saying the prayers.

21st Day of 11th Moon. — We spent the day with our regular services. In the evening sister-in-law asked me to help her dress her hair. I protested that it was already late, but she insisted, and so I gave in and helped her. Then she explained: "I have long wanted to enter the Buddhist life; I am glad that I have met Sister Chin Kuang, for you have strengthened my decision. When my husband was here he admired my hair greatly. I am going to cut it off and have it buried with him in his grave. There is no time to wait for a regular initiation, and so I am going to ask Sister Chin Kuang to shave my head this evening. I have not told my father and mother, for they might not agree to this, but they will understand afterward." Sister Chin Kuang gladly consented. I watched the procedure in silence. Sister-in-law put the cut braids in a black-wood box and retired to her own room.

22nd Day of 11th Moon. — This morning the servants were greatly surprised to see sister-in-law's shaven head, but she remained wonderfully calm. When our parents were up, we three went in and sister-in-law knelt before them and explained her conduct. Our parents could not but accept the *fait accompli,* and suggested that sister-in-law should give up her ordinary dress and put on nun's robes. As we had none ready, Sister Chin Kuang lent her a few pieces of her own. Afternoon we went to the nunnery and informed the Abbess. It was agreed that the initiation ceremony be held on the eighth of next Moon.

25th Day of 11th Moon. — At 7 A.M. brother Wen was buried. Sister-in-law put the blackwood box into the grave. Before doing so, she opened the box and showed the farmers who were watching the burial the contents, so as to disarm any suspicion that it might contain jewelry. We returned to the city by boat.

28th Day of 11th Moon. — Sister-in-law completed her arrangements to leave home. She turned over all her possessions to mother. Mother proposed to sell her things and let her have the money for use in the nunnery. But father suggested keeping her things and giving her $1,500 and donating 30 mao of land to the nunnery. Sister-in-law was very happy and grateful. For days I felt unhappy; I wished that I could join sister-in-law in her initiation. We talked the whole night without sleep.

29th Day of 11th Moon. — We overslept this morning. Got up at 9 A.M. and commenced my meditation, but other thoughts came in and I could not exclude them. Afternoon, sister-in-law left home with Sister Chin Kuang, never to return again. My spirit was despondent, as if having lost someone. I retired early.

8th Day of 12th Moon. — 7 A.M., accompanied mother to Paradise Nunnery. 10 A.M., sister-in-law was initiated and given the name of Chih Kuang. Henceforth I do not address her as sister-in-law, but as Sister Chih Kuang. About twenty friends attended the service. Sister-in-law looked radiant and happy.

9th Day of 12th Moon. — Last night I dreamed that Sister Chih shaved my head and I was happy, but on waking I felt my head and was greatly disappointed. Got up at 5:30 A.M., had my usual morning devotion, but felt very lonely. Helped mother in home work, but my heart was heavy. Retired early to my own room but could not sleep.

14th Day of 12th Moon. — Today is my uncle's birthday, and also the completion of the first moon of a little girl cousin. Mother, Sister Chih, and myself called to offer our congratulations. Sister Chih Kuang at first would not go, but grandmother insisted that though she had entered the Buddhist life she was still a member of the family. A number of female guests were there, and there was naturally much whispered talk about Sister Chih. It was wonderful to see how calm and self-possessed she was. When others addressed her by her family name, she suggested that she be called Sister Chih Kuang. Sister Chih spent the night with me at home, the first time after initiation. We talked late into the night. I told her that lately I had been thinking of the mystery of life—birth, reproduction, death, in endless rotation—and was oppressed by the sense of the vanity of all things.

15th Day of 12th Moon. — The talk last evening had helped me to make up my mind. Rose at 6:30 A.M., morning devotion. Saw parents and told them my wish, but they would not consent. I was told that it was natural for sister-in-law, widowed and alone, to seek the Buddhist life, but I was in my young womanhood with a glorious future before me. I went into my room and cried out my heart. Sister Chih said to hold on to my purpose and she would do her best for me to realize it.

6th Day of 1st Moon. — Morning: when I was fixing my hair, our maid Ch'ung Hsiang told me that father had selected the 18th of next moon to engage me to a certain young man of well-to-do family and a college graduate, and congratulated me. I was horrified and decided to act before it was too late. Afternoon: went hurriedly to the nunnery and told Sister Chih Kuang and Sister Chin Kuang. We agreed that there was no time to waste, and so decided upon an early initiation, provided the Abbess would agree to it. Fortunately the Abbess consented and chose the fifteenth as the day of initiation, and said that I was to go to the nunnery on the fourteenth. I returned home but said nothing to my parents.

14th Day of 1st Moon. — Afternoon: went to a photographer and had my picture taken as a memento for mother. To the nunnery: Sister Chih Kuang had prepared some nun's dresses for me and I put them on. My clothes were given away to a poor girl. Evening: Sister Chih dressed my hair into six braids, preparing for the ceremony next morning.

15th Day of 1st Moon. — Today is the day I shave off my hair and leave this worldly life to enter the "gate of law," the most memorable, most precious day of my whole life. After this day, I shall be a new person.

Rose at 4 A.M., joined morning devotion; breakfast, beans and bean curd only, but they tasted sweet in my mouth. The nuns filed into the big hall with musical accompaniment, each wearing the rubrical mantle. Sister Chih Kuang put a red mantle over me, and Sister Chin Kuang led me into a hall. Excepting the members of the nunnery, none was present, and even the outer gate was locked to prevent any outsiders from coming in (precaution against possible interruption on the part of my family).

After doing homage to "the Three Precious" and saluting the Abbess, I knelt before Buddha. Sister Chin Kuang took scissors and cut the six braids near the roots and put them in the tray held by little Sister Hui Kuang, who gave me a smile in her eyes. I was asked to prostrate myself three times and stand up. My head was washed and then shaven smooth. Some medicated stuff was put on my forehead, and six short sticks of incense (half an inch long) were stuck into it and lighted. Two nuns held my head tightly. I closed my eyes and repeated the name of Buddha; just felt slightly warm on the head and the sticks of incense were already burnt into the skin. Henceforth six scars will remain forever on my forehead. After receiving the "Five Obligations" I prostrated myself in thanksgiving before Buddha and also thanked the Abbess and Sister Chin. The service finished, all the nuns offered congratulation and I thanked them with the usual salute of "joined palms" (palms together, fingers upward). Sister Hui, with a smile, gave back the braids and shaven hair for me to keep. Sister Chin produced a mirror and asked me to look into it and see whether I could recognize myself. I could not. The head looks clean and smooth; the scars are still sore; I feel somewhat cold without wearing a hat. Afternoon: I went home with the Abbess and Sisters Chin and Chih to call on father and mother. They were visibly surprised and even angry. I knelt before them and explained. Father and mother gave me $1,000 as an endowment for my life in the nunnery. Toward evening we returned to our nunnery. . . . . Henceforth with peace in my heart I follow Buddha's way, undisturbed by worldly anxieties and regrets!

T'ZE KUANG (RADIANT BENEVOLENCE)

16.
Religious Activities in the Buddhist Monastery

The following description of the daily life in a typical Buddhist monastery is from the pen of Karl L. Reichelt, a Christian missionary who spent many years during the first half of the twentieth century working among Chinese Buddhists. Reichelt belonged to the small but distinguished group of missionaries who did not allow their Christian and Western biases to blind them to what was admirable and valuable in the Chinese culture. In the selection presented here from his book, *Truth and Tradition in Chinese Buddhism* (translated from the Norwegian by Kathrina van Wagenen Bugge; Shanghai, 1928), we see his wide acquaintance with the subject, and his warm empathy. (Selection is from pp. 272-282.)

The fixed daily services begin very early in the morning, especially in the summer. Even in the winter one can hear the first signal for the morning mass at three o'clock in the morning. The monks then get out of bed and gather, quiet and solemn, in the big temple hall. Each knows his place, either in the East party or the West party.[1] The instructor stands by the altar on the right side. He plays one of the instruments and leads the chanting in a full, clear voice . . . Farther to the right stands the drummer and the man who beats the well-known hollow "wooden fish" (*mu-yü*). Farther out in the congregation stands the one of the East party who beats the time by striking a little bell (*ch'ing-tzu*). In some places, cymbals and other kinds of strange instruments are in use, for the "time" is very difficult. It is remarkable to hear what they can achieve with these instruments in the chants, which may last for hours. The well-known daily masses are sung without any book of ritual, but during the long extra masses the inspector and the main leaders have the books in front of them. . . .

The service begins with a "prelude," the time being given by striking the different instruments. A signal is then given on the bell, and the whole congregation bows in silence on the praying stools or praying mats, not merely on their knees, but all the way down, so that the forehead lightly touches the floor. This is done in unison, and when several hundred monks in the same dress are seen doing this the effect is quite striking. They get up and then bend again, nine times in all. This is the holy greeting, three repeated three times (3 X 3). When bowing, they must remember to let the right knee touch the floor first, for the right side is the clean one, while the left is

[1]The two groups into which the monks are divided for administrative convenience. (L.G.T.)

unclean. Therefore the cloak, which is the garment used during the mass, is only worn on the left shoulder. The kneeling rug is spread out neatly during the first prostration.

Meanwhile, the abbot, accompanied by his acolytes, has come in. He also begins with the nine-fold prostration. He may be recognized by a red patch on his gown. As soon as he has finished his silent prayer, a signal is given on the bell and the instructor introduces the mass by singing, in very low chanting tones, the first words of the sutra used. As a rule, it is the formula of greeting "Nan-mo," then comes the name of the Buddha or bodhisattva concerned, and finally "fo" [Buddha] or "p'u-sa" [bodhisattva]. After "Nan-mo," all join in, supported by the beating on the instruments, and a rushing volume of chanting rises to the high temple ceilings. The first sections of praise and the holy vows which are daily renewed offer the greatest variety. Here the alternating instruments and song are most effective. Besides facing the altar, the worshipers turn several times to one side so that the parties of the West and East face each other.

Special parts of the mass are sung by the abbot. He genuflects and bends in a rather interesting way. It is when one comes to the sutra itself that the greatest demands are made upon the monks who take part. In order to get through it all within reasonable time the speed has to be increased enormously. The chant rushes along breathlessly so that everybody feels great relief when the last section is reached, where they can rest in the long tones of praise. This last part of the mass, chanted in kneeling position, is the most touching.

The chanting tones have a pronouncedly mournful character. The music and the tunes of Buddhism are known as "pei-t'iao" (tunes of woe). And yet, at times, during the great festivals, a cheerful hymn of praise may arise. To those who hear such masses for the first time the effect may be strange and eerie. But one need not have been present many times at mass in one of the larger monasteries or heard a well-drilled monk choir, before one is struck by the devotion and religious intensity of the singing. This is doubtless true of the most serious and devout of the monks, while on the other hand many only take part in a mechanical way. More than once I have spoken with monks who have talked with enthusiasm of their longing to get to certain monastaries where the singing is especially cultivated, as for instance, to Chiao Shan, the remarkable little island in the lower part of the Yangtze, where some of the best singers of Buddhism gather. I have been present with them at several of their masses and I shall never forget the impression of noble singing and religious devotion which I there received. . . .

If it be asked: "Why do we not see larger ethical results from all this religious emotion?" I will answer with my hand on my heart: "The Chinese have the same difficulty in exchanging religious rapture and emotion for a well-directed holy life as we Westerners have. But that these masses are often ethically helpful I am quite convinced." Several Buddhists have told me: "It was not till I took part in these solemn masses that I understood what Buddhism was. I felt regenerated."

The mass often closes with a quiet procession round the great temple hall. The participants walk in long rows between the stools or out into the corridors, with hands folded (*ho-chang*) and eyes half-closed, pronouncing a greeting to the different Buddhas and bodhisattvas by prefixing every name with the well-known "Nan-mo." Or all may be united in a five-hundred- or one-thousand-fold greeting to Amitabha. The final act takes place before the high altar, the abbot after the nine prostrations returning to his apartment followed by the acolytes, and the instructor singing the last hymns and making the last genuflections, after which everybody retires.

In some monasteries there are as many as three such services every day, but two are the usual rule, for there are many other things to be attended to, and such a service may last one or two hours.

After morning mass there is a chance to complete one's toilet, after which comes breakfast. This is often followed by the ordered masses for the dead, when a band of monks must serve again in the temple hall. Then guests come who have to be entertained, the daily business must be attended to, etc. In some places, there are special schools for the young monks and novices. All too soon it is eleven o'clock and the dinner bell calls the monks to the refectory. In the afternoon there is, as a rule, less to do, so it is easy then to get a talk with the monks. The evening mass is about five o'clock and is quite impressive. It differs from the morning mass only in including, as a rule, a part of the confession litany. The beautiful prayer of the "Pure Land" . . . is also chanted. The sutra used is often the little Amitabha scripture (the "O-mi-t'o Ching").

When there are no novices being educated in the monastery and all is quiet, it is considered a meritorious undertaking to have a law scholar (Fa-shih) connected with the monastery giving regular lectures or expositions of different classical writings. If the abbot himself is a law scholar he may do it, but as a rule some famous expositor from another place is engaged. This serves to bring fame to the monastery. It is announced a long time ahead, by big posters, that such and such a master is going to give lectures on some of the scriptures. "All who are devoted to Buddhism are welcomed." The master is received and treated with veneration . . . The lecture usually takes place in the afternoon. It has fallen to my lot to be present on many such occasions.

The master comes in, accompanied by the abbot, and takes his seat on a stage beside the image of Vairocana or Maitreya. When he enters, everybody stands up. A short mass is read as an introduction to the lecture. The master sits with his feet crossed under him like a living Buddha, and the choir boys arrange the folds of his gown neatly around him. In addition to the monks there gradually assemble a group of interested laymen, old pensioned officials, scholars, or even a group of venerable matrons. The young monks distribute copies of the scripture that is to be read, to every one present. First the master reads a passage. Then he begins to explain sentence by sentence, while he gives a general survey later. He sometimes launches out into the deep so that it is difficult for the "unlearned" to follow him, but often he gives out real pearls. His theme carries him away, one feels his deep emotion, but he controls himself and forces himself back to the usual academic style.

Without doubt these lectures do much good, especially among the monks who are led deeper into the great religious thoughts. They act as an antidote to the mechanical routine which constantly tends to blunt the mind. . . .

It remains now to say something further about meditation. This can be done either privately in the different cells or unitedly in the meditation hall. At the latter place, regular courses in meditation are given under the leadership of the "wei-na" [instructor] or the "t'ang-chu" [assistant instructor]. These are meant to assist the newly ordained monks to become familiar with this holy art, but one often sees older monks also, both from among the casual visitors and those who have definite occupations in the monastery, joining in voluntarily. These older monks have their seats on the left side as one enters. Here, also, the "lord of the hall" (t'ang-chu) sits. The instructor sits on the right side near the group of young monks. He has the "fragrant beating boards" (hsiang-pan) on his side, and is placed on a separate raised seat. He keeps a close watch on all, and if irregularities occur, he gives his reprimand when the period is over, at which time the "fragrant boards" may be used. By his side he has two young assistants, who help in his work.

Special beating of the big drum calls the monks together for meditation. In order to benefit fully from the holy exercise it is the rule first to take two or three quick marches to get the blood moving. The whole group makes a round of the corridors and then re-enter and take their places. At a given signal everybody gets up again, and the quick march is resumed, this time round the hall, going a certain number of times round in circles, the leader at the side of the group with a long bamboo pole in his hand. "Right about face" is ordered by a heavy stroke of the bamboo pole on the floor, after which the quick step goes in the opposite direction. This is done as many as three times. Then the big drum is again sounded, the door is shut, the participants resume their seats, and the meditation proper commences. Meanwhile, a long incense stick has been lighted in one of the outer halls. This is looked after by an attendant (hsiang-têng). Three quarters of an hour may elapse before it has burned down. When it does, the fact is announced by renewed drum beating. A new stick is then lighted, burns out, and another three quarters of an hour has passed. If the meditation is to take "three incense sticks," still another is lighted, and in this way they mark altogether two and a quarter hours. The periods in the meditation are thus divided according to the burning down of the incense sticks. This, too, expresses the thought that meditation should assist a person to concentrate his mind so that it ascends in a fine, straight line, as one sees the incense smoke rise from a stick in a closed room. . . .

It is of first importance in meditation to get the correct posture. Without this, it is difficult to attain to the right condition of mind. The posture is the same as that of the historic Buddha when he sat under the Bodhi-tree and had his great inner experience: the legs crossed under him, the eyes half shut, the hands loosely crossed in front. If one sits quietly and immovably like this, and breathes deeply and regularly, one will have bound or chained that part of the body which mostly hinders man in the free expansion of the mind. But more is required, for though it is difficult to get accustomed to the rather uncomfortable position, this is gradually learned, particularly if one begins in youth. A thousand times more difficult is the next step: to become calm and acquire concentration. To help toward this the instructor repeatedly enjoins: "Away with all unnecessary and vain thoughts," "the heart must get to rest" (hsin kuei-i). Here it is that many fight a desperate inner battle, and worst of all, one is not allowed to ask Buddha for help. No, here in the meditation hall, Buddha must in no form be invoked for mercy. Here one must "yung kung" oneself, labor on to the goal. Many have given up the effort at this, the second step, and allowed it to become a merely mechanical performance.

Where, then, shall those who would attain to this calm of mind begin? The answer is: You must begin with yourself. Think of where you have come from; what you were before you were born into the world as a man. Think until you see your original face (*pen-lai-ti mien-mu*). Then think of what you may attain to if all the illusions of the world, all the worldly and carnal desires, are annihilated. (Here drastic directions are given of how to see through the emptiness and ugliness of everything connected with the body and the senses.) Think of being delivered from all this! Think what it means to get behind all feelings of pleasure and displeasure, to be raised above the vicissitudes of life, to see clearly, to see "emptily," and face the future as one who has already conquered it. At this stage one may begin thinking of Buddha, not the historical Buddha, but the Buddha idea. And from this elevation he is seen in a new light: Buddha is not a distant personality, he is myself in my final redemption, which I now perceive from the midst of the white mist in which I am sitting. The few elect who attain to this feel as if their seats have been changed into a flowery bed of the most brilliant and fragrant lotus. Personally, I have met such persons. They long for the hour of meditation, and even continue their meditation in their own chambers until late at night.

From this it will be understood why the Buddhists call meditating "tso kung-fu" or "yung-kung"; namely, work. They often measure the spiritual worth and character of a monk by the extent to which he finds his enjoyment in meditation. . . .

17.
the imperial worship

The religious rituals of the Imperial Court might be considered as the paradigm for the State religion as a whole. In each administrative center of the vast empire the official in charge would have to see to it that the prescribed temples and altars were set up, and that the prescribed services—sacrifices in honor of State-recognized deities—were held there during the year. The temples and altars were in general small versions of the great establishments at the Capital, and the local official was the small counterpart of the Emperor. However, the Emperor did not personally act as officiant in many ceremonies, his dignity of course not permitting that he should humble himself except in the worship of the most exalted deities. These were Heaven, Earth, the Imperial Ancestors, and the Gods of Land and Grain.

We give here the vivid descriptions of Joseph Edkins (*Religion in China*, Boston, 2nd edition, 1878, chapter 2: "Imperial Worship," pp.18-38). It was written in the midnineteenth century when these services were still being carried on, and when the vast, symbolic complex of temples and altars in Peking was in actual use, and not merely an architectural museum. We give this material at considerable length, because it includes much that is of general application in the study of Chinese religion. We edit as necessary.

I. The imperial worship of China is ancient, elaborate, and solemn. At the establishment of each new line of emperors fresh regulations in regard to sacrifices are enjoined, but it is usual to follow old precedents to a very large extent. . . .

The chief center of the religious solemnities embraced in the imperial worship is the altar of Heaven. This is in the outer city of Peking, and is distant two miles from the palace. There are two altars, the southern, which is called Yüan-ch'iu, or "round hillock," and the northern, which has upon it a lofty temple, called Chi Nien Tien, "temple for prayers for (a fruitful) year."

Beside special occasions, such as the establishment of a dynasty, the conclusion of a successful military campaign, or the accession of an emperor, there are three regular services in each year. They are at the winter solstice, and the beginning of spring, and at the summer solstice. The first and last of these are performed on the southern altar, the second at the northern.

The spectacle is most imposing. The Emperor proceeds the evening before, drawn by an elephant, and accompanied by grandees, princes, and attendants, to the number of about two thousand. He passes several hours of the night within the park of the altar of Heaven, in a structure called Chai Kung, or Palace of Fasting, which corresponds to the "Lodge for passing the night while upon the road," mentioned in the classical work *Chou Li*. Here the emperor prepares himself by quiet thought for the sacrifice. He spends the time in silence; and, to remind him of the duty of serious meditation, a copper man fifteen inches high, attired as a Taoist priest, is carried in the procession, and placed before him on his right, as he sits in the fasting-hall. The image bears in its hand a tablet inscribed, "Fast for three days." It is intended to assist the Emperor to keep his thoughts fixed. The idea is, that if there be not pious thoughts in his mind, the spirits of the unseen will not come to the sacrifice. The three fingers of the left hand of the image are placed over the mouth, to teach silence to the monarch of three hundred millions of people while he prepares himself for the ceremony.

The altar of Heaven consists of three marble terraces, circular, and ascended by twenty-seven steps. The uppermost of the three terraces is paved with eighty-one stones, arranged in circles. It is on a round stone in the centre of these circles that the Emperor kneels. Odd (i.e. *Yang*) numbers only are used, and especially multiples of three and nine, in the structure of this altar.

As the visitor stands on this terrace, he sees on the north the chapel for preserving the tablets, beyond it a semicircular wall, and farther still the buildings connected with the north altar and temple. This temple is ninety-nine Chinese feet in height, and has a triple roof, with blue tiles. Both altars are ascended by four flights of steps, towards the four cardinal points. Behind the visitor, a stone's throw from the altar on the south-east, is the furnace for the burnt-sacrifice, in which a bullock is consumed to ashes. On the south-west are three lofty lantern poles, the light from which is very conspicuous in the darkness of the winter night at the solstice, when the kneeling crowd, headed by the Emperor, is engaged on the successive terraces of the altar and the marble pavement below in performing the prostrations appointed in this the most solemn act of Chinese worship.

The two altars, with the park, three miles in circuit, which surrounds them, date from A.D.1421, when the third emperor of the Ming dynasty left Nanking, and made Peking the capital. . . .

The upper terrace of the great south altar is 220 feet in diameter, and nine feet high; the second 105 feet in diameter, and eight feet high; the third and lowest is fifty-nine feet in diameter, and eight feet one inch in height. The entire height, then, is twenty-five feet two inches, but the base is already raised five feet by a gradual ascent. The low encircling wall is roofed with blue tiles.

In place of the green porcelain furnace on the south-east for the burnt sacrifice, there was anciently an altar on the south called T'ai T'an. The word *t'an,* "altar," shows that in the time of the *Li Chi,* one of the classics [compiled probably during the second century B.C.], which uses this term in describing it, it was an altar, and not a furnace.

The altar on which the Emperor kneels, and where the written prayer is burned, corresponds to the Jewish altar of incense. The furnace, or rather the altar, which it now represents, corresponds to the Jewish altar of burnt-offering. The furnace is nine feet high and seven feet wide, and is placed outside the low inner wall which surrounds the altar . . . Outside of the furnace is the outer wall, distant 150 feet from the inner. Beside it is the pit for burying the hair and blood of the victims, a ceremony instituted apparently with the idea that it would be possible in this way to convey the sacrifice to the spirits of the earth, just as the smoke and flame of the burnt-offering convey the sacrifice to the spirits of heaven.

It is impossible here to avoid seeing a striking resemblance to the Roman sacrifices which contained the burial ceremony, with a similar idea attached to it, in their worship of the terrestrial divinities. . . .

The animals are slaughtered on the east side of the altar, everything appertaining to the kitchen requiring to be upon the east side. They consist of cows, sheep, hares, deer, and pigs. Horses were formerly used, but not now. The house where these animals are kept is on the north-west of the altar, near the hall in which the musicians and dancers who take part in the sacrificial ceremonies meet to practice for these occasions.

The idea of a sacrifice is that of a banquet; and when a sacrifice is performed to the supreme spirit of Heaven, the honour paid is believed by the Chinese to be increased by inviting other guests. The emperors of China invite their ancestors to sit at the banquet with Shang Ti, the supreme ruler. A father is to be honored as heaven, and a mother as earth. In no way could more perfect reverence be shown than in placing a father's tablet on the altar with that of Shang Ti. Yet, at the same time, another idea is present: The Emperor desires, in fulfillment of the duty of filial piety, to pay the greatest possible honor to his parent . . . On the upper terrace of the altar the tablet of Shang Ti, inscribed "Huang T'ien, Shang Ti," is placed, facing south, immediately in front of the kneeling Emperor. The tablets of the Emperor's ancestors are arranged in two rows, facing east and west. Offerings are placed before each tablet.

Large and small millet, panicled millet and rice, are boiled as if for domestic use. Beef and pork in slices, with and without condiments, are presented in the form of soup. Salt fish, pickled fish, pickled slices of hare and of deer, pickled onions, bamboo shoots, pickled parsley and celery, pickled pork and vermicelli, come next. The condiments used in making the dishes are sesamum oil, soy, salt, pepper, anise, seed, and onions.

The fruits offered are such as chestnuts, sisuphus plums, water chestnuts, and walnuts.

Wheat flour and buckwheat flour are made into balls, with sugar in the middle, and afterwards stamped so as to become flat cakes.

Three cups of *chiu*[1] are placed in front. Next comes a bowl of soup. Then follow eight rows of basins, making twenty-eight in all. They consist of fruit, basins of rice and other cereals boiled, pastry, and various dishes.

Jade stone and silk offerings intended to be burnt are placed behind these twenty-eight dishes. Then there is a whole heifer, with a brazier on each side for burning the offerings.

Behind the heifer are placed the five worshipping implements of Buddhism, namely, an urn, two candelabra, and two flower jars. Behind these are more candelabra, and the table in the south-west corner at which the Emperor reads the prayer.

On the second terrace, on the east side, the tablet of the sun is placed, and also that of the Great Bear, the five planets, the twenty-eight constellations, and one for all the stars. On the west side is placed the tablet of the moon spirit, with those of the clouds, rain, wind, and thunder. . . .

Twelve pieces of blue silk are burned in honor of Shang Ti, and three of white in honor of the emperors. Seventeen pieces of silk, yellow, blue, red, black, and white, are burned in honor of the spirits of the heavenly bodies, and wind and rain.

Several kinds of incense are used. All are composed of fragrant woods gound to sawdust, and then made up into bundles of sticks or pastilles of various shapes.

The Emperor is the high-priest, who acts personally or by deputy in all the public sacrifices performed for the sake of obtaining rain or securing freedom from calamities. His position then is like that of the patriarchs in the religion of Genesis. He combines the offices of chief magistrate and high-priest. The particulars of his duty as priest of the people are such as offering prayer for a good year, presenting the offerings, and worshiping. Besides these, he previously inspects the animals in their sheds when living, and afterwards when slain and made ready for the sacrifice.

On proceeding to the robing-tent, he washes his hands and puts on sacrificial robes. He then, guided by the directors of the ceremonies, mounts the altar and stands near the kneeling cushion, while all the princes and nobles take their places on the steps and terraces of the altar or on the stone pavement below. When told to kneel, he kneels. When told to light incense and place it in the urns, he does so. When led to the tablets of his ancestors and told to kneel before each and kindle incense sticks, he does all this. He is afterwards led back to the chief tablet, and there he performs the ceremony of the three prostrations and nine knockings of the head (kotow). In this he is immediately imitated by the attendant worshipers in their various positions.

The music, which has been in course of performance by the appointed 234 musicians, stops. The Emperor is led to the table on which are placed the

---

[1]Author's note explains this is "either distilled or not distilled. It is the Mongol and Turkish *arahi* and *arrack,* and the Japanese *sake.* The number three is expressive of honor. The same mode of showing respect is employed in the sacrifices to the Earth spirit and to the Emperor's ancestors."

offerings of jade and silk which are to be burned. Here he kneels, having the heifer behind, offers the jade and silk, and rises. The officers whose duty it is to sing here interpose with a song descriptive of the presentation of the bowls of food. Other officers bring up these bowls, together with hot broth, which last they sprinkle three times on the body of the heifer. Meantime the Emperor is standing on the east side of his tent. More music is now performed, the piece being called "The song of universal peace." Upon this follows the performance of the ceremony of presenting the bowls of food before the various tablets by the Emperor. Then the first cup of wine is presented, the Emperor officiating. Appropriate music is performed.

The officer in charge of the prayer places it on the table intended for this use, and it is there read by the Emperor. It is, at the sacrifice in February, couched in such terms as the following:

"I, thy subject, by hereditary succession son of heaven, having received from above the gracious decree to nourish and console the inhabitants of all regions, think with sympathy of all men, earnestly desirous of their prosperity.

"At present looking to the approach of the day *Hsin* and the spring ploughing, which is about to take place, I earnestly look up, hoping for merciful protection. I bring my subjects and servants with offerings of food in abundance, a reverential sacrifice to Shang Ti. Humbly I pray for thy downward glance, and may rain be granted for the production of all sorts of grain and the success of all agricultural labours."

The remainder of the prayer is an encomium upon the deceased emperors worshiped on the same occasion

After reading this prayer, the Emperor takes it to the table for silk offerings and the jade scepter. Here, kneeling, he places it in a casket with the silk, and then makes some more prostrations.

The second presentation of the cup of wine now takes place, and after it the third, the Emperor officiating. The music here takes the name "The song of excellent peace," and "The song of harmonious peace."

The band of musicians on the pavement below, numerous as it is, is no larger than that of the dancers, who move in a slow step through several figures. When the songs are ended, a single voice is heard on the upper terrace of the altar chanting the words, "Give the cup of blessing and the meat of blessing." In response, the officer in charge of the cushion advances and kneels, spreading the cushion. Other officers present the cup of blessing and the meat of blessing to the Emperor, who partakes of the wine and returns them. The Emperor then again prostrates himself, and knocks his forehead three times against the ground, and then nine times more to represent his thankful reception of the wine and meat. The assemblage of princes and nobles all imitate their lord once more at this point. An officer calls, "Remove the viands." The musicians play a piece suitable to this action, and another called the "Song of glorious peace."

The spirit of Heaven is now escorted home again to the tablet chapel on the north of the altar.

The crier then chants the words, "Carry away the prayer, the incense, the silk, and the viands, and let them be reverently taken to the T'ai T'an. . . . The crier calls, "Look at the burning." The proper music is played, and the

Emperor proceeds to the spot set apart as most suitable for observing the burning. The officers upon this take the tablet on which the prayer is written, the worshiping tablet, the incense, the silk, and the viands to the green furnace, within which they are placed and burned. At the same time the silk, incense, and viands offered to the tablets of the emperors are taken to the large braziers prepared for them, and there burned.

The ceremonies here terminate, and the Emperor returns to the palace.

The spirit of the worship may be partly judged of from the hours at which it is performed. At the south altar it must be at midnight, because that is the hour called *Tzu*. Tzu is the first of the twelve hours, and was applied to the eleventh month, or December. The sun is at Tzu when he passes the winter solstice. The day was divided into twelve parts, because there are twelve lunations in a year. It was natural to begin counting the months from the time when the sun was at the lowest point. The time of the solsticial sacrifice of winter should be regulated on the principle that the hour Tzu is on this account most suitable.

When the spring sacrifice takes place near the beginning of the year, the time chosen at present is the first glimmering of the dawn. But formerly midnight was the hour.

The sun is worshiped at the Sun altar at four o'clock in the morning, and the moon on the Moon altar at ten in the evening. . . .

II. The character of the Chinese imperial worship at the Earth altar is substantially the same as at the altar of Heaven, except that instead of the worship of star gods and the sun and moon we have that of the spirits of mountains, rivers, and seas. . . .

There are two terraces to the altar. One is sixty feet square, and six feet two inches high. The other is 106 feet square, and six feet high. Only even (i.e. *Yin*) numbers are made use of in the construction of the altar. Yellow tiles are employed in roofing the walls. The steps on each of the four sides are eight in number. A ditch surrounds the altar. It is 494 feet four inches long, eight feet six inches deep, and six feet wide.

Between the altar and the ditch is a wall six feet high, and two feet thick, and within it are four open gateways. Outside of the north gateway, a little to the westward, is the pit for burying the prayer and silk, which are offered to the Spirit of Earth. Beside it is the spot where the silk offered to the spirits of the emperors worshiped at the same time is burned.

On the upper terrace, when the sacrifice takes place, are arranged the tablet of the spirit of Earth facing north, and those of the emperors facing east and west.

On the lower terrace fourteen Chinese and Manchurian mountains are represented by fourteen tablets, and the seas and rivers of China each by four tablets. Half of the mountains, seas, and rivers occupy the east terrace, and half the west. The seas are simply north, south, east, and west. The mountains and rivers are worshiped by their names, and they are selected on account of their size and sacredness.

In the sacrifice to Earth, the burial of the prayer and the silk, it is to be noted, takes place at a spot on the north-west. The tablet, according to the present arrangement, faces to the north, and the spirit, therefore, has the ceremony in sight. The west is, as being on the left hand, the position of honor.

The Emperor, after the presentation of the three cups of wine, is directed to proceed to a certain station on the altar where he can conveniently observe the process of burying, which here corresponds to the burning of the prayer and silk in the sacrifice to the spirit of Heaven.

The prayer is as follows: "I, thy subject, son of heaven by hereditary succession, dare to announce to Hou T'u, the imperial spirit of Earth, that the time of the summer solstice has arrived, that all living things enjoy the blessings of sustenance, and depend for it upon thy efficient aid. Thou art placed with imperial Heaven in the sacrifices which are now presented, consisting of jade, silk, the chief animals used for food, with various viands abundantly supplied." . . .

The spirit of Earth is the only spirit beside the spirit of Heaven to whom in prayer the Emperor styles himself a "subject."

The colour of the jade presented is yellow. The prayer is written on a yellow tablet. The twenty-eight dishes, the three cups of wine, and the solitary bowl of soup are the same as at the temple of Heaven. The gold lamps are wanting, as also the gold censers, one pair of the candelabra, and the flower-vases.

The designation Shang Ti is applied to the spirit of Heaven only. . . .

The musical instruments are the same for the spirit of Earth as for the spirit of Heaven, viz., two kinds of stringed instruments, two kinds of flutes, etc.—sixty-four in all; but the bell is gilt for the sake of having it yellow. The two hundred and four musicians and dancers, instead of blue, wear black robes embroidered with figures in gold. Blue, on the other hand, is the color used in the worship of Heaven.[2] . . .

When the emperor sends an officer to perform his duties at the sacrifice, the details are much less complex. . . . The same omissions occur if the Emperor's son is deputed to perform the ceremonies. These omissions clearly show that a priestly character is attributed to the Emperor by virtue of his office.

The presentation of food and wine to the spirits who are worshiped indicates that the Chinese idea of a sacrifice to the supreme spirit of Heaven and of Earth is that of a banquet. There is no trace of any other idea. . . .

III. The imperial worship of ancestors constitutes one of the most important portions of the official worship.

The imperial Temple of Ancestors is on the south-east of the Wu Men, or chief gate of the palace. It is called T'ai Miao, the "great temple," and is divided into three principal *tien* or halls, and several smaller. The front *tien* is used for the common sacrifice to all ancestors at the end of the year. The middle *tien* contains the most important tablets, each in its shrine. Emperors and empresses are placed in pairs. . . . All face to the south. . . . The sacrifices on the first day of the first month in each of the four seasons are offered in this hall. . . .

The times for sacrifice are not only the first of every third month and at the end of the year, but whenever great events occur. The Emperor, when

---

[2]Author's note: Yellow and brown are both expressed by *huang*. The earth color here meant is the light brown of the soil in North China, but black is the color of the north. The altar of Earth is the "north altar," Pei T'an.

informed that the time has come for inspecting the prayer, proceeds to the Pao Ho Tien or Ch'ung Ho Tien, both of them state halls in the palace. The prayer, written on a yellow tablet, is presented and approved.

The sacrifices are offered in the middle and back halls of the ancestral temple at the same time, in order that all the imperial ancestors, remote as well as near, may enjoy them. . . . The dishes are the same as those used in the sacrifices to the spirits of Heaven and Earth. They are placed before the Emperor and Empress in common. . . . The prayer is read from a table on the south-west, chosen because it is the point of greatest humility, the east being the position of honor. An officer reads the prayer upon his knees, in the name of the Emperor. The prayer states the Emperor's descent as son, grandson, etc., as the case may be. Then follows his proper name, which is not permitted to be written or pronounced by any of his subjects. The prayer proceeds to say: "I dare announce to my ancestor that I have with care, on this first month of spring (or any other of the four seasons), provided sacrificial animals, silk, wine, and various dishes, as an expression of my unforgetting thoughtfulness, and humbly beg the acceptance of the offerings." The prayer contains the titles of all the deceased emperors and empresses prayed to . . .

Six poems are sung, each to a different melody. Some of the names of these airs are the same as those used at the sacrifices at the altar of Heaven. . . . Here follows a specimen: "Ah! my imperial ancestors have been able to become guests with supreme heaven. Their meritorious acts in war and peace are published in all regions. I, their filial descendant, have received the decree of heaven, and my thought is to carry out the aims of those who preceded me, thus ensuring the gift of long prosperity for thousands and tens of thousands of years." This is sung when the Emperor presents the silk. . . .

The Emperor must not call himself "your subject." He must say "your filial descendant, the Emperor."

This ceremony being so burdensome as to entail on the Emperor the necessity of kneeling sixteen times, and knocking the forehead thirty-six times against the ground, is an indication of the importance attached to filial piety, and to the character of the Emperor as an example of virtue to all his subjects. . . .

Another ancestral temple of the emperors is within the palace. It is called the Fêng Hsien Tien, and is in the eastern portion of the palace. Besides this there is the temple at the tomb of each emperor.

IV. A very important branch of the imperial worship is the sacrifices to the gods of land and grain. The altars to these spirits are on the right hand of the palace gate. Their position corresponds to that of the Temple of Ancestors.

The altar of the spirit of land, Shê, consists of two terraces, both ascended by flights of three steps. The upper terrace is covered with earth of five colours. Yellow occupies the middle, blue the east, red the south, white the west, and black the north.

On the south-west of the altar is a spot for burying the victims. The tablet to the god of land, Shê, is on the terrace on the east. That to the god of grain, Chi, is on the west. Both face north. There are two tablets occupying the position of guests, Hsia T'u, called Kou Lung, looks west, and Hou Chi east. The last of these was superintendent of husbandry to the [mythical] Emperor

Yao; the first was officer of Huang Ti [also a mythical emperor]. They represent, it may be safely said, the founders or chief promoters of Chinese agriculture.

The worship takes place in the middle months of spring and autumn, and on occasion of important events when announcements are to be made to them.

The sacrifices are the same as in the worship of ancestors and of the temple of Earth, as regards the twenty-eight dishes, but a bullock, pig, and sheep are all offered, and the jade and silk to be burned are placed beyond the three animals. . . .

18.
most holy former master, the philosopher k'ung

Such are the words inscribed on the soul tablet of Confucius which stands above the altar in the Confucian temple. This reader is not the place to attempt a presentation of the life and teachings, much less the influence, of the Master, but we must at least give a few indications. We turn, for the following quotations, to the *Analects* (*Lun Yü*), compiled from the personal recollections of the disciples. (Selections are located by chapter and verse.)

Autobiographical

At fifteen I was determined to study. At thirty I had established [my character]. At forty I was no longer in doubt [about the Way]. At fifty I understood Heaven's will. At sixty when I heard [the Way] I could follow it easily. At seventy what my heart desires does not go beyond the bounds. (II,4)

The Master said, I can be happy even with just simple food to eat and water to drink, and only my bended arm for a pillow. Wealth and honors wrongfully acquired are to me like floating clouds. (VII,15)

The Master said, In a village of ten homes there is bound to be someone as conscientious and sincere as I, but there won't be anyone as fond of learning. (V,27)

The Master said, When three of us walk together, [the others] are bound to be my teachers. I can pick out what is good in them and emulate it, and from what is not good I can learn to change [that same thing] in myself. (VII,21)

The Master said, I have never refused to teach anyone who has come bearing his [tuition fee of] dried meat. (VII,7)

The Master said, If a student is not eager I don't begin, if he won't open up I don't explain. If I hold up one corner and he can't then figure out the other three, I don't repeat the lesson. (VII,8)

The Master said, I wasn't born with wisdom. Being fond of history I diligently seek it through studying the past. (VII,19)

The Master said, How could I dare to claim to be holy and virtuous? You might say with truth that I never give up trying, and I teach without getting tired of it — that's all. A disciple replied, That's just where we disciples are unable to come up to you. (VII,33)

Tzu-kung would judge people. The Master said, You must be a paragon! Personally, I haven't the time for that. (XIV,31)

The Master said, Tz'u, do you think what I'm after is encyclopedic knowledge? The disciple replied, Yes, is it not so? The Master said, No, what I seek is the unifying principles. (XV,2)

The Duke of Shê asked Tzu-lu (a disciple) about Confucius. Tzu-lu had no answer. The Master said, Why didn't you tell him, He is simply a man who is so enthusiastic that he forgets to eat, so happy that he forgets his troubles, and doesn't realize that old age is coming on him. (VII,18)

Through the Eyes of the Disciples

The Master was entirely free from four [faults]: He was not biased, he was not arbitrary, he was not obstinate, and he was not selfish. (IX,4)

The Master said, The Way of the noble man (*chün-tzu*) has three qualities I am not able to claim: He has a perfected moral character (*jen*) and therefore no anxieties; he is wise and therefore has no doubts; he is brave and therefore has no fears. Tzu-kung replied, But that is in fact your own Way, Master. (XIV,30)

[The disciple] Yen Yüan said with a sigh [of admiration]. . . The Master methodically encourages men to become better. He broadened me with culture and disciplined me with the codes of social behavior (*li*). Even if I should want to stop at this point I cannot. Although I've given it all I have, it's as though the goal were still before me, and try though I may to reach it, it still eludes me. (IX,10)

An official once expressed admiration for a disciple of Confucius, saying, Tzu-kung is greater than Confucius. This being reported to Tzu-kung, the latter said, If we use the comparison of a house and its wall, then my wall is only shoulder-high; one may look over it and see whatever is valuable in the house. But the wall around the Master's house is hundreds of feet high. If you don't find the gate by which to enter, you cannot see the beauty of the ancestral temple or the abundance of officials in attendance. But there may be only a few who have found that gate . . . (XIX,23)

The same official spoke ill of Confucius. Tzu-kung said, That's no use. Confucius cannot be slandered. The greatness of other men is like mounds which can be stepped over, but Confucius is like the sun and moon, and one can never jump over them. Even though you break your neck trying to do so, what harm is done the sun and moon? It only shows your own bad judgment in trying to do so. (XIX,24)

Some Words of Wisdom

The Master said, Study as if the goal were just beyond your grasp and you feared to lose it. (VIII,15)

The Master said, I have tried spending the whole day without eating and the whole night without sleeping in order to think. It was useless. It is better to study. (XV,30)

The Master said, Man is by nature upright. If he lose this character and yet go on living, he's just lucky to avoid [death].

The Master said, the man of moral character (*chün-tzu*) makes demands on himself, the petty man makes demands on others. (XV,20)

The Master said, When it comes to moral character (*jen*) don't yield to your teacher. (XV,35)

The Master said, If a man is not Good (*jen*), what good is it if he goes through the correct social forms? If a man is not Good, what good is it if he has the correct ritual performed [at the sacrifices]? (III,3)

The Master said, Is virtue (*jen*) far off? I have but to wish to be virtuous, and virtue is at hand. (VII,29)

The Master said, The man of moral character (*chün-tzu*) brings out the good in others, and not their bad side. The man of petty character does the opposite. (XII,16)

The Master said, The noble man (*chün-tzu*) hates to think that he will leave no name to posterity. (XV,19)

The Master said, Gentlemen of determination, moral men (*jen jen*), will not seek life at the expense of virtue (*jen*). They will give their lives for their moral principles (*jen*).

Tzu-kung said, Does the man of moral character (*chün-tzu*) also hate? The Master said, He does. He hates those who talk about how bad other people are. He hates moral delinquents who slander those of higher character. He hates men who are bold but have no manners. He hates those who are obstinate but narrow-minded. (XVII,24)

Yen Yüan asked about moral perfection (*jen*). The Master said, To subordinate the self and in all things act according to the codes of social behavior is moral perfection. If one could for a single day subordinate oneself to these codes the whole world would become morally perfect. Now, does moral perfection derive from oneself, or from others? (XII,1.1)

Chung-kung asked about moral perfection. The Master said, When you are in public be as polite as though receiving a distinguished guest. When you are in charge of the people be as scrupulous as though conducting a great sacrifice. What you don't like done to yourself, don't do to others. [Acting in this way] you will arouse no resentment either at home or abroad. (XII,2)

Ssu-ma Niu asked about moral perfection. The Master said, Moral perfection lies in choosing one's words with care. The disciple exclaimed, Choosing one's words with care — this is moral perfection? The Master said, Living a moral life is difficult. Can one be other than careful in talking about it? (XII,3)

Ssu-ma Niu asked about the man of moral character (*chün-tzu*). The Master said, The man of moral character is neither anxious nor afraid. The disciple exclaimed, Neither anxious nor afraid — this is the man of moral character? The Master said, On examining himself he finds no moral fault. So why would he be anxious or afraid? (XII,4)

The Master said, Virtue (*tê*) is not solitary — it is bound to have company. (IV,25)

The Master said, I've never seen anyone who loved virtue as much as he loved women. (IX,7)

The Master said, The goody-goodies are the ones who sabotage virtue (XVII,13)

An officer in power asked Confucius about government. Confucius replied, To govern (*chêng*) is to correct (another *chêng*). If you, Sir, lead them correctly, who will dare not to be correct? (XII-17)

The same official, being concerned about robbery in his state, consulted with Confucius. The latter replied, If you, Sir, were not avaricious, then even if you paid them your people would not steal. (XII,18)

The same official again asked Confucius about government, saying, What do you say to slaying the bad to save the good? Confucius replied, Sir, in governing why use slaying at all? If you, Sir, seek to be good, all your people will be good. The virtue of the nobleman (*chün-tzu*) is like the wind, while the virtue of the common people is like the grass. As the wind blows, the grass must bend. (XII,19)

Tzu-kung asked, What do you say about a man who is liked by all his neighbors? The Master said, We can't judge him by that. Tzu-kung then asked, What if he is hated by all his neighbors? The Master said, We can't judge him by that, either. A better test is if the good people of his neighborhood like him, and the bad people hate him. (XIII,24)

Fan Ch'ih asked about wisdom. The Master said, Do your duty to men, and while paying due respect to spirits keep your distance. This may be called wisdom. [The disciple] asked about virtue (*jen*). The Master said, The victory [of right] in the [moral] struggle [within a man's heart] may be called virtue. (VI,20)

The Master said, Yu, shall I teach you about wisdom? When you know it, know that you know it; when you don't know it, admit you don't know it. That's wisdom. (II,17)

The Master said, Don't worry about not having a position — worry about making yourself fit to hold one. Don't worry that you aren't famous — try to act so you will deserve to be famous. (IV,14)

The Master said, Don't worry that men won't know you — worry about your lack of ability. (XIV,32)

The Master said, If a man does not constantly ask himself, What should be done? What should be done? I really don't know what should be done about him! (XV,15)

[The Master said,] When the Way prevails in a country one should be ashamed of being poor and undistinguished. When the Way does not prevail in a country one should be ashamed of being rich and exalted. (VIII,13.3)

The Master said, Seeing a great man, aspire to equal him; seeing an ignoble man, take a good look at yourself. (IV,17)

[The Master said,] To see what is right but not do it is cowardice. (II,24.2)

The Master said, Make conscientiousness (*chung*) and sincerity (*hsin*) your chief principles. Have no friends not equal to yourself. Don't hesitate to correct your own faults. (IX,24)

Tzu-kung asked, Is there a single word that may serve as the guide for one's whole life? The Master said, Will reciprocity (*shu*) do? What you don't like yourself don't do to others. (XV,23)

Someone asked, What do you think of the principle that one should requite injury with kindness? The Master said, Then with what should one requite kindness? One should requite injury with justice, and kindness with kindness. (XIV,36)

The Master said, Men by nature are similar. Through practice they come to diverge. (XVII,2)

The Master said, It is only the wisest and the stupidest who never change. (XVII,3)

The Master said, Young people should be respected. Who can tell but that they will be as good as we? Only if someone has no reputation by the age of forty or fifty, then he may not merit our respect.

The Master said, It is man who makes the Way greater, not the Way that makes man greater. (XV,28)

The Master said, If a man could realize Tao in the morning, he could die that evening [without regret]. (IV,8)

China's "Herodotus," the great Ssu-ma Ch'ien, eloquently summed up the Chinese feeling about Confucius, in his biography of the Sage (*Shih Chi, Historical Memoirs, K'ung Tzu Shih Chia*):

When I read the writings of Confucius I imagine I can see the man. When I went to [his home state of] Lu I saw the ancestral temple of Chung-ni (his given name), the carriages, robes, and ritual implements. There were students who performed the rites at his home at the proper times. I started to leave, only to return again; I could not tear myself away. There have been many rulers and eminent men in this world, who were honored while they lived, but forgotten when they were dead. [The doctrines of] Confucius, who only wore a common cloth garment, have been transmitted for more than ten generations, and all the scholars honor him. Whenever the Six Arts (i.e. all learning) are discussed in China by anyone — from the Son of Heaven, kings, or lords [on down] — the words of the Master are the final authority. We can say that he is Most Holy!

19.
Confucius as a patron saint

The general resistance on the part of the literati to deification of their Master, Confucius, cannot negate his vast importance in Chinese religion. His teachings formed the moral character of the nation. His worship was, at least during the later centuries, most prominent in the state cults throughout the country. His birthplace at Ch'üeh-li and the ancestral home of his clan at Ch'ü-fu (these are in Ch'ü-fu county, southwestern Shantung province) have through the ages been preserved as shrines, visited by countless pilgrims and honored by the inscriptions of emperors.

Following are a brief description of these shrines, a general description of an official Confucian Temple, a discussion of the music and dancing (or posturing) in the ritual, and some visual illustrations. The first item is extracted from a volume by E. H. Parker, entitled *Studies in Chinese Religion*, Chapman & Hall (London, 1910). He is quoting in turn from a report by James Stewart Lockhart, who paid a visit to Ch'ü-fu in 1903, where he was received by the Yen-sheng Kung ("Duke who propagates holiness"—official title of the current head of the K'ung clan; in this instance the 76th lineal descendant of the Sage). (We condense and slightly edit this material, which is found on pages 192-197).

On Sunday, the 10th of May, I went in uniform[1] to the Temple of Confucius to show my respect for China's Great Sage. I was conducted by descendants of the Sage to that portion of the temple where Chinese have to kneel and perform the kotow to their great teacher. Having raised my hat, I read in Chinese a short encomium of Confucius. I then proceeded to the main building of the temple, where the Duke and his suite were waiting to receive me. . .

On Monday, the 11th of May, we proceeded to the Temple of Confucius, and were met at the entrance by two of the uncles of the Duke and his steward, who conducted us all round the buildings.

The grounds of the temple cover about thirty-five acres, and are well wooded with fine old cypress, yew, and fir trees of great age. Among the trees are one planted by the Sage himself, and two planted during the T'ang (A.D. 618-907) and Sung dynasties (A.D. 960-1126).

The temple is divided into a series of courts, of which there are six, before the main temple is reached. Each court is separated from the other by a gateway, but has steps leading into the court on either side. The main

[1]Lockhart was paying an official call as a British Commissioner. (L.G.T.)

temple is built upon the spot where Confucius . . . lived. In front of the entrance to the main temple are thirteen pavilions covering tablets with inscriptions written by various emperors of China. The main temple itself consists of ten buildings and an altar: Each building has a court to itself.

After passing through the entrance to the main temple, the altar called the Hsing T'an is reached. It is open on four sides, and is so named because Confucius received those who came to seek his instruction at a place so called. Behind the Hsing T'an is the Ya Ch'eng Tien, a great hall containing a statue of Confucius, sixteen feet high, seated on a throne and screened with curtains embroidered with dragons. The hall is supported in front by white marble pillars with deeply carved dragons, and in the north, east, and west by pillars of black marble carved in cameo-work. The floor is lined with black marble, and the roof is covered with yellow tiles. The ceiling consists of 486 panels, square in shape, gilded at the edge, and ornamented with dragons.

In front of the statue is a table on which are displayed enamelled vases and bronze urns and tripods, presented to the temple by the Emperor Yung Chêng (A.D. 1723-1736), and which are said to date back to the second year of Yüan Ho, of the Han Dynasty (A.D. 85). In the hall are suspended four gilded tablets and three pairs of scrolls presented by emperors of the present [Ch'ing] dynasty, and there are also statues of Yen Tzu and Tsêng Tzu, his favorite disciples, of his grandson, of Mencius, and of twelve of his chief disciples. At the east and west of the great hall are two corridors containing the tablets of his disciples and the philosophers who have supported his teaching from the earliest times up to the present dynasty. Behind the grand hall is a building in honor of his wife, and in the rear of it is a building panelled with black marble, in which are depicted scenes in the life of Confucius, and in one of which is a picture of the Sage. On the west are three buildings, the first being the hall in which the music is played at the worship of Confucius, the instruments used being kept in a building still further to the west. The second contains the statue of the father of Confucius; the third is in honor of his mother. On the east are three buildings. The first is in honor of the classics [which Confucius is supposed to have written and edited], and the other two are in honor of his ancestors. In the court in front of these two buildings are a tablet on which is engraved the genealogical tree of the family of Confucius, but which is so affected by age that it is not possible to obtain from it satisfactory rubbings; the well used by Confucius; and a pillar marking the spot where the Confucian classics were found in the wall of the house formerly inhabited by Confucius, having been hidden there to save them from the general burning of Books ordered in 213 B.C. by the first Emperor Shih Huang Ti. . . .

In the afternoon we went to the tomb of Confucius, which is situated to the north of the city, and is distant from it about a mile and a half. . . . The approach to the tomb is through a fine avenue lined with cypress trees, symbolical of the immortality of the fame of the Sage, and leads up to the gates of the cemetery, which covers a large area of ground, thickly wooded with trees of large size and great age.

After passing through the entrance, the road, which is lined with pillars inscribed by various emperors, winds to the west until a brook called the Chu Shui, "the Red Water," is reached. This brook is crossed by three bridges, the center one of which leads to an avenue of trees, one of which is the famous tree planted by Tzu Kung, one of the most distinguished of Confucius' disciples. At the end of the avenue are six stone figures, four of animals and two of men, sixteen feet in height, which are immediately in front of a hall, containing an incense table, in which the ceremonies in honor of Confucius are performed. This hall opens by four folding doors into the enclosure, in which are three mounds, marking the last resting-place of the Sage, his son, and his grandson.

The grave of Confucius is a mound about thirty feet in height and one hundred in circumference, covered with trees and brushwood. In front of it are a stone urn and altar, and a tombstone with the following inscription in seal characters: "The most holy ancient Sage, the Prince of Culture."

To the west of the tomb is a small building erected on the spot where Tzu Kung, the beloved disciple of the Sage, mourned for his master six years.

To the east of Confucius's tomb is the grave of his son, and to the southeast that of his grandson. Both are high mounds with stone urns and pillars, and in front of the grave of the grandson are two colossal stone figures. The tombstones bear the following inscriptions in ordinary characters: "The tomb of the Marquis of Ssu Shui" (the title by which the son is known to posterity). "The tomb of the Transmitter of the Sacred Sage, of the State of I" (the title by which the grandson is known to posterity). . . .

The following description of a Confucian Temple is taken from the Introduction (pp. v-vii) to Thomas Watters's book, *A Guide to the Tablets in a Temple of Confucius,* American Presbyterian Mission Press, (Shanghai, 1879). The material is given complete with slight editing.

According to the laws of China there must be a Wên-miao or Temple of Confucius attached to every Prefecture, Sub-Prefecture, District, and in every market-town throughout the empire. Consequently not only has each town its temple but all Prefectural cities contain two and some three.

A Wên-miao may be built on any convenient site within the wall of a town but it must in all cases face the South. There are differences of detail from place to place but the essentials of the temple are much the same everywhere, and vary only in size and completeness. It must consist of three Courts which generally follow in a line from South to North. The outermost of these is called the P'an-kung, from the name given to the state College of a feudal principality during the period of the Chou dynasty. It is bounded on the South by a wall called the Hang-ch'iang, a name which recalls that of the Government Colleges during the Han period. The colour of this wall, as of the temple generally, is red, that having been adopted by the Chou rulers as their official colour. It is not provided with a gate until a student of the district to which the temple is attached succeeds in obtaining the title Chuang-yuan, that is, first among the Chin-shih (i.e. the recipients of the highest, or "doctoral" degree, awarded after extremely competitive examinations conducted in the imperial capital) of his year. When this occurs the middle portion of the wall is taken away and a gate substituted, through which, however, only a Chuang-yuan and an Emperor or Prince may pass. A little to the north of this wall is an ornamental arch of wood or stone called the Ling-hsing-mên and beyond this is a pond called the P'an-ch'ih. This pond is of semicircular shape properly, and extends from East by South to West according to the rule established for state colleges during the Chou period. These had "half-ponds" while the Emperor's College had a complete circular pond. . . . The pond is spanned by the Yuan-ch'iao or Arched Bridge, also reserved for the use of a Chuang-yuan or Emperor, and often called the Wang-ch'iao, or Royal Bridge. The chief entrances to the Court are by two gates, one in the east wall and one in the west. At the upper end on the west side is the Tsai-sheng-t'ing, a room in which the animals for sacrifice are kept, and at the opposite corner is a chamber for the private use of the chief worshiper. In this he rests for a short time, on coming to the temple, and it is hence called the Kuan-t'ing or Official Pavilion. It is known also as the Kêng-yi-so because the mandarin here changes his ordinary robes for Court uniform.

The north side of this Court, which is usually planted with trees, is occupied by a large hall in the middle of which is the Ta-ch'êng-mên, opened only for a Chuang-yuan or an Emperor. This is also known as the Chi-mên or Spear Door, because for some time it was adorned by two stands of antique spears. On each side of this is a small door leading into the next or principal Court, on entering which two long narrow buildings are seen extending along the east and west walls. These are called respectively the Tung-wu and Hsi-wu, and they contain the tablets of the Former Worthies and Scholars arranged in chronological order. Between these buildings is an open space called Tan-ch'ih or Vermilion Porch, that having been the name of a corresponding open square in front of a palace during the Chou dynasty. This part of the Court is usually planted with cypresses or in their absence with oleas and other handsome trees. Here all ordinary worshipers kneel and prostrate themselves when celebrating the worship of Confucius. Above the Tan-ch'ih is a stone platform called the Yueh-t'ai or Moon Terrace, also a survival from the Chou times. This adjoins the Ta-ch'êng-tien or Hall of Great Perfection, the Temple proper. In many places this is an imposing structure with massive pillars of wood or stone and embellished with quaint devices in painting. In the middle of the north wall, "superior and alone," sometimes in a large niche and sometimes merely resting on a table, is the Sage's tablet. Before it stands an altar on which are usually a few sacrificial vessels, and overhead are short eulogistic inscriptions. Next below the Sage are the Four Associates,[2] two on his left hand and two on his right. Their tablets are in niches or frames and have altars before them. Lower in the Hall and arranged along the walls are the tablets of the Twelve "Wise Ones," six on each side, also furnished with altars.

The next Court, which is behind the principal one, or, if space requires, at its east side, contains the Ch'ung-shêng-tz'u, Ancestral Hall of Exalted Sages. In it are the tablets of five ancestors of Confucius, of his half-brother,

---

[2]Yen Hui, favorite disciple of the Master; Tzu Ssu, his grandson, and putative author of *Chung Yung;* Tseng Tzu, another favorite disciple; and Mencius, the Second Sage. (L.G.T.)

of the fathers of the Associates and of certain other worthies. With a few exceptions the men worshiped there have been canonized on account of the merits of their posterity and not from any great virtue in themselves.

The official residence of the Director of Studies is in close proximity to the Confucian temple which is under the care of that mandarin. Certain buildings for the use of government students and chambers for the worship of deceased local celebrities, or deserving officials, are also sometimes found either within the temple precincts or immediately outside. The Wên-ch'ang-kung, moreover, or Hall of the God of Literature, is now often found close beside the Temple of Confucius.

As we have in *Chinese Religion: An Introduction* (pp. 72-74) quoted from John K. Shryock a vivid picture of the ceremony held in the *wen-miao*, we shall not give a complete description here, but shall excerpt a few remarks from Watters, *op. cit.*, pp. xii-xvi, which may shed further light on its meaning.

The first *Ting* day (referring to the numbering of days by "stems" and "branches") in the second month of Spring, and the same day in the second month of Autumn, are fixed as the times for the worship. The *Ting*, which comes under the element of Fire (referring to the *wu hsing*), is the fourth of the Ten Stems or Cyclical signs and so the first *ting* occurs within the first third of the month. These two were the days on which, during the Chou period, the Spring and Autumn Sessions of the State Colleges were opened by the Minister of Music. . . .

All the ceremonies of this service recall the golden age of Chinese antiquity, the days of Wu Wang and Wên Wang and Chou Kung (founders of the Chou dynasty, anc particular heroes of Confucius), and the times of simpler virtue long before. The same airs were played with the same sort of accompaniment, four thousand years ago, and the sacrifices and worship have meanings brought from a far-off period. Nearly everything in them is a type or symbol. The white silk, emblem of faithful purity, was the present by a chief to the man whom he wished to take into his service. The ox, head of domestic animals, leaves broad, lasting footprints; the pig, as its bristles symbolize, has a will of its own; and the sheep, plump for food, is also soft with wool to make woolen clothing. The incense typifies the fragrance of virtue, and the wine and food the abundance of a happy Kingdom. The music is supposed at one time to rouse the hearer to valiant deeds and at another to lap him in soft measures expressing peace and harmony. The boys who perform the curious moving accompaniment (i.e. the dancers, or posturers), are dressed in the old uniform of Hsiu-ts'ai's or graduates of the first Degree. They bear a flute in the left hand and a pheasant's feather in the right, the former the symbol of the refinement produced by music and the observance of social laws, and the latter of the adornment of learning.

The performances of these boys cannot be understood without a reference to the old Chinese writings. In the Great Preface to the *Shih Ching* we read that when the "prolonged utterances of song are insufficient" for excited feelings, unconsciously the hands and feet begin to move. This tendency was turned to practical account and the movements were adopted and regulated to be the visible representation of what music was supposed to express. Hence in very early times we find a Kan-wu and a Wên-wu, that is, a warlike and a peaceful accompaniment. The actors in the former held a bow in the left hand and an arrow in the right, and imitated the gestures of an archer shooting in the presence of his chief. The performers in the latter held a flute and pheasant's feather. When the [legendary] Emperor Shun failed in his attempt to conquer the Miao (a non-Chinese tribe) by arms, he resolved to win them over to submission and allegiance by gentle persuasives. So he had an exhibition of "war and peace posture-makers" in the Court before his palace and within two months the savage chief tendered his submission. During the Chou dynasty, exhibitions of these performers were held at the sacrifices to deceased Kings and Emperors, and on all grand festive occasions of state. Their numbers were also settled by law, sixty-four being allowed to an Emperor and thirty-six to a Prince or Chief. These *wu* (dances) were originally, perhaps, athletic and military exercises performed at the end of a war or at a military review before the ruler. When a Chou Emperor held a durbar, the feudal chiefs showed their skill in archery in the Court before the Palace. There was an established etiquette for them in taking up the bow, advancing from their position, bowing, and retiring, and the boys at the Confucian worship still, to some extent, imitate these actions. But only the civil performance of posture-making takes place in the temples of the Sage, the idea of war being inconsistent with the solumnity of the place and the nature of the service.

. . . The ceremonies used at his service are the same as those used in the Temple of Kings and Emperors. It has been the custom in China, from a very remote age, to pay posthumous worship to the great benefactors of the country, and especially to the promoters of learning and culture. Hence Yao, and Shun, and Yü (legendary rulers of the Golden Age) were all worshiped after death, and similar honor was paid to Chou Kung not only in his own country but also in Lu (the native State of Confucius). These, however, were all summed up in Confucius who was the actual founder of learning, the teacher not for one age or country but for all time and all the Empire. So the titles and honors of Former Sage and Former Teacher were transferred to him, and scholars and officials were required to do him homage. In process of time the rank of Prince or King, was conferred on him, and the worship offered to him then took the character of that offered to a feudal chief of the time at which the Sage lived. It is not as a king, however, but as their great teacher and pattern, that the Chinese worship their Sage. The idea involved in the ceremonies is to forget for the time that he is dead and to treat him as though he were present in the flesh. . . . Offerings are presented to him at other seasons besides those mentioned above, and his birthday is observed as a solemn fast in all the public departments. But he must be worshiped in his own temple and it is forbidden to set up any image or likeness of him in a Buddhist or Taoist temple. The schoolboy may do him obeisance in the school, and the student in the College, for these are institutions which are eminently the result of Confucius's teaching and influence.

The importance of music and posturing in the Confucian ceremony has been emphasized by the above quotation; here we give a transcription of the melody of the hymn played and sung in unison on this occasion, the lyric in translation, and some drawings of the postures of the dancers which accompany it. This material is taken from J. A. van Aalst, *Chinese Music*, The Chinese Maritime Customs Service, (Shanghai, 1884; reissue Peking, 1939, The French Bookstore), pp. 27-33.

Very slow.

Ta tsai K'ung tzŭ. Hsien chüeh hsien chih.
Yü t'ien ti ts'an. Wan shih chih shih.
Hsiang chêng lin fu. Yün ta chin ssŭ.
Jih yüeh chi chieh. Ch'ien k'un ch'ing i.
Yü huai ming tê. Yü chên chin shêng.
Shêng ming wei yu. Chan yeh ta ch'êng.
Tsu tou ch'ien ku. Ch'un ch'iu shang ting.
Ch'ing chiu chi tsai. Ch'i hsiang shih shêng.
Shih li mo ch'ien. Shêng t'ang tsai hsien.
Hsiang hsieh t'ao yung. Ch'êng fu lei hsien.

SACRIFICIAL HYMN TO CONFUCIUS

1. Receiving the Approaching Spirit

Great is Confucius!
He perceives things and knows them before the time;
He is in the same order with Heaven and Earth
The teacher of ten thousand ages.
There were lucky portents, and on the unicorn's horn a tuft of silk.
The rhymes of the song correspond to the sounds of metal and silk.
The sun and moon were unveiled to us;
Heaven and Earth were made to look fresh and joyful.

2. First Presentation of Offerings

I think of thy bright virtue.
The jade music ends. The music of metal is first heard.
Of living men there never was one like him;
Truly his teaching is in all respects complete.
The vessels are here with the offerings, the same as during thousands of years.
At the spring and autumn equinoxes, on the first Ting day,
clear wine is offered.
The sweet smell of the sacrifice now first rises.

3. Second Presentation

The regular sacrifices should be offered without deficiency.
The chief sacrificer advances in the hall and presents the second offering;
The harmonious sounds are heard of drum and bell;
With sincerity the wine cups are offered.
Reverently and harmoniously
Approach the sacrificers, men of honourable fame.
The ceremonies are purifying, the music cleanses the heart;
They work on each other and reach the point of perfect goodness.

4. Third and Last Presentation

From antiquity through all the ages
Primitive men have done this.
They wore skin hats; they offered of the fruit of the ground.
How orderly was the music!
Only Heaven guides the people;
Only the Sage conforms his instructions to the day and the hour.
The moral duties are arranged in their proper order.
Till now the wooden clapper sounds.

5. Removal of the Viands

The ancestral teacher said in his instructions:
"Those who sacrifice obtain happiness."
Throughout the four seas, in students' halls,
Who would dare not to be reverential?
The ceremony concluded, the removal of the offerings is announced.
Let none be neglectful or show want of respect;
Let their joy be in him who is the source of their culture;
Let them remember the poem of the beans in the fields (from *Shih Ching*),
    and imitate him.

6. Escorting the Spirit Back

The Fu and Yi mountains are very high;
The Chu and the Ssu spread their waters far,
So thy beautiful acts extend their influence above and around,
Causing benefits without end.
Now has been seen the glory of the sacrifice;
The sacrifice has been made to appear great and beautiful.
He renovates the thousands of our people;
He fosters our schools and halls for instruction.

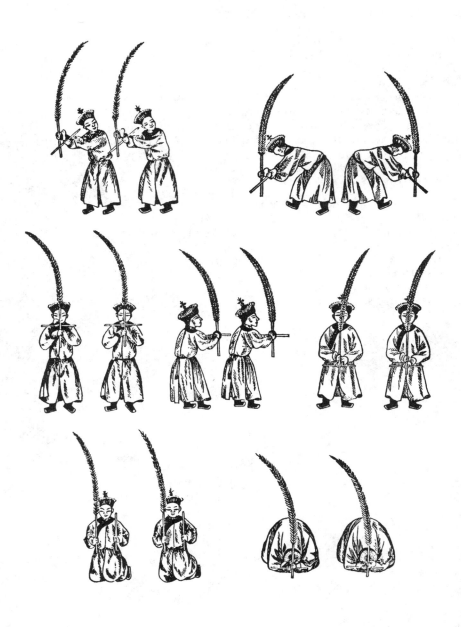

**EVOLUTIONS MADE BY DANCERS DURING THE
HYMN TO CONFUCIUS**

20.
ancestor festivals

The following description of the household shrine and the Seventh Moon festival in the ancestral cult is taken from the notable study by anthropologist Francis L. K. Hsu, *Under the Ancestors' Shadow* (Columbia University Press 1948), pp.182-191. This book was based upon the author's field investigations, during 1941 to 1943, of the "small semirural community" of West Town in the far southwestern province of Yunnan.

Each household has a family shrine. The shrine is situated in the central portion of the second floor of the west wing of the home. It is installed on the ground floor only when the house is a one-story structure. Occasionally the shrine is for ancestors only, but more often it houses a number of popular gods.

Ancestors are represented in such a shrine either on a large scroll or on separate tablets. The scroll is a large sheet of mounted paper containing names, sex, and titles of the ancestors who are (theoretically) within *wu fu*, or five degrees of mourning . . . [but] this rule is not always observed. On the scroll of a poor and illiterate Ch family only a small number of the ancestors were represented, because "the old scroll was destroyed by fire and these are the only ones we can remember." On the scroll of a Y family many ancestors beyond the five degrees were represented, because they "have not had another scroll made yet." The tablets are made of wood, but if there is no time to have one made, a paper one will be substituted.

The popular gods in all family shrines are three: *Kuan Kung* [often called *Kuan Ti*] (the warrior from Three Kingdoms), Confucius, and one or more Buddhas. A fourth popular figure is the Goddess of Mercy or Fertility.[1] As a rule these gods are represented by images. In addition, there are often other spiritual figures in family shrines which the family members cannot identify. In at least one shrine there was a large tablet for Confucius as well as his supposed image. Before the shrine is an offering table, on which there are two incense burners, one for ancestors and one for the gods, two candlesticks, and a flower vase or two. At the foot of the table are two round straw cushions for the kneeling worshiper.

[1]Kuan-yin, presumably. (L.G.T.)

Incense is offered in each burner daily, usually by a woman of the house. This act is performed every morning just before breakfast. There is no offering of food except on occasions of marriage, birth, division of the family, and during the ancestor festival.

The festival occurs around the fifteenth of the Seventh Moon, but in effect it begins on the first of the month and ends on the sixteenth. On the first of the month the portion of the house containing the shrine is cleared of nonessential articles and cleaned. Offerings of the following items are made: fruit, preserves, candies, two or more bowls containing fragrant wood, some lotus or other flowers in the vase, and a number of dishes or bowls of cooked food. Red candles are inserted in the candlesticks. A new cloth, as well as a front cover, is placed on the offering table. If the tablets are encased, their covers are removed. The offerings and arrangements may be made by both men and women. The offerings may be replaced with fresh ones from time to time throughout the fifteen days.

If the family can afford it, as many West Town families can, one or more priests are invited to read scriptures and perform certain rituals before the shrine during this period. Such priests may be hired for one day or for several days, depending on how much the family is willing to spend. The greater the number of priests and the longer they are utilized, the more beneficial it will be for the dead and for the living. If only one priest is hired, he sits on a stool at the right of the offering table. His equipment consists of a wooden "fish," a pair of cymbals, many volumes of scriptures, the family's complete genealogical record, as well as the names and birthdays of all its living members. These data are written on a long folder of yellow paper. The priest recites the scriptures and performs all the pertinent rites continuously for the entire period of his employment, stopping only for meals and opium, but uninterrupted by the family's work on the shrine.

The function of the priest in connection with the dead ancestors was clear to all informants: to report the names of the dead to superior deities and to uplift them by scripture reading so that they will be able to proceed to the Western Heaven of Happiness as soon as possible. The reason for a complete list of the names of the family's living members is not clear to all. Some insist that it is to bless the living; others say that it will make the dead happier by showing them what worthy descendants they have. . . .

Some time during the first thirteen days of the month a married daughter makes a visit to her parents' home. She takes with her the following gifts: a number of loaves of sweetened bread; two or three pounds of pork; pears or other fruit; and a number of bags filled with ingots made of paper for members of the parents' family who have died within the last twelve months. She will be entertained at a specially prepared meal upon her arrival. She presents these gifts to her parents, pays proper ritual homage before the family shrine, and is supposed to remain for three days. In practice, however, most married daughters have to leave sooner because of the pressure of work in their husbands' households. After a woman has died, her daughter-in-law makes this visit on her behalf. When the latter has also died, then the grand-daughter-in-law will make the visit. Informants agreed that this ceremonial relationship was always kept up for several generations. Every married woman must return to the home of her husband before the fourteenth of the Seventh Moon for the big ceremony.

If a member of the family has died within a year of the Seventh Moon, the family will make a special offering and ritual homage to the recently deceased. This occasion always includes the burning of a quantity of ingots made of paper and sealed in bags, each inscribed with the names of the recipients and their immediate descendants. This ritual is generally designated as *shu* (burn) *hsin* (new) *pao* (bags).

If there has been no death within the last twelve months, the family worship takes place on the afternoon of the fourteenth. The service is performed in one of two ways, depending upon family habits. Members of the several branches of the household can perform the worship together, with joint offerings of food, wine, and incense, or they can perform it separately, with individual offerings. The dishes offered on this occasion are all elaborately prepared and contain chicken, pork, fish, and vegetables. Each dish is topped with a flower design. If the household worships as one unit, all dishes, together with at least six bowls of rice, six cups of wine, and six pairs of chopsticks are laid on the offering table in advance. Members of the household then kowtow one after the other before the altar. Generally men kowtow first, followed by women and children. But this rule is not rigidly kept. . . .

If several branches of the household perform the ceremony separately, each branch will use its own offering trays. One tray contains six or eight bowls of chicken, meat, fish, etc., and a second tray contains two bowls of rice, two pairs of chopsticks, and two cups of wine. These trays are presented at the shrine by one or two male members of the branch, followed immediately by the other members. They kowtow before the altar, the elder before the younger, and men before women. The usual number of kowtows appears to be four, but often individual members perform this obeisance five, nine, or even more times. Various branches of the household may come into the shrine room with their trays at approximately the same time, or representatives of one branch may arrive before those of another have completed the ritual. Indeed, the whole second floor of the wing may be crowded and noisy.

The atmosphere among the worshipers on this occasion appears to be greatly influenced by whether or not the male members of the family or household are scholarly. If some of them are, the atmosphere is more serious than otherwise. In all cases the West Town worshipers seem to be much less serious than the families in North China which I observed before 1937 on such occasions. . . .

When the offerings and homage at the family altar terminates, the same dishes are taken by a male member of the household (or branch of the household) to the clan temple. There the food is briefly offered at the main altar, and the male who delivers it kowtows a number of times. After this, the offering food is taken back to the house, and all members of the household come together to feast on it. If it is not enough for everyone, more food will be added until all are satisfied. Male and female members of the household eat at the same table.

During the day incense sticks are inserted at numerous places in the family home: on the lintels of all portals, special parts of the walls, and in many sections of the courtyard. During the ceremony at the family altar practically equal amounts of homage are given to ancestors and to the gods beside them. In some families the offering dishes are placed between the two groups. In others, identical offerings are placed before each group. In some families, all kowtows are intended to be shared by both; in others, all members prostrate themselves twice, once before each group.

After the meal, the *shu pao* (burning the bags) ceremony begins. Each bag contains a quantity of silver ingots and bears the name of a male ancestor and his wife, of the descendants who are providing the bag for them, and the date on which this is burned, together with a brief plea entreating the ancestors to accept it.

In general it is the custom to provide one bag for every direct male ancestor of the lineage (whether he is in the family shrine or not) and his wife or wives. By the word "direct" I refer to those deceased members, however remote, who are lineal ancestors of the person who is providing the bags. In other words, they are father, father's father, father's father's father, etc., not father's brother, father's father's brother, etc. Most families keep a list or a separate book containing the names of those ancestors who figure largely on this occasion. If first and second cousins live in the same household, each will thus provide for his own parents and grandparents until they come to a common ancestor. For the recently deceased, the number of bags per ancestor is at least doubled and may be much larger and more elaborately decorated. Each bag is burned with some coats and trousers cut out of paper.

In very rich families, music may accompany the ritual homage before the family altar as well as the *shu pao* ceremony, but this is unusual. A big container with some ashes and a bit of fire is placed in the middle of the courtyard just outside the west wing of the house. A young member of the household then kneels on a straw cushion beside the container, facing the west wing. The rest of the household may be sitting or standing around him. All the bags are heaped beside the kneeler. He first picks up the bag for the most ancient lineal ancestor, reads slowly everything that is written on it, and then puts it on the fire. As he does so, another member will throw on the same fire one or two suits of the paper coats and trousers. This procedure is repeated with all the bags, and in many cases it may take one or two hours to complete the ceremony. After all bags are burned, the ashes are poured into a stream which finally carries them into the lake.[2]

Shortly after the household ceremony and sometimes while it is still going on, the worship in the clan temples begins. Families who have no clan temples omit this ceremony; those who have them never fail to perform it. Although this is more formal than the worship at the family altar, the degree of formality varies from clan to clan. I watched such ceremonies in five temples in the years 1942 and 1943 and have had several informants describe for me the ceremonies in four others. The most elaborate and formal ceremony appears to have taken place in Y temple.

In 1943 the clan was represented by one or two male members from each household, totaling about 140 individuals. Two men were elected in

---

[2]Burning carries the messages and the gifts to the spiritual realm, as the smoke disappears into the atmosphere. The ashes are disposed of carefully. (L.G.T.)

advance each year from among the senior and more active members of the clan to act as treasurers as well as general managers of the ceremony. With the help of junior members of the clan they had the temple cleaned before the occasion, the altars decorated, and the kitchens made ready for use. A team of volunteer cooks who prepared a number of special offering dishes was chosen from among the clan members. In the temple a pair of big candles was lighted on the table before the center altar. The tables before the side altars held incense burners, but no candlesticks. Large numbers of lighted incense sticks were inserted in each burner.

As soon as the hired bugler and drummer arrived, the ceremony was begun. All male individuals present, including those who had cooking and other duties to perform, stood in six or seven rows of about twenty each facing the main altar in the hall. Without regard for wealth, power, or learning, the rows were arranged in order of seniority with regard to generation and age. The older men of the senior generation came first, followed by the younger ones of the same generation, and then the older men of the succeeding generation. One member stood aside and acted as master of ceremonies. After giving an order for the rows to be formed and another order for them to kneel down, the master of ceremonies knelt down too and proceeded to read aloud from a document written on yellow paper. This was a general report about the clan and its prosperity. It was called Piao and contained the names of all living male descendants of the clan. The names were included by order of seniority in generation and age, as in the formation of the rows. After the reading, the document was burned. While it was being burned, the master of ceremonies gave orders for the kneeling congregation to kowtow: once, twice, thrice, and a fourth time. He then shouted "Stand up," and pronounced the completion of the ceremony.

Musicians played during the ceremony, except for the period when the general report was being read aloud. As soon as the ceremony was completed, five bags of paper ingots were burned to the ancestors. One large bag with some special decoration was marked for the "very first ancestor" (the ancestor of origin). The other four were marked for "all ancestors of all generations." All five bags were provided by "all descendants of the Y clan." After this event the company sat down at various tables to eat a hearty meal. The seating was also more or less in accordance with seniority of generation and age.

In sharp contrast to the lack of formality at household altars, generally the temple ceremony calls for the wearing of one's best clothes. Most of the elders wore the ceremonial short coat on top of their gowns. The atmosphere during the entire proceeding was very solemn. There was no joking, laughter, or unnecessary noise or movement. . . .

. . . The ceremony at lesser ancestral temples, such as those of Ch clan and a Y clan, was performed without the accompaniment of music, but with much solemnity. . . .

21.
funeral Rites in taiwan

Death in the Chinese society means becoming an ancestor. As the ancestral cult is central in this society, so the rites connected with death and its aftermath are the most protracted and serious of all Chinese religious practices. The rituals (*li*) were written into elaborately detailed codes before the beginning of the Christian era, and those codes have been in force down to the twentieth century. While there are variants on the rituals at different times and places, and in accordance with the social and economic status of the family, in essentials they conform to the prescriptions in the sacred Li texts.

What follows is an outline of the funeral rites in Taiwan as they would ideally be carried out by the Hoklo Taiwanese (i.e. those Chinese natives of the island province whose ancestral homes were in the mainland province of Fukien, across the Strait of Taiwan). Readers interested in studying a much more detailed account, with extensive interpretive commentary, should consult J. J. M. de Groot, *The Religious System of China*, Vol. I (Leyden, 1892; reprinted in Taipei, 1964).[1]

(1) *Moving the bedding.* The time of death of all males and females who are of middle age and above, married, and have posterity, is called "the end of long life." When death seems imminent, the dying person is moved into the main hall (the room where guests are entertained), where upon two long trestles are placed boards, covered with a mat. For males this deathbed is placed on the left side, and for females on the right side of the hall. However, if there are those of the older generation still living in the household, then they do not "move the bedding," or else they only move it to a side wing of the main hall. In the case of minors who die untimely, they do not "move the bedding."

The icons of the household deities, including the soul-tablets of the ancestors, which are enshrined in the main hall of every home, are covered to avoid contamination from the evil influences of death.

When breath ceases the pillow is replaced by a stone or with "Hades paper" (paper stamped to resemble banknotes, negotiable in

[1]Our summary is taken principally from Ts'ao Chia-yi, "Taiwan chih sang-tsang (Taiwanese funerals), in *Taiwan Wen Shian* (a quarterly journal) IX, 4, Dec.1958, pp.61-66. This is supplemented by information from two articles by Ho Lien-k'uei: "Sang-tsang" (funerals), in *Taiwan Feng-t'u Chih* (Taiwanese Life and Customs), Taipei, 1956, pp.80-84; and same title in *Taiwan-sheng T'ung-chih Kao* (Draft Local History of Taiwan), Taipei, 1955, *chüan* 2, pp.28f. We have also utilized Ch'en Han-kuang, "Taiwan Fu-lao-jen chin-chi chih tiao-ch'a" (Taboo among the Fukienese in Taiwan), in *Taiwan Wen Shian*, XIII, 2, June 1962, 24-38; and Wang Chin-lien, "Taiwan-ti sang-su" (Taiwanese funeral customs), in *Ibid.*, VI, 3, Sept.1955, pp.57-60.

purgatory), and the body is covered with the "water bedding" (a coverlet red on top—red is auspicious—and white on the bottom—white is the color of death).

Below the feet of the dead one is placed "rice at the tips of the feet": the rice is heaped up in the bowl to overflowing, in the shape of a pointed hilltop; on it is placed an egg and a chopstick. An oil lamp is lighted and kept alight day and night. It is said that these prevent the soul from starving or from losing its way on the road to purgatory through the *yin* region. In addition, Hades paper, "money to buy the way" from the malicious devils along this road, is burned on behalf of the deceased.

The entire household let their hair go unkempt, kneel, and wail.

The rice bowl of the deceased is broken. A paper figure of a boy and a girl are placed one on either side of the corpse, with incense sticks; these are called "slave spirits."

(2) *Guarding the bedding.* It is believed that if a cat should jump over the corpse prior to its coffining, it will surely rise up as a vampire. Therefore the family members guard against this very strictly. The sons and grandsons sleep beside the corpse at night. This act "exhibits the utmost filiality" and "prevents untoward happenings."

(3) *Sending over the small sedan chair.* A small sedan chair is made from paper and filled with Hades paper money. This is burned before the corpse. The purpose is to inform Heaven of the death.

(4) *The fingertip money.* When a person realizes his death is near he will keep some coins on his person. (This is according to Ts'ao; but according to Ho, it is the family members who put 120 coins in the sleeve of the deceased.) The sleeve is shaken and the coins caused to drop out into a wooden rice measure. This is called "releasing the fingertip money." The family head then divides these coins among all the family members, each of whom strings his or hers together (the old Chinese "coppers" had a hole in the center). The idea is that these will enrich the survivors. Some of the clothing and personal effects of the deceased will also be distributed among the close family members; the idea here is similar, and also includes the thought that the dead will not be forgotten.

(5) *The washing of the corpse.* All the family don mourning garments. The "filial son" (eldest son of the deceased) takes an earthenware basin to a stream (or it may be taken for him by a Taoist priest), throws in some coins, scoops up some water, wails, and returns. This is called "begging water" or "buying water." With this water the corpse is washed by family members: if a male, by sons and grandsons; if a female, by the daughters-in-law.

(6) *Announcing the death.* Since everything connected with funerals is white, this is called "announcing the white" and white cards are sent to relatives and friends. When making an oral announcement the word death is not used; the messenger says, "drink a cup of water for me," and immediately leaves the home of relative or friend without looking back.

(7) *Wailing in the street.* When the close female relatives are coming to condole, as they approach the house they must wail, using certain sorrowful words.

(8) *Meeting the "outside family" guests* (those to which a family is related by marriage). A table is set before the gate of the bereaved house, covered with a cloth, and set with candlesticks and incense brazier holding unlit sticks of incense. The filial males kneel there and greet the relatives from the wife's family and the uncles, who lift one corner of the tablecloth and enter the house.

(9) *The "buriers."* Prior to the coffining only the closest relatives and friends come to condole; they are called "buriers." After addressing some words of condolence to the chief mourner, these will light a pair of incense sticks (two sticks are used in almost every funeral rite), kneel by the corpse, and wail. The filial son and daughter (his wife) kneel and wail also, in appreciation for the buriers' condolences.

(10) *Setting up the soul-silk.* Prior to the making of a permanent soul-tablet one is made of paper, about a foot high and three inches thick, in the shape of a blunt-tipped sword. On this are written the surname, tabu personal name, and public appellation of the deceased, together with his rank, posthumous name, the year, month, and day of death. This is placed before the deceased for his soul to receive the prayers of the survivors. Buddhist and Taoist priests are asked to set up this "soul-silk."

(11) *Paying respects.* The relatives and friends present elegiac scrolls (pairs of vertical paper scrolls with appropriate sentiments in matched words); or packages wrapped in white paper containing such items as white candles, Hades money, certain pastries, incense sticks; or rolls of brocade material; or money to help defray the funeral expenses. These are arranged before the corpse, with labels on them saying "with respect," or "funeral articles."

(12) *Putting on the grave-jackets.* The grave-jacket is called "longevity jacket," or "old person's jacket." They are mostly prepared after the age of fifty, in expectation of death. They are made of white material, their number varying with age and wealth, from three (for the young) to seven (for the middle-aged) to eleven or more (for the aged). Nine, however, are never worn, as the word for nine sounds in the local dialect like the word for dog.

The grave-jackets are not directly put on the corpse. The filial son first puts a "coolie hat" on his own head. Around the top of the hat is an encircling bamboo fillet into which are inserted two small, red candles. He seats himself on a bamboo stool which is set on a winnowing basket outside the house. The idea is thus expressed that the deceased will never "wear" the pure sky over his head, nor will his feet ever again tread the pure earth. The filial son holds his arms outstretched, with a piece of hemp rope across his shoulders, and an old woman who is considered to have led a blessed life puts the grave-jackets on him inside out. He is fed with "longevity noodles." The grave-jackets are transferred from the son to the corpse by slipping them off of either end of the rope; the coolie hat is hung up on the rooftop by means of a bamboo pole. After the filial son has climbed down from the bamboo stool, he kicks it behind him and re-enters the house without a backward look. The grave-jackets have no buttons, and those of the males are in the style of the Han dynasty.

(13) *Meeting the coffin.* When the empty coffin nears the house, a peck and two pints of rice are pressed onto the cover of it to "repress" the evil influences of the coffin. The filial son and daughter welcome the coffin, kneeling and saluting it, burning paper Hades money. They wail, and follow the coffin into the house.

(14) *Opening up the soul-road.* Soul masses are said by Buddhist and Taoist priests so that the soul will not go astray on its journey to purgatory.

(15) *Taking leave of life.* After the washing and garbing with the grave-clothes, the mouth of the corpse is filled with rice, a table is set with "twelve dishes" (six vegetable and six meat), and the Buddhist and Taoist priests chant. Putting the rice into the corpse's mouth is called "taking leave of life."

(16) *Filling the corpse's mouth.* In addition to rice, jade or jewels may be put in, so that their precious influences may serve to protect him if he is attacked by demons.

Ho mentions another custom at this point: Every family member takes hold with one hand of a long, hempen rope, one end of which is attached to the sleeve of the dead person. They then ask the augur (who has come to select an auspicious time for the coffining) to cut off the portion held by each; whereupon each person wraps up his portion in a sheet of silver Hades money and burns it. This is called "cutting off lots," and represents the idea of separation from the soul of the deceased.

(17) *Encoffining.* The bottom of the coffin is fitted with a board in which are carved seven holes in the form of the seven stars of the constellation Great Bear. Over this is placed some Hades money. The corpse is put into the coffin, being provided with paper hat and boots. The sides of the coffin are further stuffed with more Hades money to prevent the body from shifting about.

Should the deceased be a young person who has not been married he must also be provided in the coffin with a cooked egg, a stone, and salted beans.[2] Some wood ashes are sprinkled in the bottom, which will protect the deceased from enemies. The outside relatives are asked to observe the coffining (to ensure that there will be no later lawsuits over any irregularities), and the coffin is nailed shut. Any persons whose zodiacal birth-animal is opposed to that of the deceased will avoid this moment as unlucky. Everyone is also careful not to let his tears or his shadow enter the coffin as it is being closed, lest this endanger his own health and luck. The coffin should be placed with its head to the south and foot to the north, orientation of the hall permitting.

(18) *Striking the tub.* The interval elapsing between the encoffining and the burial will vary according to the circumstances of the family. In poor families it will not be more than one to three days, while in wealthy families it may be several months or even several years. During this interval the outside wood is oiled every few days by people from the coffin shop to make it more waterproof and airtight; this is called "striking the tub."

---

[2]Symbols respectively of rebirth, transformation, and sprouting.

(19) *Taking out the coffin.* The coffin is taken out to the roadside where it is the object of the sacrifice of a pig's head and other viands. The place in the main hall where it had been resting is sprinkled with salt and rice to dissipate the evil influences. After taking the coffin outside, five or seven bowls of white rice are placed on it, with a single chopstick stuck therein. The women accompany the coffin in their mourning garb, wailing.

(20) *Offering sacrifice.* Two kinsmen from the outside family lead in the formal sacrifice to the departing coffin's inmate: Incense is burned, the mourners drop to their knees and kotow (letting the forehead touch the ground) thrice; rise and repeat the kneeling and kowtowing; hasten forward to make a libation of wine, pouring the wine into a pan full of sand which sits in front of the spirit table; again kneel and kotow, at the same time wailing. Needless to say the filial sons also accompany them. After the outside relatives, it is the turn of the family members and friends. During all of this ceremony there is a continual accompaniment of music from the funeral band.

(21) *Circumambulating the coffin and sealing it.* Upon the conclusion of these sacrifices the filial son and his wife, led by Buddhist and Taoist priests, circumambulate the coffin thrice, wailing. The purpose is to indicate that they cannot bear to part from its inhabitant. Then the coffin is sealed by someone from the outside family, this nailing down being accompanied by auspicious sayings which by puns augur well for the family in such matters as sons and wealth.

(22) *Thanking the guests (i.e. the outside family).* When the procession has gone down one or two streets the coffin is halted, and the guests are thanked for their trouble in coming from afar. The guests thereupon bow to the coffin and take their leave. The procession goes on to the cemetery.

(23) *The funeral procession.* This is commonly called "going to the hill." On the day of the burial all the relatives and friends gather. In the morning the Buddhist and Taoist priests start their chanting and worshiping. The elaborateness of the procession of course varies according to the financial means of the family; here is how a full-fledged parade would be arranged:

First comes what is called "the deity who clears the road." This a paper and bamboo figure of a man, in whose hollow interior are hung the innards of a pig. He is borne by a rabble of beggars and "Lohan-feet" — riff-raff who make a living by this sort of thing — until the grave is reached, at which time they must make off with the pig innards, fleeing without a backward look lest they be struck dead by the spirits.

Then comes a five-colored banner, followed by two pairs of lanterns, bearing the name of the deceased on one side, and the words "a hundred sons, a thousand grandsons" on the other. The characters are written in red on the first lanterns and in blue on the second. After the lanterns there comes a "straw dragon" made from rice straw, whose head emits smoke as it is set afire. Hades money is scattered along the way to distract evil spirits.

Musicians come next, striking a big drum and a gong, and playing on the *la-pa* (a Central Asian trumpet). They are followed by sons and daughters of the deceased who carry red silk "spirit banners," while grandsons and granddaughters carry yellow silk banners.

Then come white parasols, signifying death, and two palanquins each carried by four men; on the first there is a large incense brazier, and on the second there is a drum. Behind the palanquins there are borne elegaic scrolls supplied by relatives and friends on which are written such sentiments as "Riding the crane he returns to the West"; or "Now he is an ancient."

More palanquins now appear, on which ride girls dressed up as "the twenty-four paragons of filiality." Behind these there comes a paper sedan chair in which are pasted paper figures of the deceased attended by four mourners of his nephews' generation. The chair is followed by baskets of flowers and by animals which are simulated in paper or sometimes consist of live pigeons who would fly back by themselves when released at the grave.

A most important member of the procession is the sedan chair for the soul. It is carried by four mourners of the deceased's nephews' generation. In it are a rice peck-measure, the "soul silk," and a pair of "soul sedan chair lanterns." When the burial is finished the eldest grandson rides home in this chair, carrying the peck-measure and the soul silk.

This chair is followed by Buddhist and Taoist priests, who in turn precede the coffin itself. The coffin is covered with a more or less elaborately embroidered cloth. The coffin of a poor person will be carried by four men; the common coffin will require eight to sixteen men; while the coffin of a family of wealth with many relatives may use thirty-two to sixty-four pallbearers. The "filial son," wearing sackcloth and grass sandals, walks behind the coffin, weeping. His eldest son carries a soul flag which is like a small mandala. Then follow the other sons, carrying small white paper lanterns in one hand and a mourning staff in the other (this is about a foot long, made of bramble or bamboo tipped with a bit of red cloth or hemp). After the sons come the close relatives of the deceased, all dressed in mourning.

The end of the procession is brought up by the rest of the mourners, friends and relatives, who in the old days would wear white mourning bands on their heads, and in later days wear the bands on their left arms. In Japanese times (1895-1945) they would wear paper badges below the breast.

(24) *Opening up the grave.* Prior to the funeral the eldest son has, in consultation with an augur, selected the gravesite. There, incense and candles are lit, and gold Hades paper money is burned in sacrifice to the earth gods—the "god of the hill" and the "local earth god." (There are two kinds of mock paper money: the gold is for the *shên*, or beneficent dieties, and the silver for the *kuei*, or maleficent spirits.) These sacrifices are to pray for their protection of the deceased. They are called "the opening [of the grave] omens." The actual construction is called "opening up the grave."

(25) *Putting [the coffin] in the grave.* When the coffin reaches the cemetery, the "soul-silk" or spirit tablet, which has of course accompanied it during the funeral procession, is placed upon the altar which stands in front of the tombstone. The funeral pennants are stuck into the ground to either side of the grave, and sacrificial meat and wine is set before it. The coffin is put down in front of the grave and the filial son on its left, the filial daughter-in-law on its right, pay their last respects and wail. When the coffin is lowered into the pit, all must avoid standing close enough for their shadows to be trapped as the dirt and stones are piled over it. During this time there is

a continuous music from the funeral band, and the Buddhist and Taoist priests chant.

The filial son again sacrifices to the local earth god, and then, bearing the spirit-tablet, kneels in front of the grave, where some dignitary (according to one source this would be the head of the clan) has been invited to "dot the *chu*" (i.e. with a brush dipped in vermilion ink, to place the final dot on the character *chu*, which signifies that the tablet is now the actual residence of the soul of the deceased). The spirit tablet is then set on a rice measure in front of the grave, where it receives the libation of the one who has dotted the *chu*, accompanied by the burning of incense, kneeling of all parties, and the din of music from the band. Led by the Buddhist and Taoist priests the funeral party circumambulates the grave, wailing, and then they return home.

The spirit-table is borne by the eldest grandson,[3] seated in the sedan chair. The route taken on the return must be exactly the same as that going to the cemetery, in order that the soul shall not lose its way. Some earth from the grave is carried home in an incense brazier and put on the spirit table. The soul-silk is put in back of this. The Buddhist and Taoist priests again burn incense and Hades money and chant sutras.

(26) *Thanking Earth.* Three or seven days after the burial the filial son and other close relatives go to the cemetery to sacrifice. This is called "thanking Earth," or "paying off the [lime] ashes," or "completing the tomb." After performing a sacrifice a venerable person is asked to "scatter the five grains"; besides the grains he also scatters small nails and copper coins. The filial son and daughter-in-law pick these up in their mourning garments and carry them home. They will give wealth and sons (through punning correspondence with the Chinese words). The daughter of the deceased should leave money for the gravediggers and musicians on top of the grave.

(27) *Settling the spirit.* The soul-silk is placed on a sackcloth-covered table at the side of the main hall. With it on the table there are incense, candlesticks, and a spirit-table lamp; there are also a male and a female figure made out of paper. The male holds a water pipe (Chinese version of the hooka) and the female holds a tea tray and teacup. Sacrificial meats and wine are provided. Buddhist and Taoist priests are asked to chant sutras and burn incense, and to settle the soul in its place, while the filial son and other family members kneel and wail during the sacrifice. This is commonly called "settling the spirit." After this the seven weeks sacrifices commence.

(28) *Sacrificing by weeks.* The days following the death are divided into seven periods of seven days each—although after the first week the periods are actually shortened to six days, on the theory that "time passes quickly for

---

[3]This is a vestige of one feature of the ancient rites which has not survived: the personator. At sacrifices to the deceased the grandson would sit silently as the representative of his grandfather to receive the sacrifices. It is an obvious symbolization of the continuity of the family line, the grandson actually conceived as the "reincarnation" of the ancestor in the generation before his father. This alternation of generations was futher symbolized in the alternation of tablets on the shelves of the ancestral temple. It is thus not merely the natural affection between the old and young which accounts for the special closeness of grandparents and grandchildren in China, as contrasted with the formal distance maintained between father and son.

the dead." Some say that after seven days the dead return to inspect, and so they are thus sacrificed to. During the first week the filial son and his wife sacrifice; during the third week the filial daughter sacrifices; during the fifth week the filial grandson and granddaughter sacrifice.

These sacrifices are all accompanied by the "sounds of clashing cymbals" (i.e. the services of Buddhist and Taoist priests). During the sacrificial periods rice and side dishes are offered morning and evening to the spirit of the deceased. When the women sacrifice they wail. The sacrifice is called "filial rice" or "proffered rice." After the seven weeks are over there is the "sending of rice": A bag of rice about five inches long by three inches wide, and a small bundle of firewood are placed on the spirit-table (i.e. the altar on which the temporary soul-silk stands).

(29) *Riding the horse to seek forgiveness of sins.* During the first, third, and fifth week sacrifices, Buddhist and Taoist priests are called in to say soul masses, which is vulgarly called "making good karma." There are "three-mornings" services (i.e. beginning one morning and terminating on the third morning) and "noon-night" services (beginning at noon and terminating the same day at midnight).

The ritual called "sending off the horse [to seek] forgiveness" is as follows: A paper horse and paper official are made and set on a stand in an open place atop a long bench, underneath which is placed a charcoal brazier with live coals in it. The priests rapidly circumambulate this bench, and then ask the village head or a schoolmaster to read a document begging Heaven for forgiveness of the sins committed by the deceased; this person will be attired in a long gown and riding jacket (of the old style). The opening section of the document he reads has the following lines (the original is in verse):

> With both hands I accept a document,
> Not knowing what is contained in it.
> Before the hall of the forgiving-official I open my mouth to read it.
> The spark of light of this soul penetrates the nine [realms of] sunya (emptiness).

The closing section has the following lines:

> Before the reading of the opening of this prayer for forgiveness had been completed
> The sins and enmities of the deceased's soul had been forgiven.
> The sons and daughters will carry on their filial conduct forever,
> Protect the sons and grandsons and give them all blessings and long life.

After the reading of this document the priests again circumambulate the table swiftly, and then they burn the "forgiveness official," the "forgiveness horse," and the "forgiveness petition" together. Following this ceremony the priests perform on their musical instruments.

Then before daybreak there is the dedication to the deceased of the numerous replicas made with paper—houses, furniture, everything he will need in the nether world; plus such deities as the god of the hill and the local earth god, and "the twenty-four paragons of filiality"—which are also transmuted into the etherial dimension by burning.

(30) *Expelling the spirit.* This ceremony takes place at one of several intervals after the death: either on the last day of the seven weeks; on the

hundredth day; on the first death anniversary; or on the second death anniversary. Again Buddhist and Taoist priests are called in to chant scriptures, and then they perform the rite of burning the soul-silk (this is now replaced by the permanent wooden tablet), and getting rid of the altar on which it has been standing. The altar-table is thrown outside the house by the roadside. When this is done there must be men made up to resemble dragons and tigers, called "dragon and tiger fighters"; otherwise the men who move the altar-table, and the bereaved family will suffer from the evil spirits. Also, anyone carelessly stepping on the oil which was in the lamp on the altar-table will get sick, so the children are taught not to walk on the side of the road where it was thrown. On this occasion wealthy people again have a service held "to make good karma."

(31) *The soul-tablet.* The permanent wooden tablet is inscribed like the soul-silk and placed in the main hall on the altar beside the other ancestral tablets. A pinch of the ashes from the incense brazier on the altar-table of the recently deceased is put into the brazier before these ancestral tablets, this commonly called "joining the braziers." Those who are unable to ask Buddhist and Taoist priests to perform this rite will usually do it themselves on New Year's Eve.

(32) *The tombstone.* On this is carved the date and tabu personal name of the deceased. According to one source the number of characters in an inscription must correspond to the five characters "birth, old age, sickness, death, suffering," which is of course the Buddhist summary of existence; the native Chinese attitude shows up in the same requirement, which goes on to specify that the words "sickness," "death," and "suffering" are themselves tabu.

(33) *Hanging up filiality.* The death is made known by special announcements pasted on the gate posts. Special cards of thanks are later sent to all the relatives within the five degrees of mourning, thanking them for their condolences.

(34) *Avoidance of certain days for funerals.* Certain double dates according to the Chinese calendar, and conflicting horoscopic days must be avoided or bad luck will follow; hence an expert is consulted to decide on auspicious times and days.

(35) *Changing the burial.* Those who believe in the theories of *feng-shui* (geomancy) or heed the words of Buddhist and Taoist priests and soothsayers, call the burial of the corpse the "unlucky burial," and the burial of the bones the "lucky burial."

In eleven or twelve years, or as early as five or six years after the original burial, on an auspicious day, they will offer sacrifices, and have the workmen who specialize in such matters open the tomb and break open the coffin. The bones will be removed and washed and dried in the sun. Then they will be properly arranged and placed in a "golden peck-measure" — an earthenware jar about three feet high and one foot in diameter. This is temporarily stored in the grave pit, or else in a small shrine called "temple of Yu Ying Kung" (collective name for spirits bereft of their due sacrifices), or "repository of all good [spirits]"; such temples usually being on a hillside or in the cemetery by the roadside. A small red marker is fastened to the little temples saying "ask and ye shall receive" (*yu ying* literally meaning the latter), or "repository of all good [spirits]." Afterwards the bones are reburied in another place selected as auspicious by the *feng-shui* expert.

(36) *Beckoning-the-soul burial.* In the case of those whose corpses cannot be found for burial, such as those who have been killed in war or died by drowning, it was formerly the practice to make a silver tablet five inches long by three inches wide, to inscribe on it the name of the deceased, the filial son to dot the *chu* with blood from his finger, and to bury this tablet inside of a "golden peck-measure."

22.
religion and magic in the middle ages

In their preoccupation with the intensely interesting philosophical thought of Buddhism and with the exacting self-discipline of the Dhyana School (Ch'an or Zen), modern Western students are apt to overlook—even perhaps to prefer to overlook—the "grassroots" aspect of Buddhism. Some scholars have gone so far as to assert that Buddhism is only a philosophy, not a religion. Similarly, to those whose picture of Taoism is based upon the endlessly intriguing apothegms of Lao Tzu (*Tao Te Ching*) or the lofty, imaginative flights of Chuang Tzu, it may not be pleasing to descend to the level of magic and superstition characteristic of religious Taoism among the masses. Of course, recollection of the world of magic and superstition in the European Middle Ages may help us to accept this as a situation that is not, after all, so strange. Like professional religious everywhere, except perhaps in the modern, secularized West, the Chinese monks and priests were regarded by the multitudes as men of special, secret, supernormal powers. They might be feared, or they might be admired, but they had about them a charisma by virtue of their particular sort of learning and their vocation. Even a slight acquaintance with the Buddhism manifest in Chinese history, art, and literature quickly disabuses one of the notion that it was primarily either an intellectual game or a practice confined to masters of yogic concentration. In popular stories and dramas, the monks and their Taoist confreres are always cast in the role of workers of magic. It was, in part, because of such powers that Buddhism originally won the confidence of the Chinese. As J. LeRoy Davidson puts it: "The Buddhist missionary had more than philosophic abstraction to offer the Chinese. Magic was part of his stock in trade; it was needed to compete with the host of popular superstitions current in China."[1] E. D. Edwards, from whose work we extract material for this chapter, speaks of "the collections of tales of magic which formed the chief propaganda used by

[1]*The Lotus Sutra in Chinese Art* (Yale University, 1954), p. 14.

Taoists and Buddhists to win converts among the people during the T'ang period."[2]

In a religion like Taoism, which centers upon the attainment of immortality through techniques, hope and faith are supported by the examples of those who have been successful in the quest. There are in fact countless stories of such persons in the Chinese literature since Later Han times. It goes without saying that anyone who has achieved the supreme power will concurrently have the ability to work deeds of lesser caliber; thus it is only reasonable to accept the workaday magical powers of Taoist Adepts. We give here a few instances, as translated by Lionel Giles in his *A Gallery of Chinese Immortals*, John Murray (Publishers) Ltd., (London, 1948 — Wisdom of the East Series). The notes are in the original.

Where Fu Lü came from is not known; but he constantly stayed at Chü [in Shantung], and wandered about among the temples along the seacoast. In one temple he found three hsien (adepts who have attained immortality) gambling for melons. Seeing Fu Lü, they bade him bring them a few dozen yellow and white melons, and then told him to shut his eyes. When he opened them again, he found himself in the island of Fang-chiang, which lies to the south of P'eng-lai.[3]

Afterwards, when he revisited Chü, he brought out a quantity of pearls and jade and other precious things which he had taken from Fang-chiang, and offered them for sale. Time went on, and one day he appeared in reddish brown garments,[4] with shaven head and all the look of an old man. On being questioned, he said that he had been convicted of stealing objects from a temple. A few years later, however, he resumed his youthful appearance and his hair grew long again as it was in the days gone by. (28-29)

The real names of T'ai Shan Lao Fu ("The Old Gaffer of Mt. T'ai") are not known. When [Emperor] Wu Ti of the Han dynasty was on a hunting expedition in the east, he saw an old man hoeing the ground near the roadside, round whose head there was a halo of light several feet in breadth. This astonished the Emperor, and he stopped to question him. The old fellow appeared to be about fifty years of age, but his face was fresh-colored like a boy's, and his skin was unusually smooth and clear. Asked by the Emperor what Taoist method he had employed to this end, he replied: "When I was 85 years old, my body was decaying fast and death was at hand; my hair was white and my teeth were gone. Then I met one possessed of Tao who taught me to abstain from cereal food, to eat nothing but *shu* (Atractylis root) and drink nothing but water. He also made me a magic pillow, stuffed with 32 ingredients . . . I practiced this regimen, and lo! my age was turned to youth; black hair grew again on my head, new teeth filled the place of those that had gone; I was able to travel 300 *li* in one day. Your servant has now reached the age of 180."

[2]*Chinese Prose Literature of the T'ang Period* (full citation following) p. 49.
[3]Two of the Isles of the Blest, placed by Lieh Tzû at fabulous distances from the coast of China.
[4]The usual garb of a criminal.

The Emperor, having received this prescription for longevity bestowed upon him jade and silk. The veteran afterwards retired into the fastnesses of Mount T'ai, only returning to his village at intervals of five or ten years. When 300 years had elapsed, he returned no more. (38-39)

Tso Tz'û, styled Yüan-fang, was a native of Lu-chiang [in Anhwei]. While yet a boy, he possessed supernatural powers. Once when he was at a banquet given by Ts'ao Kung (i.e. the famous general Ts'ao Ts'ao), the latter looked smilingly round at his assembled guests and said: "I have made but poor provision of delicacies for this noble company today. What we lack are some perch from the Wu-sung River, with which to make a mince." Said Fang: "That is easily obtainable"; and, calling for a bronze bowl full of water, he began angling in it with a bamboo rod. After a little while he pulled out a perch, whereupon Ts'ao Kung clapped his hands vigorously, and the whole company was much astonished. "One fish," said Kung, "won't go around. It would be nice to have two." So Fang cast his line again, and soon drew up another fish. Both were over three feet long, and deliciously fresh. Kung had them minced up before his eyes, and handed round the dainty to his guests sitting at table. "Now that we have got our perch," he said, "it is a pity that we have no raw ginger from Shu to go with them." "That too can be procured," said Fang. Suspicious lest he should buy some in the vicinity, Ts'ao Kung then said: "Some time ago I sent a man to Shu in order to buy brocade. Please instruct your messenger to tell my agent to purchase two extra lengths of it." Fang's messenger departed, and in a twinkling was back again with the raw ginger. "I saw your agent, Sir," he said to Ts'ao Kung, "in a brocade shop, and gave him your order." More than a year afterwards Kung's agent returned, and sure enough he had got the two extra lengths. On being questioned, he said that the year before, on such and such a day of such and such a month, he had met a man in a shop who acquainted him with Kung's order.

On a later occasion Ts'ao Kung, accompanied by some hundred scholars, went for an excursion not far outside the city. Fang provided a single jar of wine and a single piece of dried meat. Tilting the jar with his own hands, he poured out wine for all the assembled guests, not one of whom but ate and drank to repletion. Kung thought this very strange, and caused an investigation to be made. On sending round to inspect the wine-shops, he found that the day before they had all been cleared of their stocks of wine and meat. This angered him, and he secretly determined to put Fang to death. The latter was just about to be arrested as he was sitting in Ts'ao Kung's private apartment, when he walked straight into a wall and incontinently vanished. Then Kung hired a number of men to capture him. One of these saw him in the marketplace, and was on the point of seizing him when suddenly all the people there were transformed into his exact likeness, so that no one could tell which was really he.

Later on, some of them met Fang on the brow of the Yang-Ch'êng Hill, and again pursued him, whereupon he ran amongst a flock of sheep (it is implied that he turned into a sheep himself).

Kung, realizing that he was not to be caught in this way, told his men to go among the sheep and make the following announcement: "Ts'ao Kung does not want to put you to death. He has only been making trial of your magical arts; and now that they have stood the test, his desire is simply to have an interview with you." Then suddenly one old ram, bending its two forelegs, stood erect like a man and began to speak, saying: "What a fluster you're in!" Ts'ao Kung's men cried out: "That ram is the one we want," and all made a dash for him. But lo! the whole flock, numbering several hundreds, now turned into rams, all bending their forelegs, standing erect and calling out: "What a fluster you're in!" The result was that no one knew which of them to capture.

Lao Tzû said: "The ills that afflict me are due to my being encumbered with a body. Once I succeed in freeing myself from my body, what ill can befall me?"[5]

Those who are of Lao Tzu's persuasion may be said to have the power of freeing themselves from their bodies. How can they fail to keep misfortune at a distance? (76-78)

Chinese civilization was most vigorous in the T'ang period. After centuries of division between ephemeral barbarian dynasties in the north, and scarcely less unstable Chinese dynasties in the south, the whole country was reunited under a strong Chinese house. The boundaries of the empire were more far-flung than ever before in history. China was open to foreign contacts, and its great capital of Ch'ang-an in the northwest was undoubtedly the most sophisticated and cosmopolitan city in the world. The society seems to have been unfettered by the moralistic, even puritanical, code implanted by the Neo-Confucianists of Sung and later times. In particular, the position of women was still relatively free. As we have noted elsewhere in this reader, it was in T'ang that Buddhism attained its greatest worldly glory, which then led to its fall in the midninth century; and it was likewise in T'ang that Taoism held a place of unprecedented power, as may be judged from the fact that the very emperors themselves claimed descent from Lao Tzû on the basis of their surname, Li, which was supposed to be that of the Sage.

If we wish to study the general religious climate of those times, we can turn to a great deal of source material aside from the official documents of the dynasty. In particular, short fiction, which was just then developing into a true art form, reveals the beliefs and practices of the people. E. D. Edwards has analyzed the anthology called *T'ang Tai Ts'ung Shu (Collected Reprints of the T'ang Dynasty)*, containing both fiction and miscellaneous essays of all sorts, in her work, *Chinese Prose Literature of the T'ang Period, A.D. 618-906* (2 vols., London, 1937-38), from which we extract some illuminating remarks.

. . . The most popular belief, illustrated by stories in the anthology, is undoubtedly the Taoist idea that the souls of dead men take up their abode

[5]See *Tao Tê Ching*, chap. 13. This cryptic saying may have given the impulse to many later developments of Taoism which would hardly have met with the approval of Lao Tzû himself.

in material objects. Belief in transmigration, although present, is less strong. Another phase of this belief which the stories show is that inanimate objects possess souls. The character of these tales suggests that it is some quality of the object itself which gives rise to the belief that it is as it were "alive."

Of the philosophical aspect of Taoism scarcely a trace is found in T'ang stories. Exorcism and magic are their theme; no religious ideals are portrayed and no moral principles enunciated. Taoist recluses are depicted not as spending a life of contemplation, but in an everlasting search for the elixir of life; they had no thought for the good of others, and philanthropic persons usually prove to be immortals temporarily banished to earth to expiate a crime. "Miracles" were performed either for display and gain or to refute and destroy rivals. Magic was a weapon employed primarily for personal aggrandizement and not for the benefit of the doctrine. Buddhist tales, though definitely instructive, especially in relation to the slaughter of animals, the theory of reward and retribution, and the efficacy of reciting Buddhist sutras, are by no means free from superstition.

The beliefs contained in the anthology may be briefly summarized as follows: The world is governed by a Supreme Being, most often called Ti, or Sovereign Ruler. He does not appear to be omniscient or omnipotent. In the story of Miao-nü, his daughter having been banished, he is said to be "seeking" her, being evidently unaware of her whereabouts after two or three reincarnations, while in the story which tells of the loss of his two Medicine Spirits, he is completely outwitted by a Buddhist priest. References to this Being are comparatively few, but it is stated that he inhabits as his inferior dwelling-place part of the desert near the K'un-lun Mountains, and that the hosts of the spirits dwell there also.

The spirit-world is all around, and to it go the souls of the dead. Many become officials there, occupying positions similar to those they held on earth, and these spirit-officials may be appointed to govern definite and special districts. The functionaries of the underworld have specific duties in relation to the world of men. Submarine palaces may be inhabited by dragons, but they are similar to the palaces of earth. So close is this likeness between the two worlds and so exactly does the one imitate the other that the spirits even have wives.

Persons who commit suicide or die by violence or accident are not escorted to the nether world and cannot find their way, but wander about disconsolate until they can find a substitute. *Yao-kuai* are ghosts more powerful and cleverer than the average, and belong to the category of beings who injure with intent. To the class of harmful spirits belong also the *yehch'a*, the Buddhist *yakshas*.

The soul of man is two-fold, the inferior (*po*) appertaining to his mortal clay, and the superior (*hun,* or *shên*) representing his spiritual self. According to the Confucian theory the latter dissipates after death but according to the Buddhists it is reincarnated, while the Taoists say it goes to live in the underworld. That is why the theories in the anthology seem to be contradictory. All three religions accept the principle of the reincarnation of the soul. It may occupy its own body again if it is not decomposed, or it may enter into the body of a man just dead, or into an unborn child, or it may take possession of a living person. The superior soul may also leave the body and live a separate and distinct life apart from it, while the body, kept alive by the inferior soul, remains more or less inert, even for years, awaiting its return. Vampires are explained as embodiments of inferior souls which, having contrived to preserve themselves overlong after the death of the body, go about in a variety of forms, ferocious demons devouring men. It is possible for the soul to visit heaven, or it may return to earth after the death of the body to requite an injury or repay a debt.

There is a spirit in every object, and most are prone to evil, but even the most evilly disposed spirits are comparatively powerless against the devout, safety being in direct ratio to virtue.

The dead have their loves and their hates, and enjoy precisely the things which they enjoyed on earth. Many instances are related of spirits living the normal life of human beings and behaving as men, and the anthology contains a large number of stories of love between men and spirits . . . (Vol. II, pp. 31-33)

These stories . . . are not stories of the supernatural; tales of spirits and gods, where no human agency is assumed, do not form part of the present inquiry, which is restricted to marvels and "miracles," performed by Taoist and Buddhist priests and sorcerers, or even by Confucian scholars versed in magic arts. . . .

Performances in which no reference to the origin of the magician is made are generally less marvelous than those conducted by foreigners. Nevertheless, many magical practices are attributed to Chinese. The theory that matter could be changed or modified at will, although Taoist in essence, was frequently illustrated by laymen versed in the art of modifying the Five Elements.

A certain Shih Wei-t'ui, for example, was the master of many magical arts. One evening when drinking with friends he remarked, "Would you like me to show you a trick to amuse you?" Knowing his skill, they assented, whereupon he took a piece of paper and cut out the figure of a boy who danced and cut capers while Shih sang an accompaniment. . . . At least one story goes a step beyond causing a pictured person to come to life: *Huan ying chuan* contains the story of a man who transformed himself into a figure in a picture and spoke to those who searched in vain for him.

Perhaps the best instance of complete control over matter is the following, the magician being neither priest nor scholar but a beggar[6]:

During the reign of Tê Tsung of the T'ang dynasty, there appeared in the marketplace at Yang-chou a certain Hu, asking for alms. As he was a skillful magician his gains were enormous. One day he appeared with a bottle, large enough to hold perhaps half a pint. To his request for enough money to fill the bottle a bystander responded with a gift of a hundred cash. Hu threw these into the bottle with a rattle, although the neck of the bottle was no larger than an ordinary reed, and the astonished spectators saw the cash become as small as grains of rice. A thousand, ten thousand, twenty thousand cash were contributed. So also were a donkey and a horse, which appeared in the bottle no larger than flies. Lastly there arrived upon the scene

[6]However, it may not be going beyond the bounds of probability to assume that this "beggar" was in reality a Taoist Adept — who are fond of such amusements. (L.G.T.)

a string of official horses and carts, which quickly followed the earlier offerings into the magic bottle and were in turn followed by the magician himself. The bottle then disappeared, but some months later Hu was seen with the string of horses and carts in another part of the country.

Invisibility, one of the strongest evidences of power over matter, was an art greatly coveted and frequently attempted by the emperor Ming Huang. He could not, however, achieve it alone, but only in the company of his instructor, the bonze, Lo Ssû-yüan. Failure was the invariable result when anyone not within the charmed circle tried to imitate such tricks. . . .

Instances of the transmutation of base metals, although not frequent, occur in the present collection. . . . Wang K'o-jung used to tell a story of the time when he was a Buddhist priest. During a period of heavy snow he and a dozen others were without food for about ten days, being unable themselves to venture out to beg alms, and having no money wherewith to send a servant to buy food. At last one of their number took a long-handled pan, set it on the stove, poured into it some quicksilver from a bottle, and added a little powder which looked like mud from the wall. These ingredients he heated together, finally producing a cake of silver several ounces in weight with which the servants were able to purchase food for the starving priests.

During the T'ang period Ts'ui Yüan-liang, magistrate of Hu-chou, approached a certain priest who was an adept at alchemy and begged instruction. The priest agreed to give a demonstration. He sent Ts'ui for an axe, which he put into an earthen crucible with a purple pill. Covering the crucible with a square tile, he piled charcoal over it until it was completely buried. He then worked the bellows till the fire blazed and told Ts'ui to think of an object, which, he said, would appear in silver in the crucible. After a while the priest removed the crucible from the fire to a bowl of water and laughing, asked Ts'ui what object he had thought of. "Myself," was the reply, whereupon the magician lifted out a silver image of Ts'ui, complete to the last detail.

Both Buddhists and Taoists claimed power not over matter only, but over spirits also. Many were skilled, though not always successful, exorcists. On the other hand there are tales of Taoists who succeeded in expelling demons which an ordinary witch (*wu*) had failed to expel. Both invoking and expelling spirits came of long practice and experience and were matters of art rather than virtue. The popularity of exorcism was largely due to the fact that many diseases were regarded as demon-possession, and therefore could be more appropriately treated by magic than by drugs. Such cases are rarely described in detail, and little is said of methods of exorcising. There is, however, a story in *Huan i chih* which explains both the nature of the disease and its cure: An unfortunate woman had for years been surrounded by the evil aura which marks persons possessed by demons. Often she would weep all day and shout incoherently all night. At length her family appealed to a Buddhist priest, well versed in the Disciplinary Rules, skilled in modifying the Five Elements, a capable charm-writer and an expert in controlling spirits. His method of curing the patient was as follows: First he twisted straw into the shape of a woman, then dressed the figure in bright colors, and set it upon a pile of earth. Thereafter he recited incantations until, after a time, a voice spoke from the straw figure, begging that its life might be spared. In answer to stern inquiry the demon explained its nature. The priest, knowing that it was too dangerous to be at large, sent for a large jar which he laid upon its side and into which he drove the demon with a whip, while it emitted faint bleating sounds. The jar was then sealed with a charm and buried in a mulberry grove, the family being charged to see that it was not disturbed. . . .

Amongst specifically Buddhist arts was the Great Wheel Spell, used for the cure of sickness. It was not, however, very efficacious, being liable to engender in a patient a form of madness, which drove him to climb upon the rafters and eat crockery.

Power over matter, that is to say the practical application of alchemy to the production of wealth and the enjoyment of a long life in this world, forms one of the principal themes of these stories. . . . the majority of instances relate, as is only natural, to "external" alchemy (*wai tan*). "Internal" alchemy (*nei tan*) and the attainment of immortality were for the few, who practiced rigorously a variety of spiritual exercises and used medicinal herbs and drugs to etherealize their bodies. To most men only the practical benefits of long life and wealth appealed, and it is therefore this type of story which is commonly found in these records. . . .

Neither Taoists nor Buddhists were uniformly successful in the working of magic. The present Anthology relates the sad end of a Buddhist priest who claimed to be able to cause rain to cease. During the year A.D. 710, when Ch'ang-an had been deluged with rain for more than two months, a certain Ouigour priest offered his services to end the downpour. After prohibiting the slaughter of pigs, he set up an altar, and recited sutras and incantations. In the course of fifty days he sacrificed twenty sheep and two horses; but the rain still continued. Thereupon the priest was himself dispatched and the rain ceased forthwith. . . .

From Confucian sources come tales which show the darker side of magic, for Taoists in particular were hated by the official class, on account of the favour they enjoyed at Court. *Huan i chih*, for example, contains a bitter denunciation of a Taoist priest versed in magical arts, whose reputation was of the worst. He is accused of leading astray the youth of wealthy and honorable families, by evoking, and allowing his followers to see Hsi Wang Mu, the Fairy of Mt. Wu, and the Fairy Pao of Ma-ku, for, in response to his invocation, "all the fairies responded and came." So bitter was the resentment against him that he was eventually executed. A good deal of the bitterness of Confucian invective sprang of course from jealousy. During the T'ang period the Taoists enjoyed imperial favour and were extremely powerful. Several emperors were ardent Taoists, and more than one, accepting an *elixir vitae* at the hands of a priest, cut short his own life in attempting to lengthen it indefinitely. (Vol. I, pp. 49-59)

23.
the cult of mount t'ai

The connection between mountains and religion is a very old and universal one. Mountains are one of the most imposing of natural phenomena, which the premodern mind invariably saw as living, divine powers. In China five mountains have since antiquity been singled out as "sacred peaks" of more than local fame: Sung Kao in the Center, T'ai Shan (Shan means mountain) in the East, Heng Shan in the South, Hua Shan in the West, and Heng (a different word in Chinese) Shan in the North. Besides these there is of course any number of mountains with sacred connections, such as O-mei Shan in Ssuchuan province, and Wu-t'ai Shan in Shansi, famous centers of Buddhist pilgrimage. Of the five sacred mountains of the ancient Native Tradition, T'ai Shan is by far the most important, its cult dating back as far as the Shang dynasty, and continuing to modern times. As one of the vital cults of both popular and official religion, enduring through the entire span of Chinese history, it will obviously be of great interest in the study of Chinese religion. It has been the subject of a lengthy monograph by the noted French Sinologist Edouard Chavannes, and it is from this work, *Le T'ai Chan: Essai de Monographie d'un Culte Chinois* (Paris, 1910; reprinted in Taipei, 1970), that we translate the following material. It is taken from the first chapter, called "The Cult of T'ai Shan", (pp. 3-43).

Mountains, in China, are divinities. They are considered to be natural forces that act in a conscious manner and who can, in consequence, be rendered favorable by sacrifices and touched by prayers. But these divinities are of diverse importance: Some are small, local genie whose authority is only exercised in a small territory; others are majestic sovereigns who hold immense regions in dependence. The most celebrated are five in number. . . . Among these five mountains, there is one yet more renowned than the others; this is T'ai Shan or the Peak of the East . . .

T'ai Shan, which raises its heavy silhouette just to the north of the prefectural capital of T'ai-an-fu, is not a very imposing mountain; its altitude is in fact only 1545 meters above sea level. It is, however, the highest mountain in eastern China, and thus is considered to govern all the surrounding heights and to preside over the East. . . .

Folklore also informs us that the mountains are the habitat of personages who are endowed with marvelous faculties; fairies and gnomes frolic there. In China, under the influence of Taoism, these genies of the mountains have been conceived to be men freed from all the fetters which hinder our existence and cut it short. These are the immortals, the blessed ones among whom one will be able to take nourishment from marvelous utensils of jade, and who give one ambrosia to drink, as it is said in the inscriptions of three Han [dynasty] mirrors.

But the mountain is not only the place where celestial deities and immortals appear; it is itself a divinity. (Beginning with the Chou and coming to Ming times — fourteenth century — T'ai Shan has been given official ranks and titles by various emperors.) The general attributes of a divine mountain are of two sorts: On the one hand, indeed, it presses by its bulk on all the surrounding territory and is the principle of its stability; it is the regulator which prevents the soil from moving and the rivers from overflowing; it prevents earthquakes and floods. On the other hand clouds accumulate around the summit which seems to produce them and which merits the Homeric epithet, "assembler of clouds"; the divine mountain has then under its orders the fecund clouds which shed fertility upon the world and cause it to bring forth harvests.

Numerous prayers of the Ming period show us that T'ai Shan is indeed invoked by virtue of these two attributes. In the spring, it is begged to favor the growth of the grain; in autumn, thanks are offered for the harvest which it has protected. It is asked to help men by its invisible and powerful action which distributes rain and clear weather in the right proportions and which permits the nutritious plants to attain their maturity. In case of drought, it is very natural that it should be addressed, for "to see to it that the rain comes to the worker at the right time is the secret task for which it has the responsibility". Thus, when the rains are awaited, the [budding] ears of grain stud the fields like stars, and the peasants begin to fear famine, the sovereign of men has recourse to the majestic Peak which can and should put an end to this misfortune. In the same way, in case of earthquake or flood, prayers appropriate to the circumstances recall to T'ai Shan its functions as ruler of the whole region and ask it to restore order.

In texts which are of interest for the history of Chinese religion, one will notice the relations which are supposed to exist between the emperor and the god of T'ai Shan. Whenever there is trouble in the world, the emperor begins by accusing himself of lack of virtue. It is, in fact, a leading idea in the religious psychology of the Chinese, that, on the one hand, physical calamities have as their first cause moral faults, and, on the other hand, the sovereign is responsible for the sins of all men, for, if he governed well, all the people would act properly. However, at the same time that he confessed his offenses, the emperor reminded the god of T'ai Shan that he also was not safe from reproach. If sacrifices are offered to him and if he is loaded with honors, it is because his protection is counted upon. By betraying the confidence that has been placed in him, he ceases to merit the regard that has been evinced for him.

No doubt, the god of T'ai Shan is not the cause of the misfortunes which have befallen the people; but, as he has as his duty to collaborate with Heaven for the prosperity of living beings, it is reprehensible when he does not promptly remedy the scourges that have been pointed out to him. "If it is by my faults that I have drawn down calamities," said an emperor to him in 1455, "assuredly I do not decline the personal responsibility; but, for the turning of misfortune to good fortune it is truly you, oh god, who has the duty to apply yourself to it. If a fault has been committed and you do not perform a commendable act, you will be as guilty as I. If, on the contrary, you transform misfortune into good fortune, who will be able to equal your merit?" The same emperor said in 1452, on the occasion of a flood of the Yellow River, "Whose is the responsibility? Assuredly, it is due to my lack of virtue; but you, oh god, how could you alone be exculpated? You should so act that, when the waters flow, this is beneficial, an advantage and not a torment to the people; then you and I will have acquitted ourselves of our respective duties; towards Heaven we will have no fault; towards the people we will have nothing to be ashamed of."

Thus, the emperor and the god of T'ai Shan appear to be like two high dignitaries, almost equal in rank, who have been designated by Heaven to assure the welfare of the people, the one by his sage government which establishes harmony and virtue among men, the other by his regulative influence which maintains good order in the physical world. Moreover, both are accountable for their acts to Heaven, which has invested them with their functions, and to the people, who look to them for their prosperity. By the constant cooperation of a moral power which is the Emperor with the powers of nature such as the god of T'ai Shan, droughts, earthquakes, and floods would be avoided and the people would be happy.

The god of T'ai Shan is also invoked in other cases where his intervention appears less easily explicable at first sight. We find, indeed, in the Ming era prayers, some announcements to this divinity of the imminent departure of the imperial armies for some remote military expedition. The sovereign first takes the precaution of declaring that he knows the gravity of all warlike enterprise. He enumerates the grievances which oblige him to have recourse to arms, despite his repugnance to using coercive means. Having thus justified his decision, he indicates that his troops will abandon their families to brave the perils and the fatigues of a long road; he supplicates the divinity to so act that the soldiers will be free from pestilential emanations which could decimate them, and asks him to permit all the men to return safe and sound to their hearths.

The question arises as to why T'ai Shan should be brought into the case on such occasions; how is it that this local god, who presides in the east, can act at a distance to safeguard the armies which are going to chastise rebels in Kwangsi or Tonkin? The answer is furnished by the clause which ends these prayers: "As I do not dare to address myself inconsiderately to the Emperor on high," we read in one of these pieces, "it is you, oh god, who are willing to take this request into consideration for transmittal to him on my behalf". In another, it is said: "I ardently hope that you, oh god, will transmit and forward to the Emperor on high (my request)". Or again: "I hope eagerly that you, oh god, will take into consideration my sincerity and that you will inform the Emperor on high of that." Thus, in all these cases, the god of T'ai Shan is not asked to perform acts which are beyond his jurisdiction; he simply plays the role of intermediary between the sovereign of men and the supreme divinity, the Emperor on high, who alone is qualified to preside over the general direction of the universe. As this supreme divinity is too distant and too majestic for one to dare to address him directly, one asks a subordinate divinity to intercede with him. T'ai Shan is moreover well chosen to fulfill this task since his height brings him near to heaven.

The religious attributes enumerated thus far are common to the god of T'ai Shan and to the other mountain divinities of China . . . But there are other attributes which pertain only to T'ai Shan; it is these that we shall now study.

T'ai Shan is the Peak of the East. It presides in this capacity over the East, that is to say, over the origin of all life. Like the sun, all existence commences in the East. The *yang* principle, which makes the sap rise in green plants, is concentrated in the Peak of the East from which emanate vivifying influences. In 1532, when an emperor prays to have a son, he addresses himself to T'ai Shan because this mountain is the inexhaustible source of births.

At the same time that T'ai Shan carries in its womb all future existences it is, as a logical consequence, the receptacle to which lives return when they have come to an end. As early as the first two centuries of our era it was a widespread belief in China that, when men die, their souls return to T'ai Shan. In the popular literature one finds a whole series of stories which inform us about a sort of Elysian Fields where the dead continue to speak and act as they did in life. There they intrigue for official position, and the recommendations of influential personages are very useful — it is another subterranean China which spreads out under the sacred mountain.

Since T'ai Shan creates lives and takes in the dead, it has therefore been concluded that it governs the longer or shorter duration of human existence. It joins in itself the attributes of the Three Fates, giving, sustaining, and terminating life. Thus one prays to it for the prolongation of one's days, as for example in the case of a certain Hsu Chun (circa A.D. 100) who, being gravely ill, turns to T'ai Shan to ask for life. A poet of the third century of our era writes with melancholy: "My life is declining; I have a rendezvous with the Eastern Peak."

Tradition localizes precisely the place where the souls of the dead are assembled at the foot of T'ai Shan: It is on a small hill, called Hao-li Shan, which is about two kilometers to the southeast of the town of T'ai-an-fu. In the immediate vicinity of this hill there was celebrated in bygone times the solemn sacrifice *shan*, addressed to the earth, and that is why the kingdom of the dead which is in the earth is located there. A temple has stood here for more than a thousand years. Today, it is more popular than ever. When one visits it, one is immediately struck by the innumerable funeral steles which form long rows as in a cemetery. These steles have been erected by families or by village communities to mark the spot where their dead ancestors have been reunited.

In the temple of Hao-li, which is comprised of several very magnificent buildings, one sees, just as in the principal temples consecrated elsewhere to the god of T'ai Shan, a series of seventy-five chambers arranged all along the walls of an interior court. These are so many tribunals in which the trials of the infernos are represented by means of mud statues. The cult of T'ai Shan seems to us here, then, to be associated with the rewards and above all with the punishments of the other world. This poses a problem in religious history: Until this point, indeed, the god of T'ai Shan has appeared to us to be a divinity of nature. In that he governed the rains and the stability of the soil, that he was the principle of life and death, he was only concerned with the natural phenomena which did not involve any moral element. This is moreover the reason for which his cult is a Taoist cult, for Taoism is principally a nature religion, to the contrary of Buddhism which is above all a moral religion. Throughout the whole extent of the Chinese empire, it is the Taoist priests who officiate in the sanctuaries of divinities symbolizing the forces of nature. If this is so, how is it that in the cult of T'ai Shan there enters the moral idea that souls are punished or rewarded in the other world according to their good or bad deeds?

It is perfectly certain that this idea is not inherent in the cult, and that it was introduced only by the T'ang period, the seventh or eighth century of our era. One can explain this intrusion as an influence of Buddhism on Taoism. In Buddhism the idea of retribution for deeds is early and essential. It is, one can say, the very basis of this religion which neglects nature entirely in favor of ethics. Now Buddhism, an ethical religion imported from India into China, was there implanted by the side of Taoism, a nature religion of purely Chinese origin. Coexisting thus, the two systems have over a long time reacted with each other. Taoism has then borrowed from Buddhism its ethical theory of punishments and rewards and has copied its infernos exactly from those of Buddhism. Having made this addition to its religious foundations, it has then sought for some cults to which to attach it. It has found two: One is that of the *Ch'eng-huang,* the god who presides over the wall of the town and who is the magistrate charged with judging the conduct of the citizens; the other is the cult of T'ai Shan by which this divinity presides over the souls of the dead. That is why one finds in China representations of the tortures of hell in two sorts of Taoist temples, the one being those of the god of the city (*Ch'eng-huang miao*), the others being those of T'ai Shan (*Tung-yüeh miao*). This also explains why, in these two sorts of temples, one often perceives, suspended above one of the doors or against a wall, an enormous abacus. The presence of this calculating machine signifies that the divinity of the place has for his mission to keep the accounts of human actions and to balance up the good and the evil.

We omit here the author's study of the imperial sacrifices called *feng* and *shan,* which were at several times in history—from 110 B.C. to A.D. 1008—held on T'ai Shan.

The cult of T'ai Shan, as we have studied it to this point, is the official cult; the documents of which we have availed ourselves in order to set forth its diverse aspects derived for the most part from the imperial administration. It remains to indicate what it has become in popular practice.

The cult of T'ai Shan is one of the most widely spread in China. In every town of any importance, one finds a temple of T'ai Shan which is called either the temple of the Eastern Peak (*tung-yüeh miao*), the temple of He who is equal with Heaven (*t'ien ch'i miao*), or finally, "traveling palace of T'ai Shan" (*T'ai Shan hsing kung*). In these buildings, a multitude of votive tablets eulogize the divinity in four-character [inscriptions]. Some recall his names:

The Peak, the ancestor, the *T'ai,* the *Tai.*

Others liken his influence or his height to those of Heaven:

> His saintly virtue equals Heaven.
> His height reaches to Heaven.
> The Peak of the mountain matches Heaven.

Others again recall that T'ai Shan is the principle of all existence, that he sustains life by his beneficent action, finally that he is the master of life and death:

> To all beings he gives life.
> His authority governs the mechanism of life.
> His bounty extends to living people.
> His bounty is lavished upon the multitude of the living.
> The depth of his grace is a second creation.
> He shows as on the palm of his hand life and death.

but the largest number of these tablets allude to the judicial functions of T'ai Shan who controls rewards and punishments in the world of the dead:

> He judges without partiality.
> All is reflected in the mirror of *T'ai*.
> Here it is hard to cheat.
> He terrifies those who are far, he affrights those who are near.
> His divine power rewards and punishes.
> He does good to the good, he does evil to the evil.
> He gives good fortune to the good, he sends calamity to the wicked.
> The wicked do not endure.
> When he glances down, it is frightening.
> It is difficult to escape his penetrating gaze.

Certainly it is this role as judge of hell that is now in the popular imagination the essential role of the god of T'ai Shan. The seventy-five courts of justice which, in the Temples of the Eastern Peak, display along the walls of the principal court the frightful torments reserved for wicked men after their death, are well calculated to strike sinners with religious terror. This is why multitudes flock to the temples where the clever monks promise them that with some money and much incense they will get into the good graces of the terrible arbiter of their destinies beyond the tomb.

However, an attentive observer will not be slow to realize that in certain temples of the Eastern Peak the god of T'ai Shan is not alone in drawing homage to himself. I recall that, when I was visiting the *Tung yüeh miao* in Peking, which is outside the most northerly of the two eastern gates, my attention was attracted by some women who were betaking themselves to the temple in a strange manner. Scarcely had they taken three steps than they prostrated themselves at full length on the dusty road in the midst of the hubbub of chairs, wheelbarrows, mules and donkeys which crowded the way. They stood up to take three more steps and then make the same prostration. Now, the destination of their painful route was *not* the principal hall in which the god of T'ai Shan was enthroned; they were headed towards other sanctuaries occupied by female divinities. We have now to investigate the goddesses who are the object of such ardent devotion.

The most important among them is one called *Pi hsia yuan chün*. The term *pi hsia* designates the colored clouds which herald the dawn. As for the term *yuan chün*, it is a title that the Taoists give to female divinities. It is thus that *Hsiu Wen-ying*, goddess of lightning, is called by them *Hsiu yuan chün*. *Pi hsia yuan chün* is then the princess of the colored clouds: She is the goddess of the dawn and is considered to be the daughter of T'ai Shan, god of the East. This cult is not very old. It seems to have begun with the discovery on the summit of T'ai Shan, in the year A.D. 1008, of a large stone statue. The emperor Chen-tsung immediately had a replica made in jade which was placed near the pool where the first statue had been found; the pool was after that known as "the pool of the jade woman." The idol soon attracted numerous worshipers; the sanctuary consecrated to her was continually enlarged and it has become today the most magnificent of the temples that cover the summit of T'ai Shan. It was above all during the Ming era that the cult of the goddess flourished. It became, in the north of China, the equivalent of the cult of Kuan-yin in the provinces of the south. They were not satisfied to assign her a subordinate place among the temples of the Eastern Peak, but they erected special buildings for her . . . In our day, one finds in the north of China a great number of temples devoted to the princess of the colored clouds; they are called *niang niang miao*, "Temple of the Lady," or *Pi hsia yuan chün hsing kung*, "Traveling palace of the princess of the colored clouds," or in abbreviated form, *Pi hsia kung*.

. . . Most often she is accompanied by two other goddesses: One holds in her hands an emblematic eye; she is the lady of good eyesight (*yen ching niang niang* or *yen kuang nai nai*) who prevents eye diseases. The other is the lady who gives babies (*sung tzu niang niang* or *sun tzu nai nai*). . . . In the various temples that I have visited, the statues of these two acolytes were covered with votive offerings, eyes made of cardboard and dolls of plaster, which attested to the fact that multitudes of women had received help from the good goddesses, healers of the bad eyes of infancy and guarantors of fertility.

But the three goddesses are not always alone and one finds them sometimes accompanied by six other ladies who are like fairies that protect motherhood. The first favors gestation; the second makes delivery easy for a woman; the third makes the child normal; the fourth prevents the fatal smallpox of infancy; the fifth opens the intelligence of the newlyborn; the sixth governs the mother's lactation. . . .

This group of *Pi hsia yuan chün* and her acolytes, which plays a great role in the religious life of the women of northern China is, in our day, the center of attraction of the cult localized on T'ai Shan. It is towards them that the crowds of worshipers press who, during the first four months of each year, hasten to the sacred mountain on pilgrimage. All religions are explicable by psychology and are but the crystalizations of human feelings. So it often happens that after man has produced a god in his own image, woman in her turn creates a divinity which better satisfies her aspirations. This is what has happened here, and by the side of T'ai Shan who is a god useful to men, the good goddesses have appeared because the women have desired them with all the ardent faith of their maternal hearts.

Pi hsia yuan chün and her cortege are not the only divinities who have been associated with T'ai Shan. If we visit the great temple *Tai miao* in the town of T'ai-an-fu we will note, beyond the edifice in which the god of T'ai Shan is enthroned and that where *Pi hsia yuan chün* is worshiped, a hall dedicated to the spouse of T'ai Shan. Another is dedicated to three brothers of whom the eldest is named *Mao Ying*, still another is dedicated to *Ping-ling*, who is the third son of T'ai Shan, yet another is dedicated to a little-known personage who bears the military title of *t'ai-wei*. And finally there are the seventy-five courts of justice each of which has its own president. All these divinities and some others besides are enumerated as forming the court of the god of T'ai Shan in a Taoist treatise entitled "The true book of the discourse pronounced by the venerable god *Yuan shih* on the subject of the Eastern Peak who delivers from evil and acquits from sins." . . .

T'ai Shan with its pantheon of gods and goddesses succors not only the thousands of pilgrims who each year come to visit the holy mountain. It is not even absolutely necessary, in order to assure the deity's good will, that one should go to one of the temples which has been raised to him in each town of northern China. One can obtain his aid in an efficacious and constant manner by having recourse to amulets which are impregnated with his supernatural energy. The traveler who journeys through northern China often has occasion to remark the stones which, encased in a wall, or set up at the entrance to an alley or opposite the gate of a house, show the inscription *T'ai Shan shih kan tang*. This phrase signifies that "the stone of T'ai Shan is able to cope," which is to say that it can oppose the evil spirits who try to work mischief in the home or to penetrate into the street. The stones which have this magical power are not always from T'ai Shan except metaphorically, for they are made, according to the locality, from the most diverse rocks. They prove, nevertheless, the power that is attributed to T'ai Shan in warding off demons. Another way of having constantly at one's disposal the protective force of T'ai Shan consists in tracing its image according to certain mysterious rules, which makes a sovereign charm against all evil. To tell the truth I have never come across the diagram of T'ai Shan by itself; but one often sees engraved in stone, modeled in bronze, or painted on porcelain the "Tableau of the true form of the five Peaks," which shows the conventional images of the five mountains among whose number T'ai Shan is found. By carrying this marvelous talisman on oneself one can brave the greatest perils without fear.

24.
puRGatORy

In many places in the essays which comprise this book the reader will come across the Chinese belief that the deceased must undergo a harrowing journey in the nether world to the courts of purgatory, there to suffer appropriate punishment for sins and crimes committed during the mortal span; then the soul will be reborn in a condition morally commensurate with the deeds of its former existence. The modern student of penology may be skeptical about the deterrent effect of punishments, but most religions have coupled the promise of paradise with the threat of hell, or used the principle of the carrot and the stick, in the belief that both are needed by weak and wayward man. In China the popular conceptions of purgatory resulted from the common understanding of karma and rebirth brought in by Buddhism,[1] in combination with certain notions of the folk religion and—most notably—with the assumption that trial and punishment in the nether world must be the counterpart of trial and punishment in the magistrate's yamen of the Chinese empire. The Ten Courts of Purgatory are pictured in books and tableaux (in many temples) in all the graphic detail of the worst imaginings of a prisoner condemned to face the harsh justice of the magistrate—but a justice whose punishments include tortures no mundane magistrate could dream of applying.

We give below some excerpts from a popular tract of a type which was widely circulated, the equivalent of the "hellfire and damnation" tract of the West. One notes that the first part is devoted to an earnest plea to the sinner to repent; while the second reveals what is in store for him if he does not. The translation of this text, the *Yü Li Ch'ao Chuan* (or what the translator renders as the *Divine Panorama*, in allusion to Dante), is the work of Herbert A. Giles, and is found as Appendix I to his book, *Strange Stories from a Chinese Studio*, Kelly & Walsh, Ltd. (Shanghai, Hongkong & Singapore, 1926, 4th rev. ed.), pp. 467-485.

---

[1] The cycle in Buddhism is birth-life-death-rebirth (for the possibilities in the latter see note to follow on the Six Paths). Devout believers will hope, however, to escape rebirth entirely by the mercy of Amitabha Buddha, who will take the soul to the Western Paradise. (L.G.T.)

THE DIVINE PANORAMA, PUBLISHED BY THE MERCY OF YÜ TI,[2] THAT MEN AND WOMEN MAY REPENT THEM OF THEIR FAULTS AND MAKE ATONEMENT FOR THEIR CRIMES.

On the birthday of the Saviour P'u-sa,[3] as the spirits of Purgatory were thronging round to offer their congratulations, the ruler of the Infernal Regions spake as follows: "My wish is to release all souls, and every moon as this day comes round I would wholly or partially remit the punishment of erring shades, and give them life once more in one of the Six Paths.[4] But alas! the wicked are many and the virtuous few. Nevertheless, the punishments in the dark region are too severe, and require some modification. Any wicked soul that repents and induces one or two others to do likewise shall be allowed to set this off against the punishments which should be inflicted." The Judges of the Ten Courts of Purgatory then agreed that all who led virtuous lives from their youth upwards shall be escorted at their death to the land of the Immortals; that all whose balance of good and evil is exact shall escape the bitterness of the [worst three of the Six Paths], and be born again among men; that those who have repaid their debts of gratitude and friendship, and fulfilled their destiny, yet have a balance of evil against them, shall pass through the various Courts of Purgatory and then be born again amongst men, rich, poor, old, young, diseased or crippled, to be put a second time upon trial. Then, if they behave well they may enter into some happy state; but if badly, they will be dragged by horrid devils through all the Courts, suffering bitterly as they go, and will again be born, to endure in life the uttermost of poverty and wretchedness, in death the everlasting tortures of hell. Those who are disloyal, unfilial, who commit suicide, take life, or disbelieve the doctrine of Cause and Effect (i.e. karma), saying to themselves that when a man dies there is an end of him, that when he has lost his skin he has already suffered the worst that can befall him, that living men can be tortured, but no one ever saw a man's ghost in the pillory, that after death all is unknown, etc., etc.,—truly these men do not know that the body alone perishes but the soul lives for ever and ever; and that whatsoever evil they do in this life, the same will be done unto them in the life to come. All who commit such crimes are handed over to the everlasting tortures of hell; for alas! in spite of the teachings of the Three Systems (i.e. Buddhism, Taoism, and Confucianism) some will persist in regarding these warnings as vain and empty talk. Lightly they speak of Divine mercy, and knowingly commit many crimes, not more than one in a hundred ever coming to repentance. Therefore the punishments of Purgatory were strictly carried out and the tortures dreadfully severe.

[2]The Jade Emperor, highest deity of the popular pantheon (L.G.T.)

[3]P'u-sa is the Chinese abbreviation for Bodhisattva; the "Saviour P'u-sa" here referred to would be Ti-tsang, Sinicized version of Ksitigarbha; his special concern is the salvation of suffering souls in Purgatory. (L.G.T.)

[4]That is, the six realms of sentient existence: in the worlds of the gods *(shen)*, humans, demons *(asuras)*, souls in purgatory, hungry ghosts, and animals. (L.G.T.)

But now it has been mercifully ordained that any man or woman, young, old, weak or strong, who may have sinned in any way, shall be permitted to obtain remission of the same by keeping his or her thoughts constantly fixed on P'u-sa and on the birthdays of the Judges of the Ten Courts, by fasting and prayer, and by vows never to sin again. Or for every good work done in life they shall be allowed to escape one ward in the Courts below. From this rule to be excepted disloyal ministers, unfilial sons, suicides, those who plot in secret against good people, those who are struck by thunder, those who perish by flood or fire, by wild animals or poisonous reptiles (the latter cases being obviously divine punishment for unforgivable sins) — these to pass through all the Courts and be punished according to their deserts. All other sinners to be allowed to claim their good works as a setoff against evil, thus partly escaping the agonies of hell and receiving some reward for their virtuous deeds. . . .

(When God—that is, the Jade Emperor—saw this proposal, he said:) "Good indeed! Good indeed! Henceforth let all spirits take note of any mortal who vows to lead a virtuous life and, repenting, promises to sin no more. Two punishments shall be remitted him. And if, in addition to this, he succeeds in doing five virtuous acts, then he shall escape all punishment and be born again in some happy state—if a woman she shall be born as a man. But more than five virtuous acts shall enable such a soul to obtain the salvation of others, and redeem wife and family from the tortures of hell. Let these regulations be published in the *Divine Panorama* and circulated on earth by the spirits of the City Guardians (i.e. the *ch'eng-huang,* or spiritual magistrates). In fear and trembling obey this decree and carry it reverently into effect."

The First Court

His Infernal Majesty Ch'in Kuang is specially in charge of the register of life and death both for old and young, and presides at the judgment seat in the lower regions. . . . Every man and woman dying in old age whose fate it is to be born again into the world, if their tale of good and evil works is equally balanced, is sent to the First Court, and thence transferred back to Life, male becoming female, female male, rich poor, and poor rich, according to their several deserts. But those whose good deeds are outnumbered by their bad are sent to a terrace on the right of the Court, called the Terrace of the Mirror of Sin, ten feet in height. The mirror is about fifty feet in circumference and hangs towards the east. Above is the inscription: "No good person comes before the terrace of the mirror of sins." There the wicked souls are able to see the naughtiness of their own hearts while they were among the living, and the danger of death and hell. Then do they realize the proverb,

> Ten thousand taels of yellow gold cannot be brought away;
> But every crime will tell its tale upon the judgment day.

When the souls have been to the Terrace and seen their wickednesses, they are forwarded into the Second Court, where they are tortured and dismissed to the proper hell.

[Those who commit suicide out of any other reason than loyalty, filiality, chastity, or friendship] shall be escorted to this Court by the Spirits of the Threshold and of the Hearth. They shall be placed in the Hunger and Thirst Section, and every day from seven till eleven o'clock they will resume their mortal coil, and suffer again the pain and bitterness of death. After seventy days, or one or two years, as the case may be, they will be conducted back to the scene of their suicide, but will not be permitted to taste the funeral meats, or avail themselves of the usual offerings to the dead. Bitterly will they repent, unable as they will be to render themselves visible and frighten people, vainly striving to procure a substitute. . . . Any soul which after suicide shall not remain invisible, but shall frighten people to death, will be seized by black-faced, long-tusked devils and tortured in the various hells, to be finally thrust into the great Gehenna, forever to remain hung up in chains, and not permitted to be born again.

Every Buddhist or Taoist priest who receives money for prayers and liturgies, but skips over words and misses out sentences, on arriving at this, the First Court, will be sent to the section for the completion of Prayer, and there in a small dark room he shall pick out such passages as he has omitted, and make good the deficiency as best he can . . .

O ye dwellers upon earth, on the first day of the second moon, fasting turn to the north and make oath to abstain from evil and fix your thoughts on good, that ye may escape hell! The precepts of Buddha are circulated over the whole world to warn mankind to believe and repent, that when the last hour comes their spirits may be escorted by dark-robed boys to realms of bliss and happiness in the west.

The Second Court

His Infernal Majesty Ch'u Chiang reigns at the bottom of the great Ocean. . . . he has a vast hell, many leagues in extent, and subdivided into sixteen wards, as follows:

In the first, nothing but black clouds and constant sandstorms. In the second, mud and filth. In the third, *chevaux de frise*.[5] In the fourth, gnawing hunger. In the fifth, burning thirst. In the sixth, blood and pus. In the seventh, the shades are plunged into a brazen cauldron of boiling water. In the eighth, the same punishment is repeated many times. In the ninth, they are put into iron clothes. In the tenth, they are stretched on a rack to regulation length. In the eleventh, they are pecked by fowls. In the twelfth, they have only rivers of lime to drink. In the thirteenth, they are hacked to pieces. In the fourteenth, the leaves of the trees are as sharp as swordpoints. In the fifteenth, they are pursued by foxes and wolves. In the sixteenth, all is ice and snow.

[Candidates for these wards include] those who lead astray young boys and girls, and then escape punishment by entering the priesthood; those who filch letter, pictures, books, etc., entrusted to their care; those who injure a fellow creature's ear, eye, hand, foot, fingers, or toes; those who practice as doctors without any knowledge of the medical art; those who will not ransom

---

[5]Posts covered with spikes. (L.G.T.)

grownup slave-girls (which must be done that they may be married); those who, contracting marriage for the sake of gain, falsely state their ages; or those who in cases of betrothal, before actual marriage, find out that one of the contracting parties is a bad character, and yet do not come forward to say so, but inflict an irreparable wrong on the innocent one . . .

O ye men and women of the world, take this book and warn all sinners, or copy it out and circulate it for general information! If you see people sick and ill, give medicine to heal them. If you see people poor and hungry, feed them. If you see people in difficulties, give money to save them. Repent your past errors, and you will be allowed to cancel that evil by future good, so that when the hour arrives you will pass at once into the Tenth Court, and thence return again to existence on earth . . .

The Third Court

His Infernal Majesty Sung Ti reigns at the bottom of the great Ocean . . . This Hall is many leagues wide, and is subdivided into sixteen wards, as follows:

In the first everything is Salt; above below, and all round, the eye rests upon Salt alone. The shades feed upon it, and suffer horrid torments in consequence. When the fit has passed away they return to it once again, and suffer agonies more unutterable than before. In the second, the erring shades are bound with cords and carry heavily weighted *cangues*.[6] In the third, they are perpetually pierced through the ribs. In the fourth, their faces are scraped with iron and copper knives. In the fifth, their fat is scraped away from their bodies. In the sixth, their hearts and livers are squeezed with pincers. In the seventh, their eyes are gouged. In the eighth, they are flayed. . . .

Those who enjoy the light of day without reflecting on the Imperial bounty; officers of State who revel in large emoluments without reciprocating their sovereign's goodness; private individuals who do not repay the debt of water and earth (i.e. do their duty); wives and concubines who slight their marital lords; those who fail in their duties as acting sons, or such as reap what advantages there are and then go off to their own homes; slaves who disregard their masters; official underlings who are ungrateful to their superiors . . . all these, even though they have a setoff of good deeds, must pass through the misery of every ward. Those who interfere with another man's Fêng-Shui;[7] those who obstruct funeral obsequies or the completion of graves . . . those who incite others to commit crimes; those who promote litigation . . . those who forge deeds and other documents . . . those who injure posterity in any way—all these, and similar offenders, shall be punished according to the gravity of each offense. . . .

The Fourth Court

The Lord of the Five Senses reigns at the bottom of the great Ocean . . . His Court is many leagues wide, and is subdivided into sixteen wards, as follows:

[6]Wooden collars. (L.G.T.)

[7]Disturb the good-luck producing features of topography of his ancestors' graves or his home. (L.G.T.)

In the first, the wicked shades are hung up and water is continually poured over them. In the second, they are made to kneel on chains and pieces of split bamboo. In the third, their hands are scalded with boiling water. In the fourth, their hands swell and stream with perspiration. In the fifth, their muscles are cut and their bones pulled out. . . .

Those who cheat the customs and evade taxes; those who repudiate their rent, use weighted scales, sell sham medicines, water their rice[8] . . . those who do not make way for the cripples, old and young; those who . . . steal bricks from walls as they pass by, or oil and candles from lamps; poor people who do not behave properly and rich people who are not compassionate to the poor; . . . those who know good prescriptions but keep them secret . . . those who try to bewitch their enemies, and those who try to frighten people in any way, all these shall be punished according to the gravity of their offenses . . .

The Fifth Court

His Infernal Majesty Yen Lo (i.e. Yama) said, "Our proper place is in the First Court; but, pitying those who die by foul means, and should be sent back to earth to have their wrongs redressed, we have moved our judgment seat to the great hell at the bottom of the Ocean . . . and have subdivided this hell into sixteen wards for the torment of souls. All those shades who come before us have already suffered long tortures in the previous four Courts, whence, if they are hardened sinners, they are passed on after seven days to this Court, where, if again found to be utterly hardened, corruption will overtake them by the fifth or seventh day. All shades cry out either that they have left some vow unfulfilled, or that they wish to build a temple or a bridge, make a road, clean out a river or well, publish some book teaching people to be virtuous, that they have not released their due number of lives, that they have filial duties or funeral obsequies to perform, some act of kindness to repay, etc., etc. For these reasons they pray to be allowed to return once more to the light of day, and are always ready to make oath that henceforth they will lead most exemplary lives . . . But now ye have come to my Court, having beheld your own wickedness in the mirror of sin. No more—bull-headed, horse-faced devils, away with them to the Terrace that they may once more gaze upon their lost homes!"

This Terrace is curved in front like a bow; it looks east, west, and south. It is eighty-one *li* (Chinese miles) from one extreme to the other. . . . No good shade comes to this Terrace; neither do those whose balance of good and evil is exact. Wicked souls alone behold their homes close by and can see and hear what is going on. They hear old and young talking together; they see their last wishes disregarded and their instructions disobeyed. Everything seems to have undergone a change. The property they scraped together with so much trouble is dissipated and gone. The husband thinks of taking another wife; the widow meditates second nuptials. Strangers are in possession of the old estate; there is nothing to divide among the children. Debts long since paid are brought again for settlement . . . He sees his children become corrupt, and his friends fall away . . . All souls, after the misery of the Terrace,

[8]To make the grain heavier when weighing it for sale. (L.G.T.)

will be thrust into the great Gehenna, and when the amount of wickedness of each has been ascertained, they will be passed through the sixteen wards for the punishment of evil hearts.

[The usual variety of sins are enumerated which will subject the guilty shades to the unpleasantries of sixteen wards—such sins as disbelief in karma, injuring religion, leading immoral lives, bullying and sycophancy, etc.] Those who in life have not been guilty of the above sins, or, having sinned, fasted on the eighth day of the first moon, and registered a vow to sin no more, shall not only escape the punishments of this Court, but shall also gain some further remission of torture in the Sixth Court. Those, however, who are guilty of taking life, of gross immorality, of stealing and implicating the innocent, of ingratitude and revenge, of infatuated vice which no warnings can turn from its course—these shall not escape one jot of their punishments (the details of which we have omitted).

The Sixth Court

In the first (of the sixteen wards), the souls are made to kneel for long periods on iron shot. In the second, they are placed up to their necks in filth. In the third, they are pounded till the blood runs out. In the fourth, their mouths are opened with iron pincers and filled full of needles . . .

[Subject to such punishments are such sinners as] rail against Heaven and Earth . . . who steal the gold from the inside or scrape the gilding from the outside of images; those who take holy names in vain, who show no respect for written paper, who throw down dirt and rubbish near pagodas or temples . . . who obliterate or tear books which teach man to be good, who carve on common articles of household use the symbol of the origin of all things (the yin-yang symbol), the Sun and Moon and Seven Stars, the Royal Mother and the God of Longevity on the same article (thus improperly associating male and female), or representations of any of the Immortals; those who embroider the Svastika (Buddhist symbol) on fancy work . . .

The Seventh Court

His Infernal Majesty T'ai Shan reigns at the bottom of the great Ocean . . . His is a vast, noisy Court, measuring many leagues in circumference and subdivided into sixteen wards . . .

[The most interesting sin in the catalogue for this Court is that of "eating red lead and certain other nauseous articles":] All things may not be used as drugs. It is bad enough to slay birds, beasts, reptiles, and fishes, in order to prepare medicine for the sick; but to use red lead and many of the filthy messes in vogue is beyond all bound of decency, and those who foul their mouths with these nasty mixtures, no matter how virtuous they may otherwise be, will not only derive no benefit from saying their prayers, but will be punished for so doing without mercy . . . Ye who hear these words, make haste to repent . . . every morning when you wash your teeth mutter a prayer to Buddha . . .[9]

[9] Thus strongly is the Buddhist character—albeit a folk-Buddhist one—of the Purgatory emphasized; the sin mentioned is precisely the raison d'être of religious Taoism: attainment of immortality through the elixir (alchemy) which contains red lead. (L.G.T.)

The Eighth Court

His Infernal Majesty Tu Shih reigns at the bottom of the great Ocean . . . in a vast, noisy Court many leagues in extent, subdivided into sixteen wards . . .

In the first, the wicked souls are rolled down mountains in carts. In the second, they are shut up in huge saucepans. In the third, they are minced. In the fourth, their noses, eyes, mouths, etc., are stopped up. In the fifth, their uvulas are cut off . . . In the eighth, their viscera are fried . . . In the thirteenth, their chests are torn open . . . In the fourteenth, their skulls are split and their teeth dragged out . . .

[Those punished here include the unfilial and those who indulge in magic and sorcery.] But those who believe in the *Divine Panorama*, and on the first of the fourth moon make a vow of repentance, repeating the same every night and morning to the Spirit of the Hearth, shall, by virtue of one of three characters, *obedient, acquiescent,* or *repentant,* to be traced on their foreheads at death by the Spirit of the Hearth, escape half the punishments from the First to the Seventh Court, inclusive, and escape this Eighth Court altogether . . . To this God added, "Whosoever may circulate the *Divine Panorama* for the information of the world at large shall escape all punishment from the First to the Eighth Court, inclusive. Passing through the Ninth and Tenth Courts, they shall be born again amongst men in some happy state."

The Ninth Court

His Infernal Majesty P'ing Têng reigns at the bottom of the great Ocean . . . His is the vast circular hell of A-pi, many leagues in breadth, jealously enclosed by an iron net, and subdivided into sixteen wards . . .

In the first, the wicked souls have their bones beaten and their bodies scorched . . . In the third, ducks eat their heart and liver. In the fourth, dogs eat their intestines and lungs. In the fifth, they are splashed with hot oil . . . In the seventh, their brains are taken out and their skulls filled with hedgehogs . . .

All who on earth have committed one of the ten great crimes, and have deserved either the lingering death, decapitation, strangulation, or other punishment shall . . . be brought to this Court, together with those guilty of arson, of making *ku* poison,[10] bad books, stupefying drugs, and many other disgraceful acts. . . .

O ye who have committed such crimes as these, on the eighth of fourth moon, or the first or fifteenth (of any moon), fasting swear that you will buy up all bad books and magical pamphlets and utterly destroy them with fire; or that you will circulate copies of the *Divine Panorama* . . . Then, when your last moment is at hand, the Spirit of the Hearth will write on your forehead *He obeyed* . . .

---

[10]Translator's note says that this is concocted by throwing all sorts of insects into a container and letting them stay without looking at them for a year. "The insects will have killed and eaten each other, until there is only one survivor, and this one is *Ku*."

The Tenth Court

His Infernal Majesty Chuan Lun (i.e. He who "turns the Wheel of Life") reigns in the Dark Land . . . There he has six bridges, of gold, silver, jade, stone, wood, and planks, over which all souls must pass. He examines the shades that are sent from the other courts, and, according to their deserts, sends them back to earth as men, women, old, young, high, low, rich, or poor, forwarding monthly a list of their names to the judge of the First Court for transmission to Feng-tu (capital of the Infernal Regions).

. . . Those scholars who study the Book of Changes, or priests who chant their liturgies, cannot be tortured in the Ten Courts for the sins they have committed. When they come to this Court their names and features are taken down in a book kept for the purpose, and they are forwarded to Mother Meng, who drives them on to the Terrace of Oblivion and doses them with the draught of forgetfulness. Then they are born again in the world for a day, a week, or it may be a year, when they die once more; and now, having forgotten the holy words of the Three Religions, they are carried off by devils to the various Courts, and are properly punished for their former crimes.

All souls whose balance of good and evil is exact, whose period of punishment is completed, or whose crimes are many and good deeds few, as soon as their future state has been decided—man, woman, beautiful, ugly, comfort, toil, wealth, or poverty, as the case may be—must pass through the Terrace of Oblivion. . . .

The place where the Wheel of Fate goes round is many leagues in extent, enclosed on all sides by an iron palisade. Within are eighty-one subdivisions, each of which has its proper officers and magisterial appointments. Beyond the palisade there is a labyrinth of 108,000 paths leading by direct and circuitous routes back to earth. Inside it is as dark as pitch, and through it pass the spirits of priest and layman alike. But to one who looks from the outside everything is seen as clear as crystal, and the attendants who guard the place all have the faces and features they had at their birth. These attendants are chosen from virtuous people who in life were noted for filial piety, friendship, or respect for life, and are sent here to look after the working of the Wheel and such duties. . . .

Birds, beasts, fishes, and insects may after many myriads of *kalpas* again resume their original shapes; and if there are any that during three existences do not destroy life, they may be born amongst human beings as a reward . . .

Mother Mêng was born in the Earlier Han Dynasty. In her childhood she studied books of the Confucian school; when she grew up she chanted the liturgies of Buddha. Of the past and the future she had no care, but occupied herself in exhorting mankind to desist from taking life and become vegetarians. At eight-one years of age her hair was white and her complexion like a child's. She lived and died a virgin, calling herself simply Mêng; but men called her Mother Mêng. She retired to the hills and lived as a *religieuse* until the Later Han. Then . . . God commissioned Mother Mêng to build the Terrace of Oblivion, and appointed her as guardian, with devils to wait upon her and execute her commands.

It was arranged that all shades who had been sentenced in the Ten Courts to return in various conditions to earth should first be dosed by her with a decoction of herbs, sweet, bitter, acrid, sour, or salt. Thus they forget everything that has previously happened to them, and carry away with them to earth some slight weaknesses . . .

The Terrace is situated in front of the Ten Courts, outside the six bridges. It is square, measuring ten (Chinese) feet every way, and surrounded by 108 small rooms. To the east there is a raised path, one foot four inches in breadth, and in the rooms above mentioned are prepared cups of forgetfulness ready for the arrival of the shades. Whether they swallow much or little it matters not; but sometimes there are perverse devils who altogether refuse to drink. Then beneath their feet sharp blades start up, and a copper tube is forced down their throats, by which means they are compelled to swallow some. When they have drunk, they are raised by the attendants and escorted back by the same path. They are next pushed on to the Bitter Bamboo floating bridge, with torrents of rushing red water on either side. Halfway across they perceive written in large characters on a red cliff on the opposite side the following lines:

To be a man is easy, but to act up to one's responsibilities as such is hard.
Yet to be a man once again is perhaps harder still.

For those who would be born again in some happy state there is no great difficulty;
It is only necessary to keep mouth and heart in harmony.

When the shades have read these words they try to jump on shore, but are beaten back into the water by two huge devils. One has on a black official hat and embroidered clothes; in his hand he holds a paper pencil, and over his shoulder he carries a sharp sword. Instruments of torture hang at his waist, fiercely he glares out of his large round eyes and laughs a horrid laugh. His name is *Short Life.* The other has a dirty face smeared with blood; he has on a white coat, an abacus in his hand and a rice sack over his shoulder. Round his neck hangs a string of paper money; his brow contracts hideously, and he utters long sighs. His name is *They have their reward,* and his duty is to push the shades into the red water. The wicked and foolish rejoice at the prospect of being born once more as human beings; but the better shades weep and mourn that in life they did not lay up a store of virtuous acts, and thus pass away from the state of mortals for ever. Yet they all rush on to birth like an infatuated or drunken crowd; and again, in their early childhood, hanker after the forbidden flavours. Then, regardless of consequences, they begin to destroy life, and thus forfeit all claims to the mercy and compassion of God. They take no thought as to the end that must overtake them; and finally, they bring themselves once more to the same horrid plight.

25.
the cult of matsu

Of the numerous deities which have throughout history been prominent in Chinese religion, few have been thoroughly studied by modern
scholars. Yet the nature of the religious beliefs and practices of the folk
and the communities can only be understood if these cults are analyzed.
In the following essay we present information about one cult, which is particularly useful for our purposes for several reasons: First, it was officially
sanctioned by the imperial government, and hence may illustrate one
aspect of the State religion; second, it was an immensely popular cult, and
not merely kept up by official support; third, it was primarily concerned
with protection of seafarers, and thus its deity may serve as an example of
an occupational or "professional" tutelary god; fourth, it demonstrates
how people become gods in China; and fifth, it continues to be a vital part
of present day religion over a wide area of China.

Matsu or Matsu-p'o is a Fukienese localism, an affectionate family term
something like "Granny." The goddess thus familiarly called by the people is
formally known as the Holy Mother in Heaven (t'ien-shang sheng-mu), and
holds the high titles of Imperial Concubine of Heaven (t'ien-fei) or Imperial
Consort of Heaven (t'ien-hou). A deity prominent for centuries particularly in
the southern coastal provinces, Matsu is in Taiwan today second in popularity among Taiwanese only to Kuan-yin. The religious census of 1960 states
that she is the chief deity of 383 temples throughout the island province.[1]
    While above all the protectress of those who must venture upon the wa-
ters, her spiritual power was more generalized to include broader protective
and merciful functions. She is not only the patroness of sailors, but long ago
became a universally worshiped deity who was included in the official cults
as early as the reign of the Mongol Emperor Kublai Khan (during the 1280s).
    It is in Taiwan today that we are able to get our clearest look at this cult,
so we shall advert especially to that case. First we may mention briefly examples of her prominence elsewhere. In a book published in 1865, the missionary Justus Doolittle remarked that the image of this deity would always be
found as patron in the local guildhalls of out-of-town businessmen visiting
Foochow.[2] According to John Shryock, the only provincial and trade guide-
hall mentioned in the Local History of Huai-ning, an important city of Anhui
province, is that of Fukien, which is entered as the T'ien-hou Temple.[3] C. K.

[1]L. G. Thompson, "Notes on Religious Trends in Taiwan," Monumenta Serica,
XXIII, 1964.
[2]Justus Doolittle, Social Life of the Chinese, N.Y., 1865, I, p.262.
[3]J. K. Shryock, The Temples of Anking and Their Cults, Paris, 1931, p.26.

Yang mentions "the large variety of accounts [about Matsu] given in inscriptions of temple steles found in local gazetteers . . ." and states that "there were temples dedicated to this goddess in all coastal provinces as well as in localities along major navigable rivers." Yang explains that "the high percentage of official cults among temples of craft and trade deities is due to the official status of the large number of temples along the southern coast dedicated to T'ien-hou . . ."[4] Col. Valentine R. Burkhardt, in his fascinating volumes of personal observations concerning the beliefs and practices of the Hong Kong Chinese, has much to say about the cult of the Queen of Heaven. For example, among "the Boat People, the birthday of the Queen of Heaven . . . is the most important of their religious festivals." He states that "the temples to the Queen of Heaven are by far the most numerous in the Colony . . . So great is her popularity that twenty-four temples in the Colony are dedicated to her."[5]

Her close resemblance to the popularized Buddhist deity Kuan-yin has been noted by many writers, and Reginald Johnston, in his description of P'u-t'o-shan, the island center of Kuan-yin's cult, has pointed out that shrines to Matsu are found there as well.[6]

Matsu is popular in geographical designations. There is a small group of islands off the Fukien coast bearing the name. The capital town of the P'eng-hu islands (Pescadores) was called Ma-kung, or Matsu's Temple. An old temple to Matsu is one of the sights of Macau, and it seems that the very name of Macau was derived by the Portuguese from this temple.[7] There is a temple to Matsu even in San Francisco's Chinatown. It is especially interesting to note that in the initiation ceremonies of the Triad Society (T'ien-ti Hui, or Hung League), most prominent of the secret societies in modern and recent times, Matsu appears several times. There is for instance the description of the "ferryboat for the valiant Hungs," where she stands on the stern of the vessel and Kuan-yin stands in the hold. In fact, according to Ward and Stirling, an earlier name of this secret society was "The Family of the Queen of Heaven."[8]

Turning now to Taiwan and a few examples of the substance of the cult, we find the first historical evidence only with the late arrival of Chinese rule over the island—the conquest of the Dutch by Cheng Ch'eng-kung (known in Western writings as Koxinga) in 1662. Cheng believed his victory was aided by the supernatural intervention of Matsu, and so he had her temple at Luerh-men (the port for the capital town of Taiwan, now Tainan City) renovated and supplied with a new image and other furnishings.[9]

[4]C. K. Yang, *Religion in Chinese Society*, Univ. Calif., 1961, pp.72f; 147.

[5]V. R. Burkhardt, *Chinese Creeds and Customs*, Hong Kong, 3 vols.: Vol.I (1953), p.13; Vol.III (1958), pp.110 and 154.

[6]R. F. Johnston, *Buddhist China*, London, 1913, p.268.

[7]See, for example, Ping-ti Ho, *The Ladder of Success in Imperial China*, Columbia Univ., 1962, p. 196; Søren Egerod, "A note on the origin of the name of Macao," *T'oung Pao*, 47 (1959), pp.63-66.

[8]J. S. M. Ward & W. G. Stirling. *The Hung Society or the Society of Heaven and Earth*, London, 1925, Vol.I, pp.79ff; Gustave Schlegel, *Thian Ti Hwui. The Hung League or Heaven-Earth League*, Batavia, 1866, pp.70; 108f; 131.

[9]See especially Lin Heng-tao, "Lu-erh-men t'ien-hou-kung chen-wei lun-chan chih chieh-chüeh" (the upshot of the dispute over the genuineness of the T'ien-hou Temple at Lu-erh-men), in *Taiwan Feng-wu*, XI, 5 (May 1961), 3-5.

Cheng Ch'eng-kung was a loyalist in the cause of the Ming dynasty, which was toppled by the Manchu invaders who founded the last dynasty called Ch'ing. He took Taiwan because the Manchu forces had made the mainland untenable and he needed a base. Twenty-one years later the Ch'ing government was ready to attack Taiwan, and now Matsu showed her impartiality: Several stories of her aid to the Ch'ing forces have been preserved in written sources. She was observed bearing a banner and urging on the Ch'ing warriors during the battle for P'eng-hu. Credit for the victory was due to the inspiration this sight gave to the hard-pressed attackers. Again, when the victors landed in the almost waterless Pescadores, Matsu caused a small well to produce enough water for all of them. These miracles were not totally unexpected, however, as the Ch'ing admiral had before the invasion dispatched several officials from the Board of Rites to burn incense, make offerings, and pray for aid before the image of Matsu in her home temple on the island of Meichou; following which, the admiral himself had made a pilgrimage to her shrine. It may be that the goddess was finally persuaded of his sincerity and the justness of his cause when, upon seeing that the living quarters of the attendant monks were not in good repair, he generously donated 200 taels of gold to rectify this situation.[10] It was in gratitude for Matsu's help in the Ch'ing victory that she was by Imperial decree raised in rank from Imperial Concubine to Imperial Consort of Heaven.

More typical perhaps of incidents in which Matsu protects mariners is the story of the return of a ship bearing the captured Taiwanese rebel Lin Shuang-wen to Amoy in 1787. When the vessel arrived at Ta-tan Men, a tiny island in midstream of the entranceway to the great bay, it was already dusk. The skipper wanted to anchor and wait for daylight to go on in, but having spent four days at sea the official in charge was impatient to reach Amoy, which could already be seen in the distance. He gave the order to proceed. A gale had started to blow, the junk began to list, and soon it was so dark they could not see where they were going. The crew were in a panic. Two anchors were dropped, but they would not hold. When all seemed lost they suddenly saw a gleaming light ahead, and the cry went up, "Matsu has come!" The light moved as if someone were guiding them through the rocks in a small boat, and indeed, by following its guidance, they finally entered the harbor safely. This was all the more extraordinary in that for a vessel to enter Ta-tan Men in the dark was unheard of, because of the menace of rocks.[11]

It is said that there are three temples in Taiwan today where Matsu's spiritual power is generally recognized as most potent: One is in P'eng-hu, one at a town called Pei-kang, and one at a place called Kuan-tu near the hot springs resort of Pei-t'ou, outside of Taipei. The tale of the founding of the Kuan-tu Temple may serve as an example of the continuing credibility of Matsu's powers.[12]

---

[10]Story as in *T'ien-fei Hsien-sheng Lu (A Record of Miracles of the Holy Mother in Heaven)* (TWTK No.77), Taipei, 1960, pp. 44f.

[11]Story as in *ibid.*, pp.71f.

[12]Story as in Hsieh Chin-hsuan, "Shen-mi ti Kuan-tu Ma-tsu" (The mysterious Matsu of Kuan-tu), *Taiwan Feng-wu*, IV, 3 (Feb.1954), pp.15f.

According to this story, the image of Matsu at the Kuan-tu Temple was once the protective icon aboard a large junk. The vessel was caught in a typhoon and sunk in the Taiwan Strait, and the image floated into the bay at the mouth of the Tan-shui River. The people of the villages in the vicinity pulled it out of the water and set it up in a certain temple. After several days had passed, Matsu appeared in a dream to one of the local men and asked him to see to the construction of her temple. She told him she had already selected the site, and instructed him that wood from a certain hill was to be used for the building.

The next day the image was gone from the temple where it had been deposited, and it was found at the place in Kuan-tu where the temple now stands only after four days of searching by the villagers. This naturally convinced the people that Matsu had indeed chosen her own place of residence, and they subscribed funds for construction of the temple. The man who had had the dream went to the hill as directed and asked the landowner for the lumber. To his surprise the landowner replied that he was a man of his word, and fully intended to honor the contract which had already been made the day before with a mysterious young woman. Upon being informed that this was obviously the goddess herself, the landowner immediately donated all the necessary lumber.

It was estimated that three days would be required for workmen to cut down the trees. To their amazement, however, that very evening a storm uprooted the trees and even chopped them into boards, then hurled them down the hill to the site of the temple. The news of Matsu's miracles spread far and wide, and in a short while several thousand believers had assembled at the spot to participate in the work of construction. This of course made the work go faster, but created a shortage of food. However, this crisis was overcome when the resident monks discovered behind the rising building a small cave, from which cooked rice was flowing. The amount produced was exactly enough for the workers. Needless to say this made it easy for the temple to be completed in record time.

The story is completed with the addition of a parable involving the well-known mythical theme of the inexhaustible food supply. One greedy fellow tried to get more out of the miraculous rice-producing hole so that he could sell it for a profit. In the dead of night he stole out to the spot and began digging to enlarge the opening. The result of course was that the flow of rice ceased entirely, which everyone realized was Matsu's punishment for his greed.

These stories illustrate the beliefs of the cult, and we may next turn to the question of its historical origin and evolution. This question does not much concern her devotees, whose faith is securely anchored in reports of such miracles. They may commonly have heard a biography of the goddess that goes something like this:

She was born in the small island of Mei-chou, which is off the coast of Fukien province. She was the sixth daughter of a petty official named Lin. She was born at the beginning of the Sung dynasty (about A.D. 960). She was of course a remarkably intelligent, pious, and studious girl, devoted to religious practices. One day, seated at her loom, she fell into a trance in which she saw three ships carrying her father and two elder brothers. The ships were storm-tossed and about to founder. She took her father's ship into her mouth, and seized her brothers' ships with either hand, dragging them toward the safety of the shore. Unfortunately her mother called to her just at the critical moment, and as she roused and answered her, the ship with her father aboard fell from her mouth, and he was lost. This turned out to be not just a nightmare, but an actual miracle, when her brothers returned in a few days to tell of their narrow escape and the sad fate of their father. The girl refused to marry (very remarkable behavior in the Chinese society). She spent her short life in continuing service to her mother (the most commendable behavior) and in perfecting her religious powers. At the age of twenty-eight she was transformed into a spiritual being. After that time she was seen very often by those in danger on the sea, and became famous as their savior.[13]

The journal of a well-educated merchant who paid a visit to Taiwan at the end of the 17th century attests that belief in the goddess was not confined to the simple folk, but was generally accepted:

> Matsu is the most puissant of the deities of the seas . . . Whenever a junk is in danger, if they pray to her she will answer their prayers. Often her spirit soldiers will be seen guarding them, or the goddess herself will come to save them. Her miracles are too numerous to recount. In the middle of the ocean, when wind and rain obscure [everything], when the night is black as ink, at the tip of the mast there appears the light of the goddess, manifesting her divine help. Or in the vessel there will suddenly shine forth a glowing fire like the gleam of a lamp, which will rise up the mast and then be extinguished. The mariners say this is the fire of Matsu, and if it leaves, [the ship] will inevitably meet with disaster—a prophecy which is always strangely fulfilled. In the vessel they store a "Matsu staff," and whenever a great fish or sea monster tries to come near the ship they fend it off with the Matsu staff. . . .

After giving a sketch of the traditional biography, and some particulars about later miracles, the author continues:

> Up to the present time when the women of the Lin clan in Meichou are going out to their fields, they simply place their children in the temple saying, "Auntie, watch them carefully!" They are commonly gone all day, but the children don't cry or get hungry, nor do they go beyond the threshold of the temple. When the women return in the evening each finds her own children and takes them home.[14]

It seems that the goddess loves the children of her clansmen.

Careful scholarly examination of the Matsu legend in its several variants had not been undertaken until as recently as the 1950s, when a Taiwanese named Li Hsien-chang began publishing his findings in several Japanese journals. From a meticulous examination of the extant historical sources, Mr. Li has shown clearly how the legend built up through gradual accretions, as later writers added details to the materials they found in earlier documents.

[13]See, for example, Chuang Te, "Ma-tsu shih-shih yü T'ai-wan ti hsin-feng" (The history of Matsu and the religious beliefs in Taiwan), *Taiwan Feng-wu*, VIII, 2 (June 1957), pp.5-16. J. J. M. de Groot already gave the common version in *Les Fêtes Annuellement Célébrées à Émoui (Amoy)*, Paris, 1886, Vol.I, pp.260-267.

[14]Yü Yung-ho, "Hai-shang chi-lüeh" (Brief account of [journeying] on the sea), in his *P'i-hai Chi Yu (Small Sea Travel Journal)*, TWTK No. 44, Taipei, 1959, pp. 59f.

If the film is run in reverse, so to speak, we come to the earliest stage, and the four simple facts—or apparent facts—which are all that the Sung sources can tell us: (1) that Matsu was from Mei-chou; (2) that she was a daughter in the Lin family; (3) that she was versed in fortune-telling; (4) that after she died she was worshiped. The rest of the story, so much more interesting and detailed as we come to Yuan and Ming and Ch'ing writings, is, so far as can be discovered from documentary evidence, entirely an embroidering of these four facts.[15] Of course there must be adequate reasons why the cult should have arisen in the first place, but these reasons must remain conjectural in view of the lack of any further historically attested facts.[16]

A note may be added concerning the attendants of the goddess. In her temples one will find two subordinate figures (aside from any other notable deities who may have been invited to share the temple with Matsu), whose names are Thousand-league Eyes (Ch'ien-li Yen) and Favoring Wind Ears (Shun-feng Erh). With slight variations, their images will conform to the following description: Both are standing, to left and right of Matsu, in attitudes respectively of looking and listening afar. As one writer puts it, "they seem strange but not fierce, martial but not frightening." One shades his eyes with one hand, the other has a hand to an ear, to indicate their functions. They have short beards or no beards. They wear earrings, bracelets, and ankle bracelets. Their colored jackets are perhaps blown open to reveal the chest. They have red feet. They may hold weapons or be empty-handed. Eyes has a green face and body; Ears has a red face and body. Their faces may be decorated here and there with gold.[17]

Although they look like "barbarians"—perhaps barbarian seamen—they are in fact derived from ancient mythology, and may be traced through many centuries of transmogrifications. The latest, as in the case of so many of the characters in the modern Chinese pantheon, is the version to be found in the famous *Canonization of the Gods,* a work of the Ming dynasty which is a melange of myths concerning the struggle between the last, wicked ruler of the Shang dynasty and the founder of the Chou.[18] In any case, these figures are appropriate symbols for two powers essential to the miracle-working capacity of Matsu: the ability to see across the seas and to hear how the winds are blowing.

[15]See Chinese translations of Li's work in *Taiwan Feng-wu,* seven articles published between Dec. 1960 and Dec. 1963.

[16]The first major study of the subject is now available in a Western language: Bodo Wiethoff, "Der Staatliche Ma-tsu Kult," *Deutsche Morgenländische Gesellschaft Zeitschrift* (Wiesbaden), 116, 2 (1966), pp.311-357.

[17]Chang Ching-ch'iao, "Ch'ien-li yen ho shun-feng erh" (Thousand-league Eyes and Favoring Wind Ears), *Taiwan Feng-wu,* V, 8/9 (Aug.1955), 43f.

[18]One should consult Liu Ts'un-yan, *Buddhist and Taoist Influences on Chinese Novels, Vol I: The Authorship of the Feng Shen Yen I,* Wiesbaden, 1962.

26.
the lung-hua sect:
a secret religious society

How much of the true religious life of the Chinese has been carried on in sects or societies popular among the masses we shall never be able to determine because—all sectarian organizations of this sort being illegal in the Chinese polity—their membership, beliefs, and practices have usually not been documented. Certain of the secret societies have indeed played a prominent role in history; but there must have been countless others which came into existence and eventually ended without any historical notice. It has been remarkably difficult to obtain detailed information even about those known by name. Nevertheless, we believe that the need for religious life, felt by the Chinese as by every other people and unsatisfied by any other institution of the traditional civilization, must most commonly have found its expression through participation in these clandestine groups.

One of the most circumstantial accounts available to us is that of two closely related sects, the Sien-t'ien [Hsien-t'ien] and the Lung-hwa [Lung-hua], which came under the expert scrutiny of J. J. M. de Groot in Amoy in 1887. Through great good luck Dr. de Groot was made privy to all the details concerning these sects, which he then included in his book, *Sectarianism and Religious Persecution in China*, E. J. Brill, (Leiden, 1901; reprinted in Taipei, 1963, Literature House, Ltd.). The second of the two sects seems likely to be the more representative of the type, and we therefore extract from de Groot's account some particulars about the religious character of the group. This condensation comes from chapter seven, pp.197-241.

[The Lung-Hwa sect] worships a great number of gods and goddesses, and makes painted or carved likenesses of them. At the head of the Pantheon are the three Apexes of the Hsien-t'ien sect,[1] mostly represented in watercolors on large scrolls, as three old men, each holding in his hands the eight trigrams, arranged in a circle . . . In some meeting places I saw these pictures suspended on the wall for worship during the religious exercises. The

[1]These have earlier been described by the author as the Wu-chi, the T'ai-chi, and the Huang-chi; they are abstract philosophical concepts rather than personalities—the first means Limitless (or in de Groot's interpretation, Apex of Nothingness), the second Extreme Limit (or in de Groot's translation, Grand Apex), and the third Omnipotence (or what de Groot calls Apex of Imperiality). The first two terms have a long and complicated history in Chinese philosophy; but here they are deified and anthropomorphized. (L.G.T.)

Wu-chi or Apex of Nothingness is the principal person of this Triad, and thus the chief god of the sect. He is the sovereign ruler of the Nirvana-Paradise, and regulates the admission thereto. . . . As in the Hsien-t'ien sect, we find among the deities of the Lung-hwa society the Triratna of Buddhism [i.e. the Three Jewels: Buddha, Dharma, Sangha], and moreover, all kinds of Buddhist, Confucian and Taoist saints. The chief of these dii minores [minor deities] are the God of Heaven (T'ien-kung) and the Goddess of Earth (Hou-t'u), the sun, the moon, Avalokiteśvara, Amitabha, Śakyamuni, Dharmapala. In some meetingplaces I also saw a tablet inscribed with the name of the tutelary god of the City-walls and Moats (Ch'eng-huang Yeh), . . . Besides, I also saw a similar tablet dedicated to the far more ancient, homebred god of the Domestic Fireplace (Tsao-shen), and also tablets of four generals of an imaginary army by means of which the God of Heaven maintains order and peace in the Universe, which is incessantly disturbed and harassed by evil demons. . . .

For their common services in honour of these deities, and for their religious meetings in general, the sectaries use the principal apartment or hall (*t'ang* or *miao*) in ordinary dwelling-houses, with the full consent, of course, of the owner, often himself a leader. Such places they call at Amoy, ts'ai-tug (*ts'ai-t'ang*), "vegetarian halls," because the Buddhist command against the killing of living beings makes the sectaries altogether vegetarians. [There follows here an explanation of the hierarchy of the organization, which we omit.]

Looking upon each other as brothers and sisters [the members of the sect] generally denominate one another familiarly as ts'ài-iú (*ts'ai-yu*) or "vegetarian friends," the men as ts'ài-kong (*ts'ai-kung*' or "gentlemen vegetarians," the women as ts'ài-ko (*ts'ai-ku*) or "lady vegetarians"; the leaders they simply call ts'ài-t'âo (*ts'ai-t'ou*) or "vegetarian chiefs." Each parish or hall has a leader, who most often is the master of the house. He has charge of the altar which bears the images of the Triratna, Avalokiteśvara, and whatever other Saints the brotherhood may worship, as also a tablet inscribed with the names of the seven latest deceased leaders, and held to be inhabited by their souls. . . . All communities of the Lung-hwa society are zealous in enlisting new members. A chief encouragement to this work is the great reward held out to all who bring in neophytes, namely, promotion to a higher religious rank. . . .

[The author next describes in detail the initiation ceremonies, whose overall character is summed up thus:] As a matter of fact it is nothing else than a subdivision of the consecration-ritual of Buddhist monks. . . . Besides the intrinsically Buddhistic character of the sect, the ritual of the initiation shows us the syncretic spirit of it. The five fundamental Commandments of Buddha [against killing, theft, sexual immorality, lying, drinking alcohol] are, indeed, brought in connection with the five Constant Matters (*wu ch'ang*) or Confucian fundamental virtues: benevolence, righteousness, ceremonies and rites, knowledge, and trustworthiness, which from time immemorial have played an important part in classical ethics. Following Mencius, who boldly declared that the first four of these virtues are innate, philosophers have always identified them with man's character, his *hsing*, bestowed by heaven, and therefore intrinsically good. Hence they are, like this natural character, emanations from the Way of heaven, the Tao . . . The ground theme of Confucian ethics being thus essentially Taoistic, the Lung-hwa sect by adopting it gives itself a Taoistic character. Its syncretism goes further still, for novices are admonished by the Initiator to identify themselves with the five Elements [*wu hsing*][3] of which the universe is composed. . . . And finally, the syncretism of the sect is evident from the compulsion laid upon the neophytes to obey six precepts of the Sage Edict [promulgated by the first emperor of the Ming dynasty]. . . . The initiation or first consecration in reality changes the recipients into Devas [divine powers], unless they break their vow, renounce the Triratna, and sin against the commandments. . . .

As already noticed, the members of the Lung-hwa sect at Amoy, in order to promote their individual and mutual Salvation, hold quiet meetings for the worship of their Saints and Buddhas, and for the reciting of Sutras,[4] liturgical prayers, and powerful Tantrani [magical utterances]. These meetings do not generally take place on fixed dates, but at the convenience of the participators . . . Moreover, the sect has a number of so-called *pài-kìng jît (pai-ching jih)* or "days of worship," being calendar days devoted to the worship of special Saints. These are:

1. Fifth of first month, in commemoration of the Patriarch Lo, the founder of the sect.
2. Ninth of first month, in honor of the God of Heaven.
3. Fifteenth of first month, in honor of the Rulers of the three Worlds.
4. Nineteenth of second month, in honor of Kwan-yin.
5. Nineteenth of third month, in honor of the Lord of the Great Light *(t'ai-yang kung),* the Sun.
6. Eighth of fourth month, birthday of the Buddha Śakyamuni.
7. Sixth of sixth month, the opening of Heaven.
8. Nineteenth of sixth month, in honor of Kwan-yin.
9. Last of seventh month, birthday of the Lord of Hell, Ti-tsang Wang.
10. Fifteenth of eighth month, chief festival of the Moon.
11. Nineteenth of ninth month, in honor of Kwan-yin.
12. Seventeenth of eleventh month, birthday of the Buddha Amitabha.
13. Twenty-third of twelfth month, on which the gods ascend to heaven.

In this list the syncretic character of the sect is especially conspicuous. No less than five of these thirteen days are . . . calendrical festivals of the people in general, viz. the second, third, seventh, tenth and thirteenth . . . Buddhistic yearly feasts of the laity are the fourth, eighth, and eleventh; and the sixth, ninth and twelfth days are taken from the calendar of Buddhist monastic life. The first alone is the special property of the sect. The list shows that the principal Saints of the sect are the same as those of the Chinese Mahayana church in general. . . .

In the early morning of the feastdays cups of tea are placed upon the altar of the hall, to refresh the Saints residing there. . . . Successively more members make their appearance, until the male or female leader is of the opinion that enough of them are present to commence the great service. Rice, vegetables, fruit and tea are now placed upon a table in front of the altar,

---

[2]Water, fire, wood, metal, earth. (L.G.T.)

[3]Discourses, or sections of discourses, by the Buddha. (L.G.T.)

together with fragrant incense, for the benefit of the Saint whose festival is being celebrated. A smaller portion is in like manner allotted to each of the other principal Saints of the hall, and the members range themselves in one or more long rows along the sidewalls of the apartment, the men, attired in the long ceremonial robe and with a conical straw hat overlaid with red fringe, to the left of the saints, and the women to the right. In both rows the highest graduates are nearest to the altar. With closed eyes, and the palms of the hands pressed together before their breasts, all mumble unanimously a series of formulas and extracts from the Sutras, one of them tapping with a wooden knocker on a hollow wooden bowl at every syllable pronounced. And the first word of every strophe is marked by a stroke on a metal bell. When this pious work has been continued for some little time, the men come forward, two by two, and kneel in front of the sacrifice, respectfully saluting the Buddhas and Saints on the altar by touching the ground nine times with their foreheads. After them the women do the same, only at a somewhat greater distance from the altar. This act of devotion ended, the dishes with food are removed from the altar, and converted into a vegetarian meal, of which all the brethren and sisters may partake. . . . When the meal is over, each member takes leave of the head of the parish with a courteous bow, thanks him, and departs.

On the four annual days specially devoted to Kwan-yin and Amitabha, and, if desired, on any other festival, either immediately after this first meeting, or later on in the day, the fraternity assembles again. This second meeting is called that of the *pan-jo ch'uan*, "the Ship of Prajna or Wisdom," i.e. the highest of the Parami or perfections by which Nirvana is reached.

A small barge or boat of bamboo and paper, intended to convey departed souls to the Paradise of the West, is placed in the open court in front of the hall. The sails, flags or pennons, and other parts of the rigging are decorated with inscriptions bearing upon this spirit-journey. At the rudder is a paper effigy of Kwan-yin, the high patroness of the Mahayana church, and as such, supreme guide of its members on the road to Salvation. Her satellite Hwan-shen-tsai holds the sheet, her female attendant, called the Dragon's Daughter, stands on the fore-ship, holding up a streamer on which is written *chieh-yin hsi-fang*, "be admitted and introduced into the West (the Paradise)." Several other Buddhist saints, such as Brahma, and Wei-t'o-shen or Indra, do duty as sailors. Round this Bark of Mercy *(tz'u-hang)* the members of the sect range themselves, and under the guidance or not, as the case may be, of one or more of their number, who are consecrated monks, they hold a series of Sutra readings, interspersed with invocations and Tantrani, to induce the holy Kwan-yin to take souls on board and convey them to the land of bliss. And finally, under the shout of *O-bî-tô (O-mi-tô)* repeated many hundred times, the ship with all its contents is burned on the spot. Thus, through fire and flame, the Bark of Wisdom plies right across the sea of transmigration to the promised Nirvana, where the highest Intelligence prevails. If the seashore is near, the bark is sometimes launched there on a plank, and allowed to drift away with the tide. . . .

Another solemnity, performed on many of those festivals, is called *pài ts'ien hût (pai ch'ien fo)*, "Veneration of the thousand Buddhas." All present stand in rows, with the palms of their hands pressed together before their breasts. Some who can read have a small table in front of them, on which the

Sutra lies. They mumble an All-saints litany, every sentence of which is, "Namah Buddha So and So" followed by a slow semigenuflexion. In this manner, at least a thousand names are recited, even two or three times successively; but as it is impossible to keep up the knee-drill long, the litany is now and again broken off, and the interlude filled up with a piece of another Sutra, or with invocations without genuflexions. The object of this litany is to obtain pardon of sins by exciting internally, at the invocation of each name, a feeling of deep repentance. It is therefore called "The Sutra of Repentance of the Names of a thousand Buddhas." The members who cannot read the litany and do not know it by heart, only mumble in their mind. This act of repentance plays an important part in monastic life, and is performed in many different forms. . . .

As in the meetinghalls, so in private houses Sutra readings form an essential part of the great practice of Salvation. These readings are performed either standing or kneeling, and often the worshiper accompanies himself by tapping rapidly on a hollow wooden bowl, and at intervals on a metal bell, as the monks in Buddhist convents are wont to do. Very few sectaries understand what they recite. Most of them have only learned by heart the sound of the characters . . . The understanding has nothing to do with the meritoriousness of this pious work. For the Sutras are the sacred books which make known the roads that lead to Salvation, and to proclaim them at all times, together with the Vinayas or religious rescripts which serve to keep mankind in those roads, is the highest duty imposed upon the sons and daughters of Buddha . . . He who fulfils this duty is deserving in the highest degree. What then does it matter whether he understands what he recites? The mighty salvation power contained in the Sutra or Vinaya loses nothing by it, and moreover—who can tell?—perchance there are myriads of unseen spirits on the spot listening to the recital, and obtaining Salvation thereby. . . . It is the quantity of the recited matter that is of chief importance. . . .

If the members of the sect are asked for the reason why Kwan-yin occupies so prominent a place among their patron saints, the ready answer is to the effect that she has constantly proved herself a faithful deliverer of all victims of misfortune and oppression who invoke her. . . . The stories about deliverance brought by Kwan-yin, most of them centuries old, generally represent her appearances to have been called forth by the reading of Sutras dedicated to her.

Very zealous sectaries recite at least once a day; many do so twice, in the morning and in the evening, not counting the extra readings on calendar feastdays and sundry special occasions. When a sick man or woman is to be comforted or cured by means of Sutras, the reading of these is benevolently performed at the bedside by one or more brethren, who, in conclusion, burn a written prayer on behalf of the patient, addressed to Kwan-yin.

For those who cannot read, or cannot learn Sutras by heart, there exists an easy, and therefore very popular method of obtaining Salvation. This consists in repeating hundreds and thousands of times one and the same Saint's name, with the prefix *lam-bû* (Namah). And here the name of Amitabha (Amit'o), the Lord of Paradise, is of paramount efficacy. [On the sail of the Bark of Mercy and Wisdom previously described, which is depicted on woodcut prints used in keeping track of the number of times one recites the formula, the following is written:] "The mere word Amit'o is a precious sword cutting down all heresies. It is a brave general who defeats hell. It is a bright torch shedding its light in the blackest darkness. It is a bark of mercy into Paradise; the shortest path to lead us out of the wheel of transmigration; a salutary means to help us out of existence. It is a mysterious, magic word which makes us immortal, a remedy imbued with spiritual power, which renovates our bones. The 84,000 schools of the Dharma are contained in those six words (Na-mah A-mi-t'o-fo); those words are one sword-stroke which cuts through 1700 dolichos stalks. If one mutters nothing but the word Amit'o, one need not even trouble to clap one's fingers, in order to reach the West."

Other prints of this kind . . . bear similar inscriptions, but represent Salvation somewhat differently. Here Amit'o stands in the ship, which sails in a shower of flowers, while several devotees, recognizable as people of either sex and of various social position and age, in kneeling attitude, and with hands folded as in prayer, crowd a strip of light which emanates from his hand. Thus the bark in full sail draws them along by this Buddha's light of Salvation towards Paradise.

The foregoing pages have shown, that the pious work of saving the dead by prevailing upon Kwan-yin to convey them into the Western Paradise of Amit'o, forms one of the chief items in the religious program of the Lung-hwa sect. Doubtless this work is its vital point, as the prospect of being piloted by brethren and sisters in Buddha to those regions of supreme felicity must be the strongest motive for most neophytes to join the sect. What will become of my soul and body after death? is the great question which occupies the minds of the whole Chinese people, and *a fortiori* of those who strive after ideals, the realization of which lies in a future world. Is it to be wondered at that so many childless concubines and widows take refuge with the sect? They know well, that in the human society in which they live, where begetting sons is one of the highest moral duties, they are looked upon as worthless creatures, only deserving of being buried in a poor style by indifferent relations, or even by public charity; they know well that, but for the religious community to which they entrust themselves, only a trifling sum will be spent on religious ceremonies on behalf of their souls.

[The author now describes the washing and dressing of the corpse, which is clad in what is essentially a Buddhist clerical garb. This being done by the sectarian brothers (for males) or sisters (for females),] the saving process of the dead begins. Candles are lighted in the apartment, and particularly near the body; incense is burnt in considerable quantities, and some sectaries recite together various sanctifying Sutras, repeating the name of Amit'o hundreds and hundreds of times. The death of a Buddhist who walked in the path of Salvation is called deliverance from the ocean of earthly woe, transition from an existence of imperfection and misery to one of perfection and felicity, therefore a most joyful event. Hence—unless they do not share the views of the sect—the relatives of the deceased do not spend the day in loud wailing and weeping, as the old and orthodox Confucian doctrine urgently prescribes; none of the inscriptions on red paper, adorning the outer and inner doors, are pasted over with white as sign of mourning; no furniture is removed from the apartment where the corpse lies, not even the domestic altar is taken away, to save the Saints whose animated images stand thereon, the spectacle of death, which might possibly bring them disaster. Mock paper money, which no true Confucian will omit to burn in large quantities to enrich his departed in the other world, is not used by the sect. The Buddhist, who forsakes the world and keeps the Commandments, ought to loathe riches, and shall he mar the felicity of his dead co-religionists by forcing treasures upon them? . . .

With the body in the coffin there are deposited three letters, or certificates, to facilitate the reception of the deceased into the Western Paradise. We give some excerpts from one of these documents, in de Groot's translation:

> Most humbly we hope that the defunct, on going home (to Nirvana), may be exempted from entering again any terrestrial wombs, and may enter into the womb of sanctity.
> This is to certify about an inhabitant of the place Amoy . . . By worshipping the Buddhas, and by abstinence from forbidden food he has been drawn up to Salvation and carried to a higher condition. . . . He was born in this life on [such and such a year, month, day, hour]. Humbly bowed down to the ground, he saw the gates of the Dharma opened wide for him by the Highest Apex of Nothingness, the Sage Patriarch; he took refuge in the orthodox doctrine, and accepted the excellent laws of the Tathagatas, which lead to the nine religious degrees . . . and so having accepted the Religion, he earnestly applied himself to this day to the keeping of the five Commandments; and the ten Commandments too he steadfastly kept. Now he has gone home. . . . His great destiny is herewith settled, and the years of his life in this world of light are accomplished; so we turn towards Thee, most high Apex of Nothingness, Sage Patriarch, to declare all together before Thy Lotus-throne that he, an offspring of the beautiful Religion, has followed the instruction of his teachers and thus obtained degrees; that he has burnt no (paper) money (for the spirits and gods) on high, nor (paper) horses for (the souls in) the infernal regions; that he has promulgated the admirable principles come to us from the West [India], and has felt sorrow and remorse over the iniquities of the East (China). . . .
> We give this good certificate to the wise soul of [so-and-so], graduated in our Religion. He will travel with it first to the Mountain of the Souls (i.e. T'ai Shan), and have it examined there for determination of the share of felicity to be allotted to him; and then he will return to his origin (Nirvana), to be rooted and grounded therein for everlasting kalpas, to sorrow over the sins and vices of the present life, and to gather inexhaustible blessings. . . .

Under the guidance of members who are consecrated Buddhist priests, a service is now celebrated which has for its object to convey the soul into Paradise. It is called *téng se-hong (chuan hsi-fang)*, "going or sending home to the West." . . . The altar erected for the occasion, is adorned with portraits in watercolors of some principal Saints of the sect. Those of the three Apexes may on no account be absent. The chief of this triad, the Apex of Nothingness, the personification of the Nirvana-Paradise into which the deceased is expected to be received, hangs in the middle. . . .

On the way to the grave the following verse is recited at intervals:

For several dozen years thou hast kept the fast unbroken,
And now thou travellest home, and returnest to thine origin.
At the assembly on the Mountain of Souls [T'ai Shan] mayest thou have pleasant
    meetings;
We hope that in the West thou mayest be seated on a precious lotus.
Today, on this journey homeward, all things cease for thee to exist,
Thou hast nothing further to do with springs and autumns of human life;
Depart then to-day quickly to the West,
There take thy stand on a lotus-throne, to ascend step by step ever higher thereon.
Namah, Buddha Amit'o. . . .

27.
ReliGion in the RuRal communities of Recent times

Experienced students of China have always recognized the danger of attempting to generalize in descriptions of the land and its cultures. It may be permissible to make one grand generalization: The Han culture—that of the "Chinese Chinese" as against the numerous ethnically distinct groups that have historically been included within the political boundaries of China—is basically homogeneous, with many greater and lesser variants. The homogeneity is the result of a similar economic basis in intensive agriculture; a single language (although modified by extreme dialectical variations); a single writing system based upon meaning rather than sound, thus enabling the classical writings of ancient times to be fairly intelligible to all literate persons; a common system of cosmology and ethics; and other factors. Not the least important of these shared cultural factors is the assemblage of religious beliefs and practices. The existence of the local variations makes it difficult to give a sample in our readings that will not be misleadingly parochial—especially when we are dealing with religion in the community. As is quickly discovered from reading community studies of different places in China, the details of religious conditions are as diverse as every other aspect of community life. What follows, therefore, must be taken merely as suggestive. We have brought together observations from several authors who have studied communities in widely separated areas of China, and at different times, and whose personal points of view are quite disparate.

Our first selection comes from one of the earliest avowed attempts at a "sociological study" of Chinese villages, *Village Life in China* (Fleming H. Revell Co. New York, Chicago, Toronto 1899) by the Protestant missionary, Arthur H. Smith. While this work would hardly pass muster today as a piece of objective scholarship, one can extract some useful information from it. We take a few passages from chapter 9, on "Village temples and religious societies," pp. 136-140.

The process by which the inconceivably great numbers of Chinese temples came to be is not without an interest of its own. When a few individuals wish to build a temple, they call the headmen of the village, in whose charge by long custom are all the public matters of the town, and the enterprise is put in their care. It is usual to make an assessment on the land for funds; this is not necessarily a fixed sum for each acre, but is more likely to be graded according to the amount of land each owns, the poor being perhaps altogether exempt, or very lightly taxed, and the rich paying much more heavily. When the money is all collected by the managers, the building begins under their direction. If the temple is to be a large one, costing several hundred taels, in addition to this preliminary tax, a subscription book is opened, and sent to all the neighboring villages, and sometimes to all within a wide radius, the begging being often done by some priest of persuasive powers, dragging a chain, or having his cheeks pierced with spikes, or in some way bearing the appearance of fulfilling a vow . . . Lists of contributions are kept in the larger temples, and the donors are expected to receive the worth of their money, through seeing their names posted in a conspicuous place, as subscribers of a certain sum. . . .

It is seldom safe to generalize in regard to anything in China, but if there is one thing in regard to which a generalization would seem to be more safe than another, it would be the universality of temples in every village throughout the empire. Yet it is an undoubted fact that there are, even in China, great numbers of villages which have no temple at all. This is true of all those which are inhabited exclusively by Mohammedans, who never take any part in the construction of such edifices . . . The most ordinary explanation of a comparatively rare phenomenon of a village without a temple, is that the hamlet is a small one and cannot afford the expense . . . In the very unusual cases where a village is without one, it is not because they have no use for the gods; for in such instances the villagers frequently go to the temples of the next village and "borrow their light," just as a poor peasant who cannot afford to keep an animal to do his plowing may get the loan of a donkey in planting time, from a neighbor who is better off.

The two temples which are most likely to be found, though all others be wanting, are those of the local god [*t'u-ti*], and of the god of war [Kuan-ti]. The latter has been made much of by the present dynasty, and greatly promoted in the pantheon. The former is regarded as a kind of constable in the next world, and he is to be informed promptly on the death of an adult, that he may report to the city god ("Ch'eng Huang"), who in turn reports to Yen Wang, the Chinese Pluto. In case a village has no temple to the T'u-ti, or local god, news of the death is conveyed to him by wailing at the crossing of two streets, where he is supposed to be in ambush.

Tens of thousands of villages are content with these two temples, which are regarded as almost indispensable. If the village is a large one, divided into several sections transacting their public business independently of one another, there may be several temples to the same divinity. It is a common saying, illustrative of Chinese notions on this topic, that the local god at one end of the village has nothing to do with the affairs of the other end of the village.

When the temple has been built, if the managers have been prudent, they are not unlikely to have collected much more than they will use in the building. The surplus is used partly in giving a theatrical exhibition, to which all donors are invited — which is the only public way in which their virtue can be acknowledged—but mainly in the purchase of land, the income of which shall support the temple priest. In this way, a temple once built is in a manner endowed, and becomes self-supporting. The managers select some one of the donors, and appoint him a sort of president of the board of trustees (called a *shan chu,* or "master of virtue"), and he is the person with whom the managers take account for the rent and use of land. . . .

The temples most popular in one region may be precisely those which are rarely seen in another, but next to those already named perhaps the most frequently honoured divinities are the Goddess of Mercy (*Kuan Yin P'u Sa*), some variety of the manifold goddess known as "Mother" (*Niang Niang*), and Buddha. . . .

It is impossible to arrive at any exact conclusions on the subject, but it is probable that the actual cost of the temples, in almost any region of China, would be found to form a heavy percentage of the income of the people in the district.

The Rev. Smith wrote mostly from his years of residence in Shantung province; our next author, also a missionary but in addition a professional sociologist with the more objective standards of a later generation, writes about a village in the southern province of Kwangtung. Daniel H. Kulp's *Country Life in South China* (Teachers College, Columbia University, 1925; reprinted in Taipei, 1966) is a milestone in scientific community studies in China. From the chapter on "Religion and the spiritual community" (pp. 284-314) we extract the summary section entitled "Religious attitudes."

Sufficient data have been presented to show that religion colors every aspect of life in Phenix Village. The living person must constantly be alert if he would refrain from injuring or offending the hosts of spirits all about him. He consumes much time and money in constant effort to maintain a harmonious participation in his plurality of communities: the living, the departed ancestral spirits, and the spirits of nature that work their will through the operation of natural forces. Each of these communities [is] equally real. Out of all his religious practices he wins satisfaction for his wish for security and achieves a sense of solidarity with his folk, natural, human, living, departed, present or historical. To break with these communities, to refuse to conform to the customary demands made upon one by the mystical members of the communities was a thing unheard of until the introduction of Christianity and modern science.

Thus all matters, projects, plans, behavior of every kind are measured by community norms first founded in favor of the family, its head, and back of all, its spiritual head or departed ancestor. What these norms are and how they grew up can be seen in the ancestral worship and in the filial duties of everyday life. The wise sayings of a powerful and learned *chia-chang* [defined earlier by author as the head of a particular kin-group—moiety or branch-family], after his death, are repeated and transmitted from generation to generation, providing fixed norms and schematized behavior patterns for the living. Out of the mystical assumptions of the living, the sanctions of the dead become powerful means of control of the conduct of the living. Attention centers on ancestors and not descendants; the look of the community is backward and not forward in any mundane sense; continuity, conservatism, traditionalism, institutionalism, familism are the great societal values. The individual person is of value only as he, while living, enhances and defends these values. Human prosperity is worth while only as it makes possible the happiness of the spirits, who, in turn, can produce human prosperity. There is an interaction between the human and the spiritual that creates a fundamental interdependence of the two and places religion at the center of all familist practice.

That these attitudes are based on error makes no difference sociologically. They motivate behavior and illustrate how in human conduct the notions that people hold in their minds about themselves and the roles they play in various groups are the real and immediate determiners of action. The man participating in ancestral worship is constantly projecting himself into the future world; he sees himself in the situations and conditions that he believes his departed ancestors are now in; he also sees himself in relation to the living descendants who later will be called upon to worship him; the guaranteeing of that status in the future life is his central problem. Out of this objective has developed the whole complex of familicentrism. That is why religion is not individual and personal religion so much as it is collective and group religion. Individuals pray not for themselves but for their families.

The culture complex of religion in Phenix Village is made up of attitudes, values and practices of all the various religious systems to be found in China. Until Christianity was introduced, there was no sectarianism whatever in the village. The same person followed animistic practices, spiritist seances, Buddhist adherence, Taoist customs and Confucian standards; but the important thing to note is that there were no sectarian adherents who marked themselves off from other religious groups and refused to follow certain practices as not belonging to their religion. The essence of sectarianism is the refusal to compromise. Strictly speaking, the sects exist but not in any practical way in Phenix Village. There is no Buddhist, nor Taoist, nor Confucian temple. For the laity, then, religion is a mingling of the practices of all these religions together with the familist religion of ancestral worship.

Lacking the knowledge to criticize any of the religions, the ordinary person frankly believes whatever religious faiths he encounters. The scholars of the village are sceptic about Buddhism and Taoism but they do not interfere with the people in following Buddhist or Taoist practices. The scholars are advocates of Confucianism. They keep quoting Confucius or his disciple Mencius until gradually the norms of conduct that the great sage enunciated seep down to the last man or woman in the village. So it is that the people believe in animism and worship the spirits of objects of nature. They have strong faith in the Buddhas, for they practice Buddhist customs and contribute money to erect Buddhist temples; they follow Taoism, for they call upon the Taoist priest of the region to perform ceremonies for the dead, use Taoist charms for protection against demons, and on certain days observe vegetarian diets.[1] Lastly, they proudly refer to the teachings of Confucius as moral standards for familist practice and close every debate by quotations from his classics as to what is proper.

We further quote from the same chapter the paragraph labelled "Village philosophy":

Part of the philosophy of the people of Phenix Village has been illustrated by their notions of religion and ancestor worship. Briefly, opinion is shaped and action undertaken according to whether they will please the gods they worship or glorify their ancestors. Fate rules all. The people do not entirely subscribe to a laissez-faire social policy for they think that collective action in worship and ceremony will either control the gods and so their own future well-being or ameliorate their condition by changing the mood of the gods. They constantly alternate from fatalistic laissez-faire-ism to a practical magic. They manipulate charms, mutter formulas, spread mystic characters to the wind, wear amulets and in all sorts of ways try to control their environment to meet their wishes, as best they can. But when all their effort, individual and collective, fails, when floods come in spite of prayers and death carries off their kin, worship notwithstanding, then they acquiesce and call it *Ming* or Fate.

Our third selection is from the field report of Bernard Gallin, an anthropologist who spent sixteen months during 1957-58 in a village of west-central Taiwan. His book is entitled *Hsin Hsing, Taiwan. A Chinese Village in Change* (University of California, 1966); this selection comes from pages 248-256.

The lunar calendar forms the base for the schedule of calendrical rituals—the *pai-pai* [religious worship festivals] which are celebrated by the whole village on set days. One such important rite is the *pai-pai* for unworshiped, anonymous ancestors. Such forgotten and neglected ancestors wander about the countryside looking for sustenance, becoming negative powers or harmful spirits (*kuei*) which often make trouble for people. Although they are regarded as demons, the Taiwanese follow universal custom and refer to them euphemistically, calling them good brothers (*hao hsiung-ti*) to avoid antagonizing them.

Pai-pai for the good brothers are held regularly on the second and sixteenth of each lunar month by all the villagers of the area. On these dates each household worships individually, but outside of its house since "one does not invite negative powers or spirits into the *kung t'ing* [main room]." The sacrifices for this occasion are usually quite simple and consist of vegetable soups and perhaps some cut-up pork and/or fish . . .

[1]Vegetarianism is usually considered a Buddhist, rather than a Taoist, custom. (L.G.T.)

The villagers also tend the spirits of other unknown people.

In addition, the villagers also worship spirits of the unknown dead which have been confined for long periods of time or even permanently to the underworld for having led immoral lives. During the seventh lunar month these spirits are released and permitted to journey to the surface, where they roam about for the entire month. At this time they must be offered sustenance. The villagers refer to them as good brothers also, but unlike the good brothers worshiped on the second and sixteenth of each lunar month, these good brothers are "criminal" good brothers.

Until a few years ago each community in the Hsin Hsing area and the city of Lukang worshiped them with large *pai-pai* on different days of the seventh lunar month. The many *pai-pai* held throughout the month made it possible for the people in one place to invite people from elsewhere to share in their feast. . . . [The sacrifices] are offered not only to the good brothers but also to an underworld god known as P'u Tu Kung who watches over the good brothers. The villagers call this occasion, the fifteenth of the seventh month, Chung Yuan.

The most frequent *pai-pai* which villagers define as calendrical are the four which are held independently by all village families on the same days of each lunar month. On the first and fifteenth, all the gods and their soldiers and horses are worshiped. On the second and sixteenth days of each month, as mentioned above, offerings are made to the good brothers. . . .

One of the most important family holidays of the year is celebrated in winter in the first lunar month — the Chinese New Year. . . . The New Year's celebration actually begins on the twenty-fourth day of the twelfth month, when the villagers send the gods off to heaven. They burn incense and a special paper money called *chia ma* and shoot off firecrackers. The paper money bears a picture of a horse which symbolizes the horse on which the gods ride to heaven. The families sacrifice fruit and cake at a very simple ceremony.

On New Year's Eve the villagers worship their ancestors in the *kung t'ing.* . . . The next day the worship of the ancestors begins anew and is repeated daily until the third day of the first month. On these three days the villagers also worship the three brother gods (San Chieh Kung),[2] and many of them, including men, young women, and children, spend their time gambling during the period of rest from work.

The fourth day of the first month is called Chieh Shen or "welcome the gods." On this day the gods who went to heaven come back to earth. The villagers offer sacrifices and burn incense and paper money to welcome them back.

The ninth day of the first month is the birthday of T'ien Kung, the highest of the gods. Although the villagers consider him a vegetarian, they nevertheless sacrifice pork, duck, and chicken in addition to vegetable dishes and cakes, explaining that T'ien Kung eats only the vegetables, but his friends and the other gods eat the meats.

The fifteenth day of the first month, called Shang Yuan or "the first full moon of the New Year," is the occasion for worship of all the gods and ancestors with sacrifices of meat, vegetables, incense, and paper money by each individual family.

[2]T'ien Kuan, god of heaven; Ti Kuan, god of earth; Shui Kuan, god of waters. (L.G.T.)

Late in the second month or early in the third is Ch'ing Ming Chieh, "one hundred days after Tung Chieh" (the winter solstice). On this day, village families go to the cemetery to clean and sweep the graves and worship their ancestors. If a family has built a new house, married a son, or produced a baby boy during the year, they will hold a special ceremonial and offer many sacrifices at the grave site. In addition, for three years following the death of a member of the family, a special ceremonial takes place at which the female members of the family wail as they did at the funeral. . . .

The twenty-third day of the third month is the birthday of the goddess Matsu [for details concerning her cult, see the separate article by Thompson]. . . . Each year many people from far-off villages and even cities travel to Lukang in long processions by hired trucks, bicycles, pedicabs, sedan chairs, and on foot to worship Matsu on her birthday. Some Hsin Hsing villagers also go to Lukang to worship Matsu on this day, but most worship her at home because they are too busy to travel to Lukang. However, Lukang is considered a very exciting place when it is filled with tens of thousands of people who have come to worship Matsu, and many villagers, especially young people and women, go there in the evening to watch the festivities.

In addition to the recognition which is accorded Matsu on her birthday, for at least the last forty years Hsin Hsing and eleven other villages in the area have held a joint procession each year to worship Matsu some weeks after her birthday. . . . On the day of the procession, the villagers assigned to carry the sedan chairs assemble at a prearranged spot to begin the circuit through the twelve villages. A large statue of Matsu, borrowed for the occasion from her temple in Lukang, is carried in a big sedan chair by several villagers. As the procession passes through the village, the residents worship the goddess, and a local shaman invites her to eat. Village teams of performers accompany the procession. They dance, give exhibitions of traditional boxing and sword play, act out little incidents or excerpts from traditional Taiwanese operas or stories, or do a dragon dance in which a large, green paper dragon is carried over the heads of many men who weave in and out to simulate his sinuous movements. The whole occasion is extremely gay and entertaining and, it is felt, most rewarding. Many food offerings to the goddess are displayed in each village along the route. They are provided by each village family and are eaten at dinner in the evening, after the Matsu procession has passed. . . .

The twenty-fourth day of the fourth month is the birthday of the Hsin Hsing village god, Ta Shih Kung. Those villagers who have been working elsewhere normally come home for this *pai-pai*, and even some of the members of village families whose business or work has required them to move to the city return for this day and stay overnight or several days with relatives in the village. The main reason for this influx is that the celebration is one of the gayest and most festive of all those held during the year.

All families worship Ta Shih Kung in a joint *pai-pai* held in the courtyard of one of the largest *tsu* [clan] houses in the village. A shaman is present to exorcise any devils that may be near and to invite the god to eat the sacrificed food, the best the villagers have all year. Guests are invited from all over the area to join in the festivities, and for weeks or even months in advance the villagers issue invitations to relatives and friends. . . . The entertainment includes not only the good food and the contact with different people, but also a puppet show performed by a professional group hired from a city. The puppet show is based on stories from dynastic history and is a source of delight to the villagers and their guests . . . . The carnival atmosphere of the occasion is augmented by the presence of vendors of food, sweets, sugarcane, and betel nut who come from Lukang and surrounding villages to sell their wares.

The puppet show and other communal expenses of the *pai-pai* are paid for with money collected from each village family by the pot master for Ta Shih Kung and his assistants, who also arrange for the show. Each village household is assessed an amount calculated on the basis of land operated (whether owned or rented) and the number of people in the household. The families of village shamans are not required to contribute any money on such occasions. . . .

During the fifth and sixth months, the busy agricultural season, there are no important village *pai-pai* other than the usual four to worship the gods, their soldiers and horses, and the Good Brothers. Most festive holidays and calendrical rites fall in months when the farmers are not busy with agricultural chores. . . .

The fifteenth day of the eighth month is the birthday of T'u Ti Kung, the Earth God. On this day the villagers hold a *pai-pai* at his temple which is located on the road in front of the village. Each village family worships individually with sacrifices of pork, vegetable dishes, and moon cakes. No guests are invited to dinner on this occasion. . . .

In the ninth month there are no special *pai-pai*, but around the middle of the tenth month, the village has one of its largest joint *pai-pai* of the year on the occasion called *tso p'ing-an* [literally, "making peace"]. By the time of this *pai-pai*, the farmers have harvested their rice, and at the ceremonial worship of T'ien Kung, his soldiers, and many lesser gods, they thank T'ien Kung for giving them a good crop and "peaceful days." The ceremony is held in the courtyard of one of the largest village *tsu* houses, and a shaman invites the gods to partake of the sacrifices. Huge amounts of paper money are offered to the god . . .

Each village in the area arranges to hold its *tso p'ing-an pai-pai* on a different day. Thus, for a period of almost two weeks, the villagers busy themselves with visits to relatives and friends to help them celebrate their *tso p'ing-an* festival. Hsin Hsing village alone entertains hundreds of guests on this occasion. . . .

Some time during the first half of the eleventh month, the villagers celebrate Tung Chieh. Each family worships its ancestors in the *kung t'ing* with steamed round dough cakes and other simple sacrifices. Some families also worship at the village Earth God temple, and others go to the Matsu temple in Lukang.

The sixteenth day of the twelfth month is called Wei Ya and is the last day of the year on which the Good Brothers are worshiped by each family. On this day the villagers also go to the Earth God temple to ask T'u Ti Kung to protect their livestock. The average family does not have guests to dinner, but landlords are supposed to invite their hired men to eat on this occasion. . . .

By the twenty-fourth day of the twelfth moon, as already indicated, the villagers begin to prepare for the New Year's celebration by sending the gods off to heaven. . . .

Most clearly classifiable as noncyclic rites of passage (crisis rites) are those associated with life-cycle events . . . such as the ceremonies held at a birth, on a boy's sixteenth birthday, upon marriage, and at death. Though they are rites of passage, they function also as rites of intensification, since they draw together family and *tsu* groups, including relatives and friends from the surrounding area, and often large segments of the village.

Functioning similarly are the times when a villager is seriously ill or when young men are being sent off for military service. While both situations are of immediate concern only to a particular family, the entire village may be requested to participate in a *pai-pai* and offer its prayers and sacrifices for the well-being of each person thus endangered. In case of a serious illness, the patient's family requests the villagers' participation by sounding a gong at dawn of the day on which the *pai-pai* is to be held. It would be rare for any village family (no matter what its relationship with the sponsoring family) to be unwilling to participate.

Still another noncyclic *pai-pai* which clearly functions as a rite of intensification rather than a rite of passage occurs when a god from some distant place comes to the village for an unscheduled visit. The villagers may be notified of the impending visit by a local god speaking through a shaman while he is in a trance. On the day of the announced visit, the entire village holds a joint *pai-pai* to welcome and worship the god. The occasion may become a regular *pai-pai* event as a result of the shaman's earlier announcement and may eventually become a part of the village's regular cyclic calendar of rituals.

Our final selection in this group is an article by Jack Potter, entitled "Wind, Water, Bones and Souls: The Religious World of the Cantonese Peasant," which we reproduce in extenso from the *Journal of Oriental Studies* (University of Hong Kong) VIII, 1 (Jan 1970), pp. 139-153. It brings together the several most important ingredients of the peasant religion, and further shows that the yang force which fêng-shui endeavors to utilize is in fact the universally found principle of *mana*. Research for this study was carried on by the author during 1961-63 in the village of Ping Shan in the New Territories of Hong Kong. (The Cantonese terms used in this paper are romanized following the Chao system of Cantonese romanization. Yuen-ren Chao, *Cantonese Primer* (Cambridge, Mass.: Harvard University Press, 1947). We omit the Chinese characters appearing in the original paper.)

Much has been written about Chinese peasant religion, but there have been few attempts to show how these diverse 'superstitions' (as they are sometimes called) function as a meaningful system in the lives of Chinese peasants.[3] In this paper I present an interpretation of the religious and magical beliefs of the villagers of Ping Shan, a Cantonese lineage in Hong Kong's New Territories.[4] I attempt to show how their basic social values and supernaturalistic beliefs and practices interrelate to form a meaningful and fairly consistent worldview and philosophy of life. The intense drive for success and security in this world, the mainspring of a dynamic and highly competitive society, was intimately related to the villagers' view of their place in the universe and their relations with the superhuman forces and beings which inhabited this universe.[5] If the villager was able to bind these supernatural forces to his will, or enlist the aid of supernatural beings, it was possible to achieve a long life, success and fortune. If he did not deal with these forces and beings in a proper fashion, thus alienating or disturbing them, and if he did not receive their aid in his worldly affairs, life could be a continuous series of disasters and failures. Those ordinary persons who simply 'lived along' with average success had achieved a kind of neutrality in their relations with the supernatural world. They succeeded in passing through life without incurring the ill effects that would have resulted if they had alienated or disturbed the supernaturals, but they had not obtained supernatural aid; their mediocrity was mute testimony to this failure.

From the villager's point of view, all success was the result of luck or fortune and all failure—including death, the ultimate failure—was due to bad luck and ill fortune. That everyone would exert maximum effort to succeed was taken for granted; but success in this world could not be assured by hard work and effort alone. For no matter how hard one tried one could not be assured of success unless one was lucky, and one was lucky only if he could utilize supernatural power in his worldly affairs. Consequently, most religious and magical action was an attempt to avoid the unlucky supernatural elements of the universe and to control or enlist the aid of supernatural forces and beings which could bring one luck.

[3]Notable exceptions are the works by J. J. M. De Groot, *The Religious System of China*, 6 vols. (Leiden: E. J. Brill, 1892-1910); Francis L. K. Hsu, *Under the Ancestors' Shadow* (New York: Columbia University Press, 1948), and C. K. Yang. The interpretation of Chinese religion given here, although based on different data, is similar to the one given by De Groot.

[4]The field research on which this article is based was carried out in Ping Shan, a Chinese lineage in Hong Kong's New Territories, from August 1961 through January 1963. The Ping Shan lineage is made up of eight villages centred around a central ancestral hall dedicated to the lineage founder. The Tangs of Ping Shan have inhabited this area since the twelfth century and although many changes have taken place in village culture over the past fifty years since their incorporation into the British Colony of Hong Kong, enough of the old beliefs still remain to allow a reconstruction of these major features of their belief systems.

[5]Unlike many peasant societies which have a world view characterized by what Professor George M. Foster, in 'Peasant Society and the Image of Limited Good', *American Anthropologist*, 67:193-315 (1965), has called the Image of Limited Good, the Cantonese and Chinese peasants in general exhibited an intensive achievement orientation. I do not mean to imply that the Image of Limited Good model is entirely inapplicable because many aspects of Chinese peasant life do correspond with this model.

In a sense, one's fate was sealed by the concatenation of astrological influences present at birth and noted in a person's 'eight characters',[6] but in spite of this the Cantonese peasant attempted to overcome cruel fate by enlisting supernatural aid. The Cantonese peasant's *weltanschauung* was not a fatalistic one, except in complete failure, nor was it an optimistic one, except as seen from the pinnacle of success. The universe was essentially a stage on which human beings, impersonal supernatural power, and supernatural beings interacted in a constant drama of life and death, success and failure. A person's fortunes were determined by how he fared in this complicated drama of life.

A belief that the universe contains as its essence an impersonal supernatural power lies at the base of the villager's cosmology and plays an important role in his religious and magical beliefs. According to several of the more educated and sophisticated villagers, the *hey shae*, a kind of primordial energy, is the vital animating principle of the universe. The villagers sometimes called it *dey mat*, or 'pulse of the earth', and conceived of it as flowing or pulsating through the land configurations that form the earth's surface. This primordial energy has two manifestations: *yang* (Cantonese *yeung*) the bright and active male principle; and *yin* (Cantonese *iam*), the dark and passive female principle. The *yin* and *yang* are not two separate substances; they are simply two aspects of the *hey shae*. In a sense, the *yin* is merely the absence of *yang*, and vice versa. An analogy can be drawn with electricity: the universe has two 'poles'; the positive or *yang* pole, and the negative *yin* pole. The *hey shae* is manifested in the *yin* and *yang* which in turn give rise to the five elements: gold, water, fire, wood, and earth. These elements, in various combinations and permutations, make up all things in the phenomenal universe.

Allied to this conception of the *hey shae*, are the pervasive beliefs and practices centering around *fung shui*, literally 'wind and water', which is the Chinese term for the set of geomantic influences that lie at the core of their magical system.[7] The essence of this idea is that the configurations of land forms and bodies of water on the face of the earth direct the flow of the *hey shae* and that this has great implications for the fate of the world's human inhabitants. When discussed in the context of *fung shui* this primordial energy is sometimes called *lung hey* or 'dragon vapors'. *Fung shui, dey mat, lung hey*, and *hey shae* are all terms used by the villagers to refer to this fundamental and all-pervasive supernatural power.

[6]The eight characters denote the exact time of a person's birth. They are important in that they are believed to hold the key to a person's fate in life.

[7]Maurice Freedman (in chapter 5) of his *Chinese Lineage and Society: Fukien and Kwangtung* (London: Athlone Press, 1966) has discussed *fung shui* in much more detail. The description he gives there of geomantic beliefs in the New Territories tallies in most important respects with the description given here. And I refer the reader to this book for an interesting analysis from a somewhat different point of view and a good bibliography on the subject. However, as is apparent from what I have written in this paper, I do not completely agree with Freedman's statement (p. 124) that *fung-shui* is not like most of the rest of Chinese religion; there is no reliance on the will of a deity; there are no gods to serve or placate. I agree that *fung shui* is not like *some* other elements of Chinese religion; but I would tend to emphasize the interrelationship between *fung shui* and the rest. I would stress that *fung shui* is governed by some of the basic ideas that are found elsewhere in Chinese religion and magic.

Fung shui is the source of all luck and efficacy. A successful man, family, or lineage is successful because they have 'good *fung shui*'; if they are not successful, it is because they have 'bad *fung shui*'. *Fung shui* can be a beneficial force if properly handled, but it can also be an extremely dangerous and destructive force if improperly dealt with. If one gets too large a dose of *fung shui* it may cause disease or even death, not only for an individual family, but an entire village or an entire lineage group. Handling *fung shui* is like dealing with a high voltage electric current; the benefit one receives from its power is directly proportional to the technical skill employed. The occult pseudo-science of *fung shui* has been developed over the centuries by the Chinese into what is undoubtedly one of the most complicated magical systems in history. Since ordinary villagers could not hope to understand the finer points of the science, practised and experienced experts were usually consulted in important *fung shui* matters. These specialists, called *fung shui sin shaang* or '*fung shui* teachers', were common in the rural areas of China and were frequently consulted by the villagers. The *fung shui sin shaang* learned their trade by reading the ancient texts on the subject written to train professional practitioners and interested scholarly amateurs and by serving as apprentices of a recognized specialist.

It is difficult to convey the extent to which the thoughts and actions of the villagers of Ping Shan revolve around *fung shui* matters. Almost all important actions, whether they be individual or collective, must be adjusted to and guided by the *fung shui* influences that might affect or be affected by these actions. In the New Territories, and probably in Kwangtung Province as a whole, entire villages were set up according to *fung shui* prescriptions to ensure the prosperity and safety of future generations. Villages had to be constructed at the foot of a hill if possible so that the *fung shui* could flow gradually from the higher mountains along the crests of smaller hills to concentrate on the village. Village sites had to have bodies of water standing in front of them to balance the flow of *fung shui* coming down from the mountains. The height of village houses, the plan and layout of the village, the shape of house roofs—even the maximum size that the village could safely attain—were all theoretically governed by *fung shui* requirements. Since villages required special groves of *fung shui* trees as a curtain at the rear of the village, some villages had to postpone construction for several years to allow the *fung shui* trees to reach a proper height! The exterior and interior construction of village houses, including the exact size and location of doors and the direction in which they were to open, were determined by *fung shui*. *Fung shui* is so important that even today quarrels frequently occur in the village over such seemingly innocent matters as opening up a new window in a village house. If the neighboring household should suffer illness or misfortune it would definitely be blamed on the *fung shui* disturbances created by the new window. Even a man's face can be said to have good or bad *fung shui*. Some of the villagers in the New Territories even go so far as to grow sizeable handle-bar mustaches during certain periods of their lives because a *fung shui* specialist told them that their luck and money would flow away from them during these years if protective measures were not taken.

The flow of invisible *fung shui* currents follows the pull of gravity like water and these ethereal currents that flow through the mystical environment of the Cantonese peasant are even more difficult to control than streams or rivers. To obtain maximum benefit from a *fung shui* current it must be captured and restrained in exactly the proper amount. If the concentration of the 'dragon vapors' upon a house, a village, or an ancestral grave is too powerful it may lead to the death or impoverishment of the people involved; if it is too weak the inhabitants will at best have only mediocre luck. To contain the flow of magical power and to ward off unpropitious currents, retaining walls are erected in front of buildings, villages and ancestral halls.

It is a cardinal rule of the science of *fung shui* that moving bodies of water can conduct *fung shui* power rapidly away from a given site. For this reason, a good *fung shui* site must never be so situated as to see water flowing away from it. Water is needed to balance the power of the *hey shae* flowing down to concentrate on the site, but it must be standing or flowing inward towards the location. If a locality has bodies of water flowing away from it sometimes remedial steps can be taken. In Ping Shan an entire village and a large pagoda were constructed as a retaining wall to prevent the *fung shui* of the main villages and the central ancestral halls of the lineage from being swept out to sea by a river that once flowed by the front of the village.

Fung shui requirements vary for different structures. What might be proper *fung shui* for an entire village or a large ancestral temple might be terribly destructive if concentrated upon a single ancestral tomb. There is a proper balance of *fung shui* for individual houses, for whole villages, for ancestral halls, for ancestral tombs and for temples. *Fung shui* is an exact science, like Newtonian physics, and the traditional prescriptions for different purposes are set down to the smallest detail. A difference of a few feet in the location of a grave or a difference of a few inches in the height of an ancestral tomb might spell the difference between success and fortune for entire generations of descendants. Even apparently minor matters like the digging of a village well might be so disturbing to the flow of the village *fung shui* as to kill everyone in the village. The villagers of Ping Shan claim that numerous people who once dwelt at the rear of their village died off because the Hong Kong government erected a police station on the hill behind their village which cut off their flow of *fung shui*.

The officers of the New Territories Administration are continually beset with difficulties concerning *fung shui* matters because the construction of a road or the erection of a new building inevitably harms the *fung shui* of nearby villages and results in interminable litigation by the villagers who demand compensation for the damage done to their *fung shui*. Most roads in the New Territories have a serpentine quality that is due more to *fung shui* requirements than to bad engineering. Everything in the lives of the villagers, then, from the construction of a village latrine to the determination of the direction in which bridal sedan chairs were placed was determined according to *fung shui* criteria.

However, the principal way that *fung shui* affected the lives and fortunes of the villagers was not so much through the propitious location of houses and temples as it was through the ancestral cult, one of the other important pillars of Chinese peasant religion. The family ancestral spirits enshrined on household altars were the foci of the family ancestral cult. More distant lineage ancestors of earlier generations, enshrined in central and branch ancestral halls, were the foci of lineage and lineage subsegments. Family ancestors were worshipped daily, on the major holidays throughout the year, and especially during the Ching Ming grave-cleaning ceremony in the spring. More distant ancestors of the lineage were worshipped in ancestral hall rites twice yearly, in the spring and fall, and the tombs of lineage ancestors located in the surrounding hills and mountains were worshipped collectively by groups of descendants during a period of several weeks in the autumn of each year.

In ancestral rites the descendants honored their ancestors and furnished them with food, drink, and money that they could use in the nether world of hell. Ancestral spirits of the family who went back for only a few generations were remembered as individual personalities and were basically benevolent beings who watched over and protected their immediate descendants. Lineage ancestors seated in the ancestral halls and tombs were for the most part not remembered as individual personalities. Ancestors this far removed were regarded almost as deities. Villagers frequently referred to more distant ancestors by the term *poosat* (Mandarin *pu-sa*), the general term used to refer to temple deities of Buddhist or Taoist origin. Family ancestors were also sometimes called *kwae* the term used to refer to the malicious spirits from hell, indicating that even they could be malevolent if not properly treated and cared for.

An important element in the ancestral cult of Kwangtung Province and other areas of South China is the elaborate and peculiar burial practices and cult of the dead that is distinctive of this region. Cantonese funerals are similar to those found in other parts of China but the Cantonese have an additional set of practices associated with the dead that is more elaborate than those found elsewhere. The usual practice of the villagers of Ping Shan is to first bury the body in a wooden coffin on a special burial hill near the village. Then after a period of from five to ten years has elapsed the coffin is disinterred and the skeletal bones of the ancestor are ritually washed. The remains are then placed in a ceramic funerary vessel, about two feet high and one foot in diameter, called a *kam taap*. These ceramic pots are then placed in neutral *fung shui* spots on the hillsides in the vicinity of the village.

Even the *kam taap* were theoretically only temporary resting places for the ancestral bones. The ideal was to finally bury them in one of the elaborate circular masonry and brick tombs that were the preferred final resting places for the villagers' ancestral spirits. However, for most ancestral spirits, the ceramic funerary vessels were the final resting places because only families of some means could afford the expense of hiring a *fung shui* specialist to undertake the sometimes lengthy process of locating a tomb site in the surrounding mountains which had excellent *fung shui*. The fee of the *fung shui* specialist was high, the tomb site would be expensive if it was a good one, and the expense of constructing an elaborate tomb was out of the question for most village families. Consequently, most *kam taap* were left permanently exposed on the hillside where they were worshipped every spring by the immediate descendants of the enclosed ancestral spirit. After a few generations, however, most of the *kam taap* were lost and the ancestral spirits they contained would be forever forgotten. The *kam taap* might be overgrown with vegetation or they might be kicked open by a stray buffalo and the bones scattered. Even if the *kam taap* were not lost or broken the descendants would after a period of time discontinue the yearly worshipping and grave cleaning ceremony because only seldom was ancestral property attached to a *kam taap* burial and the villagers soon ignored a burial that had no property attached to pay for the worshipping expenses and to purchase roast pork to be divided among the male descendants. Most ancestral spirits ceased to be important as a focus for collective worship after a few generations if they were not buried in a permanent tomb.

It was only the wealthier villagers who were able to achieve a real immortality. Their families had sufficient wealth to transfer their ancestral spirits to a permanent tomb endowed with property where descendants could worship down through the generations. Furthermore, they were able to locate the tomb on an excellent *fung shui* spot that would ensure succeeding generations of continuing fame and prosperity.

The transfer of the *kam taap* to a permanent tomb was a lengthy and critical process that had to be undertaken with extreme care. After the *fung shui* specialist had located a burial plot with promising *fung shui*, the family would purchase the site and under the direction of the *fung shui* teacher proceed to build a tomb whose size and shape exactly fitted the *fung shui* of the site. The *fung shui sin shaang* took special care to trace out the flow of the magical currents in the surrounding countryside so that he could locate the tomb on the exact spot where the lucky influences were concentrated. The grave was ideally surrounded by two enclosing spurs of hills on the right and left side of the grave, called the 'green dragon' and the 'white tiger' respectively, which held the tomb in their protective embrace. Water should be visible flowing in towards the tomb and the winds should be neither too strong nor too mild. The villagers described a good grave site as being 'comfortable' for the ancestor buried there. The *kam taap* containing the ancestral bones was buried a few feet below the ground at the rear of the semi-circular tomb, facing outward through the arms of the grave and the encircling hills. Above and to the rear of the *kam taap* was placed the tombstone on which was carved the birth and death day of the deceased and any special honors he may have achieved during lifetime, such as passing the imperial examinations or serving as an official.

Every detail of the tomb's construction and the arrangements for transferring the *kam taap* to the tomb were planned with painstaking care. The direction in which the ancestral bones faced outward from the tomb and the depth at which the *kam taap* was buried were determined with precision by the specialist. The direction in which the ancestral skull faced from the tomb was important because on this depended, among other things, which of his sons and their lines of descent would receive most benefit from the *fung shui* of the grave. If the entombed ancestor faced in one direction the line stemming from the eldest son might prosper; if it faced in another direction the second son's line would prosper, and so on. Often the situation was made even more complicated because one direction might bring them increased numbers, while a third direction might ensure that certain descendants would pass the imperial examinations and become high officials. Since the consequences of each direction were explained in detail by the *fung shui* specialist before the burial, sons often quarrelled over the position in which the *kam taap* was to be placed in the tomb. The depth of the burial and the exact moment when the *kam taap* was lowered into the grave were also important because if the timing was not exactly suited to the grave's *fung shui* the entire effect might be lost.

So strong was the belief in the importance of *fung shui* that even the entombment might not be permanent if the family of the entombed person ran into a period of bad luck. The quality of a grave's *fung shui* was often tested several years after burial by digging up the *kam taap* and examining the condition and color of the skeletal remains. If the bones were golden in colour this showed that the *fung shui* of the grave was good; however, if the bones were found to be black, this showed that the *fung shui* was bad and they might be removed and buried in a different location. If a set of brothers had differential success in the years following the burial of their father the unsuccessful sons would suspect that the *fung shui* of the grave would doom them to poverty while promoting the success of their brothers. In this case quarrels and even violence might ensue, with some of the brothers wanting to move the bones and others opposing their efforts.

The system of logic behind *fung shui* beliefs was self-fulfilling. If a group was successful then the *fung shui* of their graves must be good; if the descendants were not successful, then the grave must be a bad one. As an added prop to the system, it was believed that certain graves were good for only certain periods of time, thus explaining any marked changes in the fortunes of a group. This elaborate pseudo-science was perfectly consistent, given certain assumptions, and could never be disproved. The *fung shui* specialist could always think up some reason why his predictions did not work out and in any case the effects were only noticeable over generations, long after the specialist had died. The system was remarkably persistent because it did give *some* explanation for the differential success of family lines in a society which encouraged achievement and yet could award only limited amounts of wealth, prestige and power. After all, there had to be some explanation for the fact that some branches of a lineage over the centuries increased in numbers and produced officials and wealthy merchants, while other branches of the lineage ended up as a few families of poor tenant farmers.

One important effect of the system was that a person's or a family's success did not necessarily imply the inferiority of other less successful members of the village community because in the last analysis success could be attributed to the impersonal whims of fate or the character of one's ancestral tombs. This was especially important in a community as tightly knit as a Chinese lineage where envy and jealousy might seriously damage the solidarity of the community. The Chinese lineage rested upon an ideology which held that all lineage members were brothers and a fiction which held that all were social equals. The magical and impersonal explanation for differential success furnished by the *fung shui* system softened to some extent the effects of great social differentiation which was a feature of many communities. In functional terms, *fung shui* plays somewhat the same role in Chinese villages that the civil-religious hierarchy plays in the village communities of Latin America. Both mechanisms help to maintain the solidarity of the village community; one by eliminating wealth differences and the other by attributing such differences to impersonal fate.[8]

[8]Cf. G. Foster, p. 305 and Eric R. Wolf, *Sons of the Shaking Earth* (Chicago: University of Chicago Press, 1959), p. 216.

The extreme care taken in this lengthy and costly process of burial, reburial, and entombment gives some indication of the importance attached to *fung shui* by the villagers. So much care was taken because a man's fortunes and those of his descendants were believed to be largely determined by the character of his and his lineage's ancestral graves. If the *fung shui* of the graves was good, then all or part of the descendants would become wealthy, achieve high official position, increase in numbers — or all of these things. On the other hand, ancestral graves with neutral or poor *fung shui* might lead to the impoverishment or even the physical extinction of a line of descent.

In addition to the complicated magical system of *fung shui* the Cantonese peasant had a well-developed system of beliefs involving anthropomorphic supernatural beings. The world of the villager was inhabited by myriads of gods, ghosts and devils who profoundly affected his life on earth. The supernaturals were endless in their variety but, in the eyes of the villagers fell into a limited number of functional categories defined on the basis of how they affected human fortunes.

The first category consisted of the *zan* and *poosat* which included ancestral spirits and other deities of Buddhist, Taoist or Confucian origin. The *zan* and *poosat* were basically benevolent beings from whom the villagers could expect aid in the form of magical power or supernatural intervention. The second category of supernaturals was the *kwae*, malevolent spirits which were to be propitiated and avoided if at all possible. The *kwae* caused directly or indirectly all misfortune, failure, illness and death in the world.

As might be expected, supernatural beings also participated in the fundamental dualism of Chinese cosmology. The *zan* and *poosat* embodied the *yang* principle and were spoken of as 'bright' and 'lucky' beings. The *kwae* embodied the *yin* principle and were dim and unlucky creatures from the world of the shades who returned to earth to haunt and torment humans. This dualism is also found in the closely related cosmological beliefs of the villagers, whose universe was divided into three layers: (1) the lower *yin* world of hell and purgatory; (2) the upper *yang* world of heaven; and (3) the phenomenal world of earthly existence in which supernaturals from the other two layers interacted with living humans.

These three sections of the universe are closely interrelated to form one unitary system. Living humans after death become *kwae* and go to be judged by the ten judges of hell. Those persons who had lived moral lives passed through hell and entered heaven where they waited to be born again as bugs or men, depending upon the chacter of their previous life on earth. Those persons who died unnatural or unfulfilled deaths — such as being executed or murdered, committing suicide, or dying in childbirth—and those persons who committed evil deeds during their lifetime, spent more time in hell, where they underwent hideous and unmerciful torture. The poor souls in purgatory became the *kwae* that returned at night to torment human beings and cause them misfortune and death. Another important source of *kwae* were those persons who died without male descendants to worship them and provide them with the food, clothing, and money necessary for life in hell. These people also became hungry, wandering ghosts who preyed upon hapless humans and forced them to give them sustenance.

The *zan* and *poosat* were, like the *kwae*, basically human in character and origin, whether they were ancestral spirits or Buddhist and Taoist temple deities. Many deities enshrined in local temples were famous men who accomplished such great deeds that they were deified after death. In many cases, the only difference between ordinary mortals and deities was that the deities had been men of extraordinary ability and power.

This basic kinship between deities and men can also be illustrated by a curious practice that the villagers have of referring to particularly successful men as *shang poosat*, usually translated as 'living buddha'. This, however, is not an accurate translation of the term because it implies too close an association with Buddhism and idols. *Poosat* is the term used to refer generally to any powerful benevolent deity, whether it be an ancestral spirit or the Buddhist deity *Koon Iam*, the Goddess of Mercy. The use of this term to refer to successful men signifies that living men, if they command enough magical power, can approach the status of deities. It also implies that such men are treated much like deities; they are persons to whom one shows deference in the hope of receiving a favor; and they are men with whom one likes to associate in the hope that some of their luck will, literally, 'rub off'.

Supernatural beings play an important role in the religious life of the villagers. Each year there is a complex ceremonial calendar in which worship at local shrines and household altars plays an important part. Deities and ancestral spirits are worshiped in the hope that these supernatural beings may help the villagers to get rich and have a healthy and secure life. The propitiation of the *kwae* has an equally important place, with several major festivals designed to bribe them with offerings and force them to leave the village. The central conception on all religious worship is to obtain power and help from benevolent supernatural beings and to ward off the attacks of the *kwae*.

At this point, to complete the system of thought, it is necessary to introduce the villagers' beliefs concerning human souls and to relate these beliefs to other parts of the system. All villagers agree that a person has ten souls: three *wan* and seven *p'aak*. The villagers are no more certain about the exact nature of all these souls than are most Christians about their similar belief and were unable to explain clearly just what happened to these multiple souls after death. Some of the more sophisticated villagers suggested that the seven *p'aak* souls represented the animal senses of the body (the seven bodily orifices) and disappeared at death, whereas the three *wan* souls were aspects of one major soul called the *ling wan* which after death went to heaven or hell. The villagers also spoke of a person as having one major soul, the *ling wan*. However much puzzlement and disagreement there was about the significance of these multiple souls and what happened to them after death, all agreed that a person's fortunes in this life were closely related to the quality of his *ling wan*.

In the view of the villagers, a person's soul represented his life force and vital spirit. Illness was commonly believed to be caused by the temporary loss of one's soul, and death was believed to result from the permanent separation of the soul from the body.

The state of a person's soul was said to be either lucky or unlucky, bright or dim. A person with a bright soul was lucky and succeeded in everything he attempted. Since a person with a luminous soul was imbued with the *yang* principle, the *kwae* shrank back from him in fear and were unable to cause him harm. Most villagers were afraid to wander out at night because this was the time when the *kwae* returned from hell. But persons with bright souls could wander out at night unafraid since the *kwae* were repelled by his soul-light. A person with a bright soul-light had in effect captured a portion of the vital *yang* spirit of the universe and could use it to accomplish anything he wished. The *kwae* were almost as much afraid of him as they were of the powerful temple deities who were imbued with even more power.

On the other hand, a person whose soul-light was dim was an unlucky person who failed in almost everything he attempted. His family were continuously beset by the *kwae* which resulted in sickness, poverty, and even death. Instead of repelling the *kwae*, people with dim soul-lights actually attracted *kwae* to them. They had to feel their way carefully and cautiously through life and had to employ every magical means available to guard against the incursions of the ghosts and devils. But, even with all these precautions, the most they could hope for would be to achieve an ordinary existence with a minimum amount of security; they could never become successful or powerful people.

Fung shui, the cult of the dead, the belief in supernatural beings, and the conception of souls — all key elements of the Cantonese peasant's religious and magical beliefs — are not simply disconnected superstitions. On the contrary, they are mutually interdependent elements in a meaningful view of the universe and man's place in this universe. Furthermore, the villagers' supernaturalistic beliefs and practices are intimately related to their cultural values and to their cosmological and philosophical beliefs.

The basic goals of the villagers were the pursuit of wealth, power and prestige. The pursuit of these goals took place within a universe that was basically divided into two opposing impersonal forces: the *yin* and the *yang*. Everything in the universe, at any given point in time, was affected by its mode of interaction with these two ultimate forces.

The villagers' beliefs concerning the *yang* principle are by no means unique for they are based on a concept similar to that of *mana*, an idea which plays an important role in many religious systems of the world. *Mana*, as conceived by the peoples of the Pacific and by various American Indian tribes (although here it is called by different names), is an impersonal supernatural power that is the source of all efficacy in the world. A man is successful because he possesses *mana*: a warrior is a great warrior because he has obtained 'power'. In Durkheim's theory of religion the belief in an all pervasive supernatural power is the essence of the sacred and is the basic and original element in all religious systems.[9] The Cantonese peasant's conception of a basic supernatural power which is the driving force of the universe, whether it be called *yang*, *hey shae*, *fung shui*, or 'luck', is basically the same as the belief in *mana* held by other people of the world.

[9]Cf. Emile Durkheim, *The Elementary Forms of the Religious Life*, trans. J. W. Swain (Glencoe: The Free Press, 1954), chapter 6.

The *mana* principle underlies the entire Cantonese system of religion and magic. The pseudo-science of *fung shui* is merely one involved method of capturing *mana*. Most ritual practice involving deities and ancestors were attempts to obtain power from these beings. Supernatural beings were more powerful than humans principally because they control more *mana* than ordinary humans. A lucky person was lucky because he possessed *mana*, and the amount of *mana* possessed was evidenced by the brightness of his soul. *Kwae* were dangerous because they were dim creatures who stole the vital power of human beings.

The elaborate cult of the dead involving ancestral bones and *fung shui* was merely another important method of capturing magical power for the use of living descendants. Two aspects of the ancestral cult make this clear. First, a person must actually participate in the yearly ancestral sacrifices at the tombs of his ancestors to receive benefit from the grave's *fung shui*. Second, among the most important ritual paraphernalia used in the ancestral sacrifices are the roast pigs placed on the altar as offerings. This ritual pork is divided among all male descendants present at the sacrifices, with equal shares given to each man present. The ritual pork is not an ordinary offering because once it has been placed before the ancestors it takes on a sacred, magical quality and is believed to be especially lucky. All Chinese like to eat pork from a good grave and sometimes even nonlineage members are offered some as a prized gift. What is even more revealing, bits of this sacrificial pork are pressed into the mouths of small children who are too young to eat solid food.

The significance of these practices, I believe, can be interpreted as follows. The ancestral bones located in a good *fung shui* site receive the full force of the *fung shui* or *mana*, that pulsates through the earth's surface. If the *fung shui* is potent, the ancestral bones turn a bright yellow color and are considered extremely efficacious. The yellow coloring of the bones result from the *mana* infused into them, the same *mana* that lights a lucky person's soul. During the ancestral sacrifices the magical power of the ancestral bones is transmitted to the sacrificial pork; and this is why the pork is considered lucky. When consumed by the members of the kinship group, this magical power is absorbed by the souls of the members of the group. If the *fung shui* is really good, great quantities of *mana* will be absorbed by the descendants, their soul-light will be bright, and they will be successful in every aspect of their lives. Most importantly, such lucky persons will then give birth to sons at propitious times, ensuring that they have good 'eight characters'. And so the explanation runs full circle and the system is complete. Wind, water, bones, and souls all fit together in one fairly consistent system of religion and magic that enables us to understand many aspects of Cantonese culture.

As is evident in this paper, however, Cantonese peasant culture exhibits several contradictory themes; and not all elements of the villagers' belief system can be understood by using this cognitive model. If all success is due to fate, then the logical behavioral consequences of such a belief would be a fatalistic acceptance and resignation to fate. This is certainly not the prevailing attitude of the Cantonese who exhibit a strong motivation and drive for achievement. There is then a contradictory theme in Cantonese culture which holds that effort and ability are necessary for success and that all is not left to fate. I do not think that this is at all unusual for I suspect that few cultures are so well-integrated that all elements can be subsumed under one model. Most cultures are a complex of different cognitive models that interrelate in complex fashion and are often mutually contradictory. The contradictions in Cantonese culture are no more inconsistent than the Calvinistic ethic which held that a person's fate is predetermined but that the only way one could know whether he was among the saved was his success in doing God's will in his calling on this earth.

There is at least one other important cognitive model in Cantonese culture which fits into neither of the models discussed above and that is the Buddhist idea that a person's fate is based upon the morality of his actions in life. This Buddhist theme is different from both the fatalistic system of magic and the achievement orientation of the villagers. They represent three different aspects of the villagers' world view that are contradictory to the analyst but apparently do not worry the people who act in this system, who easily jump from one cognitive map to the other in different life situations. A complete account of the values and world view of the Cantonese peasants would include all three of these different cognitive models with some account of how they intersect in the lives of the villagers. In this paper I have outlined only one of these basic systems which allows us to understand a great deal of what goes on in the culture.

28.
postscript: religion under communism

One of the scholarly debates that has engaged sinologists during the early period of the Communist regime in mainland China is the question of just what, and how much, of Chinese communism is really new in the context of Chinese history, and what, and how much, is tradition in a different guise.

Atheism, following from the well-known "scientific" dicta of communism's founders, is certainly a novelty in the dogma of the Chinese state—although Confucian orthodoxy was generally described as "humanistic" rather than theistic. But the cults of the Chinese traditional state, whatever the tendencies of the literati officials, embraced many basic beliefs and practices of genuinely religious character, as our reading selections show. There is further the repressive and manipulative aspect of Chinese communist state policy towards religion. This is in sharp contrast to the several decades of general indifference towards religion during the period between the fall of the Manchu dynasty (1911) and the conquest of the communists (1949). During that confused interim, one could have concluded that Chinese religion would probably fade away, ever so slowly, as the society and culture of which it was an expression suffered the inevitable changes of modernization. As a matter of fact, this was the expectation of the Communists also, as our first selection will show. But religion, like every other feature of Chinese life, would not be simply allowed to drift onto whatever paths it was pushed by the currents of modern times; it would move towards its doom under the close guidance of the regime.

Is Chinese communism's surveillance, crippling regulation, and persecution something new? The answer must be no. Throughout China's last two thousand years, the State has held absolute right of control and intervention over religious, as well as other activities. Sometimes the right has not been exercised—but it often has been, with terrible effect, and it has always been in reserve. That despite all, religion has survived and flourished during that long period might be thought to offer a sobering pause to the new despotism. But one must remember it is communist dogma that the new age is not simply a continuation of the old, but is in fact a quantum change; that religion is a "function" of a sort of "feudal" society that will soon be destroyed; and that the society which will take its place will simply have outgrown it.

Our first selection comes from an article written at the end of what might be considered the first period of communist religious policy. It was a decade and a half after the assumption of control, and just before the outbreak of the Great Proletarian Cultural Revolution. The article, by Rennselaer W. Lee III, is entitled "General aspects of Chinese communist religious policy, with Soviet comparisons," and it appeared in the *China Quarterly*, 19 (July-Sept 1964) pp. 161-173. Because our intention here is merely to indicate the basic Chinese policy, we omit the Soviet comparisons from this carefully considered discussion.

The Chinese and Russian Communists, as Marxist-Leninists, are fundamentally hostile towards religion, and are committed to its ultimate eradication. Although their attitudes towards religion are similar, their prescriptions for dealing with it are different. In essence, this difference arises from two divergent conceptions, one optimistic, the other pessimistic, regarding the progress of religion towards oblivion in a situation where the Communist Party has assumed leadership and where the "social" roots of religion have supposedly disappeared. The Chinese hold the optimistic view, a position which may be explained in part by the fact that institutional religion has traditionally been weak in China . . . When the Chinese Communists came to power, therefore, they were not confronted with indigenous religious institutions which could offer any effective resistance. . . .

Religion, according to the Chinese Communists, has two sets of roots: "social" and "cognitive." The social roots of religion are found in the class struggle. Religion is a weapon used by the exploiting classes to drain the masses of their revolutionary energy. In the Chinese context "exploiting classes" would mean the landlords, the upper bourgeoisie, and the agents of Western imperialism. The exploiters, speaking through the medium of priests or missionaries, tell the masses to be submissive to their fate, which is preordained in accordance with divine wishes. They also tell the masses that life on earth, although miserable indeed, is simply a way station along the road to eternal happiness in the heavenly kingdom. These "pernicious" doctrines lull the masses into abandoning the class struggle waged for a better life . . . hence the phrase "opium of the people. . . ."

Religion also has so-called "cognitive" roots: namely, extreme poverty or economic backwardness, and man's failure to understand or to conquer the forces directing nature and society. In the former case, the Chinese Communists consider that a rise in living standards will bring about a general weakening of religious faith among the masses. However, the ideological awareness of the masses often lags behind the improvement in their economic well-being. . . . The Chinese say that eventually "the most profound mysteries and the most dreadful natural forces will no longer be mysterious or dreadful." As man grasps and uses the objective laws which govern his existence, he learns to overcome his fear of nature. As his fear of nature disappears, he is able to view objective reality from a scientific and materialistic standpoint. As his ideological awareness grows, his propensity for religious belief dwindles. Ideally, when his ideological awareness — and his economic well-being — reach a certain level, he will be freed from religious influences.

The Chinese Communists feel that they have destroyed the social roots of religion in China by eliminating the exploiting classes. They believe that with the "eradication of exploitation of man by man" religious influence has steadily become weaker. They also feel that with a general improvement in living standards, the increased dissemination of knowledge of natural and social sciences, and the resultant emancipation of the masses from the "enthralment" of natural forces, religion will gradually "die a natural death." . . . The current party line emphasizes the naturalness or inevitability of the progress of religion towards oblivion. . . . The Chinese Communists do not consider religion so dangerous a force that an intensive atheistic propaganda struggle must be waged against it. . . .

The Chinese Communist policy towards religion is officially described as one of "seeking common ground while retaining differences." In the old China, says the Chinese Communist Party, religion had a two-fold purpose: to serve the ends of Chinese reactionaries and foreign imperialists. Now, religion has "basically shaken off their influence," and the government solicits the "wholehearted cooperation" from religion in creating the new China. In the theoretical terms of Maoism, an "antagonistic" contradiction has been basically transformed into a "nonantagonistic" contradiction. The ideological difference between religion and "scientific" Marxism-Leninism is a contradiction among the people. Religion and the Chinese Communist Party can find a political basis of cooperation in building Socialism. Chinese Communist religious policy emphasizes "the provision of a common political basis to enable the believer to join the people throughout the country in a grand union and render services to Socialism. This common political basis is "anti-imperialist and patriotic and follows the road to Socialism." The difference in "ideological awareness" between believers and nonbelievers must be "no deterrent" to their mutual relations within the framework of the struggle for socialist construction.

Religious associations follow the pattern of other Chinese mass organizations in that their main purpose seems to be both to exercise political control and to mobilize support for the State. The meetings of these associations are held primarily for the purpose of displaying adherence to the Communist party's "general line" in domestic and foreign policy, and only secondarily, if at all, to discuss matters pertaining to religion. . . .

The Chinese Communist regime's religious policy in a sense has been dualistic. The Party line makes a sharp distinction between "superstition," as manifested in the proliferation of local gods and spirits, and "integrated religious systems," as represented by Islam, Buddhism and Christianity. The policy of "freedom of religious belief," i.e., of soft-pedaling atheistic propaganda at least for the present, and bringing believers and nonbelievers into a common front for the task of Socialist construction, does not extend to "superstition." An article in *Red Flag* (*Hung Ch'i*) in March 1958, entitled "A Major Victory for Atheism," revealed that in the first part of that year the Communists had conducted an all-out campaign to "smash gods and spirits" and obliterate superstitious beliefs in the villages. *Red Flag* stressed that the antisuperstition struggle "grasped the basic desire of the masses" which was "to raise production and improve livelihood." Many superstitious practices, apparently, were extremely wasteful, and contributed to economic backwardness of the peasants by keeping them in a state of complete subservience to nature, e.g., by causing them to take a passive attitude in the face of natural calamities. The constant reference, in the *Red Flag* article, to the wastefulness of certain kinds of superstition indicates that the motive behind the Communist campaign to eradicate superstition was primarily economic rather than atheistic.

The "integrated religious systems," such as Islam, Buddhism and Christianity, did, as I indicated earlier, enjoy a certain measure of official tolerance from the government. However, the policy of "freedom of religious belief," as defined by the Party, did not prevent the Communists from persecuting believers. Indeed, there was considerable religious persecution in China. But it is important to note that this persecution was not directed against religion in name. It was directed against that category of religious believers which was unwilling or unable to reconcile devotion to one's faith with loyalty to the Chinese Communist régime. Its basis was apparently political, not atheistic. . . . The Party considers that there is not only "no contradiction" between religion and "patriotism" (i.e., loyalty to the Communist régime and support for its policies) but that the latter is a necessary precondition for the survival of the former. The Communists say pointedly: "It is the duty of every citizen to be patriotic and patriotism is in accord with devotion to one's faith. Only by being patriotic will it be possible to lead a good religious life. . . ."

The Chinese Communist policy of "freedom of religious belief" is designed to purge religious groups of rightist or antiregime elements — e.g., "parasitic monks," "reactionary" imams, and "imperialist" missionaries and their "running dogs" in China — and to spur believers to active and productive efforts on behalf of Socialism. To this end, the regime has instituted a sort of "brainwashing process" to force believers to "speed up self-remolding and cultivate socialist ideology."

The ideological remolding process which the Communists have instituted for believers has four interrelated objectives: first, to extirpate all remnants of feudalist or, in the case of Christianity, imperialist thought; secondly, to develop Socialist consciousness and love of country; thirdly, to stimulate the desire to participate in tasks of Socialist construction; fourthly, to eliminate those religious practices which interfere with Socialist construction, and, as far as possible, to harmonize religious teachings with Communist doctrine. Here the general pattern seems to be an attempt on the part of believers to play down the other-worldly aspects of religious teachings, and to stress instead the creation of an ideal state through the implementation of Communist principles. Religion in China is acquiring a strong activist emphasis, in response to the exigencies of Socialist construction.

The techniques used by the Chinese Communists to implement this ideological remolding process follow a fairly well-defined pattern. First, there are the "accusation meetings" which are aimed at purging the most outspoken anti-Party elements. Following this preliminary cleansing process, the imams, monks, preachers or priests, as the case may be, are herded into study sessions where they "enhance their political awareness," "surrender their hearts to the Party," and "resolutely take the road to Socialism." The study sessions are also intended to expose remnant reactionaries and to destroy lingering tendencies among believers to follow reactionary, feudalist or imperialist channels of thought. The study sessions have the further effect of molding or adapting religious thought to suit Communist ideology. This adaptation involves an increasing emphasis on salvation through material progress, and on unification of the concepts of Communism and paradise. . . .

Of course not all scholars are as restrained as Lee in describing the implementation of this policy. Some have been considerably more cynical, and others have been more forthright in detailing the severity of the repression. Joseph Levenson, among the first group, emphasizes the determination of the Chinese Communists to relegate religion to the status of a museum piece—on Taoism, for example:

. . . contemporary Taoists have been given the spades to dig their grave in history. A Taoist Association exists. What is it to do? It decided in 1961 to compile the history of the Taoist religion. It took charge of Taoist monuments. And so the Taoist temples, no longer active and therefore no longer nests of 'deceivers,' have ceased to be 'feudal' in the sense of moralistic epithet; they are feudal just in the nomenclature of 'scientific history.' A temple is not a disgrace, but an antique. Communists, instead of exhorting the masses to crush the infamy, urge them to preserve the relics. That is crushing enough.[1]

On Buddhism:

The destinies of Buddhism and Taoism under the communists could not be very different. The curators were waiting for both. Buddhism, culturally richer and more sophisticated, has been, if anything, more attentively restored. But the Buddhist restoration, like the Taoist, was not to life. It was historical restoration, an invitation to see it as it was, and to leave it, then, in the past tense. . . .

Religious personalities remain, and they go through ritualistic charades at a few selected sites. They staff the Chinese Buddhist Association, which is as tame as its various Christian and Taoist counterparts. Like them, and like the 'democratic parties' in the political field, the Association exists to praise the communists from the outside (the highest accolade), to bear witness to the fact that the revolution is not over, and to give the world a spectacle of communist patience and forbearance. . . . All that remains is the historically significant, aesthetically valuable, religiously drained antiquities. . . .[2]

[1] "The Communist attitude towards religion." (A chapter in Werner Klatt, editor, *The Chinese Model. A Political, Economic and Social Survey*, University of Hong Kong, 1965), p. 25.

[2] *Ibid.*, pp. 25 and 26.

The severity of religious repression has been felt most naturally among the Christians, whose "imperialist" connections are too obvious to require explanation. As we have not included Christianity within the purview of our book, we shall not consider the innumerable testimonies of both foreign and Chinese communist sources on this matter.

We must now note the sudden abandonment of the "let it die by itself" policy just described, with the shambles of the Great Proletarian Cultural Revolution. Some may doubt, of course, that the anti-religious activities of that frenetic movement were directed by State policy, but nevertheless the effects were the same. We shall instance here only the case of Buddhism, as discussed in an article by Holmes Welch in the *China Quarterly* 40 (Oct-Dec 1969), entitled "Buddhism Since the Cultural Revolution," pp. 127-136.

On 3 August 1966 a brief dispatch was included in the English service of the New China News Agency. That day, it said, the Chinese Buddhist Association had given a banquet in honor of a group of visiting Japanese Buddhists, members of the Shingon sect . . . The day before, they had joined in performing a religious ceremony at the principal Peking monastery; and the day after, 4 August, they were received by Kuo Mo-jo.

So far as I can discover, these were the last items of news on Buddhism to be printed in the Mainland press for three years. Not only was there no further mention of foreign Buddhist delegations (including this one, which was headed for Sian when it dropped out of sight), but nothing more was heard of the Chinese Buddhist Association or its members or of the activities of monks or lay devotees. Buddhism, along with other religions, appears to have abruptly vanished from the Chinese scene.

This did not happen without warning. For one thing, Chinese Buddhist leaders had suffered a series of setbacks in their effort to show that they could serve foreign policy. For years they had been trying to win control of the main international Buddhist organization, the World Fellowship of Buddhists. They had been rebuffed at its sixth conference, hosted by friendly Cambodia in 1961, had protested in vain when its headquarters moved to unfriendly Thailand in 1963, and only advertised their failure by boycotting its seventh conference at the end of 1964. . . .

In the meantime, there had been an ominous development on the domestic scene. From 1963 to 1965 — perhaps in reaction to a recrudescence of domestic religious activity in 1960-62 — a debate was carried on in the pages of several Mainland journals about the past and future roles of religion in Chinese life. It reached its denouement in October 1965, with an article in *New Construction*. Previously the official line had been that religion would disappear automatically once socialism had removed its causes. Now, with a flurry of mixed metaphor, a new thesis was enunciated: "religion . . . will not disappear of its own accord . . . it will rely on the force of custom to prolong its feeble existence and even plot to make a comeback. When a dying cobra bites a man, it can still wound or kill him. Therefore no matter how little of religion's vestigial poison remains, it is necessary to carry on a rigorous struggle against it on all fronts and to pull up and destroy all of its poisonous roots." This suggested a basic change in policy that was already, in fact, under way.

At the beginning of 1965 the official organ of the Chinese Buddhist Association, *Modern Buddhism (Hsien-tai fo-hsüeh)*, had ceased publication . . . October 1965 saw the publication of a new *People's Handbook* which, unlike the previous editions, listed the Chinese Buddhist Association without the names of its officers. . . . On 30 November 1965 its President, Shirob Jaltso (Hsi-jao Chia-ts'o) was dismissed as Vice-Governor of Tsinghai . . . the second Tibetan Buddhist leader to fall from grace in a year. (The Panchen Lama had been attacked and demoted in 1964.)

In retrospect one can see that all these events formed a pattern. The failure to win a role in the World Fellowship of Buddhists or to set up a rival organization, the disintegration of the Buddhist movement in Vietnam, China's deteriorating relations with Asian Buddhist countries, the uselessness of Buddhism in pacifying Tibet—these negative factors were confronted by the developing needs of the Socialist Education Campaign and by the increasing impatience of the regime, perhaps of Mao himself, to see the next generation do as predicted and smash the idols of their own accord. It would not have been rash to predict that the Buddhist structure erected by the regime since 1953 was about to be dismantled.

During the great rally of 18 August 1966, when the Red Guards first appeared, Lin Piao called on them to eradicate the old ideas, old culture, old customs and old habits of the exploiting classes. A campaign against [these] "Four Olds" spread through Peking and many other cities within the next two weeks. Most sources agree that by the end of September every Buddhist monastery—and every temple, church and mosque—in China's metropolitan areas had closed. . . . this was the first time since A.D. 845 that nearly all the monasteries in China ceased to function. Some were simply closed; some also had their walls covered with revolutionary slogans; some were stripped of images and religious paraphernalia; some were converted into factories, offices, apartments or barracks for Red Guards. . . .

Most of the Buddhist clergy had already returned to lay life when their landed income and religious fees were cut off in 1950-52.

Although there have been rather lurid reports of the physical destruction of Buddhist art and architecture, I am inclined to think that it was rare . . . One reason for the locking up of the monasteries and the posting of "no entry" signs may have been precisely to avert damage. . . . However, the policy of protection did not extend to articles of little artistic value and it cannot be doubted that during the campaign against the "Four Olds," many popular images were destroyed. Shanghai, for example, had a famous temple of the city gods, in one hall of which were sixty wooden statues representing the cyclical years of the old Chinese calendar. It had been customary to burn incense to the year in which one was born. Before the temple was closed, according to a Shanghai resident, Red Guards forced devout old women to break up the statues with hammers and sticks. A somewhat more bizarre story appeared in a Taiwan newspaper. During the Cultural Revolution in northern Kiangsu (where Buddhism had particularly deep roots) big-character posters were pasted over images in local temples; a city god would be labelled "tyrannical landlord"; Kuan-yin (the goddess of mercy) "ruined woman"; Tathagatha (the Buddha) "robber"; and so on. Then the Red Guards would bind the images with ropes and put them on a platform, where they would be struggled against like any other counterrevolutionaries. People were encouraged to curse them and vent their indignation and anger. After this, the images had paper dunce caps put on their heads, placards hung around their necks, and were pulled through the streets to the beating of gongs and drums—sometimes for several days on end. Finally a meeting would be held to announce the verdicts: This or that bodhisattva would be sentenced to be "shot to death." In the words of the ex-Red Guard who told this story, "how queer it was!" . . . [The relative of an overseas Chinese] saw Buddhist monks being forced by Red Guards to parade through the streets wearing the dress of Christian ministers (and vice versa). There were, of course, reports of much harsher treatment.

The effect of all this on the Buddhist laity is obvious. Quite aside from the fact that they were frightened half to death, they could not offer incense in temples that had been closed and sealed, nor have rites performed by monks who had gone back to their native places. Actually, except for elderly women, fewer and fewer Chinese had dared to patronize these temples since 1962. It had not been uncommon to bring incense home and burn it in front of an image in the kitchen, perhaps of the kitchen god, or perhaps of Kuan-yin, Maitreya, Kuan-ti or Chi-kung, who had once stood on an altar in the front part of the house, but had been moved into the kitchen during the 1950s so as to arouse less comment. But in August 1966 there began a campaign to search people's houses for feudal, bourgeois or superstitious objects: images were therefore hidden or destroyed. . . .

What we are most ignorant about is the fate of Buddhism in the countryside. Rural and mountain monasteries have been the real strongholds of orthodox Buddhism for a thousand years—in places like Wu-t'ai, P'u-t'o, Chiu-hua, O-mei, T'ien-t'ai, Pao-hua and Chung-nan Shan. Japanese visitors could not go there or even find anyone who had gone there, and concluded that the monasteries there were closed as they were in the city. Overseas Chinese have had the same experience, and refugees are no better informed. . . . Diplomats stationed in Peking as late as June 1969 report that, so far as they could see, all religious institutions—except the mosque—were still shut down. . . .[3]

Finally, if it is true that man is by nature and circumstances religious, if he may be called *homo religiosus,* can it be possible for religion either to fade away with the triumph of the new dispensation, or to be extirpated if that fadeout seems unduly prolonged in China? Many observers have, of course, held the view that Communism is itself a religion, or at least a "quasi-religion." They would agree that its very success, in fact, is due to its religious character. Richard C. Bush, Jr., to cite only one scholar, at the

[3]Welch did hear of a few cases of continuing activity on a limited scale, from first-hand sources he considered reliable. (L.G.T.)

end of the first full-scale study of our subject (*Religion in Communist China*, Nashville & New York, 1970), speaks of "the 'new religion' which has been developing over the past half century. . . . Suffice it to say here that one does not grasp the significance of communism, particularly in China, if one does not recognize its religious character. I for one am prepared to go beyond talk of religious 'character,' 'analogy,' or 'aspects,' to drop the quotation marks when speaking of communism as a religion, to delete such prefixes as 'pseudo-' or 'quasi-' and say that Chinese communism *is* a religion." (p. 424)

If such is the case, then who is its god? The Founders, Marx, Engels and Lenin, are of course Saints—but after all, they were foreigners. As all the world knows, the Chinese Communist God can be none other than Mao Tse-tung. The assertion scarcely needs substantiation, yet we shall give here some comments on this phenomenon by a sinologist-sociologist, Lucy Jen Huang. Her study appeared in the authoritative *Asian Survey* (XI, 7, July 1971, pp. 693-708), under the title, "The role of religion in Communist Chinese society." We shall limit ourselves to only a few of the keen insights offered in this paper.

Every religious revival movement requires the true believers to spread the "word," in this case mainly selections from the little red book, *Quotations of Mao Tse-tung*. Soon after the beginning of the Cultural Revolution, Red Guards, in the role of missionaries and disciples of the religious movement, traveled all over China. An excerpt from an article in the *Canton Red Guard News* exemplifies the spirit of young Red Guards during this period of the Cultural Revolution.

> Many revolutionary teachers and students and Red Guards from other parts of the country brought the thought of Mao Tse-tung to the fore, observed the Three Main Rules of Discipline and Eight Points for Attention, and carried out their task of a study force, a propaganda force, and a fighting force, wherever they they might be . . . They wrote essays and poems of their impressions and the good characters and good deeds they had met with after coming to live with the residents, and pasted them on the walls. They spared time every day to help the teenagers and children study quotations from Chairman Mao, teach them to sing revolutionary songs, and help the residents do household work. They were warmly welcomed by the revolutionary residents.

. . . Maoism, by this time, had taken the form of extreme adulation of the great leader, sage, poet, philosopher, military genius, statesman, worthy successor to the mightiest of Emperors, and the great prophet of Marxist-Leninist thought. . . . As the heart and soul of the younger generation of Chinese was aroused by this Maoist religious experience, activities began to support their unequalled zeal for the cause. . . . The purge of the unbelievers was made in the form of public attacks on rightist elements via the pages of press and magazine . . . Purgers spared few in attacking those who did not pledge undying devotion to their great god, Mao, or practice Maoism as their daily devotion. . . .

A charismatic leader is one of the important symbols in any youth move-ment. The youth-movement leader has grown up in the movement and perpet-uates the spirit of defiance against authority and regularity, typical of any proletarian revolutionary activities. In their search for meaning, Chinese Communist youth showed the quality of romantic selflessness that had con-tempt for adult's concern over traditional values of individual interests and security. It is claimed that the emotional appeal of Communism lay precisely in the sacrifices — both material and spiritual — which it demanded of the convert. . . .

In the drastically changing society under Communism, the impact of conflict and confusion experienced by the masses, especially adolescents and young adults, tended to be monumental. In their search for self-identity and meaning in life they found the Cultural Revolution a convenient outlet for their anxiety. The participation in the Red Guard movement resembled, for many youth, an adolescent religious conversion experience fulfilling needs in a maturing process, though at times somewhat pathological. . . .

One of the outstanding characteristics of the worship of Mao has been the attribution of the Messianic quality. . . . Most Messiahs have claimed supernatural powers and generally their followers have believed in such powers; the worshipers of Mao are no exception. They deified Mao and believed that his thoughts could help them grow better watermelon crops and perform successful operations on patients. . . .

Radio Moscow on January 29, 1969 described the shortage of raw material in Mainland China causing industry to come to a standstill. But one industry, the business of Maoism, was still booming. The industry produced nothing but Mao books, Mao pictures, Mao statues and Mao medals. . . .

In order to spread the "gospel" of Maoism, Red Guards urged that quotation boards be erected in every street and Mao's portrait and quotations in every household. Everyone should carry a copy of *Quotations from Chair-man Mao,* study such quotations, and carry out work according to them. All vehicles should bear quotation placards and all schools should form propa-ganda teams for instruction from the highest quarters, so that everyone could hear Chairman Mao's teachings at any time. Furthermore, quotations of Chairman Mao should be broadcast in every cinema house, and all parks and main streets should set up broadcasting stations and place them under the charge of Red Guards for propagating the doctrine of Mao Tse-tung. It is without doubt that *Quotations from Chairman Mao* has been used as the "Bible" of the socialist nation. . . .

William James, in discussing the varieties of religious experience, refers to the psychological sentiment of confession. "It is part of the general system of purgation and cleansing which one feels one's self in need of, in order to be in right relations to one's deity. For him who confesses, shams are over and realities have begun; he has exteriorized his rottenness." The Socialist revolution in China during the last two decades employed confession as one of the chief means of converting rightists and "bourgeois" elements into deserving members of the Communist society. . . .

The religious dimensions of Chinese Communism consist of military missionaries, a puritanical and ascetic style of life, service to the masses, the employment of confessions and struggles to cleanse the soul, a daily reading of the Bible in terms of Mao's quotations, the exaltation of miracles performed through faith in the teachings of their "Messiah" and the extreme adulation of Mao. . . .

The religious elements of the Socialist revolution in Communist China . . . seem to have been latent functions unintended by leaders of the regime. The official policy of the Maoist regime has been antireligious and antisuperstitious in nature. However, paradoxically, there are undeniably religious dimensions in the official tactics and ideology resembling the very phenomenon of religion and superstition which the regime claims to oppose. Mao, as the symbol of god and prophet; Maoism the Bible, in the form of quotations of Mao Tse-tung; and the faith in Mao and his teachings, which have supposedly achieved superhuman feats and miracles, have stirred the religious zeal of Mao's followers to further produce unintended consequences. The concept of "good" and "evil" in the form of Maoist vs. capitalist and revisionist spurs young Red Guards and other followers to unite to destroy the enemy, many of whom were Mao's old cohorts and former friends. Here the integrative factor of religion appears to be supplemented by the unintended consequence of a legitimate release of frustration and conflict of young Chinese Red Guards, persecuting and destroying Mao's old friends and enemies in a gesture of patriotism. At the same time, they, not Mao, are blamed for the ruthless treatment of some of the fellow travelers from the Yenan Cave days.

While the Communists attacked religion as the opiate of the people, Maoism seemed to have similar euphoric influence on the masses, chanting and reciting Mao's quotations at every important occasion and believing it could perform feats and miracles. The unification of the nation is more effectively achieved if the masses possess religious zeal and dauntless faith in Maoism. At the same time, through the worship of Mao, the insecure and the alienated find a sense of identity, belonging and esprit de corps in the common struggle and dedication of a common cause. . . .

. . . For many followers of Maoism they may have found in the Communist regime a seeming dedication to justice, international brotherhood of the laboring peoples and tireless service to mankind. They are no longer confused and alienated. But for others who are overly idealistic and impractical, Maoism may turn out to be "the God that failed." It has challenged and fired their enthusiasm but may be unable to satisfy their cherished dreams and idealism.